Contemporary Asian Art and Exhibitions
Connectivities and World-making

Contemporary Asian Art and Exhibitions
Connectivities and World-making

Michelle Antoinette and Caroline Turner

ASIAN STUDIES SERIES MONOGRAPH 6

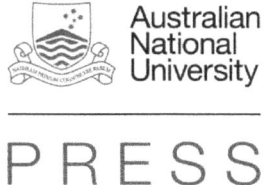

PRESS

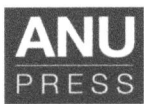

Published by ANU Press
The Australian National University
Canberra ACT 0200, Australia
Email: anupress@anu.edu.au
This title is also available online at http://press.anu.edu.au

National Library of Australia Cataloguing-in-Publication entry

Author: Antoinette, Michelle, author.

Title: Contemporary Asian art and exhibitions : connectivities and
                world-making / Michelle Antoinette and
                Caroline Turner.

ISBN: 9781925021998 (paperback) 9781925022001 (ebook)

Subjects: Art, Asian.
                Art, Modern--21st century.
                Intercultural communication in art.
                Exhibitions.

Other Authors/Contributors:
                Turner, Caroline, 1947- author.

Dewey Number: 709.5

All rights reserved. No part of this publication may be reproduced, stored in a retrieval system or transmitted in any form or by any means, electronic, mechanical, photocopying or otherwise, without the prior permission of the publisher.

Cover illustration: N.S. Harsha, *Ambitions and Dreams* 2005; cloth pasted on rock, size of each shadow 6 m. Community project designed for TVS School, Tumkur, India. © N.S. Harsha; image courtesy of the artist; photograph: Sachidananda K.J.

Cover design and layout by ANU Press

This edition © 2014 ANU Press

Contents

Acknowledgements vii

Introduction Part 1 — Critical Themes, Geopolitical Change and
    Global Contexts in Contemporary Asian Art 1
    Caroline Turner

Introduction Part 2 — Asia Present and Resonant: Themes of
    Connectivity and World-making in Contemporary Asian Art . . 23
    Michelle Antoinette

1. Polytropic Philippine: Intimating the World in Pieces. 47
    Patrick D. Flores

2. The Worlding of the Asian Modern 67
    John Clark

3. An Experiment in Connectivity: From the 'West Heavens'
    to the 'Middle Kingdom' 89
    Chaitanya Sambrani

4. The Irreverent Contemporary and Radical Tradition 109
    Pat Hoffie

5. Future Imaginaries. 129
    Charles Merewether

6. Response and Responsibility: On the Cosmo-politics of
    Generosity in Contemporary Asian Art 143
    Marsha Meskimmon

7. The Unexpected Guest: Food and Hospitality in
    Contemporary Asian Art 159
    Francis Maravillas

8. Under the Shadow: Problems in Museum Development
    in Asia 179
    Oscar Ho

9. People and Partnership: An Australian Model for International
    Arts Exchanges — The Asialink Arts Program, 1990–2010. . . 199
    Alison Carroll

10. Australia's Other Asia in the Asian Century 219
    Jacqueline Lo

Epilogue — 'My Future is Not a Dream': Shifting Worlds of
    Contemporary Asian Art and Exhibitions 233
    Michelle Antoinette

Selected Reading on Contemporary Asian Art 255

Contributor Biographies 265

Acknowledgements

This book was supported by the Australian Research Council (ARC) Discovery Project, 'The Rise of New Cultural Networks in Asia in the Twenty-First Century' (DP1096041, Caroline Turner and Michelle Antoinette), 2010–2013.

We thank Dr Debjani Ganguly, Head of the Humanities Research Centre (HRC) at The Australian National University (ANU), Canberra, for her invitation and generous support of the conference 'The World and World-Making in Art', Humanities Research Centre, ANU, Canberra, August 2011 (co-convenors Caroline Turner, Michelle Antoinette, Jackie Menzies, Zara Stanhope), which in addition to our ARC project, provided a further stimulus in shaping the ideas for our book. We thank our co-conveners, the keynote and lead speakers, and administrative staff of the HRC.

Our sincere thanks to our copyeditor, Dr Justine Molony, for her meticulous work on the manuscript, expert advice, and tremendous support and patience. We extend sincere thanks also to our image editor, Dr Ursula Frederick, for her valuable assistance preparing and advising on the images which appear throughout the book.

Our gratitude to Professor Craig Reynolds, Professor Kenneth George and Professor Li Narangoa of the ANU Press Asian Studies Series Committee for their support of the book, and especially to Professor Reynolds for his astute feedback on the book's development.

We thank the ANU Press for its support of this publication and the editorial and design staff at the Press, including Dr Duncan Beard, David Gardiner, Beth Battrick, Lorena Kanellopoulos, Nausica Garcia Pinar and Nic Welbourn.

Our thanks to the ANU College of Arts and Social Sciences and, in particular, the Research School of Humanities and the Arts, the School of Cultural Inquiry and the School of Art for supporting our ARC grant project.

Our profound gratitude to the many artists who gave their kind permission to reproduce images of their artworks throughout the volume and for their help with our research: N.S. Harsha—whose artwork also appears on the cover of the book, Nusra Latif Qureshi, Yang Fudong, Tushar Joag, Guan Wei, Janet Burchill and Jennifer McCamley, Dr Daw Khin Mar Mar Kyi, Charles Lim, He Xiangyu, Cao Fei, Araya Rasdjarmrearnsook, YOUNG-HAE CHANG HEAVY INDUSTRIES, Fiona Tan, Stephanie Syjuco, Sun Yuan and Peng Yu, Park Seobo, FX Harsono, Atul Bhalla, Qiu Zhijie, Nilima Sheikh, Tallur L.N., Qiu Anxiong, Dadang Christanto, Kwoma Arts, Graham Fletcher, Yakobus Serambi, Primus Isimin, Amatus Ahmak, Liu Xiaodong, Chen Quilin, Eunseon Park/Listentothe City, Debbie Ding, Mella Jaarsma,

Lee Mingwei, Roslisham Ismail (aka Ise), Leung Mee-ping, Tsang Kin-wah, artists involved with the Community Museum Project, Hong Kong (in particular those associated with the 'In Search of Marginalised Wisdom' Sham Shui Po Craftsperson Exhibition), Jason Wing, John Young, Miwa Yanagi, Liew Kung Yu, Phuan Thai Meng, Elly Kent, and Wong Hoy Cheong. We also thank the family of the late Roberto Villanueva, especially Eva Corazon Abundo-Villanueva and Napoleon Abundo Villanueva, and the estate of the late Santiago Bose, especially Imelda A. Bose.

We are also grateful to those who kindly assisted us in procuring and/or providing reproductions or research materials for this book, including Dr Chaitanya Sambrani and Johnson Chang, 'West Heavens' project; Dr Gene Sherman AM, Sherman Contemporary Art Foundation; Dr Claire Roberts; ShanghART Gallery, Shanghai; Professor David Williams; Professor Jen Webb; Claire Hsu, Phoebe Wong, Chantal Wong, Jaime Fang-Tze Hsu, Michelle Wong, Janet Chan, Sophie Hu, and country-based researchers Ringo Bunoan and Mohd Ahmad Sabih, Asia Art Archive (AAA); the staff at Asialink, especially Eliza Roberts and Louise Joel; Josie Browne, Kristi Jernigan and Tanya Booker, Beam Contemporary Art, New York and London; Judy Gunning, Ruth MacDougall, Maud Page, Cathy Pemble-Smith, Suhanya Raffel, Russell Storer, Chris Saines and Robyn Ziebell, Queensland Art Gallery | Gallery of Modern Art; 'Q' Nuchanart Saensa-neh, 100 Tonson Gallery, Bangkok; Aaron Seeto, Pedro de Almeida and Yu Ye Wu, 4A Centre for Contemporary Asian Art, Sydney; Michael Dagostino and Megan Monte, Campbelltown Arts Centre; Alexie Glass and Shae Nagorcka, Gertrude Contemporary, Melbourne; Luisa Tresca, Vitamin Creative Space, Guangzhou; Simon Xu Huanzhi and Chen Yun, West Heavens; Marta Zboralska, Frith Street Gallery, London; Daphne Chu and Issa Weng, Lee Studio, Taiwan; Lombard Freid Gallery, New York; Loock Galerie, Berlin and Nasuko Odate, Yoshiko Isshiki Office, Tokyo; Debbie Ho, West Kowloon Cultural District Authority; Kim Machan, MAAP–Media Art Asia-Pacific; National Art Museum of China; Agnes Lin, Jay Due and Ginie Shi Collins, Osage Gallery, Hong Kong; The National Historical Commission of the Philippines; Erwin Sebastian, National Museum of the Philippines; Siu King Chung, Community Museum Project, Hong Kong; Wu Dandan and Zandie Brockett, the studio of Liu Xiaodong, Beijing; Christine Clark, National Portrait Gallery, Canberra; Eriko Osaka, Yokohama Art Museum; Yasuko Furuichi, Japan Foundation; Raiji Kuroda and Ono Kazunori, Fukuoka Asian Art Museum; Natsumi Araki and Takahide Tsuchiya, Mori Art Museum; Singapore Art Museum, especially Tan Boon Hui, Khairuddhin Hori, Joyce Toh, Linda Lee; Lee Weng Choy; Dr Eugene Tan; Noor Effendy Ibrahim, Substation arts space, Singapore; Philip Francis, National Arts Council, Singapore; Adele Tan, National Art Gallery, Singapore; Charmaine Toh, Objectifs Centre for Photography and Filmmaking,

Singapore; Tien Wei Woon, Post Museum, Singapore; Ahmad Bin Mashadi, Shabbir Hussain Mustafa and Lim Qinyi, National University of Singapore Museum; Iskander Bin Mydin, National Museum of Singapore; David Teh, Future Perfect, Singapore; Asian Cultural Council, Hong Kong; Chinese University of Hong Kong; participants in the 'Shifting Geopolitical Ecologies and New Spatial Imaginaries' workshop, especially Workshop Directors Professor Çağlar Keyder and Professor Ravi Arvind Palat, at Inter-Asian Connections III (Hong Kong, 2012); Neil Manton; Zhang Lanshen; Safrizal Shahir; Dr Greg Lopez; Dr Gaik Cheng-Khoo; Professor Ariel Heryanto; Dr Amrih Widodo; Dr Amy Chan; Farah Wardani, Indonesian Visual Art Archive; Pak Sheung Chuen; Lam Tung Pang; Leung Chi Wo; Beverly Yong and Adeline Ooi, RogueArt, Kuala Lumpur; Professor Lily Kong, National University of Singapore; Dr Edwin Jurriens; Dr Olivier Krischer; Emily Wakeling; Dr Natalie Seiz, Art Gallery of New South Wales, Sydney; Mikala Tai and Bryan Collie, MIFA galleries, Melbourne; Elly Kent; Zara Stanhope; Dr Angie Bexley; Katie Hayne.

Our sincere thanks to the peer reviewers for kindly agreeing to review the manuscript and providing feedback.

The editors thank the contributing authors to this volume for their individual essays, but also their further collaboration and assistance with our research beyond the present book.

Finally, our warm and profound thanks to our ever supportive network of friends and family, especially Glen St John Barclay, Luke Hambly and Keir.

[Editors' Note: Asian names are presented in the manner of their country of origin except for Japanese names, which are presented in the Westernised order of personal name followed by family name, as per their common presentation in English-language publications. Korean names are generally as per country of origin, except where they are better known in the West with the family name last; i.e. Soyeon Ahn and Eunseon Park.]

Introduction Part 1 — Critical Themes, Geopolitical Change and Global Contexts in Contemporary Asian Art

Caroline Turner

This book explores cultural connections and intersections that are related to the dynamic changes in art in Asia in the late twentieth and early twenty-first centuries. It derives from an Australian Research Council (ARC) funded research project (Turner and Antoinette 2010–2013) examining new cultural networks in contemporary Asian art in the twenty-first century with a central theme of 'connectivities', from which this volume of essays takes its title.[1] The four key themes of this book, which are outlined below, are drawn from this research.

The focus of our research is contemporary Asian art, broadly defined as the art of the last 25 years. The essays in this volume provide significant new insights into contemporary art and institutions in the Asian region and into unfolding discourses in Asian art. A number of the essays are by Asian authors, thus providing important perspectives from the region, and the contributors include curators as well as scholars undertaking research in the areas of art history and contemporary visual culture.

Themes of the Book

In 2011 I was asked by Dr Debjani Ganguly, Head of the Humanities Research Centre (HRC) at The Australian National University (ANU), to convene a conference on art (with Michelle Antoinette, Zara Stanhope and Jackie Menzies) addressing the broad concept of 'the world and world-making'. That conference was planned to intersect with two other HRC conferences convened by Ganguly, one on world literature and one on history, the latter being 'Subaltern Studies: Historical World-making Thirty Years On', co-convened by Dipesh Chakrabarty, a long-term colleague and Adjunct Professorial Fellow at the HRC. Both Chakrabarty's groundbreaking book, *Provincializing Europe: Postcolonial*

---

1 Caroline Turner and Michelle Antoinette, 'The Rise of New Cultural Networks in Asia', Australian Research Council Discovery Grant (DP 1096041).

Thought and Historical Difference, and Ganguly's conceptualisation of the three conferences have been extremely influential in shaping the first theme of this current volume of essays—'world-making'.[2]

The keynote papers delivered by Patrick Flores and John Clark at the conference 'The World and World-Making in Art: Connectivities and Differences', are published in this volume. In all, nine authors in this volume gave papers and participated in discussions at the conference (Flores, Clark, Sambrani, Hoffie, Merewether, Meskimmon, Maravillas, Antoinette and Turner).[3]

The second, third and fourth themes of this book have also emerged, as indicated above, from research for our ARC grant on new cultural networks in Asia. These are: intra-Asia regional connections, Australia's cultural interconnections with Asia and, lastly, art's empathetic effects in cross-cultural engagement.

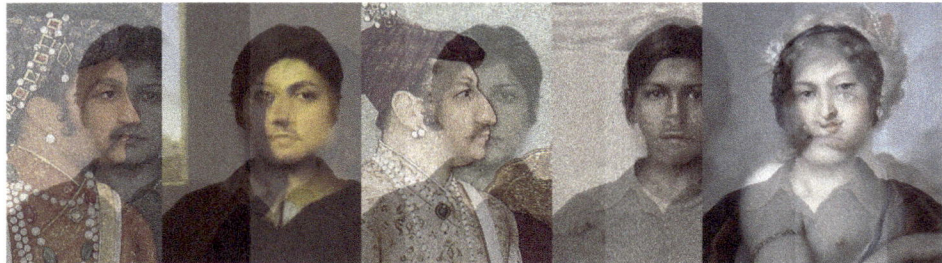

Nusra Latif Qureshi, *Did you come here to find history?* 2009 (detail); digital print. This work was shown in the 53rd Venice Biennale and in the exhibition 'Beyond the Self: Contemporary Portraiture from Asia', curated by Christine Clark and exhibited at the National Portrait Gallery, Canberra, and regional venues in Australia 2011–2013. The artist was an invited speaker at the conference 'The World and World-Making in Art', Humanities Research Centre, The Australian National University, Canberra, 2011. See www.portrait.gov.au/site/exhibition_subsite_beyondtheself_artist.php?artistID=14

Image courtesy Nusra Latif Qureshi and the National Portrait Gallery of Australia

---

2   Dipesh Chakrabarty, *Provincializing Europe: Postcolonial Thought and Historical Difference* (Princeton University Press, 2000). See also hrc.anu.edu.au/events/subalternstudies
3   'The World and World-Making in Art', conference, Humanities Research Centre, The Australian National University, 11–13 August 2011. Convened by Caroline Turner, Michelle Antoinette, Zara Stanhope and Jacqueline Menzies. See also Turner, Antoinette & Stanhope eds, 'The World and World-Making in Art', *Humanities Research* 19, no. 2 (2013), epress.anu.edu.au/titles/humanities-research-journal-series/volume-xix-no-2-2013

Introduction Part 1 — Critical Themes, Geopolitical Change and Global Contexts in Contemporary Asian Art

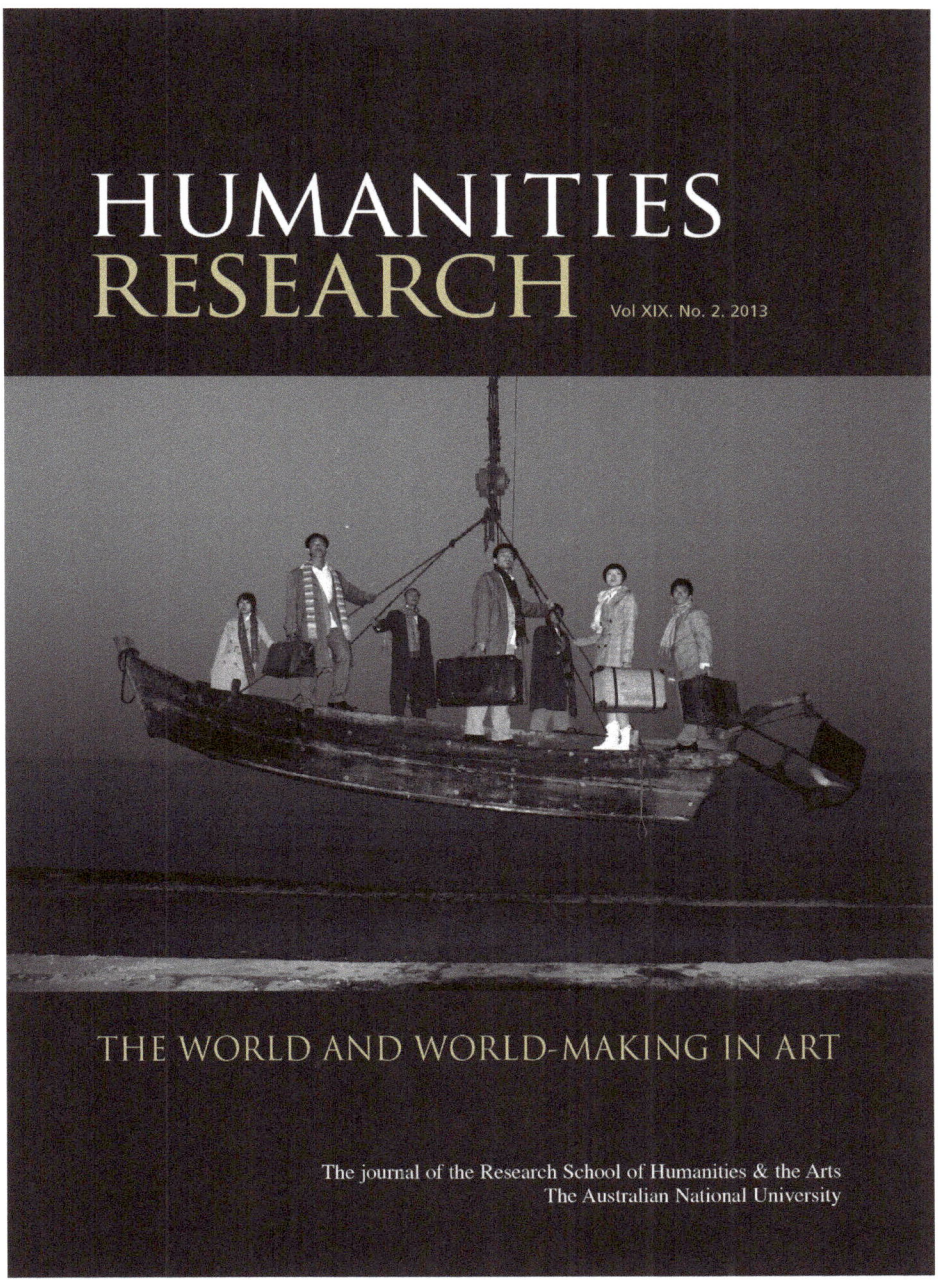

Cover of *The World and World-Making in Art*, special issue, *Humanities Research* 19, no. 2, 2013, edited by Caroline Turner, Michelle Antoinette & Zara Stanhope; featuring artwork by Yang Fudong, *Seven Intellectuals in Bamboo Forest, Part IV* 2004; photograph: black & white C-print; 120 x 180 cm; edition of 10.

Image courtesy of Yang Fudong and ShanghART Gallery

These four themes underpin this volume of essays. Our Introduction (Turner and Antoinette), is separated into two essays that outline the themes and issues and analyse historical and present developments in contemporary Asian art. The following essays by Flores and Clark offer further 'mapping' of Asian art and broad theoretical and conceptual approaches; Chaitanya Sambrani provides a case study of a specific exhibition, as does Pat Hoffie. Both also examine the critical issue of defining the 'contemporary' in art practice in Asia. Charles Merewether, Marsha Meskimmon and Francis Maravillas explore the inspiration and aesthetic contexts of the work of a number of Asian artists; Oscar Ho and Alison Carroll evaluate museum, curatorial and cultural agency approaches to intra-Asian networks, while Jacqueline Lo's essay illuminates Australia's engagement with Asia with special emphasis on Asian–Australian contributions. Michelle Antoinette provides an Epilogue and final essay to the volume.

This essay introduces the critical themes and contexts of this book and of the essays that follow within the broad framework of Asia and Asian art in a transforming world. I evaluate, in particular, the impact of geopolitical change and its effects on art and culture in the region, and also give an overview of some of the exhibitions and conferences that have helped shape the discourses about art in the Asian region over the last 25 years. I do so writing as a participant in many of these events. I also briefly discuss Australian cultural intersections with Asia in the same period. In the second part to this Introduction, Antoinette further elaborates each author's contribution in relation to our themes and to the overarching concept of 'connectivities'.

Contemporary Asian Art: Geopolitical and Economic Change

A critical question that has preoccupied those working in the field of Asian art is 'What is *contemporary* Asian art?' The Japan Foundation posed this question in the cross-cultural and transnational curatorial and exhibition project 'Under Construction: New Dimensions in Asian Art' conducted between 2001 and 2003.[4] Contemporary art from Asian countries is now seen in major international exhibitions around the world, but this is a relatively new phenomenon that parallels developing geopolitical and economic relationships. As other contributors indicate, art was dramatically transformed by the late twentieth century process of globalisation and geopolitical change that led to

---

4 'Under Construction: New Dimensions in Asian Art', Japan Foundation Forum 2002, convened by Yasuko Furuichi www.jpf.go.jp/e/culture/new/old/0210/10_07.html (accessed 3 August 2013). The exhibition was curated by nine curators from seven Asian countries. For other Japan Foundation contributions see, for example, Japan Foundation, ed., *Asia in Transition: Representation and Identity*, The Japan Foundation 30th Anniversary International Symposium 2002 (Tokyo, 2002).

Introduction Part 1 — Critical Themes, Geopolitical Change and Global Contexts in Contemporary Asian Art

a shift from an art centred in Europe and America and towards regions such as Asia. The higher visibility of contemporary Asian art in world exhibitions and forums in recent times needs to be seen in terms of a global expansion of interest in art beyond the art centres of Europe and North America. At the same time, no consideration of contemporary Asian art can be divorced from the tremendous political and economic changes in the region itself over the last two decades. As I have argued elsewhere, Asian contemporary art is under construction in an alternative sense—that is, the region is helping create a new framework for global art expressions.[5]

Geopolitical and economic transformations have led to an unprecedented growth in the middle classes in Asia, the lifting of hundreds of millions of people out of poverty, increased educational and other opportunities, revitalised intra-Asian interactions and new globalised connectivities, but at the same time, an increased consumerism and materialism and societies in which huge inequities and social issues remain to be resolved. Geeta Kapur, one of the pre-eminent writers on art today, describes the context for Indian (and by extension) many Asian artists as 'a civil society in huge ferment, a political society whose constituencies are redefining the meaning of democracy and a demographic scale that defies simple theories of hegemony'.[6]

The astonishingly rapid transformations in Asia in the last 25 years have led analysts to refer increasingly to the twenty-first century as 'the Asian century'. As Australian academic Glen Barclay has noted:

> The tectonic plates are shifting: what political philosopher Carl Schmitt called the 'identity of the period' of the last century, was the movement of the balance of world influence westward across the Atlantic from Europe to the United States. What will provide the identity of this century is the continuing westward movement of that balance across the Pacific to its logical locus, the home of more than three billion people, more than half the population of the world.[7]

This situation is described by Singaporean Kishore Mahbubani, formerly a diplomat and now Dean of the Lee Kuan Yew School of Public Policy at the National University of Singapore, as a case of the world returning to the historical normality of the place of Asian societies in the global hierarchy.[8] Significantly for one theme of this volume, that of intra-regional connections, Mahbubani

---

5 Turner, ed., *Art and Social Change: Contemporary Art in Asia and the Pacific* (Canberra: Pandanus Books, 2005).
6 Geeta Kapur, 'Dismantled Norms: Apropos other Avantgardes', in *Tradition and Change*, ed. Caroline Turner (St Lucia: University of Queensland Press, 1993), 97.
7 Glen Barclay, 'Geopolitical Changes in Asia and the Pacific', in *Art and Social Change*, 15.
8 Kishore Mahbubani, *The New Asian Hemisphere, The Irresistible Shift of Global Power to the East* (New York: Public Affairs, 2008).

also sees new connectivities as having the potential to lead to shared values and aspirations in the Asian region, mediating old rivalries and tensions that remain evident today.

Many of the artists who have come to international prominence in Asia in recent decades have done so as the region changed. For example, Japanese artists were included in major international exhibitions beginning in the 1960s and 1970s, at the time when the Japanese economy became the second largest economy in the world, although it has now been surpassed by China and has since dropped to third place. It is without question that China's extraordinary economic rise in recent times has led to world attention being focused on Chinese artists, many of whom are now superstars of the international art world. What is occurring is far more than artists from the so called 'periphery' being admitted to a 'canon' of art controlled by the West. There has been recognition for some time that Western art historical approaches cannot be the only framework for understanding and interpreting contemporary art developments in Asia. A new framework for art needs to include what Ho refers to in this volume as the development of 'languages outside a Western-dominated art world'.

Art historian Terry Smith, one of the speakers at our world-making conference, has pointed to the historical shift from Euro-American geopolitical and economic hegemony over the last 50 years. This shift has occurred, he notes, at an accelerated pace in recent years and is now affecting the context for art: 'Geopolitical change has shifted the world picture from presumptions about the inevitability of modernisation and the universality of EuroAmerican values to recognition of the coexistence of difference, of disjunctive diversity, as characteristic of our contemporary condition.'[9] Smith has also argued that '… contemporary art is—perhaps for the first time in history—truly an art *of* the world'.[10] In Asia this phenomenon has led to challenges to Euro-American values and dominance in art and is a concept that emerges strongly across the essays in this volume.

Art historian Michael Sullivan, writing in 1989, noted that the rapid flow of art and ideas from culture to culture today is now so extensive that it is no longer regarded with surprise.[11] In 1993 historian Wang Gungwu wrote that: 'The modern world has made people aware of similarities and differences

---

9   Terry Smith, 'Worlds Pictured in Contemporary Art: Planes and Connectivities', in 'The World and World-Making in Art', 12. See also Smith, 'Currents Of World-Making in Contemporary Art', *World Art*, no. 2 (2011): 20–21.
10 Smith, conference abstract for 'The World and World-Making in Art', Humanities Research Centre, ANU, 2011. See also Smith, *Contemporary Art: World Currents* (London: Laurence King and Thames & Hudson; Upper Saddle River, NJ: Pearson/Prentice Hall, 2011). For further discussion of the global in art see, for example, Hans Belting, 'Contemporary Art as Global Art: A Critical Estimate', in *The Global Art World: Audiences, Markets, and Museums*, ed. Hans Belting & Andrea Buddensieg (Ostfildern: Hatje Cantz, 2009), 38–73.
11 Michael Sullivan, *The Meeting of Eastern and Western Art* (Berkeley: University of California Press, 1989), 4. Sullivan describes the active dialogue between what he calls 'Eastern' art with Western beginning after 1500, but notes that there had been cultural exchanges long before that date.

among themselves to an extent never dreamed of in the past. Being thus more aware, people can never be the same again'.¹² The exchange of ideas that Sullivan and Wang Gungwu referred to has become more rapid, especially as new technologies, including the internet and social media, greatly expand connectivities. Globalisation has generated new debates about differences, similarities, parallel histories, art histories and art practices that necessitate multifaceted responses, as the essays in this volume reveal.

In geocultural terms the idea of 'Asia' itself is problematic, as the title of the 'Under Construction' project suggested. Asia is no monolithic entity. The idea of 'Asia' has been to a degree, as many scholars have suggested, a constructed discourse partly developed in counterpoint to the idea of the 'West', and one that cannot be used to deny the diversity of local cultures and histories in the region. It is also true, as Thai art historian Apinan Poshyananda noted when writing about Thailand, that syncretism has been a key factor in historical cultural formations in the region.¹³ The influence of fountainhead cultures, such as India and China, in historical times has been significant and Japan has been a major influence in interconnections with the West since the Meiji Restoration in the nineteenth century. Encounters with Western countries had a major impact, but we need to recall that not all Asian countries were colonised and that anti-colonial struggles in Asia have a long history. While it is clear from the essays in this volume that local, national and regional histories as well as contemporary political and social changes within countries have impacted with tremendous force on art practice, there is equally the effect of dynamic cultural engagement regionally and globally which transcends simple global/local dichotomies. These extend to minorities and multiculturalism within nations, hybridity and multiple identities, mobilities that transcend past histories and national borders, and new and extended global interactions in terms of individual lives. As Singaporean academic Lily Kong has commented: 'The reality is that our lives [today] are shaped by both the global and the local, the transnational and the nation'.¹⁴

Some of the dramatic changes evident across Asia in our times can be seen in 'West Heavens', the contemporary art and intellectual exchange between artists from India and China, which is one of the first major art exchanges between these two nations in recent times. 'West Heavens' is the initiative of Hong Kong-based Johnson Chang (Chang Tsong-Zung).¹⁵ In ancient Chinese Buddhist texts,

---

12 Wang Gungwu, 'Foreword', in *Tradition and Change*, vii.
13 Apinan Poshyananda, 'The Development of Contemporary Art of Thailand: Traditionalism in Reverse', in *Tradition and Change*, 93–100.
14 Lily Kong, 'Asian Studies and/in Asian Universities: Global Impacts?', keynote address, Asian Studies Association of Australia (ASAA) 19th Biennial Conference, 11 July 2012.
15 See Chang Tsong-Zung, 'Introduction', unpaginated exhibition booklet, 2010, and website http://westheavens.net/en/ (accessed 18 January 18, 2011). The 'West Heavens' project has been awarded the first Art Newspaper Asia Prize (2014) created in celebration of the first anniversary of the Chinese edition of the *Art Newspaper*.

India was referred to as the 'West Heavens' and was the source of Buddhist ideas. The project seeks to continue this centuries old 'cultural dialogue' and to 'compare the different paths of modernity taken by India and China'. In 2012 an exhibition *Place.Time.Play: Contemporary Art from the 'West Heavens' to the 'Middle Kingdom'*, representing artists from both nations, was held in Shanghai as part of the project. It was curated by Sambrani, who provides a fascinating personal perspective on developments in art in the region and a curator's insights into the ways the artists explored artistic connectivities and transnational cultural dialogue.

Mumbai artist Tushar Joag based his art installation in that exhibition on a performance entitled *Riding Rocinante* that involved his riding a motorcycle for 53 days from Mumbai to Shanghai. The clothes he wore on the trip and the disassembled motorcycle were used in the installation after being symbolically washed in the waters of the Yangtze, Asia's longest river and the site of the Three Gorges dam, discussed by Merewether, Sambrani and Antoinette. Joag's journey reversed those of Chinese Buddhist pilgrims Faxian (399 and 412 CE) and Xuanzang (seventh century CE) who went to India seeking sacred texts. It also referenced the journey of renunciation that the Buddha took on his horse Kanthaka, Don Quixote's journeys on his horse Rocinante in the early seventeenth century in Spanish writer Miguel de Cervantes' novel *Don Quixote* and, of course, the twentieth century motorcycle adventure of self-discovery undertaken by Latin American revolutionary Che Guevara. This artwork is, therefore, a reminder of the global interchange of ideas that characterises so much Asian art today. Joag, who has undertaken a number of art projects related to social issues in India, also wished to highlight the plight of those in both nations displaced by massive new industrial projects, such as the Sardar Sarovar Dam in India and Three Gorges dam on the Yangtze in China. These issues are also being explored by artists in China, for example, as Merewether discusses in analysing the art projects, and motivations for those projects in relation to water, of Zhuang Hui, Chen Qiulin, and Liu Xiaodong, which focus on the Yangtze.

Joag's work serves to highlight critical ideas in our research project that are explored in this volume, including globalisation and an increasing exchange of knowledge and ideas in intra-Asian contexts. As well as the dramatic geopolitical and economic transformations referred to above, his artwork reveals the effects of rapid industrialisation, including the growth of mega cities—such as Mumbai and Shanghai—and subsequent dislocation of large numbers of people as a direct result of rapid industrialisation and urban growth, and the way that artists in Asia are addressing social change.

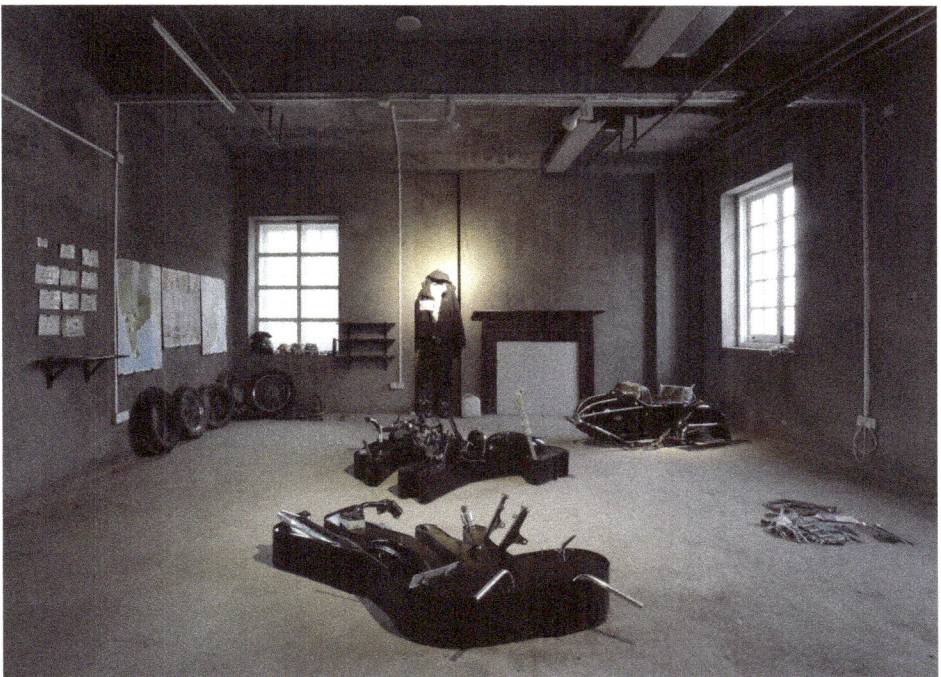

Tushar Joag, Background: *Riding Rocinante: from Bombay to Shanghai via Sardar Sarovar and the Three Gorges* 2010; maps, motorcycle spare parts and tools; dimensions variable. Foreground: *The Realisation of Kanthaka* 2010; sculptural installation; 152.4 x 100 x 365 cm.

Photograph: Thomas Fuesser; image courtesy of Tushar Joag and West Heavens

Contextualising the 'Contemporary' in Asian Art Discourses

The idea of an 'Asian' art is in part a Western classification and in part a construction developed in the countries that make up the continent. There are three critical time periods used in discourses about Asian art. First, historical or classical Asian art, which is seen and admired in museums around the world and which is generally art produced from ancient times up to the nineteenth century, but sometimes encompasses 'traditional' practice beyond that date (see Hoffie, this volume). Secondly, it is necessary to take into account the 'Asian Modern', discussed by Clark, which extends from the nineteenth century to the early 1990s. The third period is that of 'contemporary' Asian art, usually regarded as beginning in the late 1980s and early 1990s. As Sambrani points out, there is a sophisticated tradition of art scholarship in Asia, but until recently, art was largely viewed within national contexts, although links between scholars and artists existed well before the contemporary era—for example, between India and Japan.

Flores and Clark, among others, have made enormous contributions to debates about art in Asia over recent decades. Their key essays encapsulate the necessity of wider and richer historical and theoretical perspectives than those of the last 25 years. This point has also been made by other prominent scholars in the region, for example by leading Singapore art historian, T.K. Sabapathy, who also points to the need for an historical dimension in interpreting contemporary art in the region.[16]

In this volume Flores, who is a major figure in defining the 'contemporary' in Asian art and its place in global art debates, looks at the concept of 'world-making' by setting the Philippines in the context of colonial and postcolonial Spanish and American imperialism, postwar independence and the shifting political, social and economic realities of our world today. He shows the complexities for Filipinos of moving between local and global societies (historically and more recently), the often migratory economic realities that dictate life in the Philippines, and the condition of 'mediating discrepant worlds coming together in an instance that is at once belated and present …'.[17]

The idea of the 'contemporary' has been resisted by some art historians, who see the contemporary as the domain of art criticism. As art historian Miwon Kwon notes: 'Contemporary art history … marks a temporal bracketing and a spatial encompassing, a site of a deep tension between very different formations of knowledge and traditions, thus a challenging pressure point for the field of art history in general'.[18] Clark points to '… the still largely absent discourse of a worlded art history that takes account of Asia'. I would argue, however, that this is changing. The issue of whether art history can be truly global is a significant new area in art history scholarship, as evidenced by papers, including by Clark, in a session at a recent major conference in Germany in 2012.[19]

---

16 See T.K. Sabapathy, 'Developing Regionalist Perspectives in South-East Asian Art Historiography', *Second Asia-Pacific Triennial* (Brisbane, 1996), 13–17. Sabapathy elucidates the strong links in South-East Asia over the millennia and in the anti-colonial struggles between Indonesia, Malaysia and Singapore forged in the 1940s and 1950s and also cites leading Indonesian scholar Jim Supangkat's 'insistence that modernism should be "recontextualised"' (1996: 13). On the continuing need for an historical perspective, see also Sabapathy, ed., *Intersecting Histories: Contemporary Turns in Southeast Asian Art* (Nanyang Technological University, 2012).
17 Flores is the author of numerous influential articles and several books concerning Philippine art and the curator of major projects; see, for example, Flores, 'Position Papers: Turns in Tropics: Artist–Curator', in *The 7th Gwangju Biennale: Annual Report: A Year in Exhibitions*, ed. Okwui Enwezor (Gwangju Biennale Foundation, 2008), 262–85, and T.K. Sabapathy, Patrick D. Flores & Niranjan Rajah eds, *36 Ideas from Asia: Contemporary South-East Asian Art* (Singapore Art Museum, 2002). (See also Author Biography.)
18 Miwon Kwon, *OCTOBER* 130 (Fall 2009): 13.
19 The 33rd Congress of the International Committee of the History of Art (CIHA), 15–20 July 2012, Nuremberg, Germany. See http://www.ciha2012.de/en/home.html. The conference session was convened by

Clark has been one of the leading voices in drawing the distinction between the 'Asian Modern' and 'contemporary' art. In a series of seminal publications he has defined the histories and 'multiple art discourses' and practices in what he refers to 'as a particular set of geographically defined entities, which became the modern state system in Asia from the onset of late Euramerican colonialism in the eighteenth century until the end of colonial rule in the mid-twentieth century'. His essay looks in particular at the transfer of art and ideas across the region within this timeframe.

Clark's groundbreaking 1991 conference at the HRC, 'Modernism and Postmodernism in Asian Art', was the first such international conference held in a Western country. It opened up critical debates by bringing together art historians from across Asia to present developments in their different nations, on the 'Asian Modern' in particular, thus opening up new possibilities of comparative regional and transnational art histories.[20] This framework of comparative national art histories has been energetically developed since that time by scholars and curators in the region. Jim Supangkat, T.K. Sabapathy, Redza Piyadasa, Geeta Kapur, Gulammohammed Sheikh, Salima Hashmi, Apinan Poshyananda, Somporn Rodboon, Akira Tatehata, Fumio Nanjo, Eriko Osaka, Hou Hanru, Wu Hung, Gao Minglu, Kim Youngna, Soyeon Ahn, Alice Guillermo and Patrick Flores, among others, have been at the forefront of exploring the legacies of the historical and more recent past. Scholars outside Asia have also made significant contributions. These include authors in this volume and those whose work engages with the modern art history of individual countries, such as Astri Wright (Indonesia), Britta Erickson (China), Nora Taylor (Vietnam), Alexandra Munroe (Japan), and others cited in 'Selected Reading on Contemporary Asian Art' in this volume.[21] While much debate is focused on contemporary art, it has long been realised that there is a need to link the historical and modern art history of the region to its contemporary art. Further, the idea that is now broadly accepted in the international art world of 'multiple modernities', and of the 'multiple art discourses' and practices that characterise the modern referred to by Clark, has changed the cultural landscape for art globally and led to challenges to the suggestion earlier made by some Western art critics at Clark's 1991 conference, that the 'modern' art of Asia (and elsewhere outside the West) was merely 'derivative' of Western art.

Australian art historian Jaynie Anderson, another speaker at the 'World and World-Making' conference. Anderson has been President of CIHA, which will hold its next world congress in 2016 in Beijing—a significant step toward developing an art history that encompasses Asia.

20 See also John Clark, *Modern Asian Art* (Sydney: Craftsman House, 1998).
21 See citations in footnote references elsewhere in this book, as well as 'Selected Reading on Contemporary Asian Art' in this volume; essays by Salima Hashmi, Geeta Kapur, Redza Piyadasa, Jim Supangkat, Masayoshi Homma, Alice Guillermo, Nguyen Quan, Xu Hong, T.K. Sabapathy, Apinan Poshyananda in *Tradition and Change*; and by these and other authors, such as Jagath Weerasinghe, Somporn Rodboon, Yulin Lee, Soyeon Ahn and Dang Thi Khue in *Art and Social Change*.

By contrast, the essays in this volume reinforce the distinctiveness of Asian art and art histories and the distinctive voices of art experts in Asia who are shaping this new field of scholarship.

The Asian region has continued to develop its own forums for art and creative dialogue between artists, curators, and scholars. The 1990s witnessed a rethinking of cultural frameworks and hegemonies, and critiques of what then was often referred to as the 'Euro-American paradigm'. Over the next decade and into the new century new definitions of 'contemporary' Asian art were tested in various fora, including conferences, symposia, exhibitions and publications, in the region and beyond. The Japan Foundation has been a leader in these debates, as has the New York-based Asia Society. In the Australian context the conferences held in 1993, 1996 and 1999 in association with the Asia-Pacific Triennial of Contemporary Art (APT) exhibitions were also important early platforms for connecting to Asian discourses, especially for Australian artists and curators.

In referring to the 1993 APT, Hoffie draws attention to the dilemmas of defining the 'contemporary' by noting the shift that occurred 'in the understanding of the term "contemporary" as it was understood within the many accounts of the post-postmodern/postcolonial world of "international" art theory that was emerging from north of the equator', and how this 'signified cooler shifts into newness; a term that was not tied to any of the messy, resistant (often wilfully resistant) ballast of the past'. The APT exhibitions reflected this, she argues, in that the first triennial:

> … made the potentially radical proposal by suggesting, in this region at least, the 'contemporary' had not emerged mysteriously as a weightless and shadowless ghost of the eternal now, but as a force that had developed through different forms in accordance with different circumstances and in relation to particular contexts. Rather, it was presented as an active, contested zone of conflict, contrapuntals, contradictions, productive confusions, contrarieties and contrasts.

Here, I suggest, context is critical: art in Asia should not be understood by looking only at its engagement with Western art that set art in the region on a new trajectory, or in terms of Western colonialism. For example, a 2007 conference in Guangzhou, China, was entitled 'Farewell to Postcolonialism' and discussions included strongly expressed views that colonialism, the issues of Western colonialism, and Western theories of art grounded in a world view entrenched in ideas about the region viewed from the perspective of colonialism and postcolonialism, were of the past.[22] Over the last two decades scholars in

---

22 Sarat Maharaj, one of the curators of the Guangzhou Triennial 2008, entitled *Farewell to Postcolonialism, Towards a Post-Western Modernity*, for which the conference was a precursor, noted in 2007 the difficulty for a South African-born scholar of Indian descent to 'farewell' postcolonialism (author observations at conference).

Asia have examined the links between art and geopolitical change, and art and globalisation in relation to theories of art emerging from the West, as in the Japan Foundation conference 'Count 10 Before You Say Asia—Asian Art after Postmodernism' (Tokyo, Japan, 2008), at which Flores was a lead speaker. The description for the latter conference noted that: 'The integration of non-western contemporary art into the global art scene in the past 20 or so years has been rapid and explosive', but went on to suggest:

> The theoretical frame of postmodernism, proposed within the Western perspective of the modernist impasse, accelerated this process of integration in the name of multiculturalism and post-colonialism. With the increasing recognition of the possible complicity between this postmodernist discourse and the globalizing tendency of capitalist system and of its possible generation of (degeneration into) 'cosmetic' multi-culturalism, we are now standing at a historical juncture where the necessity [is] to re evaluate the achievements and problems of postmodernist discourse and its effect in relation to Asian contexts ... [23]

Asian art historical studies over the last 25 years have included examinations of specialist areas, such as women artists,[24] as well as specialist regional studies[25] and, of course, nationally focused art histories. There have been some attempts at transnational art histories comparing art movements in Asia, such as *Asian Modernism*, an exhibition organised by the Japan Foundation.[26]

As part of and in tandem with this ongoing process of re-evaluation of what is now critical in Asian art, in the last two decades the Asian region has produced an explosive growth in the exhibition and collecting practices of art museums, the projects of artist-run spaces and initiatives developed outside formal institutions, and development of biennales and other such recurring exhibitions. This is paralleled, as Antoinette underlines, by the emergence of a greatly expanded commercial gallery sector and thriving, indeed booming, art market. Important biennales and triennales in the region, and their beginning dates, include: the Indian Triennial (1968); Bangladesh (1981), Gwangju, South Korea (1995), Shanghai, China (1996) and Taipei, Taiwan (1998), biennales; the APT at the Queensland Art Gallery (QAG) in Brisbane, Australia (1993);

---

23 The conference 'Count 10 Before You Say Asia—Asian Art after Postmodernism' was convened by Yasuko Furuichi; website accessed 26 May 2011, http://www.jpf.go.jp/e/culture/new/0810/10_01.html.
24 See, for example, Dynah Dysart & Hannah Fink eds, *Asian Women Artists* (Sydney: Craftsman House, 1996); Britta Erickson, 'The Rise of a Feminist Spirit in Contemporary Chinese Art', *Art AsiaPacific*, 31 (2001): 65–71; Salima Hashmi, *Unveiling the Visible: Lives and Works of Women Artists of Pakistan* (Lahore: Sang-i-Meel Publications, 2002); Binghui Huangfu, ed., *Text and Subtext: Contemporary Art and Asian Women Artists* (Singapore: Earl Lu Gallery, 2000).
25 See, for example, Nora A. Taylor & Boreth Ly eds, *Modern and Contemporary Southeast Asian Art: An Anthology* (New York: Cornell University, 2012).
26 Tatehata Akira, Mizusawa Tsutomu & Shioda Junichi eds, *Asian Modernism—Diverse Development in Indonesia, the Philippines, and Thailand* (Tokyo: The Japan Foundation Asia Centre, 1995).

and the significant Fukuoka Triennale in Japan (1999). The last grew out of earlier, recurring Asian art exhibitions beginning in the late 1970s. In the first decade of this century many more recurrent exhibitions have been held, including the Yokohama, Japan (2001) and Guangzhou, China (2003) triennials; and the Busan, South Korea (2002); Beijing, China (2003); Singapore (2006); Jakarta and Yogyakarta, Indonesia (intermittent); and Kochi-Muziris, India (2012) biennales. The recent World Biennial forum in Gwangju hosted representatives from almost every Asian country, many of which are developing new biennale projects. Indeed there are currently more biennales in Asia than anywhere else in the world. As most of these exhibitions are focused on regional and international art, they have become important sites of engagement and dialogue about contemporary art in Asia and globally.[27]

New cultural networks in Asia have developed in association with such exhibition and museum projects; for example, the Asian Art Museum Directors' network, which is a group of directors of major museums of the region that focus on modern and contemporary art. Singapore, Japan, South Korea and China were critical in the establishment of the network, which holds symposia and works towards the exchange of exhibitions and staff. The seventh meeting was held in Jakarta and Bali in 2013. Curators in Asia have formed a similar network, the Asian Curatorial Network (ACN) (see Ho, this volume). The International Council of Museums (ICOM) has a specific Asia-Pacific branch with networks for staff of every type of museum, and ICOM's modern art committee, CIMAM, has held events in Japan, South Korea and China. As Antoinette notes (Epilogue), the Hong Kong-based Asia Art Archive is a critical source of resource material on modern and contemporary Asian art. As a result of arranging and hosting the APT, QAG has an extensive collection of art, and an archive on that art, from different parts of Asia. The Fukuoka Asian Art Museum in Japan has been collecting for longer and also has a superb collection, while the Singapore Art Museum and the new National Gallery of Singapore are collecting and documenting South-East Asian art in depth.[28] Singapore has been a key force in intra-Asian art and cultural exchange. South-East Asian art exchanges grew out of Association of Southeast Asian Nations (ASEAN) supported exhibitions and Singapore also has strong links with East Asia. Singapore has taken a lead

---

27 'Shifting Gravity', World Biennial Forum No. 1, Gwangju, Korea, 27–31 October 2012 (http://www.worldbiennialforum.org/), which I attended as an invited speaker, discussed world biennales, but the majority of attendees were from Asia. See Uta Meta Bauer & Hou Hanru eds, *Shifting Gravity: World Biennial Forum No 1* (Hatje Cantz, 2013).

28 See the catalogues of the Asian Art exhibitions, Fukuoka Art Museum to 1999 and catalogues of the first, second and third Fukuoka Asian Art Triennales, 1999 to date. See also, Fukuoka Asian Art Museum, *The Birth of Modern Art in Southeast Asia: Artists and Movements* (1997). Examples of Singapore's focus are the exhibitions *Modernity and Beyond: Themes in Southeast Asian Art* (1996); *Visions and Enchantment: Southeast Asian Paintings* (2000); and, the recent, very important survey of contemporary South-East Asian art, edited by Iola Lenzi, *Negotiating Home, History and Nation: Two Decades of Contemporary Art in Southeast Asia 1991–2011* (Singapore Art Museum, 2011).

partly because of government funding to encourage creative industry and the government's determination to make Singapore a cultural and economic hub in the region. Despite some issues related to censorship, Singapore is helped in this endeavour by having a multicultural society and international trade outlook.

China is now emerging as a strong player in the contemporary art scene with a large number of new museums, including private museums of contemporary art, being established as well as an increasingly full calendar of art fairs and biennales, museum workshops and innovative exhibitions and specialist conferences, as is South Korea. Japan experienced a museum boom from the 1970s, presaging what occurred in mainland China, South Korea, Taiwan and Singapore from the 1990s. While Japan has been an important innovator and initiator of debates for decades, as Japanese scholars have noted, it is still perceived by some as being in an ambiguous position because of Japan's wartime invasions of neighbouring countries in the 1930s and 1940s.

Museums play an important role in initiating new exchanges, but face the dilemma of pursuing a local or international orientation, as Ho demonstrates in his study of the Hong Kong-based M+ museum development. His argument presents the importance of museums connecting to local roots and local histories. The hundreds of new museums and art institutions that now exist, or are being planned, across Asia are a rich resource, providing significant infrastructure and with the potential to be shapers of public culture across the region.

Recent geopolitical changes have led museums, curators and artists in the region to initiate new transnational connections. Some have been pursued as cultural diplomacy initiatives between, for example, Japan and China, India and China and, in 2010, the Palace Museum in Beijing and the National Palace Museum in Taiwan—the latter a collaboration that would have been thought impossible a decade ago. Transnational exchange programs, such as that described by Sambrani, and the programs of Asialink in Australia described by Carroll, have taken on a renewed importance as sites for cross-cultural dialogue and for intra-Asian cultural connections.

As Merewether, Hoffie, Sambrani, Meskimmon, Maravillas, Carroll, Ho, Lo and Antoinette show, contemporary artists have been and are engaged with projects of significance beyond their own countries, especially when these relate to issues of social, political and environmental change in the region. The work of Indonesian artist Dadang Christanto, for example, is about legacies and memories of the past, the tragic hidden history of the Indonesian killings of 1965–1966, and also about recent ethnic division within Indonesia, including the killings and rapes of Chinese Indonesians in 1998. As discussed by both

Hoffie and Meskimmon, Christanto is an example of an artist whose work has been widely seen internationally, especially within Asia, and whose work has significance well beyond Indonesia and Asia.[29]

Australia and Asia

A key theme of this volume is Australia's connection with Asia, which is explored here and in essays by Hoffie, Carroll, Antoinette, and Lo. I also include here a brief case study of the APT, an Australian museum-based project that exemplifies many of the issues discussed above relating to transformations in approaches to art in the region.

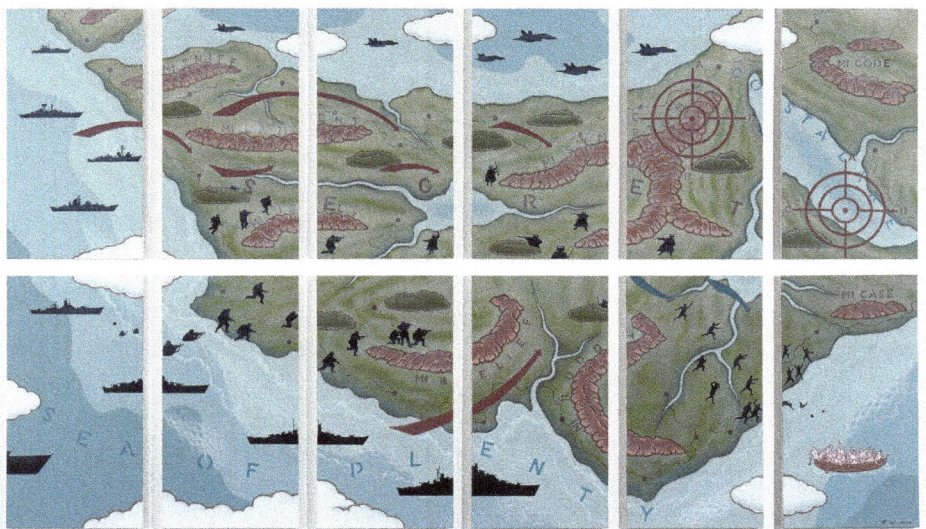

Guan Wei, *Where's Ned Kelly?* 2004; acrylic on canvas; 180 x 306 cm.

Image courtesy the artist

Australia has a long history of engagement with Asia, but also a long history, I suggest, of clinging to outdated conceptions and stereotypes of the region. Projects such as those of Asialink and the APT, both beginning in the early 1990s, were designed to counter such perceptions through knowledge of contemporary realities, not only of art but of changing societies in Asia.

Australians are not ignorant of Asia. Many Australians have been involved with Asia since the nineteenth century through trade, as travellers and adventurers,

---

29 See also Caroline Turner and Jen Webb, *Art and Human Rights: Contemporary Asian Contexts* (Manchester University Press, forthcoming).

as part of colonial administrations, and as missionaries. Asian immigration to Australia, which began in the nineteenth century with large-scale Chinese immigration, was halted by the mid-nineteenth century adoption of the White Australia policy. This policy was not officially abandoned until 1973. Australian Bureau of Statistics figures estimate that six per cent of the Australian population is Asian born, and Asian–Australians, those of Asian descent, make a major contribution to Australia's economic, political, intellectual and cultural life.[30] Lo's essay provides a fascinating exploration of the significance of this contribution and Antoinette's essay also discusses the contributions of Asian-Australian artists.

In the twentieth century numerous Australians travelled to Asia, for example as tourists, traders, maritime workers, journalists and diplomats, among others. The Second World War was a turning point in terms of growth in the numbers of Australians serving in Asia in theatres of war. Since then, Australian troops have been involved in the postwar occupation of Japan, the Malayan Emergency, *Konfrontasi* in Borneo, the Korean and Vietnam wars, Iraq, Afghanistan and, more recently, in peacekeeping roles; for example, in Cambodia and East Timor. Many Asian students began studying in Australia in the 1950s as part of the Colombo Plan, and this has continued more recently with growing numbers of Asian students, self-funded as well as on scholarships, studying at Australian schools and universities. The critical importance of economic ties with Asia is acknowledged by all sides of politics, especially relations with Japan, China, South Korea, India and Indonesia. There has been significant tourism of Australians to Asia and vice versa since the 1980s and considerable reciprocal investment between Asia and Australia, beginning with Japanese investment in the mining industry. Many Australians now work regularly in Asia. An example of expanding ties is the considerable growth in Asian studies courses in Australia, particularly since the Second World War. Asian languages are now taught in schools as well as universities and Asian history, especially Indian history, has long been part of university curricula. Much more, however, needs to be done in the areas of 'Asia literacy', a point frequently made in discussions of Australia's relations with Asia, which include evaluation of competencies required for Australia to engage effectively with Asia in the future in areas such as culture, innovation, science and technology, trade relations and economic endeavours.[31] While Australians, therefore, have knowledge of Asia, this is sometimes outdated knowledge including, as Carroll notes, in the area of art

---

30 The Australian population is 24 per cent immigrant (2000), a quarter of whom were born in Asia. Between 1981 and 2000 the Asian-born population of Australia grew to 6 per cent. Source: Australian Bureau of Statistics: http://www.abs.gov.au/AUSSTATS/abs@.nsf/2f762f95845417aeca25706c00834efa/666a320ed773 6d32ca2570ec000bf8f9!OpenDocument.
31 In 2012 the then Labor government released a white paper, *Australia in the Asian Century*, which examined Australia's relations, including cultural relations, with Asia. An example of developments since the white paper is 'Asia Literacy: Language and Beyond', a two-year national research project, which is part

history. University courses did not focus on the subject of Asian art, especially contemporary Asian art, until the 1990s. Since that decade, art schools and individual artists have been involved with Asia in increasing numbers, with the Canberra School of Art being an early pioneer in establishing links that came to be valuable to the early work of the APT. Artist exchanges since the 1990s have been greatly assisted by Asialink residencies and grants from the Australia Council for the Arts.[32]

Australians have long been exposed to the historical and classical arts of Asia through the collections of Australian art museums that were established in the nineteenth century. Exhibitions of historical Asian culture have had a strong presence in Australian museums since the 1970s. This process has much older precedents, however; indeed, exhibitions of Asian culture were shown in international fairs or exhibitions in Australia in the nineteenth century. In the twentieth century, Asia-content exhibitions became a significant new emphasis in museum and gallery programming from the 1950s onwards. The real exhibition focus on Asia, however, accelerated dramatically with a series of remarkable historical Chinese art exhibitions that were arranged under successive cultural agreements, starting in 1977 with *Recent Archaeological Discoveries from the People's Republic of China*.[33] Contemporary Asian art received some attention through initiatives such as the Artists Regional Exchange (ARX) (based in Perth) in the 1980s and the Sydney Biennale, which had shown some Asian artists

---

of the 'Safeguarding Australia's Future' program of the Australian Council of Learned Academies funded by the Australian Research Council through the Office of the Chief Scientist: http://www.acolasecretariat.org.au/ACOLA/index.php/projects/securing-australia-s-future/project-3.

32   The Canberra School of Art under David Williams was a pioneer in these exchanges. The Artists Regional Exchange (ARX), which was based in Perth, focused on South-East Asia from 1987 (see Pamela Zeplin, acuads.com.au/conference/2005-conference/article/the-arx-experiment-1987-1999-communities-controversy-and-regionality/). Australian art museums began exhibiting and collecting contemporary Asian art in the 1990s. Among the most significant museum initiatives of the 1990s was the series of contemporary Asian art exhibitions commissioned by the new Museum of Contemporary Art (MCA), Sydney, under Leon Paroissien and Bernice Murphy (for example, *Mao goes Pop: China post-1989* (1993), curated by Li Xianting & Nicholas Jose), as well as *Post Mao Product: New Art From China* (1992) curated by Claire Roberts at the Art Gallery of New South Wales (AGNSW) and which travelled to Ballarat, Canberra and Brisbane. Many Australian institutions have shown contemporary Asian art in recent years. Examples are *India Songs: Multiple Streams in Contemporary Indian Art* (1993), curated by Victoria Lynn with Indian Commissioners Manjit Bawa and Haku Shah at the AGNSW; *Edge of Desire: Recent Art In India* (2004–2007), curated by Chaitanya Sambrani and organised by the Asia Society, New York, and the Art Gallery of Western Australia, Perth (the exhibition travelled to Perth, New York, Mexico City, Monterrey, Berkeley, New Delhi and Mumbai); *Inside Out: New Chinese Art*, curated by Gao Minglu in association with the Asia Society and the San Francisco Museum of Modern Art (the exhibition was shown at the National Gallery of Australia, Canberra, in 2000); *Beyond the Self: Contemporary Portraiture from Asia* (2011), curated by Christine Clark at the National Portrait Gallery (NPG), Canberra; and *Go Figure! Contemporary Chinese Portraiture* (2012), curated by Claire Roberts at the NPG and Sherman Contemporary Art Foundation.

33   Turner, 'International Exhibitions', in *Understanding Museums*, eds Des Griffin and Leon Paroissien (National Museum of Australia: Canberra, 2011), http://www.nma.gov.au/research/understanding-museums/CTurner_2011.html.

since the 1970s, although not in great numbers until the late 1990s. In the late 1980s and early 1990s, however, Australia, Europe and North America had limited knowledge of the dynamic contemporary art of the region as a whole.

Asialink, which is discussed by Carroll with a focus on the arts program, has been a critical conduit for Australia's engagement with Asia across a broad range of activities. It was founded in 1990 to 'work with business, government, philanthropic and cultural partners to initiate and strengthen Australia–Asia engagement'. This singularly important body, a joint initiative of the Australian Government's Commission for the Future and the Myer Foundation and, from 1991, a centre of the University of Melbourne, has in the last 20 years developed crucial Australia–Asia connections through business, professional links, health, education and contemporary arts and cultural collaborations, including residencies and exhibitions in 21 countries. The Sydney-based Sherman Gallery, later Sherman Foundation, under Dr Gene Sherman, has been a major private supporter of contemporary Asian Art.

QAG, in the form of the APT, which began in 1993 and of which I was project director in the 1990s, was the first Australian art museum to make a major commitment to the contemporary art of the region (although, later, other Australian art museums began to exhibit and collect contemporary Asian art).[34] There have been seven APT exhibitions over a period of 20 years to 2012 with a total attendance of over two million visitors. These figures are substantial for exhibitions of contemporary art in a city with a population of just over two million people and in a country with a population of 23 million people. One of the APT's key objectives was to provide a series of exhibitions that could educate Australians about the dynamic changes in contemporary societies in the Asia-Pacific region and, at the same time, connect with emerging debates in the

---

34 For its first three exhibitions, the APT had a national committee consisting of Doug Hall, director, QAG; Caroline Turner, deputy director, QAG; David Williams, ANU; Alison Carroll, Asialink; Neil Manton, Department of Foreign Affairs and Trade; and Ian Howard, director of the Queensland College of Art. For a recent discussion of the APT see Hoffie, this volume; the catalogues of the first, second, third, fourth, fifth, sixth and seventh APTs, (Brisbane: Queensland Art Gallery, 1993–2012); Caroline Turner & Rhana Devenport eds, *Papers from the Second Asia-Pacific Triennial Conference* (Brisbane: Queensland Art Gallery, 1996); Caroline Turner & Morris Low eds, *Beyond the Future: Papers from the Third Asia-Pacific Triennial Conference* (Brisbane: Queensland Art Gallery, 1999); Jen Webb, 'The Asia-Pacific Triennial: Synthesis in the Making' (with Tony Schirato), *Continuum* 14, no. 3 (special issue: Synthesis) (November 2000): 349–58; and Turner, 'Cultural Transformations in the Asia-Pacific: The Asia-Pacific Triennial and the Fukuoka Triennale Compared', in *Eye of the Beholder: Reception, Audience and Practice of Modern Asian Art*, eds John Clark, Maurizio Peleggi & T.K. Sabapathy, University of Sydney East Asia Series, No 15 (Wild Peony, 2006), 221–43. See also Turner, 'Case Studies: Asia-Pacific — Part A. Asia-Pacific Triennial of Contemporary Art', *Yishu Journal of Contemporary Chinese Art* 12, no. 3 (May/June, 2013): 37–43 and 'Selected Reading on Contemporary Asian Art' and especially essays by Anthony Gardner & Charles Green, 'Mega-Exhibitions, New Publics, and Asian Art Biennials', in *Art in the Asia-Pacific: Intimate Publics*, eds Larissa Hjorth, Natalie King & Mami Kataoka (New York and London: Routledge, 2014), 23–36; Russell Storer, 'Dots in the Domain: The Asia Pacific Triennial of Contemporary Art', in Hjorth, King & Kataoka, 37–48; and references in Hoffie's essay, this volume. For a regional perspective see Sabapathy, 'Developing Regionalist Perspectives', 13–17. A full evaluation of the contributions of the APT from a regional perspective is overdue.

region and outside Asia about the nature of contemporary art in a globalising world. The APT's aim in 1993 was thus to provide a forum for discussion of diverse practices, for experimentation, and an intellectual platform for the presentation of local and regional perspectives. The exhibitions provided this platform at a time when there were few biennales or forums for debate about Asian contemporary art anywhere in the world. Many of the participants from the region met for the first time at the first APT exhibitions and conferences in the 1990s.

The APT is regionally focused on the art of Asia, Australia, and the Pacific, but excluding the Americas. As Hoffie notes, this scope encompasses provision for the representation of indigenous cultures from Australia and the Pacific. The definition of Asia-Pacific is not fixed and has included diaspora artists and, more recently, artists from countries of west Asia, such as Afghanistan and Iran. The APT also has an extensive acquisition and commissioning program, which has led to QAG building one of the world's most broadly based collections of contemporary Asian and Pacific art.

It is perhaps difficult for younger scholars and curators today to appreciate that, in the early 1990s, the APT was regarded as a radical project. To that point, contemporary art from Asia and the Pacific (except for Japan) was rarely seen in major international exhibitions. QAG had undertaken an exchange exhibition of contemporary Japanese art in the 1980s, which I negotiated. This proved to be an influential model for the later APT. QAG also showed, in 1992, Australia's first contemporary Chinese touring exhibition, which was curated by Claire Roberts. The most distinctive features of the early APTs in the 1990s were that artists and scholars in the region helped select, curate and write about the art; that the region was defined broadly; that the exhibitions served also to build a collection and archive; and that the art chosen for exhibition was not 'officially' selected. Iftikhar Dadi, the US-based academic and artist, has described the project as significant, noting that in the first decade to 1999 the APT 'emerged as a key force in formulating an understanding of emergent practices in much of the Asian region'.[35]

The first three APT exhibitions showed 220 artists from the region who were chosen by cross-cultural curatorial teams from 20 regional countries, including Australia. While this model changed after 2002, as a concept it helped build new networks and challenged outdated orthodoxies in Australia, where art was seen from mainly Western perspectives. Particularly important were three major associated conferences held in 1993, 1996 and 1999—some of the largest art conferences ever held in Australia and with speakers from the region and

---

35   Iftikhar Dadi, 'Reflections on the First Decade', in *Contemporary Visual Art+Culture Broadsheet* 42 (4 December 2012): 266.

beyond. From the first APT it became apparent that Euro-American discourses needed to be challenged. Importantly, the APT maintained a strong emphasis on art related to issues facing communities in an era of rapid social, political, and technological change and on issues of social justice and environmental degradation.

The large curatorial teams and the numbers of catalogue writers for the first three APT exhibitions, while vital to building networks and knowledge, were subject to some criticism at a time when the accepted wisdom was that one curator should provide the vision for an exhibition. The APT was shaped by collaborations between QAG and hundreds of experts and artists, from many different countries in the region and especially by the intellectual and artistic input of the artists, many of whom came to Australia for the exhibitions. This is not to say that cross-cultural curating does not pose challenges, but the many cross-cultural curatorial engagements that have occurred in the region since the early 1990s, including as part of the APT, the Fukuoka exhibitions and Japan Foundation projects cited in this essay, as well as many other regional initiatives, are generally considered to have been foundational in developing the new approaches to art exhibitions that are now emerging.

In the 1990s more Australian institutions began to develop programs to connect to contemporary art in Asia. The projects of Asialink have been critical in this respect. Another example is the Brisbane-based Media Art Asia Pacific (MAAP), which is the only organisation in the world to focus on new media art in the region and which, since its founding in 1998, has undertaken a large number of collaborative projects in Asia and Australia.[36]

As Lo notes, Asian-Australians have played a significant role in forming and maintaining Australia's connections with Asia. Senior artists, such as William Yang and John Young, who are among the founding members of the Asian–Australian artists' association, 4A, in Sydney, exemplify this influence. Today, 4A is a major site of art exchange between Asia and Australia. Lo, Maravillas and Sambrani, three of the authors in this volume, are examples of Asian-Australian academics whose work has contributed greatly to Australian intellectual life and, in recent years, many highly talented and distinguished artists from Asia have immigrated to Australia, such as Nusra Qureshi (Pakistan), Dadang Christanto (Indonesia), Guan Wei (China) and filmmaker Khin Mar Mar Kyi (Burma).

In Part 2 of this Introduction, Antoinette takes up the four key themes of our book in depth, indicating how each contribution relates to those themes and to the conclusions drawn from this volume.

---

36   http://www.maap.org.au/about-maap/. These projects include 'Light from Light' at the Shanghai Library, Hangzhou Library, National Art Museum of China (NAMOC), Beijing and in Brisbane.

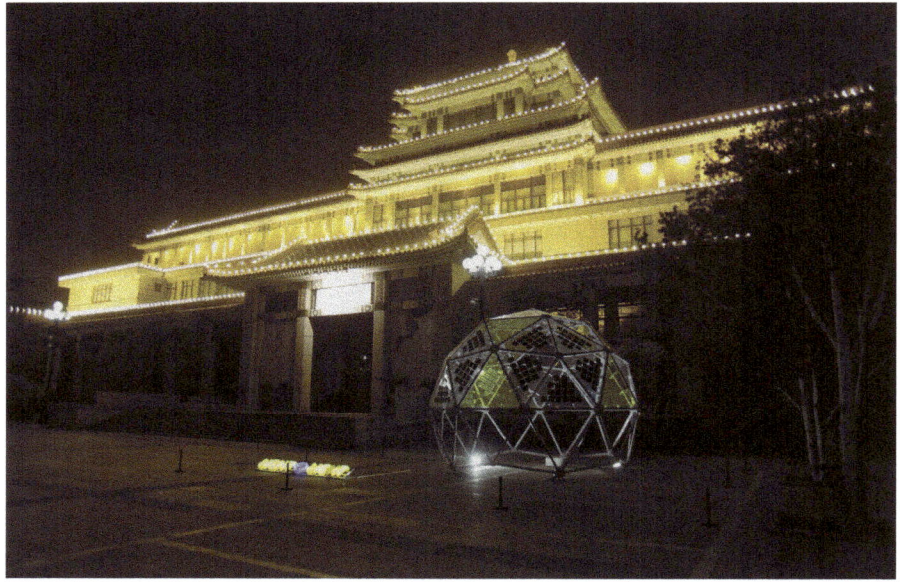

Janet Burchill and Jennifer McCamley, *'Light from Light'* 2010; National Art Museum of China (NAMOC), Beijing; self-powered geodesic dome, custom-built photovoltaic panels, acrylic, neon and aluminium frame. Part of collaborative MAAP–Media Art Asia Pacific project by Australian and Chinese artists in Beijing, Shanghai Library, Hangzhou Library and in Brisbane, with the theme of light-inspired and light-generating artworks.

Image courtesy Kim Machan and MAAP

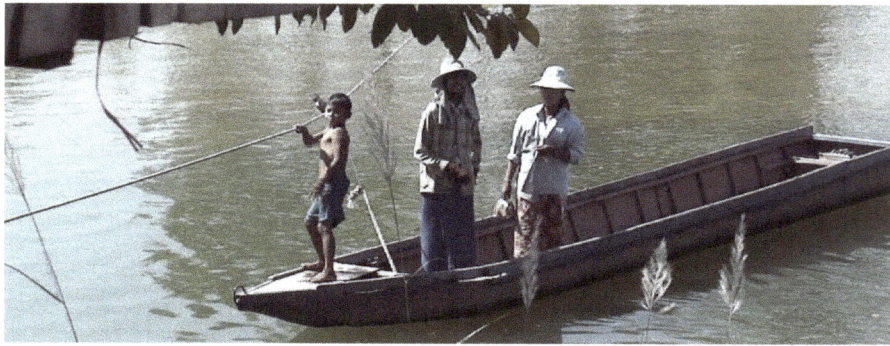

Khin Mar Mar Kyi (filmmaker), *Dreams of Dutiful Daughters* 2011 (film still). The film is about Burmese women who are illegal immigrants to Thailand. In seeking a better life to support their families, many have been forced into prostitution to survive. This film has been shown to Aung San Suu Kyi and, since the reforms in 2011, to ministers in the government.

Image courtesy Khin Mar Mar Kyi

Introduction Part 2 — Asia Present and Resonant: Themes of Connectivity and World-making in Contemporary Asian Art

Michelle Antoinette

The essays in this book provide new ways of understanding Asia and its art as sites not only of local cultural difference, but also regional and worldly connection—connections between Asia and the world, inter-Asia or intra-Asian regional connections, empathic connections forged via art's affective and sensory possibilities, and Asia–Australia connections. With its art focus, the authors engage with these four key themes to investigate what Asian art reveals about such cultural connections and examine how these issues are particular to Asia. In so doing the essays emphasise the connective medium of art itself as a vital key in forging connection for the region and between the region and the world. Art is also revealed as a means of conveying other perspectives on the world based on Asian affinities and experiences, but also for the imagination and generation of new ways of being and belonging in the world at large.

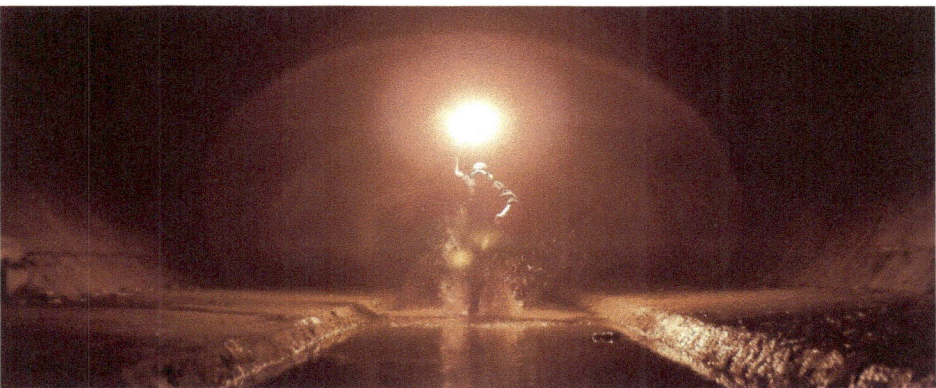

Charles Lim, *all lines flow out* 2011 (video still); video installation; 21 min.

Image courtesy the artist

Together, the essays examine the field of Asian art both as a *site* of *cultural connectedness* and a *platform for generating cultural connectivities*. They trace the multiple lines of historical and contemporary connectedness that mark Asia and which have influenced the shape of its modern and contemporary art landscape. In this, Asia itself is not a homogenous landscape, but a site of multiple and intersecting geographies, cultures, societies, histories and landscapes—*within*. Asia is thus already posited as a site of interconnection, the historical consequence of *intra-regional* crossings, but also, the historical effect of intersecting *local and global* influences.

In Part 1 of this introduction to the volume, Caroline Turner discusses the changing contexts for Asian art in a transforming world. Following Turner's mapping of contemporary Asian art's contexts, I provide here an outline of the individual essays in this volume, and more closely examine their themes of 'connectivity' and 'world-making'. The attention being given to contemporary Asian art, as Turner notes, has brought to light the predominance of 'Western' world views in the history of modern and contemporary art. Indeed, in the context of continuing debates regarding the definition and constitution of 'the modern' and 'the contemporary', the essays in this volume reveal the Euro-American bias of modern art history and demonstrate the specificity and vitality of Asian art and exhibition.

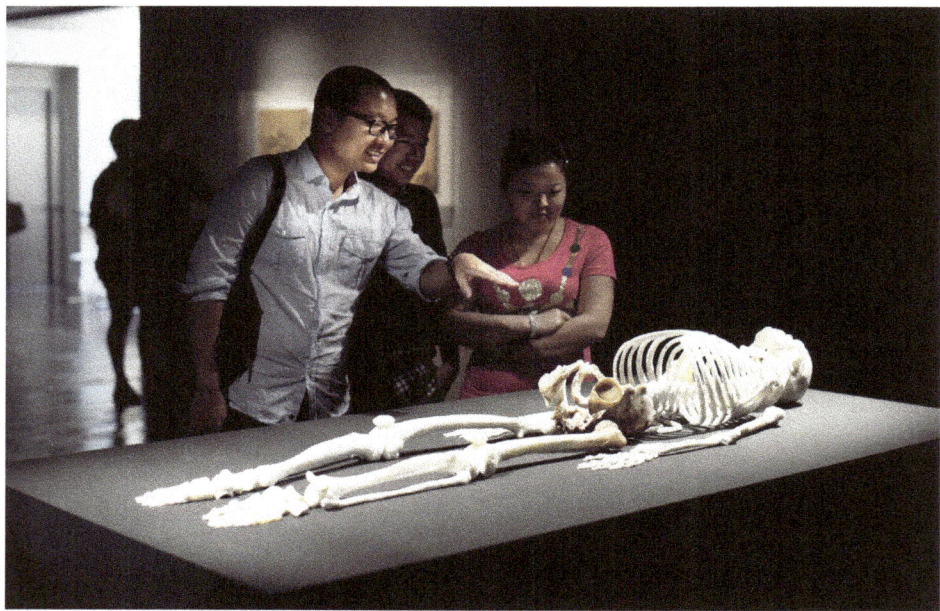

He Xiangyu, *Cola Project* 2012; installation view at 4A Centre for Contemporary Asian Art.

Courtesy the artist and White Space, Beijing; photograph: Garry Trinh

Tracing Connectedness | Connective Proposals

The essays gathered in this book coalesce around four key themes or modes of 'connectedness' and 'connectivity', which we have identified as important threads across the essays in their attention to modern and contemporary Asian art and exhibitions. The co-relation of these key themes may be read as the multi-disciplinary intersection of art history, Asian studies and cultural studies—a conjoining of areas that is provoked by the demands of understanding the interdisciplinarity and cross-cultural intersections of modern and contemporary Asian art itself. This issue, of questioning conventional disciplinary approaches to Asian art founded in Euro-American experience, is at the heart of worldwide debates on the meaning of 'contemporary art', as divergent art forms from diverse locales come into dialogue in world contexts—for example, via international exhibitions. In Asia, as cultural institutions are established to meet the burgeoning interest in cultural industries, the issue of Asian art's culturally and aesthetically 'appropriate' representation has become acute, as seen, for instance, in debates over the M+ museum project in Hong Kong (see Ho, this volume) with its competing narratives of visual culture, popular culture, globalised 'contemporary art', and local 'Hong Kong' and 'Chinese' creative histories.

Part of the motivation for gathering this diverse collection of essays is to highlight and draw attention to the range of connectivities that may be mapped in relation to Asian art. Several essays fit more than one theme and demonstrate that the kinds of projects for which Asian art is put to 'connective' tasks are many and varied. This includes art historiography (Clark, Flores, Turner, Antoinette), art exhibitions (Sambrani, Ho, Hoffie, Carroll, Turner), cultural diplomacy and exchange projects (Turner, Carroll), community and participatory engagements (Ho, Maravillas, Antoinette), forging national and world imaginaries (Clark, Flores, Turner, Meskimmon), commercial exchanges and transactions (Antoinette, Clark), intra-regional exploration and affinities (Merewether, Hoffie, Sambrani, Turner, Antoinette), eliciting empathy and provoking responsibility (Flores, Meskimmon, Maravillas, Lo) and, at its most essential level, communicating with diverse audiences on contemporary issues (Hoffie, Merewether, Antoinette), especially via the fundamental sensory and affective encounter with art (Meskimmon, Maravillas).

World-making and Making Worlds

Our volume's first theme of 'world-making'[1] not only offers a lens onto the mapping of Asia in the world—especially of Asia within the world's art histories—but also the figuration of Asia and Asian art as sites and agencies of 'worlding' and 'world-making'. Through such processes Asia is registered as an alternative viewpoint from which to imagine and make real Asia-specific visions of the world that are different from the hegemonic and undifferentiated universalisms of the West. In this way, Asia is repositioned as a critical agency and agent for 'reworlding' our perspectives,[2] allowing us to imagine the world from the position of locales that were previously overshadowed by Euro-American hegemonic universalisms, to recognise Asia and Asian art in the world, and to construct a space for Asian perspectives within world imaginaries.

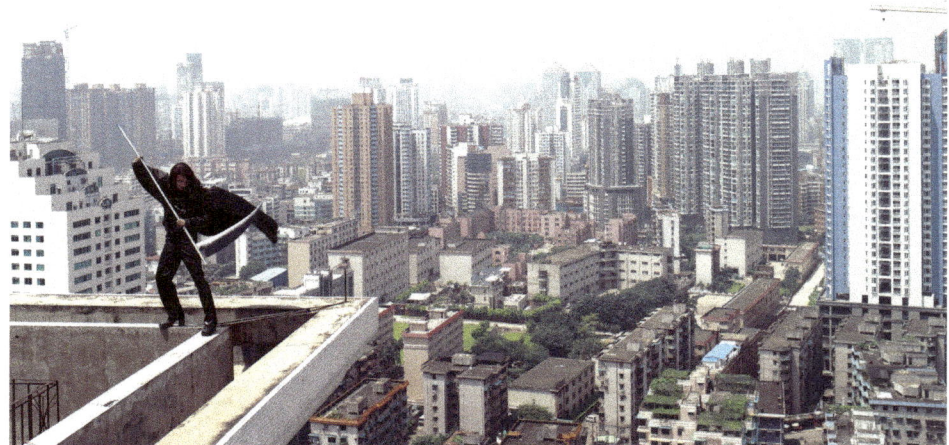

Cao Fei, *City Watcher* from the *Cosplayers* series 2004; photo; 100 x 70 cm.

Courtesy the artist and Vitamin Creative Space 2013

---

1 See Caroline Turner, Michelle Antoinette & Zara Stanhope eds, *The World and World-Making in Art*, special issue, *Humanities Research* 19, no. 2 (2013). http://press.anu.edu.au/titles/humanities-research-journal-series/volume-xix-no-2-2013; Zara Stanhope & Michelle Antoinette, 'The World and World-Making in Art: Connectivities and Differences', *World Art* 2, no. 2 (2012): 167–71.
2 Michelle Antoinette, *Reworlding Art History: Encounters with Contemporary Southeast Asian Art after 1990* (Amsterdam & New York: Rodopi, 2014).

Significantly, there is a sense that the inherent worldliness of modern and contemporary art—its generation within a world context—emphasises connectedness and connectivity within and between diverse locales. Thus, the modern and contemporary art of Asia is simultaneously Asian and of the world and, following the contemporary art theory developed by art historian Terry Smith and noted by Turner in Part I of this Introduction, is 'from the world' and potentially 'for the world'.[3] Essays in this volume by John Clark, Patrick Flores, Marsha Meskimmon, Francis Maravillas and Turner, in particular, draw our attention to this theme of worlding and world-making. In her essay, Turner discusses the geopolitical and Asia-centred contexts for a world-making and world-envisaging perspective in contemporary Asian art. Flores and Clark suggest Asia-based views of the world in history and their effect for present-day Asian art engagements *in* the world and *with* the world. By contrast, Meskimmon and Maravillas focus on the worlding processes and 'cosmopolitics'[4] that are engendered in the artistic projects of selected contemporary Asian artists.[5] The 'cosmopolitan imagination', as Meskimmon has argued elsewhere, is intimately tied not only to the new geographic crossings of contemporary artists in the world, but also to the cross-cultural communicative possibilities of their very art practice. In this sense, contemporary artists may actively create and offer alternative imaginations of the world, but also invite audiences themselves to reflect on and partake in drawing their own worlds, especially so as to map new connections with others in the world.

As Turner intimates in her essay, 'the contemporary' does not emerge from a vacuum but arises from specific histories of modern art development in Asia. With its historicising impetus, Clark's essay provides a retrospective examination of how we have arrived at the present conditions for contemporary Asian art. Clark maps a genealogy of sorts for recognising the specific connective trajectories and forms of what he calls the 'Asian Modern', a topic of long-standing interest to him.[6] He suggests that the beginnings of such modern worlding from Asian perspectives may be traced to a specific period: '"Worlding", from the outset, meant making local interpretive frames visible in a global perspective across cultural and temporal zones because, from the early nineteenth century, there was the potential

---

3   Terry Smith, 'Currents of World-Making in Contemporary Art', *World Art* 1, no. 2 (2011): 175.
4   Pheang Cheah & Bruce Robbins, eds, *Cosmopolitics: Thinking and Feeling Beyond the Nation*, Cultural Politics Series vol. 14 (Minneapolis & London: University of Minnesota Press, 1998); Edwin Jurriëns & Jeroen de Kloet, eds, *Cosmopatriots: On Distant Belongings and Close Encounters* (Amsterdam & New York: Rodopi, 2007).
5   On cosmopolitan practices in contemporary art, see Marsha Meskimmon, *Contemporary Art and the Cosmopolitan Imagination* (London & New York: Routledge, 2011); Nikos Papastergiadis, *Cosmopolitanism and Culture* (Cambridge & Malden MA: Polity, 2012); Charlotte Bydler, *The Global Art World, Inc.: On the Globalization of Contemporary Art* (Uppsala: Acta Universitatis Upsaliensis, 2004).
6   John Clark, 'Open and Closed Discourses of Modernity in Asian Art', in *Modernity in Asian Art*, ed. John Clark (Sydney: Wild Peony, 1993), 1–17; John Clark, *Modern Asian Art* (Sydney: Craftsman House G+B Arts International, 1998); John Clark, *Asian Modernities: Chinese and Thai Art Compared, 1980 to 1999* (Sydney: Power Publications, 2010).

for local discourses to penetrate the non local'. Pursuing traditional methods and aims of art historiography, Clark's essay is a periodisation of the Asian Modern, which recognises particular modernities in Asian art by refocusing attention on the specific historical conditions in which modern Asian art develops. He draws on historical documents of art, especially artists' biographies and career training and their related artworks, in order to present paradigms or 'types' for a chronological but also taxonomical mapping of the Asian Modern. In particular, Clark offers 'five generational artistic cohorts' aligning with 'five rough periods': I Transitions to Modernity, 1850s–1890s; II Academy Realism, Salon Art and the National, 1880s–1910s; III Early Modernism, 1920s–1930s; IV Abstractionism and Conceptualism, 1940s–1960s; V The Contemporary, 1980s to the Present. By tracing and mapping key artists and artworks that fall into these divisions, Clark's essay is a significant contribution to the developing history of modern Asian art. Importantly, while Clark's essay draws our attention to the specificities of the Asian world, and a larger world of art history that must recognise the unique significance of modern Asian art to world currents, it is also concerned with how the Asian Modern comes into existence through the interplay of local and global connectivities, 'emplaced in a set of relations between domestic and overseas art centres'. Clark's work, in other words, also attends to how internal and external, or 'endogenous' and 'exogenous', currents are mutually constitutive in forming the Asian Modern and points to the particular kinds of connectivities that are shaped through these contingent relations.

Essays by Clark and Flores reflect on the seemingly contradictory processes of cultural differentiation and relativisation that are often features of worlding and world-making projects. They both, however, also shift away from these conventional antinomies and, rather, encourage a recognition of their mutual connectivity as integral to the figuring of Asian art. As Clark offers, '"Worlding" is a notion which implies a coherence other than that provided by internal discourses: it posits an outside, and this depends on how the nature and extent of the outside were reciprocally conceived'. Both essays also foreground the influence of colonialism in 'worlding' Asia and this, as Clark argues, 'In a sense, […] is counterintuitive to a simple view of colonial processes as the imposition of a hegemony, rather than the collaboration with it. Such access had, at least theoretically, to include kinds of articulation of the local into the non local and vice versa'.

Similar to Clark's aims, Flores' essay is concerned with Asia-based worlding practices, but distinct from Clark's wider Asian purview, Flores focuses on the specific case of the Philippines. He uses the example of Philippine-based worlding as a 'dissent to dominant worlding'—that is, to that which casts Euro-America as the hegemonic position for viewing the world—and, rather, argues the case for worlding from the specific agency of the Philippine. Flores' essay also explores key figures in literature, film, music and theatre that illuminate Philippine experience and, in doing so, he articulates an archetypal figure— the 'polytropic Philippine'—as a legacy of a particular kind of worlding, drawn from Philippine-based experience and visions of the world. Through his examples of the national hero José Rizal, the singer Lea Salonga, the videoscapes of contemporary artist Stephanie Syjuco, and the Filipino domestic workers pictured in the Hong Kong interiors in which they work in photographs by Chinese artists Sun Yuan and Peng Yu, Flores argues the agency of the Philippine—that is, the 'Philippine remaking itself from a colonial object to a subjectivity that comprehends back'.

In particular Flores articulates a 'polytropic' condition that characterises the specific kinds of worlding enacted by these historical and contemporary Philippine cosmopolitans. He figures the life and thinking of Rizal, the Philippines' revolutionary national hero, as a key trope, but significantly, Flores casts the figure of Rizal more precisely as an emblematic 'polytrope' for the Philippine nation. He suggests the present-day veneration of Rizal as national hero is not merely a reflection of localised Philippine conditions of nationalism, but signifies the particular cosmopolitan sensibilities and aspirations of the Philippine national subject: their need to be 'compared with others' in order to gauge a 'sense of belonging to the world'.

Flores's piece eloquently argues that Philippine subjecthood is always in intimate relation to the larger world. Like the archipelago, it is in some ways deterritorialised—such as the splitting of and into the archipelago—but connected nonetheless. The 'identification, identity and imitation [of the Philippine] are instances of intimacy' that connect the Philippine with the world.[7] Thus, the Philippine is a manifestation, or more precisely, personification of the connectivity which lies in-between worlds, that interconnecting the local and non local, or outside and inside, and which 'mediat[es] discrepant worlds'. As with Clark's essay, Flores at once probes the boundaries and complex relations of the exogenous and endogenous. The polytropic Philippine is thus cast as a national subject whose experience is underlined by a complexity of both local and global connections, entanglements and affiliations.

---

7 Patrick Flores, abstract for keynote paper 'The Philippine Polytrope: Intimating the World in Pieces' presented at 'The World and World-Making in Art' conference, Humanities Research Centre, The Australian National University, Canberra, August, 2011.

Contemporary Art's Affective Impulse: Relating and Responding to Contemporary Asian Art

Essays by Flores, Meskimmon and Maravillas especially, register art's affective and sensory possibilities to bridge borders of cultural difference and point to issues of common, if differently situated, human experience in the world. Flores points to shared experiences of 'loss' that are empathetically felt and performed in the daily lives of Philippine people, whether at home in the Philippines or as part of Philippine diasporic experience:

> the polytropic Philippine is temporary, alien or exile, guest worker or second family, surrogate mother or housekeeper, first teacher or mail order bride, plural in its sympathies, assuming the grief of others and suffering its own, moving—mobile and heart wrenching, modern and melodramatic—and compassionate in many ways, that is, suffering together with passion.

Thus, Flores's essay reminds us of the real and life-sustaining co-dependencies of the Philippine and/in/of the world, as registered in the labour of the Philippine overseas contract worker (OCW) population that live beyond the nation's borders to sustain the nation's livelihood. It is more clearly via Flores's account of the affective connectivity demonstrated by a Philippine singer's rendition of the classic jazz standard *Autumn Leaves*, however, that his essay ties with the newly theorised concerns of affective response to contemporary art and which connects to other essays in the volume on this theme. As Flores argues, the lack of an autumnal season in the Philippines is no obstacle to a young Philippine singer's stunning rendition of (or in Meskimmon's terms, 'response to') a recognisably American anthem. Rather, the feeling of loss that is central to the lyric and mood of the song is harnessed by the singer as a means of connecting with the spirit of the song, and to have others respond or connect to it, through their own experiences of loss and suffering.

Likewise, Meskimmon explores themes of loss and suffering through the empathetic and sensory relation engendered through art and turns to specific instances of this in the contemporary practice of artists Dadang Christanto and Araya Rasdjarmrearnsook. Christanto, originally from Indonesia, has been resident in Australia since 1999; Rasdjarmrearnsook is a Thai woman artist. Both have made significant contributions to contemporary Asian art,[8] especially through their moving performance and installation works, and might be further framed within a 'South-East Asian' regional imaginary of

---

8 Even within Australia, Christanto is still largely framed as an Indonesian artist in the collections and exhibitions of major Australian cultural institutions.

contemporary art.⁹ While Meskimmon's exploration of these artists' practice recognises their particular Asia-based experiences and concerns, the kinds of connectivity she explores are not limited by geographical or cultural horizons. In fact, Meskimmon articulates an argument about the affective capacity of contemporary art to allow empathetic and sensory connections between people across cultural, linguistic and social borders—to allow 'a place in which we can imagine and respond to other people who are different from ourselves'.

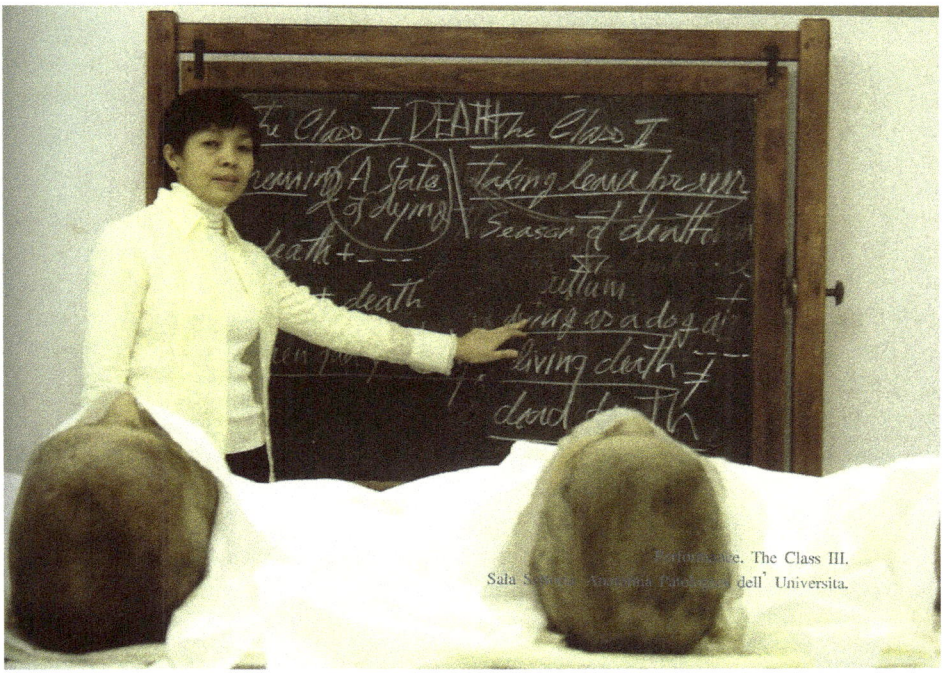

Araya Rasdjarmrearnsook, *The Class III* 2005; video installation; 16.25 min.

Work and image courtesy: Araya Rasdjarmrearnsook, with kind assistance of 100 Tonson Gallery, Bangkok

Such a space, Meskimmon suggests, is meaningful to generating a 'cosmo-politics of response' that is suggestive of both senses of 'responding to' art: that is, through the literal, sensorial reaction to art, but also the kinds of ethico-political 'answering to' that projects such as those offered by Christanto and Rasdjarmrearnsook elicit in their ability to 'touch' and 'move' others affectively and even to provoke them into political action or responsibility for fellow human beings. This kind of cosmo-politics of response also subsequently

---

9   T.K. Sabapathy, 'Developing Regionalist Perspectives in South-East Asian Art Historiography', in *The Second Asia-Pacific Triennial of Contemporary Art* (Brisbane: Queensland Art Gallery, 1996) 13–17; Iola Lenzi, ed., *Negotiating Home, History and Nation: Two Decades of Contemporary Art in Southeast Asia 1991–2011* (Singapore Art Museum, 2011); Antoinette, *Reworlding Art History*.

assists in the generation of a 'cosmopolitan imagination' that Meskimmon has articulated elsewhere,[10] a '"cosmopolitan" mode of responsibility, in which subjects simultaneously acknowledge the difference and specificity of others' experiences, yet respond generously to them'. In her essay, Meskimmon engenders connectivities via these dual meanings of response and the kinds of ethico-political responsibilities they invoke. Through this, she also shows how Christanto and Rasdjarmrearnsook 'connect the micro-stories of individuals with the macro-histories of global geopolitics ...' through what she describes as a form of 'unbidden giving'. Thus, we might trace the obligation to respond, to give, and to impel a further giving, as yet another narrative and praxis of connectivity in the art production-reception process which draws the subject of art, the subject of the artist, and the subject of the audience–participant into webs of intersubjective relation.

Subjectivity itself, as Meskimmon reminds us, 'emerges in and through its fundamental interconnectedness with others'. Christanto and Rasdjarmrearnsook's projects are argued to 'have crossed worlds, eloquently articulating local, Asian experiences of loss, mourning and reclamation while, at the same time, communicating fluently with global audiences,' revealing particular Asian stories and their larger resonance in the world. They therefore give rise to a different platform for world-making, from Asian-led perspectives that are also situated within a 'cosmo-politics' of 'transnational, transcultural generosity'.[11] Importantly, Meskimmon highlights the audience encounter with art as central to the production of art's meaning. As she argues, the art of Christanto and Rasdjarmrearnsook finally depends on the audience–participants' own sense of connection to the feelings of loss and suffering expressed and elicited through their respective art projects. For their art is not didactic in its communicative intent and call to response, but rather elicits audience response via art's affective or sensory invitation to empathic relation and dialogue with others.

Indeed, connectivities also evoke the concept of 'relation'—including 'relating to' and 'relating with', and the kinds of relationships drawn by and through art. This is central to a new stream of contemporary art theory and practice which engages artists and their publics in conscious relation with each other, variously described and debated as 'relational', 'socially engaged', 'community-engaged' and/or 'participatory' art.[12] This may be contrasted with modern notions of

---

10   Meskimmon, *Contemporary Art*.
11   Marsha Meskimmon, essay abstract for this book: 'Response and Responsibility: On the Cosmo-politics of Generosity in Contemporary Asian Art'.
12   See the key art historical work undertaken, for example, by Nicolas Bourriaud, *Relational Aesthetics* (Dijon: Les Presses du réel, 2002; Esthétique relationnelle 1998). Claire Bishop, 'Antagonism and Relational Aesthetics', *October* (Fall 2004, No. 110): 51–79. Grant Kester, *Conversation Pieces: Community and Communication in Modern Art* (Berkeley and Los Angeles: University of California Press, 2004).

the artist as individual genius, whose art is firmly framed as an autonomous product of individual authorship. Several essays draw attention to these kinds of socially connected art practice and the ways in which they resituate the conventional roles of and relations between art, artist, and audience and, in turn, generate alternative meanings about the role and value of art itself. They reflect the recent positioning of contemporary art, not merely as a signifier or mirror of the world, but as a form of relational process, collaboration and/or engagement. In this, acts or modes of connection and connectivity may be read as essential to the 'relational' process, namely between artists, their audience–participants, and the resulting 'art' they produce in collaborative and/or participatory engagement with each other. They suggest that such engagements are not necessarily smooth, harmonious or seductive connections, but can also be a field of political contestations, transgression and trespassing, where the limits to the autonomy of the artist and audience–participant or 'guest' and 'host' are tested and traversed.

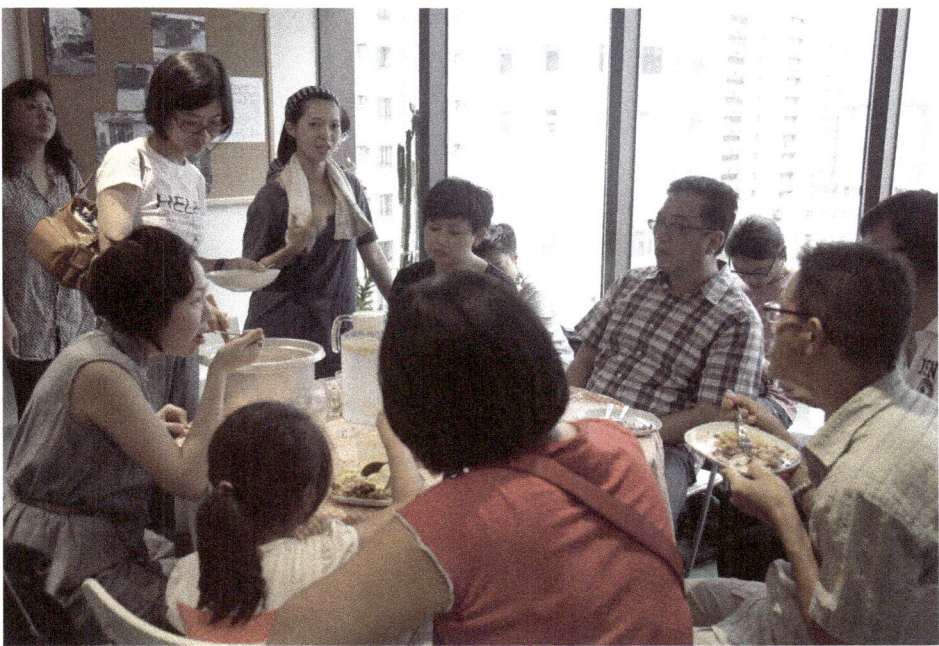

Asia Art Archive Open Weekend 2013. Spark! Programme MEALS & SHARING 'Art Tastes Salty', 7 July 2013.

Image courtesy Asia Art Archive

Like Meskimmon, Maravillas's essay highlights the intersubjective relations which are foregrounded in forms of contemporary art practice, underscored by an ethics of 'giving' and 'receiving'. Maravillas's essay, however, is especially concerned with the new kinds of relational art practices engaged in aesthetic acts of hospitality, specifically through food-based 'alimentary' art projects. Situating his reflections within a triangular field of recent theory—'relational aesthetics', 'cosmopolitanism', and 'hospitality'—Maravillas explores how contemporary Asian art might suggest 'alternative and more extensively relational frameworks for understanding home and hospitality' through the making of affective and sensuous worlds across difference. Exploring the shared subject matter of 'food' as a connective thread in various projects of contemporary Asian artists, particularly Rirkrit Tiravanija, Mella Jaarsma, Lee Mingwei, and Roslisham Ismail (aka Ise), Maravillas examines the relational dynamics of artistic projects that invite audience–participants to participate in exchanges of hospitality—that is, 'giving to' and 'receiving from' others.

In particular, Maravillas explores the ethico-political import and sensuous connectivity of these performance-based art practices, including the larger 'transnational and diasporic vectors of connection to an imagined "home"' in which they are enmeshed. He considers the value of cosmopolitan frameworks for reconfiguring notions of home, belonging and community in a region marked by the legacy of multiple colonial and postcolonial histories. Significantly, he argues that the 'performative, relational and sensuous processes of the alimentary … sets the table and the stage for the enactment of an artful hospitality and connectivity through generous and responsible acts of "world-making"'. Culturally situated practices of alimentation and world-making, Maravillas contends, are crucial to these projects' particular translations (of hospitality, home and belonging) and their connective effect (across spaces and temporalities, for instance). While the art of Rirkrit Tiravanija has become among the most well-known in this genre due to its international attention in exhibitions by the French curator Nicolas Bourriaud, Maravillas describes a wider concern with food-centred art practices among Asian artists and argues the differentiated and situated meanings of performative, participatory or relational art practices with respect to specific audiences of reception and the specific kinds of cultural translation each audience brings to interpretations of contemporary art by Asian artists.

Intra-Asian Regional Connections: Art, Exhibitions, and Curating, on Asian Terms

Another theme of this volume concerns intra-Asian regional dynamics that explore art-related connectivities within and across the otherwise discontinuous geographies of Asia. The essays addressing this theme recover the historical importance of regional connection across and within Asia and register the continuing importance of inter- and intra-regional links, especially after colonial separations and in view of new Asia-based art initiatives which (re-)connect the region in the twenty-first century. Essays which directly address intra-regional connections include those by Chaitanya Sambrani, Oscar Ho, Charles Merewether, Turner, and myself.

Recent scholarship in Asian studies, and especially intra-Asian studies, reflects theories and models of connectivity that are premised on intra-regional or 'intra-Asian' relations; these may be compared with other types of connective cultural work premised on other kinds of prefix, including 'the *inter*-cultural', the '*cross*-cultural', and the '*trans*-cultural'. As with processes of worlding and world-making, for intra-regional practices there is a basis of comparative relation based on difference, but also similitudes of socio-historical and political experience. The emphasis rests on adjacencies and networks of relation across Asia itself.[13] Often this work seeks to uphold Asia not only as an important subject of study, but attempts to recover localised tools and methods for studying Asia comparatively across the region so as to avoid hegemonic Euro-American methodologies and perspectives.[14] The work of recovering and inscribing art histories for the region as the consequence of their specific and situated contexts, may be understood in this vein.

Perhaps one of the most obvious means of new intra-regional connection is via the web-based digital technologies or ICTs (information and communication technologies), which emerged in the late twentieth century and created new channels of communication between diverse Asian societies and between Asia and the rest of the world. Web-based technologies permit day-to-day communications between neighbours in the region that were previously separated by borders of space, time, languages, history and colonialisms.[15] Furthermore, apropos of contemporary art itself, new digital and 'web art' forms have also been instrumental to the development of cross-cultural collaborative or exchange-based art projects which actively seek to creatively connect with distant others in ways that were previously restrained by physical distance. Artist groups such as Raqs Media Collective (India), tsunamii.net (Singapore), Young-Hae Chang Heavy Industries (South Korea), and House of Natural Fibre (HONF, Yogyakarta) are among those that have harnessed the so-called 'new media' technologies often towards collaborative art practices. Operating since 1998, the Brisbane-based MAAP—Media Art Asia Pacific, also mentioned in

---

13   See Chen Kuan-Hsing, with Kuo Hsiu-Ling, Hans Hang & Hsu Ming-Chu, eds, *Trajectories: Inter-Asia Cultural Studies* (London: Routledge, 1998). See also Chen Kuan-Hsing, *Asia as Method: Towards Deimperialization* (Durham: Duke University Press, 2010) and Chen Kuan-Hsing & Chua Beng Huat, *The Inter-Asia Cultural Studies Reader* (Abingdon: Routledge, 2007).
14   Chen, *Asia as Method*.
15   S.Y. Chia & J.J. Lim, 'Singapore: A Regional Hub in ICT', in *Towards a Knowledge-based Economy: East Asia's Changing Industrial Geography*, eds S. Masuyama & D. Vanderbrink (Singapore: Institute of Southeast Asia Studies, 2003), 259–98.

Turner's essay, was established 'to bring focus to "unmapped" media art activity from Australia, Asia and the Pacific.'[16] Initiatives such as MAAP have brought to light the strength of new digital art forms across many parts of Asia, especially as these forms have become increasingly inexpensive and accessible in societies that have limited public infrastructure and resources to foster art or lack the physical space for traditional art studios.

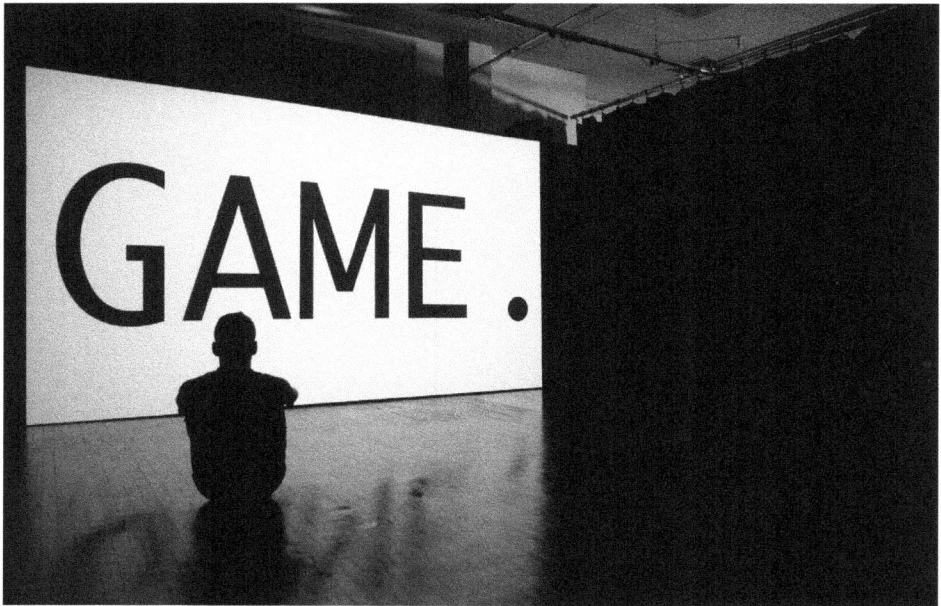

YOUNG-HAE CHANG HEAVY INDUSTRIES, *YOUNG-HAE CHANG HEAVY INDUSTRIES, THE SLICKEST LITTLE KOREAN SCUMBAG DOWN UNDER* (2012); original text and music soundtrack; HD QuickTime movie. Commissioned by Campbelltown Arts Centre and 4A Centre for Contemporary Asian Art for *Edge of Elsewhere* 2012.

Courtesy the artist; photograph: Zan Wimberley; image courtesy 4A Centre for Contemporary Asian Art

If 'new media' contemporary art forms offer new types of creative connection, as in the past, artists continue to demonstrate the concerns of their age via shared subject matter. In this volume, Merewether looks to the shared subject matter of Asia's 'seas' as a connective thread across instances of contemporary Asian art, tracing contemporary artists' common concerns with Asia's rapid industrialisation and urbanisation from the late twentieth century, and their effect for Asia's landscapes and territories. As Merewether suggests, artists are highlighting the pressing issue of Asia's changing natural environments and the socio-political consequences of this for Asia's present and its futures.

---

16   See MAAP–Media Art Asia Pacific, accessed 16 October 2013, http://www.maap.org.au/about-maap/.

This is obviously not only of increasing regional concern, but a matter of significant world interest in view of global climate change. Beyond subject matter, Merewether also considers the aesthetic connections of contemporary Asian artists who engage with Conceptual art, not merely their links to international art movements but also to their Asian Conceptual art predecessors of the 1960s and 1970s. Thus, Merewether captures multiple intra-Asian currents with effect for the region: the subject matter of art, art movements and histories, and socio-political matters of regional relevance. Moreover, his multi-sited art historical mapping and method, across different parts of Asia, allows us to view intra-Asian maps with 'up close' specificity at the same time as 'zooming out' to trace broader lines of artistic sharedness and socio-political interconnectivity across the Asian region, and beyond. As Merewether's essay highlights, the art of a particular generation often brings into relief the most urgent concerns affecting societies—in this case, how Asia's natural environments have undergone dramatic change and, in matters of governance, how Asia's territories are literally being reshaped and rezoned through land reclamations and urban projects, remaking the reality of Asian worlds for the present and the future.

Exhibitions and their curatorial motivations are also flagged as an important space for developing intra-regional cross-cultural connections. Sambrani's essay, which focuses on his own 2010 exhibition, *Place.Time.Play: Contemporary Art from the 'West Heavens' to the 'Middle Kingdom'*, suggests a renewal of intra-Asian connections through contemporary art curatorship and exhibitions—in this case, between India and China within the larger frame of the 'West Heavens' project, also discussed by Turner. Initiated by Chinese art curator, academic and entrepreneur Johnson Chang (Chang Tsong-Zung), the 'West Heavens' project seeks to probe 'how contemporary Chinese artistic and academic cultures might benefit from interactions with their Indian counterparts', with the name of the project recalling 'the ancient Chinese name for India, as the heavenly realm lying to the west'.[17] Reflecting on his own 'curatorial adventure' from the conceptualisation of the exhibition through to its final presentation in Shanghai, Sambrani offers a personal account of the development of an exhibition of contemporary Asian art from the perspective of the curator.

In particular, Sambrani's curatorial perspective directs a lens onto the complexities of conceiving and carrying out an Asia-focused, cross-cultural exhibition in a transnational context, highlighting how such projects may provide channels for forging new, intra-regional cultural connections in the twenty-first century, especially in the face of the politically complex relationship between India and China. At the project's outset Sambrani asks, 'For all their historical connections, what did contemporary artists from either country really

---

17   See the 'West Heavens' project website, accessed 6 October 2013, http://westheavens.net/en.

know of each other's work?'[18] Indeed, the 'West Heavens' project is significant in its status as the first intellectual and creative engagement across the art and academic cultures of India and China, with no substantial precedents for engagement between artist communities from these countries. As Sambrani has described, *Place.Time.Play* encouraged artists to use each other's countries as 'a laboratory in which to test new ideas for cross-cultural engagement'; artists were invited to engage in 'universal, yet locally situated, extensions of their current practice' and undertook reciprocal research trips in India and China as part of the exhibition development.[19] Sambrani argues that this cross-cultural connectivity enabled 'a different vision of "global" or "international" art, one that is premised on encountering that which is at once deeply intimate and incontrovertibly foreign'.[20] Sambrani contrasts this with the frenzied and less critically engaged commercial transactions with contemporary Asian art, now common to the global art marketplace: the growth of new Indian and Chinese art markets in the two countries has brought economic attention to contemporary Chinese and Indian art but also contemporary Asian art more generally, and the result may sometimes be an economically driven spectacularisation of Asian art rather than a critical engagement with it.[21] Importantly, Sambrani's project also reveals the obstacles and limits of cross-cultural/transnational projects and the difficulties of forging connectivities between cultures, even where there is the will to do so. As his essay points out, cultural institutions are also reflections of the unique socio-political, cultural and bureaucratic imperatives which underwrite them, and thus, may present hurdles for presenting contemporary art across cultures and connecting differently situated Asian societies. Nevertheless, as Sambrani's essay highlights, the key significance of *Place.Time.Play* and the overall 'West Heavens' project vision, is the reconfiguration of curatorial methods and exhibition models which bypass the need for Euro-American legitimation and rather attends to Asia-based experiences, and exhibitions on Asian terms.

Not unrelated to Sambrani's concerns, Hong Kong-based artist, curator and academic Ho offers a critique of hegemonic, Euro-American-influenced models of curatorship and argues their problematic effects for museum and exhibition development in Asia. Similar to Sambrani's efforts to avoid the hegemonic imaginary of a Euro-American audience for *Place.Time.Play*

---

18 Chaitanya Sambrani, essay proposal for this book: 'An Experiment in Connectivity: From the "West Heavens" to the "Middle Kingdom"'.
19 Chaitanya Sambrani, 'When India and China Engage: A Curatorial Adventure', conference paper abstract for 'The World and World-Making in Art' conference, Humanities Research Centre, The Australian National University, Canberra, August, 2011.
20 Sambrani, 'When India and China Engage'.
21 Important new art fairs in Asia, which demonstrate the increasing commercial significance of Asian art, include the Hong Kong International Art Fair (Art HK) established in 2007 and superseded by Art Basel Hong Kong in 2013; and the India Art Fair (established in 2008 and formerly known as India Art Summit).

and to instead position his exhibition for Chinese and Indian audiences, Ho contends that the kinds of curatorship required for developing exhibitions and, by extension, museums in Asia must be premised on a different set of culturally based considerations that relate specifically to Asian situations and local conditions. Thus, Ho argues, the experience of curating and exhibiting for Asian audiences within Asian contexts should be regarded as a context-specific exercise that bears specific connection to Asia and should, therefore, be premised on a different set of conditions and histories than that inscribed in hegemonic Western-influenced exhibition models. Ho cites the development of the M+ 'museum' project at Hong Kong's new West Kowloon Cultural District (WKCD) as a key case study; the long awaited M+ cultural project forms part of the recent flurry of initiatives by the Hong Kong Government to develop the economic potential of cultural industries. Examining the particular conditions and necessities of cultural institutions in Asia, Ho argues ambitious projects such as M+ are seemingly always 'under the shadow' of invited Western experts who 'play a dominant role in shaping the content and the format of presentations' in Asian cultural institutions. This situation, Ho contends, is problematic for 'efforts to create a cultural landscape that is of distinctive local characteristics' and to develop 'cultural languages and operational models that are distinctively Asian'.[22] Ho compares this with the work of independent or 'alternative' art spaces and initiatives and, more specifically, the curatorial work affiliated with such art projects, with their more experimental and locally-informed models and methods. In 2011, with the support of the Asian Cultural Council Hong Kong, Ho set up the Asian Curatorial Network (ACN) to develop an intra-regional platform for dialogue between such independent Asia-based curators and spaces, so as to provide a forum for discussing their 'alternative' methods and particular challenges (i.e. political, bureaucratic, resource-based and infrastructural) for developing exhibitions *in* Asia and *for* Asians and to exchange ideas on how to achieve their successful implementation. As Ho hints, this concern to develop Asia-specific models of exhibition must necessarily be tied to the education and training of a new generation of Asia-based art professionals in order to meet the new demands of Asia's growth in the cultural sector.

---

22 Oscar Ho, essay abstract for this book: 'Under the Shadow: Problems in Museum Development in Asia'.

Australia–Asia and 'Australia in the Asian Century'?[23]

The final theme of the volume is Asian–Australian connections, which encompasses specific Australian concerns, especially Australia's continuing interest in cross-cultural, art-based partnerships with Asia (see Turner, Carroll, this volume). The essays reflecting this theme probe particular art-related collaborations and exchanges between Australia and Asia and intersect with the topic of the Australian Research Council (ARC) project by Turner and myself on Asian art networks.[24] In varied ways, the essays explore Australia's cultural relationship with Asia now and historically and, to some degree, probe how Australia is perceived from within the Asian region and vice versa (see Lo, this volume).

This theme, which addresses specific connectivities between Australia and Asia, is especially motivated by questions about Australia's historical, present and future role with, and even, within Asia as part of an 'Asian' or 'Asia-Pacific' geo-cultural imaginary. Papers by Alison Carroll, Pat Hoffie and Jacqueline Lo, in particular, are situated within these historical and contemporary currents of Asia–Australia relations and elaborate on these issues. The white paper, *Australia in the Asian Century*,[25] for a brief period spurred fervent discussion again regarding the establishment of new cultural initiatives between Australia and Asia, but as Turner argues and other contributors attest, it should not be forgotten that over the course of recent decades various cultural agencies have been and continue to be highly active in seeking to connect Australia with Asia and vice versa. Such projects are often positioned within the realm of cultural diplomacy; for instance, as also noted by Turner, Melbourne-based Asialink is steered by a mission 'to work with business, government, philanthropic and cultural partners to initiate and strengthen Australia Asia engagement.'[26] Asialink Arts, discussed by Carroll, aims to 'develop opportunities for cultural exchange between Australia and Asia and improve the Asia capability of the cultural sector based on the principles of partnership, collaboration and reciprocity.'[27] Art-making and art exhibitions can be regarded as keys to forging new relationships with unfamiliar others, so as to relate 'Asian' experiences to 'Australians' and vice versa. Beyond the display and mirroring of culture, such projects are also spaces for the negotiation and translation of culture via the mutable text of art, with its openness to varied meanings across different

---

23 Department of the Prime Minister and Cabinet, *Australia in the Asian Century*, white paper (Canberra, 2012).
24 Caroline Turner & Michelle Antoinette, 'The Rise of New Cultural Networks in Asia in the Twenty-First Century', Australian Research Council project 2010–2013 (DP1096041).
25 *Australia in the Asian Century*.
26 Asialink, 'About Us', accessed 7 October 2013, http://asialink.unimelb.edu.au/about_us.
27 Asialink, 'Arts', accessed 7 October 7 2013, http://asialink.unimelb.edu.au/arts.

cultural contexts of production and reception. Importantly, alongside the successes of such cross-cultural exchange projects are the significant lessons learnt from the challenges or difficulties in achieving intercultural engagement and connectivity. Arguably it is through instances of the so called 'failures' of such projects that productive acts of cultural translation and negotiation are often made possible.

Along with the Fukuoka Asian Art Museum, the recurrent Brisbane-based Asia-Pacific Triennial of Contemporary Art (APT), also discussed by Turner, helped to enhance international knowledge of contemporary Asian and Pacific art at a time when there was little regard for contemporary art that was produced outside Europe and the United States. Established in 1993, the APT was preceded by other Australian initiatives to engage Asia—such as the Artists' Regional Exchange (1987–1999),[28] and the Biennale of Sydney's sporadic inclusion of Asian artists since its inception in 1973. Unlike most biennales and triennales, the APT has carved a distinctively 'Asia-Pacific' *regional* focus and assisted in forging an international presence for contemporary 'Asian' and 'Pacific' art, even an 'Asia-Pacific' art.

Hoffie explores the APT's connection to current art historical debates being played out with regard to the definition and exhibition of 'contemporary art'. More precisely, she probes changing and contested notions of 'the contemporary' both as a category of art and a marker of temporality. By recalling the history of the APT, including the original exhibition motives of the first three triennials (1993, 1996, 1999) and their means of negotiating 'the contemporary', Hoffie argues that the definition of contemporary Asian and Pacific art had changed by the time of the seventh triennial (2012–2013). To this end, Hoffie argues the necessarily interconnected currents of 'tradition' and 'change' as constituent parts of any understanding of 'the contemporary' and, therefore, influential factors in defining how such art should be presented within the space of the APT.

More specifically, Hoffie describes the inter-connectivity between 'tradition' and 'change' in terms of a 'collision' and 'morphing', whereby 'tradition', on the one hand, is 'associated with memory, history and place' and 'by implication … with the past', and on the other, 'change' is 'associated with the here and now' and 'with the tempo of movement and the blur of shape-shifting'. Borrowing from the curator Natasha Conland, Hoffie argues that the disorderly inter-connectivity underlying contemporary art is a necessarily and productively 'irreverent' manifestation, 'an active, contested zone of conflict, contrapuntals, contradictions, productive confusions, contrarieties, contrasts'.

---

28   ARX was a biennial artist exchange project established in Perth, Australia, in 1987 involving 'Asia-Pacific' artists, including a sizeable number of South-East Asian artists.

In so doing, Hoffie highlights another connection—that of contemporary Asian art to its particular socio-historical, geographical and cultural contexts, as well as the specific temporalities of its production. Moreover, she points to the creativity of indigenous Asian cultures, including via contemporary artists who bring indigenous concerns to their art practice, such as the late Filipino artists Santiago Bose and Roberto Villanueva. Such art, she argues, productively complicates established notions of 'contemporary' art, so that tradition does not necessarily signal cultural concerns of the past but lives on in active creative engagements situated in the present and future. Indeed, if the 'contemporary' is understood simply as a marker of time, then many indigenous cultures demand a reframing of the Western logic of linear time, and a dismantling of the history of art as a narrative of successive 'avant-gardes'—the ever-new which displaces the ongoing and living significance of tradition that is practiced in many non-Western cultures.[29]

The Australian interest in Asia also partly reflects the situation of Asian diasporas in Australia and their ongoing generational effect in carving a space of Asian–Australian relations and Asian–Australian identity from within Australia.[30] As essays by Lo and Turner highlight, the Australian engagement with Asia is not new; rather, it follows on from a longer history of relations *between* Australia and Asia, but also Asian–Australian relations *within* Australia. In the area of art, key pivots for revisiting what is meant by Australian art were propelled by indigenous concerns, multicultural issues and the rise of republican sentiments in the 1990s. With regard to Asian–Australian creative interventions, as discussed by both Lo and myself (Epilogue), significant density was gained around the group of Asian–Australian multidisciplinary artists (including John Young, see Lo), who formed their own collective, 4A (the Asian Australian Artists' Association)—'a non-profit organisation established in 1996 to present and promote the work of Asian and Asian-Australian artists'.[31] Alongside this has been a growing scholarship on Asian–Australian studies, especially that supported by the work

---

29 See Nicholas Thomas, 'Our History is Written in our Mats: Reflections on Contemporary Art, Globalisation and History', *The 5th Asia-Pacific Triennial of Contemporary Art* (Brisbane: Queensland Art Gallery, 2006) 24–31; Nicholas Thomas, 'Contemporary Art and the Limits of Globalisation', in *The Second Asia-Pacific Triennial of Contemporary Art*, eds Caroline Turner and Rhana Devenport (Brisbane: Queensland Art Gallery, 1996), 17–18.
30 This is not unlike the work undertaken to explore the cultural experiences of Asian diasporas in other societies, such as in the United States. See Jacqueline Lo, Dean Chan & Tseen Khoo, 'Introduction—Asian Australia and Asian America: Making Transnational Connections', *Amerasia Journal* 36, no. 2 (2010): xii–xxvii.
31 Previous affiliates of 4A include former directors Melissa Chiu (founding director) and Binghui Huangfu. Early members include: John Young, Vicente Butron, Chris Pang, Kim Moore, Philip O'Toole, Felicia Kan, Victoria Lobregat, Emil Goh, David Lui, Kate Mizrahi, Dacchi Dang, Lindy Lee, Guan Wei, Melissa Chiu, Laurens Tan, Cindy Pan, Hari Ho, Su-Lin Tse and My Lee Thi. See http://www.4a.com.au/about-4a/ (accessed October 8, 2013).

of the Asian–Australian Studies Research network (of which Lo is Chair), which includes research clusters focusing on visual culture, performing arts, and literature, among other Asian–Australian cultural practices.[32]

As Lo's essay highlights with reference to the recent art practice of Asian-Australian artists, Asia is not only 'out there', but also an already existing part of Australia's cultural fabric. These dual conditions, Lo argues, should be important considerations for Australia in its efforts to establish new narratives for engaging with Asia in the twenty-first century. Lo discusses the two artists John Young and Jason Wing in order to draw out their differently situated Asian–Australian positions, not only with effect for notions of their belonging to and in Australia, but also, belonging to and in the world. As Lo highlights, artists such as Young not only point to immediate Australian concerns but also historical issues of global resonance. From the vantage point of a diaspora artist, Young brings a transnational approach to otherwise nationally-defined histories, seeking to 'reawaken an intrinsic ethical impulse' in his audiences everywhere (and thus, corresponding with the artistic projects of Christanto and Rasdjarmrearnsook as discussed by Meskimmon in this volume). On the other hand, Lo also asks us to recognise the Asia already within Australia via the art practice of Jason Wing, whose art draws attention to the present-day legacy of historical cultural crossings between Aboriginal and Asian people, a critical and complex hybridity too often made invisible by hegemonic cultural narratives which seek to simplify, even obscure, the Asianness that is already within Australia. As Lo summarises for both artists: 'The works of Asian-Australians, such as Wing and Young, point to more nuanced ways of engaging with the complexities of Asia "out there", but also the ways in which an understanding of "Asia within" can enrich our understanding of who we are as a nation, and how we can relate in more meaningful ways with our near-neighbours.'

In the final essay in the book, the Epilogue entitled 'My Future is Not a Dream': Shifting Worlds of Contemporary Asian Art and Exhibitions', I discuss the work of a number of contemporary artists within the context of developments in contemporary Asian art over the last two decades. I return to a number of key themes raised throughout the essays in this book including the international exhibition of contemporary Asian art; new Asian art markets and cultural industries; the significance of independent art practices and curatorship in Asia in attending to local contexts; and contemporary Asian art which connects and responds to world issues. In particular, I reflect on the artwork of Liew Kung Yu, Phuan Thai Meng, Chen Quilin, FX Harsono, Wong Hoy Cheong, N.S. Harsha, Pak Sheung Chuen and Cao Fei, among others. Intersecting with the concerns of the authors represented in this volume, I consider artists' changed concerns in the twenty-first century, coinciding with shifts in Asia itself, new generations

---

32   See the website of the Asian Australian Studies Research Network, http://aasrn.wordpress.com/.

of artists and art-making, and transforming currents of contemporary Asian art practice, exhibition and historicisation. Through its engagement with Asia's pasts, contemporary Asian art, as this volume attests, is also deeply concerned with the present as a means for considering Asia's futures and, moreover, the world's futures.

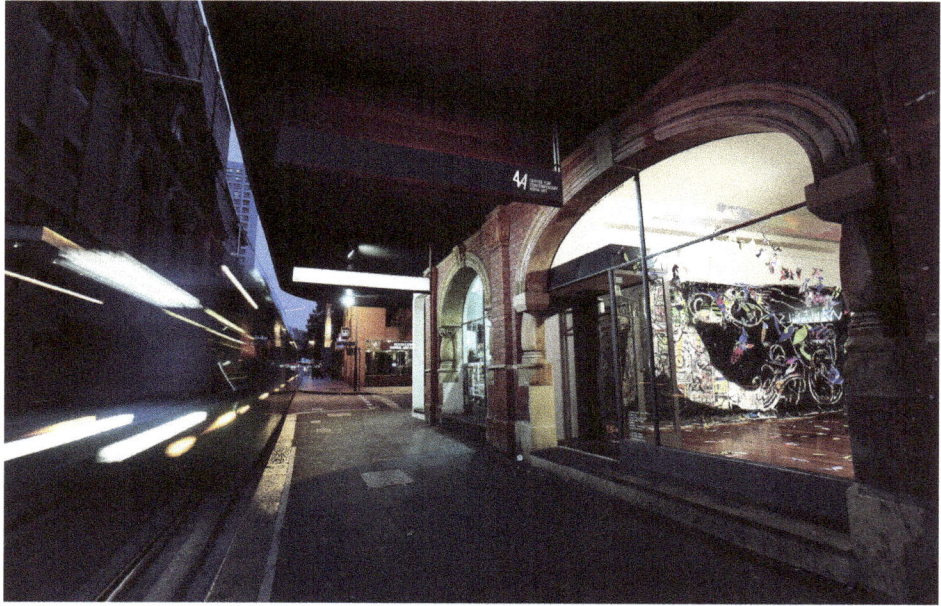

Exterior of 4A Centre for Contemporary Asian Art, Sydney.

Image courtesy 4A Centre for Contemporary Asian Art

Asian Difference and Connection in the World

Ultimately, we propose that the essays gathered here collectively ask, 'how might we think "difference" and "connection" in regard to Asia? And, in particular, the difference and connection that is inherent to modern and contemporary Asian art?' Indeed, these questions might serve as framing devices for thinking through contemporary Asian art, as readers encounter the various essays in this collection. While these are challenging questions, the essays here may be seen as efforts to examine such issues, to explore the complexities of these positionalities and their entanglements through views of the world from Asian and/or non Euro-Americentric perspectives, via empathetic and sensory engagements, across intra-regional currents of Asia itself, and in deepening diasporic and transnational networks, such as that connecting Australia and Asia. The essays not only expand our awareness of modern and contemporary

Asian art as spaces of already existing commonalities and connection, but also suggest the ongoing activity of connecting *across* Asia and *with* Asia as a project of plural and ongoing possibilities that highlight renewed forms of regional and global cultural collaboration, exchange and crossings. They emphasise Asia's diverse, ever-changing and contingent cultural landscapes and the resonant affinities, resemblances and similitudes of Asian art with other conditions and experience in the world. They also suggest specific Asian histories and contexts for modern and contemporary Asian art and exhibition, illuminating distinctive trajectories of development and passages for the future.

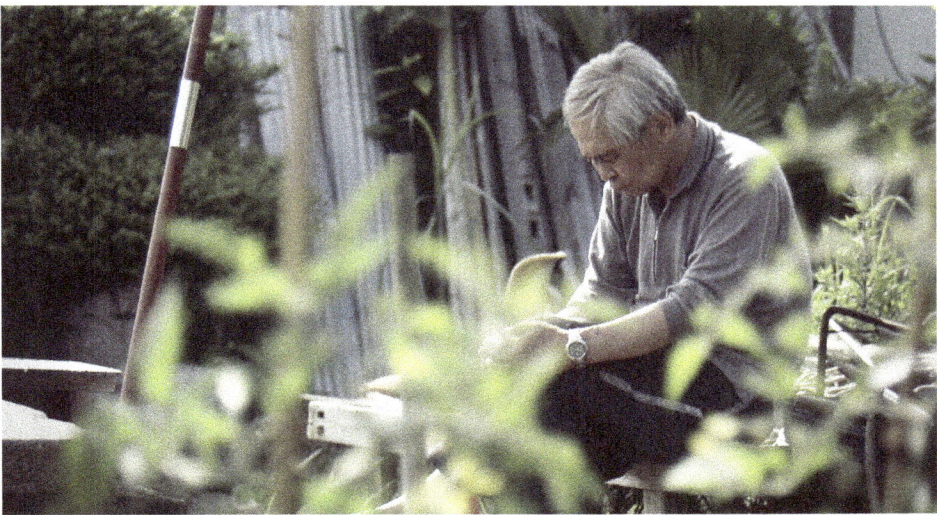

Fiona Tan, Indonesia/ Netherlands b. 1966, *Cloud Island* 2010 (still); HD installation.

Courtesy the artist, Frith Street Gallery, London and Wako Works of Art, Tokyo

1. Polytropic Philippine: Intimating the World in Pieces

Patrick D. Flores

Reflecting on the theme 'world making', I was struck by two phrases that speak of the world as radically discriminating: 'a world like no other' and 'worlds apart' authenticate the singular and the different, which invoke the other, so that distance can be marked and the incomparable imagined. On the other hand, I would be reminded of certain modes of inquiry, such as 'world history' and 'comparative religion' that tend to encompass and include, to convene a multitude under the aegis of relationality or relativisation, which in turn survives the translations of context. This essay hints at a possible shift from the apparent antinomy between discrimination and inclusion, hostility and hospitality, the exceptional and the global, the indifferent and the comparable, mastery and sympathy.

In 1884, Filipinos who called themselves *los indios bravos*, or natives of the wild, gathered in a restaurant in Madrid to toast the triumph of their peers in the 1884 Madrid Exposition. Felix Resurreccion Hidalgo was conferred a silver medal for the work *Las Virgenes Cristianas Expuestas al Populacho* and Juan Luna received one of the three gold honours for the painting *Spoliarium*. That the Filipinos convened themselves in Europe was a fraught proposition: on the one hand, they entreated for reforms in the colony by way of inclusion in the Spanish Government and, on the other, laid the groundwork for a nation founded on exception, or exclusion from the empire, the site of their prolific exile, or their progressive other-worldliness. *Spoliarium* prefigures this aspiration as well to the degree that it mingles multiple moments of coloniality itself, or the various projects that have rendered the particularities of the world singular: the empires of Rome and Spain and the space for the exposition of art in the world. The scene in the painting is the cellar of the Roman colosseum where the cadavers of gladiators and slaves are stripped of their final effects and flung into the furnace. At the same event, where glasses were raised to exalt Luna and Hidalgo, Graciano Lopez Jaena read the picture as an allegory of the Hispanic condition in the Philippines:

> For me, if there is anything grandiose, sublime in the *Spoliarium*, it is that through this canvas, through the figure depicted in it, through its coloring, floats the living image of the Filipino people grieving over their misfortunes … the Philippines is nothing more than a *Spoliarium* in

reality, with all its horrors. There rubbish lies everywhere; there human dignity is mocked; the rights of man are torn into shreds; equality is a shapeless mass; and liberty is embers, ashes, smoke.[1]

José Rizal, who would be executed for inspiring the revolution and become the country's pre-eminent patriot, sensed in *Spoliarium* a tale that was more than allegorical; for him, it was invincible evidence that the Philippine had come to belong to the world:

> Luna and Hidalgo are Spanish as well as Philippine glories. They were born in the Philippines but they could have been born in Spain, because genius knows no country, genius sprouts everywhere, genius is like light, air, the patrimony of everybody, cosmopolitan like space, like life, like God.[2]

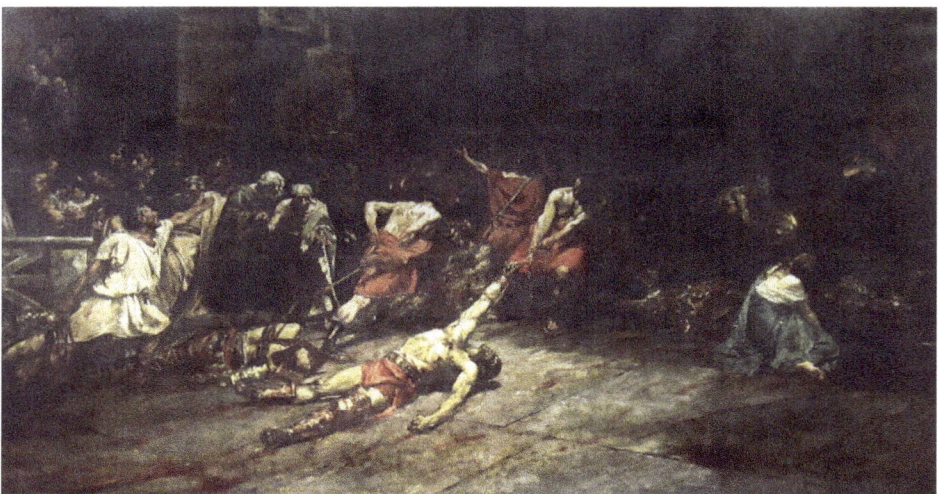

Juan Luna, *Spoliarium* 1884; oil on canvas; 4.22 x 7.67 m.

Photograph: Benigno Toda III; courtesy of the National Museum of the Philippines

Both Jaena, who felt that the locus of despoliation in Rome that was in Spain was also in the Philippines, and Rizal, who thought that the painter and the painting made the Philippine overcome the country that was colony and thus ratified its postcolonial ontogenesis, laid claim to a world at hand, in fact making it themselves because they grasped a continuum ethically and embodiedly,

---

[1] Teodoro Agoncillo, ed., *Graciano Lopez Jaena: Speeches, Articles and Letters* (Manila: National Historical Commission, 1974), quoted in *Zero In: Private Art, Public Lives* (Manila: Eugenio Lopez Foundation, Inc., Ayala Museum, Ateneo Art Gallery, 2002), 78.

[2] José Rizal, 'Rizal's Speech Delivered at the Banquet in Madrid in Honor of the Filipino Painters Juan Luna and Felix Resurreccion Hidalgo (25 June 1884)', *Political and Historical Writings / José Rizal* (Manila: National Historical Commission, 1972), 78: 18.

allegorically and performatively, immanently and imminently. It was simultaneously a repeating and a changing world, iterative like the unconscious and transformative like the politics that gripped Jaena and Rizal. But, as an astute critic would interject: 'If the unconscious is structured by repetition and the political by the desire for change … the question, still, would remain one of knowing what the unconscious changes, and what politics repeats.'[3]

In 1887, Rizal published his seminal novel *Noli Me Tangere* in Berlin. It is a microcosm of the Philippine colonial world, unfolding with the return of Juan Crisostomo Ibarra from Spain to find a ruined homeland, debased by avaricious friars and the petty elite, with his beloved woman forced to marry another man, becoming a nun, raped by a curate, and falling to her death. Early on in the novel, Ibarra walks into the narrative somewhat enchanted, or better still, bedevilled. As Rizal describes this scene of coming to Manila from Madrid, it would seem that the arrival and the arrivant were suspended in-between worlds, confounded by both 'loss and leaving':

> The sight of the botanical garden drove away his gay reminiscences: the devil of comparisons placed him before the botanical gardens of Europe, in the countries where much effort and much gold are needed to make a leaf bloom or a bud open; and even more, to those of the colonies, rich and well-tended, and all open to the public. Ibarra removed his gaze, looked right, and there saw old Manila, still surrounded by its walls and moats, like an anemic young woman in a dress from her grandmother's best times.[4]

The historian Benedict Anderson translates '*el demonio de las comparaciones*' as the 'spectre of comparisons', while the Tagalog writer Patricio Mariano nuances it as '*tukso ng pagkahawig-hawig*', or roughly, the 'temptation of affinities' or 'phantasm of semblances'. In whatever way it is discerned, the phrase describes the condition or experience of mediating discrepant worlds coming together in an instance that is at once belated and present, and in a gap or interval that is at once memory and mimicry. In this situation, the local world exceeds itself and slips into the colonial world that is incommensurate, and the imperial world to which it pretends. The perplexed personage who is Ibarra, the doppelganger of the proto-national hero Rizal, stands in the midst of this *demonio*, that is, diabolical and therefore legion. It might, therefore, be productive to construe the other world as immanent critique because it presupposes at the outset an alterity that is always-already awaiting, in other words, imminent.

---

3   Barbara Johnson, 'Lesbian Spectacles: Reading *Sula*, *Passing*, *Thelma and Louise*, and *The Accused*', in *Media Spectacles*, ed. Marjorie Garber et al. (New York: Routledge, 1993).
4   José Rizal, *Noli Me Tangere*, trans. Ma. Soledad Lacson-Locsin (Manila: Bookmark, 1996), 67.

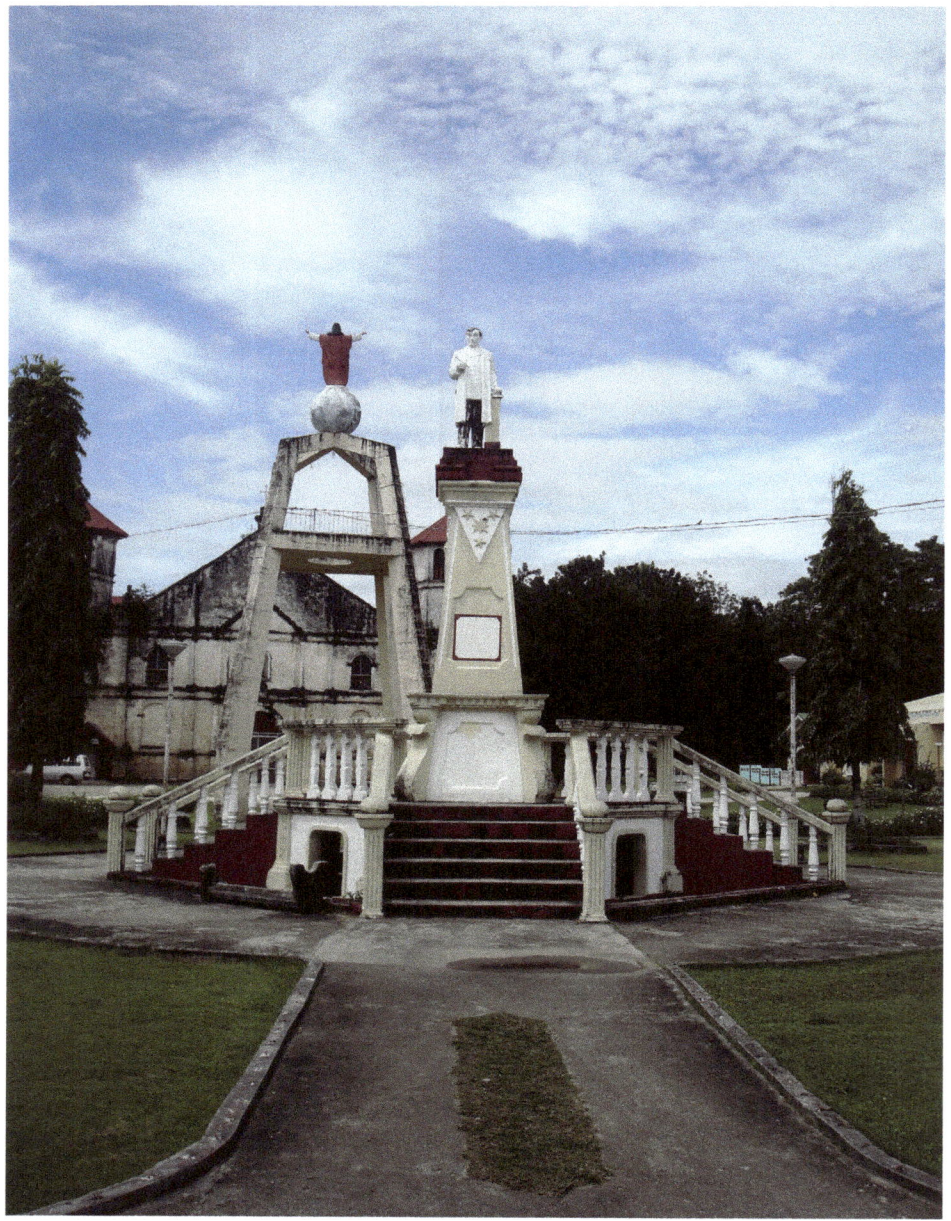

Monument of José Rizal, Dimiao, Bohol.

Photograph courtesy of the National Historical Commission of the Philippines

In 1890, Rizal wrote copious annotations on a Spanish chronicler's description of the Philippines. Antonio de Morga, a lawyer who became the colony's lieutenant governor-general, wrote *Sucesos de las Islas Filipinas*, published in Mexico in 1609, to register what he saw and observed in the islands at the time of conquest: an ancientness that tried to historicise the Philippine, this figurine of an archipelago. The esteemed Lord Henry E.J.S. Stanley translated de Morga's chronicle into English and secured the imprint of the prestigious Hakluyt Society of London. Rizal engaged with the text, which he laboured to search at the British Museum, in the same spirit of knowing the Philippine as a 'culture' and therefore as a distinct ethnic universe. In this negation, he converses not only with de Morga's fiction, but also with the imagination that underwrites it. Rizal terms this act as 'annotations', formatted as footnotes to the main text, with marginalia creeping out like a metacritique. He envisioned this tract as a confrontation with the writing of the past on the islands and anticipates the story of a nation. He writes in the introduction, addressing the potential citizens of a polity: 'If the book ... succeeds to awaken your consciousness of our past, already effaced from your memory, and to rectify what has been falsified and slandered, then I have not worked in vain, and with this as a basis, however small it may be, we shall be able to study the future.'[5] In one of these insertions, he spins a polemic around a contentious entry:

> Death was always the first sign of European civilization upon being introduced into the Pacific and God wills that it may not be its last, because, judging by the statistics, the islands of the Pacific being civilized are depopulating terribly. The first exploit of Magellan upon arriving at the Marianas, was to burn more than forty houses, many vessels, and seven inhabitants for having robbed a boat; those hapless savages saw nothing bad in robbing, which they did so naturally, just as among the civilized fishing, hunting, and to subjugate weak or ill-armed people.[6]

In this reconnaissance project, or the procedure of retrieval, Rizal enacts a redemptive process, redressing the error of colonial recordation, and inevitably asserting a self-consciousness about history and its artifice as a mode of writing the world. To a certain extent, Rizal here continues to grapple with the temptation of affinities, disconfirming the disfiguration of knowledge and refiguring the Philippine grotesque or picturesque that was to be reified as the Philippine primeval. In other words, he dwells on the particularity of ethnicity and the islands that contain it, or on the ethnographic that describes its distinction and, in doing so, affirms the universality of his being equivalently human as a native, a writer of history, and an interlocutor of empire. That he would extend this

---

5   José Rizal, *Historical Events of the Philippine Islands by Dr. Antonio de Morga* (Manila: José Rizal National Centennial Commission, 1962), vii.
6   Ibid., 64–65.

particularity to a differentiated universality through the typification of culture of the Philippine and later of the Malay is germane because it insinuates a dissent to dominant worlding. The latter may be characterised as Western, occidental or European. When Rizal states that 'despite the contact with Western nations, whose ideals are distinct from theirs, we see the Malayan Filipinos sacrifice everything, liberty, comfort, welfare, name, on the altar of an aspiration'[7] he, in a way, instrumentalises the Malay trope to galvanise a 'counter-hegemonic' project of a future 'national identity.' This is not to argue, however, that the Philippine is beyond the pale of the Malay ecumene; scholarship affirms otherwise, with one Filipino historian contending that 'Philippine forms' started to surface from 200 BCE to 1565, within a *dunia Melayu* or the Malay world.[8] Also, Rizal in his appropriation of the Malay as vector of his identity, would be esteemed as the 'greatest man the Malayan race has produced' in his time and likewise in the present in which the Malaysian dissident Anwar Ibrahim nominates Rizal as the 'first Malayan'. A noted Malay scholar considers Rizal as the first 'systematic social thinker in Southeast Asia'[9] who offered a theory of the colonial condition and a theory of emancipation.

This sequence of incidents and texts from Rizal constellates a possible worlding in which the Philippine yields manifestations of its place in the world together with the discourse of that emplacement. It posits a relationality not only by imbricating itself within the system, but by intimating that system in pieces, like islands in an archipelago—an archipelago effect. First, it casts the colonial subject as a genius that transcends country and assumes the inalienable property of nature. Second, it stages an aporetic encounter: the self recognises its origin through a colonial double vision, which is then critiqued as the basis of the origin's desolation. Third, it revises the writing of its history by presenting it and then putting it under erasure, redeeming it from a European episteme. Here, the world ceases to be outside the Philippine. As in a devotional contract, the Philippine in its toil to imitate—to identify with and resemble—and suffer the world, or that which encompasses it, becomes an intimate that secures the right to make demands of equivalence and kinship, the entitlement to importune.[10] It is this intimacy of the Philippine with the world that may have enabled it to be a country of migrants and mariners, and wherever they settle offer affective labour as givers of care and keepers of house, performers, and raisers of children and therefore suffuse the interior of well-being, emotion, and home.

---

7   Ibid.
8   R.A. Curaming, 'Filipinos as Malay: Historicising an Identity', in *Melayu: Politics, Poetics and Paradoxes of Race*, eds Maznah Mohamad & Syed Muhamad Khairudin Aljunied (Singapore: Singapore University Press, 2011), 241–74.
9   See the work of Syed Farid Alatas.
10 Fenella Cannell, *Power and Intimacy in the Christian Philippines* (Cambridge: Cambridge University Press, 1999).

It is uncanny that the Filipino author Jessica Hagedorn's 2003 novel *Dream Jungle* opens with a citation from Antonio Pigafetta, the chronicler of Ferdinand Magellan, the Portuguese discoverer who was the first person to circumnavigate the globe and was killed in the Philippine islands by a local chieftain in 1521. In the quoted account, Pigafetta (in *Primo Viaggio Intorno Al Mundo*) regards the conquered territory with derision:

> Those people are poor, but ingenious and very thievish, on account of which we called those three islands the islands of Ladroni (i.e. of thieves). Their amusement … is to plough the seas with those small boats of theirs … those boats resemble the dolphins which leap in the water from wave to wave. Those Ladroni … thought … that there were no other people in the world but themselves.[11]

In the same spirit, Hagedorn retraces the conquistador's gaze over the domain with this opening passage, as if to mimic the primal scene of colonialism:

> Zamora's gaze was steadfast and shameless. O they were beautiful, powerful, strange! Their fierce, wary eyes scrutinized him in return, taking in the brown, unruly curls on his head, the scraggly beard of his pale, unshaven face, the muscular arms and small, compact body that was, surprisingly, no taller than theirs. He had walked into a dream … The landscape of that dream—vast, ominous, shimmering blues and greens—was simply part of the loot.[12]

Here, the mingling of the ethnographic and the sublime, to form what may be framed as the 'ethnographic sublime', runs through from Rizal in the explication of wonder or astonishment over the other that is styled in an array of ways: as primitive, as civilised, as abject, as transcendent. To complicate this coincidence further is Hagedorn's heroine Rizalina (an appellation that is both the feminisation and diminution of Rizal), the daughter of a servant of Zamora Lopez de Legazpi, a rich, notorious philanderer who discovers a purportedly Stone Age tribe in the Philippines. This is obviously an allusion to Manuel Elizalde, a tycoon with interests in mining in Manila during the regime of Ferdinand Marcos, who was supposed to have discovered the Tasaday in rainforests on the southern island of Mindanao. This sensation turned out to be partly a contrivance, an attempt by a Third World nation-state to heighten its civilisational master narrative in the age of the international, and to prop up evidence of the 'original Filipino', who existed before the era of colonialism and before the reckoning of Rizal, who one biographer describes as the First Filipino.

---

11 Jessica Hagedorn, *Dream Jungle* (New York: Penguin Books, 2004), 3–4.
12 Ibid., 5.

Elizalde, who was appointed by Marcos as presidential assistant on national minorities, idealised the Tasaday as the indigene or autochthone without peer, having no acquaintance with the outside world. According to John Nance: 'They were offered corn, camote (a kind of potato), taro, and cassava. They apparently had no names for these things—staples among nearby mountain people—and indicated they had never seen them before.'[13]

The Hagedorn character Rizalina is molested by Legazpi (incidentally, the name of the Spanish official who founded the city of Manila) and, after leaving the Zamora household she becomes a sex worker in the city, where she meets an American, Vincent Moody, who is in the country to shoot the Vietnam film *Napalm Sunset*. The evocation of the primitive and of Hollywood is salient because it inevitably summons Francis Ford Coppola's 1979 US$30 million magnum opus *Apocalypse Now*, the high-flying production that the auteur filmmaker calls not a film on Vietnam but is, in fact, Vietnam—despite it having been shot in the Philippines. The conflation of Vietnam and cinema as excursions of excess, and as phantasmagoria and psychopathology may have been a conflation of Vietnam/cinema and the Philippine as well. After all, Coppola plays out his Vietnam fantasy and the hellish means of making it possible in the Philippines, which served as the material condition of filmmaking and the surrogate of the historical subject. The film, which pursues the premise of Joseph Conrad's *Heart of Darkness* (first published as a three-part serial in 1899), stages the ordeal of four men, Willard and his confreres, who are tasked to slay a renegade American soldier in Vietnam named Kurtz, played enigmatically by a hefty Marlon Brando, who has conducted his own operations in Cambodia, portrayed here as a path paved with human skulls. They find him as a lord in dominion amid the ethnic community of the Montagnards, who are fleshed out cinematically as Ifugao, a northern group in the Philippines that performs their ritual of bounty through the actual slaughter of a water buffalo. In this situation, the Philippine becomes exceptionally tropical, at once nature and ideology, inalienable and phantasmatic, bare life and sheer trace, a 'turning earth'.

Such a scenography is astutely calibrated by the Italian cinematographer Vittorio Storaro, who was enlisted by Coppola to lend grace to the film's exterior, his camera gliding or even skittering on the tension of the surface, bathing it with the ether of napalm, the quiet blaze of fire, or the luminosity of the filtered light of a surely stunning sun. This dreamscape is co-extensive with Hagedorn's recollection of her homeland, the Philippines: she remembers it as 'a sinister yet inviting apparition—on a tiny, uninhabited island in the middle of a shimmering sea. I kept trying to swim to the island but never got there, no

---

13 John Nance, *The Gentle Tasaday: A Stone Age People in the Philippine Rain Forest* (New York: Harcourt Brace Jovanovich, 1975), 13.

matter how hard or fast I swam. The house and the island kept vanishing into the distant horizon, reappearing again and again like some cruel optical illusion. I often woke from those dreams in tears, furious with myself for being weak.'[14] This interspersing between recollection and its ruse aestheticises the politics of belonging to the world or repossessing it altogether. Here, the technology of this aestheticisation partly derives from the mediation of the Philippine, the site of the deterritorialisation and the bricolage. When Hagedorn interviews the primitivist demigod and benefactor Elizalde, from whom her character in the novel is hewn and is analogue of the mythologist Coppola, her consciousness is saddened, in the register perhaps of Rizal's *demonio de las comparaciones*, by an eccentric reverie:

> In the middle of one of our long, heavy silences, a shape suddenly materialized on the parched green lawn. He was a lithe young boy with skin the color of mahogany, clad in a loincloth. A red hibiscus was tucked in his thick, black lion's mane of hair. The boy loped past us—almost dancing—on that sun-baked terrace, ignoring our presence. He warbled in a high-pitched voice as if he were singing or calling out to someone. Then with one last amazing leap, the boy vanished into the big white mansion. Elizalde didn't react. I wonder now if he had staged the performance for my benefit, if he were somehow making fun of me. Did I hallucinate the wild child with the flower in his hair, the eerie song, the entire episode? Was he a Tasaday in captivity, flown all the way to Manila to be part of Elizalde's private and intensely personal world's fair?'[15]

In the filming of *Apocalypse Now*, the helicopters that Coppola borrowed from the Philippine Government had to be withdrawn every so often because they were required for the existing conflict with Maoist insurgents in the countryside. The Philippine, therefore, was not only a *materiel* for film; it, in fact, comprised the history of the European and American theatre of operations in South-East Asia, a continuum that is denied by the reduction of the war to some kind of psychedelia, a 'rock and roll' war, according to the god–director, who himself was taken in by the irrationality of it all. In the end, with the war being conceived as out of this world, the lifeworld of the Philippine recedes into a universal whimsy of ritual and antiquity, a timelessness, the incomprehensible but irresistible exotic.[16]

---

14   Jessica Hagedorn, 'Ghost Town', *Time Magazine*, 18 August 2003, 36.
15   Ibid., 37.
16   Victor Segalen, *Essay on Exoticism: An Aesthetics of Diversity* (Durham: Duke University Press, 2002).

The contemporary Filipino visual artist Stephanie Syjuco recognises the Philippine in *Apocalypse Now*, and other Vietnam War-themed films, such as *Platoon* and *Hamburger Hill*, and seeks to recover the locale by deleting that which has encroached on it; that is, that which the film has fabricated, the very scenography of Vietnam. In the three-channel work *Body Double*, she reverses the ethnographic sublime and restores, as it were, the natural via a montage of the elements: silent, uninhabited, uncorrupted by so-called culture, the ecology of the Philippine, the diversity of which is one of the broadest in the world, that is recuperated as atmosphere. As Syjuco confides: 'This video project ignores the original filmic narrative to focus on my own attempts at discovering my place of birth—a kind of reworked "home movie". The resulting videos look like ambient, minimalist imagery of landscapes and closeups of flora and fauna.'[17] Again, the Philippine becomes figurine and intimate.

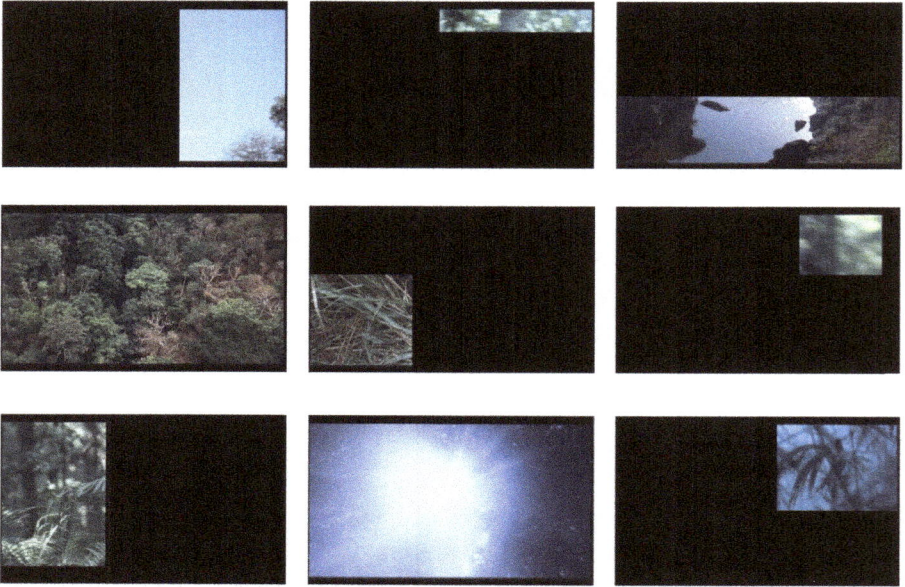

Stephanie Syjuco, *Body Double (Platoon / Apocalypse Now / Hamburger Hill)* 2007 (video still); 3-channel video installation; 120 min / 150 min / 100 min.

Courtesy of the artist and Osage Gallery

The terrain, while lush and plenty, happens to have a precarious life. The tropical is blessed by profuse parturition, on the one hand, and it is site of calamity and ruination, on the other. The Centre for Research on the Epidemiology of

---

17 Stephanie Syjuco, 'Body Double (Platoon) 2005', http://www.stephaniesyjuco.com/p_bodydouble.html.

Disasters reports that, since 1900, the 'Philippines has experienced the most events defined as requiring international assistance.'[18] Between 1900 and 1991, there was an average of eight disasters a year, making the country the hardest hit by natural disasters in 90 years. This is another condition of the 'apocalypse,' the destruction of the natural world, the decimation of population, the devastation of heritage. Such feeling of transience is key in grasping the Philippine mood for the otherworldly: migratory or millenarian, 'errant in form but firmly rooted in its essence' to borrow a phrase from the baroque philosopher Jose Lezama Lima.[19] The confluence between species and milieu, biologies and natural histories, in what the anthropologist Aihwa Ong calls 'biopolitical assemblages', bears on how global economies continue to colonise conditions of vital survival and how this very survival valiantly tries to frustrate it. As she elaborates: 'Sheer life in the tropics is becoming an ethical exception to the global cartography mapped and sustained by the biocapital regime.'[20]

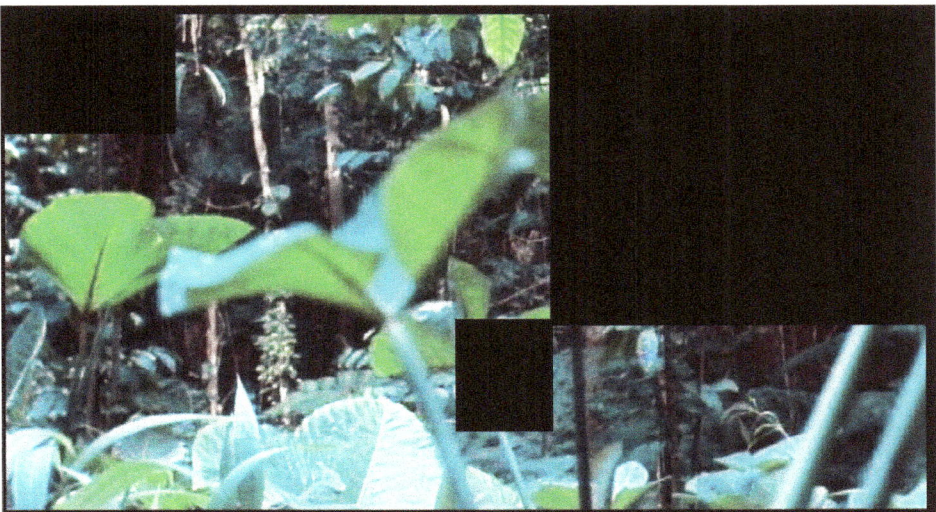

Stephanie Syjuco, *Body Double (Platoon / Apocalypse Now / Hamburger Hill)* 2007 (video still); 3-channel video installation; 120 min / 150 min / 100 min.

Courtesy of the artist and Osage Gallery

---

18 Greg Bankoff, 'Storms of History: Water, Hazard and Society in the Philippines 1565–1930', in *A World of Water: Rain, Rivers and Seas in Southeast Asian Histories*, ed. Peter Boomgaard (Singapore: NUS Press, 2007), 153.
19 Jose Lezama Lima, 'Baroque Curiosity', in *Baroque New Worlds: Representation, Transculturation, Counterconquest*, eds Lois Parkinson Zamora & Monika Kaup (Durham: Duke University Press, 2010), 213.
20 Aihwa Ong, 'Scales of Exception: Experiments with Knowledge and Sheer Life in Tropical Southeast Asia', *Singapore Journal of Tropical Geography* 29 (2008): 7.

The inclusion of the Philippine and the exclusion of the Vietnamese in Syjuco's videoscape need not be viewed in the binary terms of inside/outside, with the Philippine merely reduced as location to be animated by the cinema, which is later excised from the *mise en scène*. It might be more productive to contemplate that, in the vein of earlier reflections, the Philippine is within, internal or internalised, impersonating though neither totally assimilated nor hybridised. This is cogently articulated in the way in which Filipino performers would be conscripted by Broadway to play the role of the Vietnamese in the musical *Miss Saigon*, based on Puccini's *Madame Butterfly*, with music and lyrics by French musicians Claude-Michel Schonberg and Alain Boublil. The tale is inspired by a picture of a mother giving up her daughter in the frenzy of the fall of Saigon in 1975. The lead character is Kim, who works in a bar where she meets Chris, an American soldier stationed in South-East Asia. He leaves her and their child when he returns to America and comes back for the boy with his American wife; Kim kills herself for her firstborn. A pivotal image in this drama of love and desertion is the helicopter, the vehicle of violence and recapture. In *Apocalypse Now*, a squadron of helicopters swoops down on a school and rice fields to the operatic strains of Wagner's *Ride of the Valkyries* and, in one sequence, it hurriedly airlifts scantily clad American girls who had been brought to Vietnam to titillate the troops. At a certain point in their burlesque, the soldiers turn into a mob and nearly gang rape them. The helicopter, as a trope of escape, is central in both the film and the play, rescuing the child of the self-immolating mother and the flesh of the women defiled by men.

With *Apocalypse Now* and *Miss Saigon*, the history of South-East Asia in the Cold War emerges through the performance of the Philippine. It is the natural and ethnographic sublime of the Philippine, along with the affective labour of the Filipino, that this imaginary manifests and creates emotional capital. There is a scene in *Apocalypse Now*, which has been cut out of the original release but which was later added in the more integral version, *Apocalypse Now Redux*, that condenses the South-East Asian conjuncture. In the quest for Kurtz, Willard's group snakes its way through a river and chances on a French plantation. Willard sits with the French expatriates through a genteel dinner, during which he asks why the colonists stay, to which one of them retorts: 'Because it is ours.' This intersection between the French and the American in Indochina, as made possible through the site that is the Philippines, is emblematic to the degree that it unravels the symptoms of a possible racial melancholy, stirred up by the lost objects of both empires and their longing for them as possessions. It is at this node of the rhizome that the grisly Philippine–American war projects itself. If the Cold War is to be reckoned in South-East Asia, the American imperialism in the Philippines, beginning in 1899, must be sharply indexed, carved into high relief by the Philippine–American war that left one out of seven Filipinos dead, making it the 'first Vietnam' and also a 'proto-Iraq'. As President George W. Bush pointed out in a speech before the Philippine Congress in 2003:

> Democracy always has skeptics. Some say the culture of the Middle East will not sustain the institutions of democracy. The same doubts were once expressed about the culture of Asia. These doubts were proven wrong nearly six decades ago, when the Republic of the Philippines became the first democratic nation in Asia. Since then, liberty has reached nearly every shore of the Western Pacific.[21]

The implication of the Vietnam War is, moreover, consequential largely because it motivated the disposition of critique in Europe and the rise of its avant-garde. The 1968 student upheaval in Paris expended critical energy that infused the avant-garde, to which contemporary art turns for impetus, up to the present. It is, therefore, not to overstate that South-East Asia as a setting is exemplary because it has coordinated both the imperialism of the West and the resistance of the world against it, wherever it found itself.

When *Miss Saigon* premiered in London in 1989, it launched its star, the Filipino Lea Salonga, in the role of Kim. It opened on Broadway in New York two years later. Succeeding franchises of the play in around 25 countries and 246 cities have also had other Filipino talents in the lead. As early as 1925, Filipino soprano Jovita Fuentes played Cio-Cio San in Puccini's *Madame Butterfly* at the Teatro Municipale di Piacenza. There is a high degree of relay here from the local to the global, the self to the other in the performative utterance of, let us say, the Filipina actress essaying a Vietnamese heroine in English through a type of singing that is based on Western popular music and a musical theatre arising from vaudeville. Salonga, who auditioned for the part in Manila in an international search for the cast, was already a theatre and media personality, having appeared in *The King and I* when she was seven. While the narrative in the Philippines at that time was triumphalist, viewing the appearance of Filipino artists on the world stage as a conquest of the West, not far from the homage to Juan Luna's own conquest in Madrid a century earlier, what should not be missed is the underlying sadness of having to re-dramatise the tale of conquest so that the self could outlive the despair of its tropics, something that remarkably perturbed Rizal's persona in his novel. The global travel writer Pico Iyer was moved by the breathtaking talent of the Filipino to imitate the West by simulating 'every shade of heartbreak' and thus turning into 'musical mannequins' gripped in the vice of an 'eerie kind of ventriloquism.'[22] The

---

21 George W. Bush, President of the United States 2001–2009, 'Remarks to a Joint Session of the Philippines Congress in Quezon City, Philippines', 18 October 2003, http://www.presidency.ucsb.edu/ws/?pid=63501.
22 Pico Iyer, 'The Philippines: Born in the U.S.A', *Video Night in Kathmandu: And Other Reports from the Not-So-Far East* (New York: Vintage, 1989).

anthropologist Fenella Cannell is attentive to this kind of affect in her take on why a contestant in an amateur singing contest on a peninsula south of Manila could croon the standard *Autumn Leaves* with so much wistfulness that it gave the foreign observer the impression that the reality of autumn is deeply felt in the culture and so could be expressed so inalienably in music through a voice so unbelievably authentic. The risk of performing this alien sound requires the influence of spirit, the need to be drunk to be able to cross the gap between the everyday and the elsewhere. According to Cannell:

> It seems possible that one element in the 'sentimental' and nostalgic atmosphere of the singing is built precisely out of the origins of that risk; the loss that the author signified by 'Autumn Leaves' makes no immediate sense in the tropics, but the idea of loss itself does; in singing a song part of whose meaning escapes one, one evokes, among other losses, the sadness at not having completely understood, at being excluded in relation to a cultural register which, if one masters it, can open the doors of possibility and change one's life.[23]

Inscribed in this series of coincidences, therefore, are the history of empires and the development of nation-states in South-East Asia during the Cold War, partly through the export of human labour, the allure of economic advancement attending the desire for democracy as contrasted with the regimentation of socialism that surrounded the region. It is in this locus that the anxiety of a certain loss of ethical ascendancy via the revolution, and its negation via imperialism, that Europe and America, or Euro-America through France and the United States, distills in the performance by the Philippine in the culture industry of Broadway. The French makers of *Miss Saigon* previously staged Victor Hugo's *Les Miserables*, reinforcing the thought that, as with Coppola, Schonberg and Boublil are disillusioned by the revolutionary/imperialist double vision and appeased by the perfect(ed) Philippine performance of bereavement and benevolence. It must be noted that in 1980, a refugee processing zone opened in the Philippines under the auspices of the United Nations and the US State Department; it prepared refugees from Indochina for their settlement in Europe and America. But the Philippines also hosted the largest US military bases outside of the United States, which were utilised as platforms for naval operations during the Korean and Vietnam wars and as a strategic geopolitical foil of deterrence in the area due to their proximity to the Soviet installations in Cam Ranh Bay in Vietnam.

Mediating this convergence is the polytropic Philippine. The critic Peter Hulme remarks that the term polytropic pertains primarily to mobility, deriving from the epithet for Odysseus as a 'man of many ways' and may also mean 'much

---

23 Cannell, *Power and Intimacy*, 209.

travelled', 'given to troping', and 'cunningly intelligent'.²⁴ The latter is linked to *metis*, the idiom of quick change, originally a word from navigation signifying the 'skill needed to find one's way across a piece of water and out of sight of land … a particular kind of resourcefulness … the ability to become multiple, Protean, in order to deal with situations which are shifting and disconcerting, situations unamenable to precise measurement or exact calculation, the ability to find a way out when the way ahead is blocked.'²⁵ While Hulme uses polytropic to describe individualist ethos and colonialist duplicity, exemplified by men who 'covet the land whose inhabitants they confront, and therefore lie about the reasons for and circumstances of their coming,'²⁶ it is refunctioned here to return the look, so to speak, with the Philippine remaking itself from a colonial object to a subjectivity that comprehends back; indeed, a dissemination, like the worldly Rizal or the archipelagic effect, and the intimacies that permeate spaces which refuse the humanity it persistently intimates. In Hulme's mind, the polytropic man is an intruder, beholding his singular acts of settling. In this instance, the polytropic Philippine is temporary, alien or exile, guest worker or second family, surrogate mother or housekeeper, first teacher or mail order bride, plural in its sympathies, assuming the grief of others and suffering its own, moving—mobile and heart wrenching, modern and melodramatic—and compassionate in many ways, that is, suffering together with passion.

The polytropic may finally be gleaned as a genius transcending culture that is repatriated as a native, a self-conscious subject that needs to be compared with others. This is indicated in an anecdote shared by Rizal with his good friend, the Austrian ethnologist Ferdinand Blumentritt, with whom he had extensive epistolary exchange. In one of these letters, Rizal recounts his meeting with the eminent pathologist and liberal political figure Rudolf Virchow at an event in 1887 of the Berlin Society for Anthropology, Ethnology, and Prehistory, to which Rizal would be later admitted. Virchow was said to have told Rizal teasingly that he wanted to study him ethnographically.²⁷ Again foregrounded in this ludic encounter is the ethnographic as a measure of culture and its inherent comparisons and, surely, the comparability of Rizal and his sense of belonging to the world. In Virchow's obituary for Rizal, he considers him 'the only man with sufficient knowledge and resolution to open a way for modern thought into that far-off island world.' This leads us to ask: Was Rizal an exception or did he solicit the recognition of Europe to affirm the civilising mission and become its diffusion? Was he a convenient specimen assimilated by the liberal flank of German intellectuals in the time of the nationalist

---

24 Peter Hulme, 'Polytropic Man: Tropes of Sexuality and Mobility in Early Colonial Discourse', in *Europe and Its Others: Proceedings of the Essex Conference on the Sociology of Literature*, vol. 2, eds Francis Barker, Peter Hulme, Margaret Iversen & Diana Loxley (Colchester: University of Essex, 1984), 20.
25 Ibid., 21.
26 Ibid.
27 *Rizal's Correspondence with Fellow Reformists* (Manila: National Heroes Commission, 1963).

Bismarck who postured as espousing progressive politics? Or was Rizal so truly universal in his temperament that the foreign was hospitable to his difference or transculturality? Did someone like Rizal, a native from a colonised archipelago, finally become a worldly agent who performed the rituals of residing in the world and pursued a script of extensity, or *palabas*,[28] the Filipino term for both a dissembling or disguise and a movement towards an outside? After all, Rizal was self-conscious about how his death would transpire; he, in fact, had dreamt it and asked executioners not to shoot him in the head. When the bullets were fired, he turned to face them with dignity. This ethical and performative stance ensured that the *palabas*, the spectacle of heroism, would assume its proper potency and its effect would further inflect the Philippine consciousness, from spiritual movements who hail him as the Tagalog Christ and the emergent film industry, the early manifestations of which in South-East Asia magnified the drama of his martyrdom as both historic and cinematic.

This rumination on the polytropic Philippine tries to carve out a different circuit for the Philippines, so that it can be seen as part of a South-East Asian relay of relations. Oftentimes, the Philippines falls off the map of the region because it does not manifest the legacies or monuments of the great traditions of India and China. But a study of the other routes of encounters should rectify this notion. The widening of the latitude of the Philippine through its polytropic potential is one such effort. It recasts the condition of an at once appropriated and appropriating subjectivity and dwells within what Foucault calls the 'sudden vicinity of things', or what the theorist of visual time, Keith Moxey, calls 'productive adjacencies'.

The Philippines in 2011 commemorated the sesquicentennial of Rizal's birth, fully reminded of his ubiquity in everyday life as a national hero, even if there has been no edict proclaiming him as one. If the monument were testimony to this reverence, it would also be an index of the liberties the people have taken in portraying him in pieces, as his likeness and its mutations mark nearly every town in the country and the communities across the globe of Philippine migration in which he is a compelling cipher of identity amid the most intense of discriminations. Rizal might just be the most monumentalised person in the world, something that further complicates the term polytropic, and one can argue that Rizal is within in the same manner that the Philippine is the world within.

---

28   See Patrick D. Flores, 'Palabas', *Ctrl+P Journal of Contemporary Art*, no. 11 (2008): 8–9, http://www.ctrlp-artjournal.org/pdfs/CtrlP_Issue11.pdf.

1. Polytropic Philippine: Intimating the World in Pieces

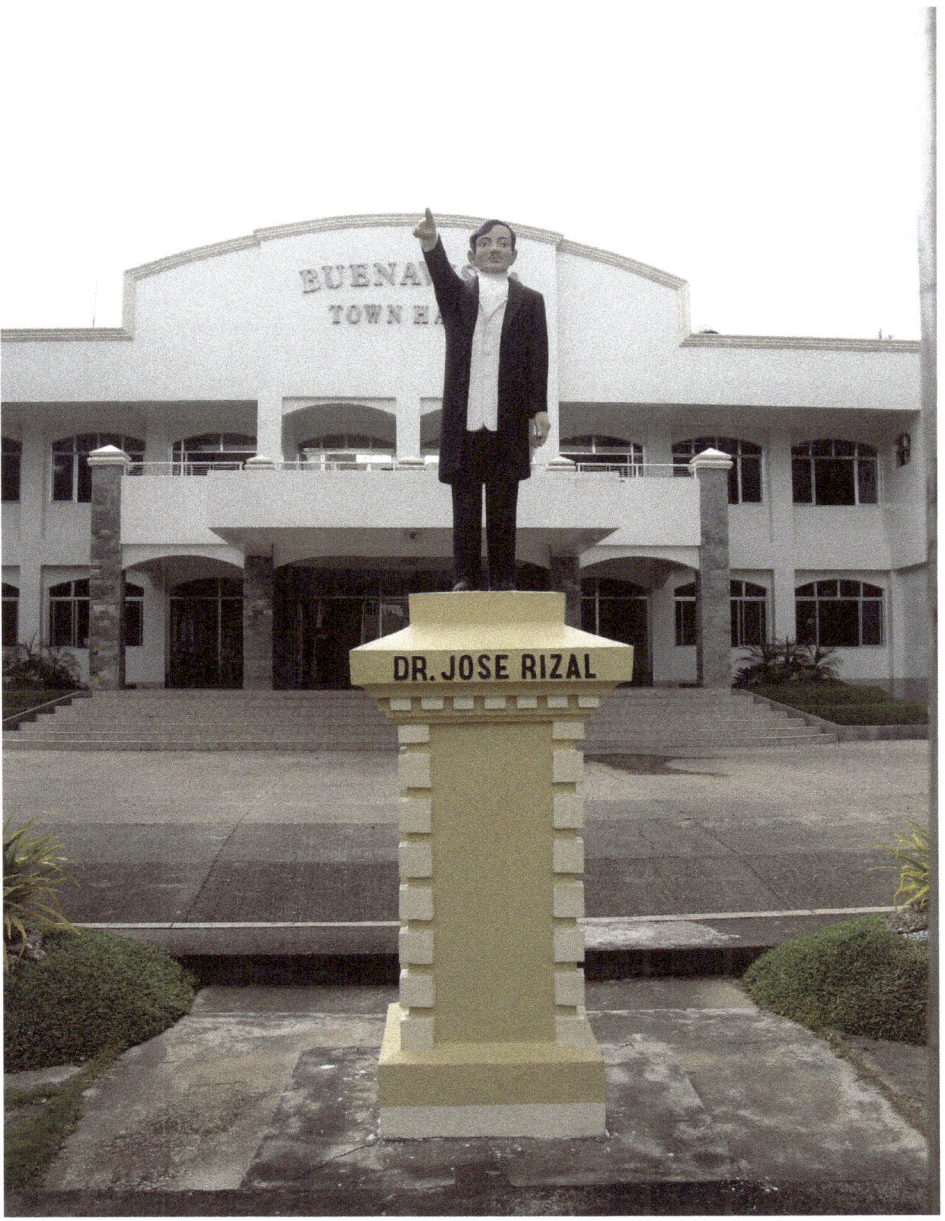

Monument of José Rizal, Buenavista, Guimaras.

Photograph courtesy of the National Historical Commission of the Philippines

This dispersal of the heroic and the intimations of the Philippine across spaces may be seen in a recent project involving Filipino overseas workers in Hong Kong, who have been called the modern-day Filipino heroes for their indispensable remittance; like Rizal, their histories are exilic, too. In 2009, the Chinese artists Sun Yuan and Peng Yu asked a hundred Filipino domestic workers, mostly women, in Hong Kong to plant a bogus grenade inside the splendid houses of their employers and photograph the tableau, the still life, the interior. This clandestine task and its tense imagery risk the imagined security and secret of the abode as well as the persons who keep it and who now guarantee the exposure of property. They are disclosed only partially in the form of bodies turned against the viewer, standing like memorials of their infiltrating deed. Through the aesthetic of the camera in the digital age, they design this unease in cohabitation, an embeddedness, the tactic of a guerilla or an interloper or a grenadier. In the multiplicity of bodies and houses and bombs, the trauma of migration, of biopolitical traffic and private life, repeats and is distributed. But this repetition and distribution, this accumulation of labour and capital, likewise ensures the settling of the human globally and, at last, a community beyond country and of aliens with the rights of others.[29] It is said that a third of the Philippine population lives beyond its islands, around 4,000 leaving every day, eight million of them toiling abroad to keep the economy on an even keel by sending home around $US20 billion a year in remittances, and countless of them coming home as corpses.

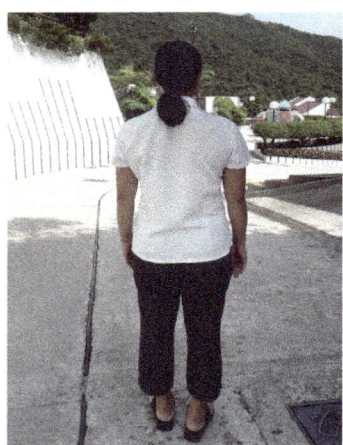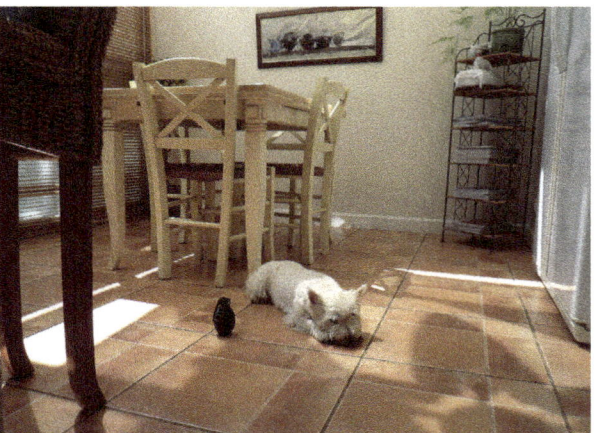

Sun Yuan & Peng Yu, *Hong Kong Intervention* 2009; 200 C-print photographs; 75 x 100 cm, 75 x 56 cm (each pair); edition 1 of 3.

Courtesy of the artists and Osage Gallery

---

29 See Agnes Lin, ed., *Hong Kong Intervention* (exh. cat.; Hong Kong: Osage Gallery, 2011).

The body of Filipinos is a ticking migrant force in the accommodations of their masters. The volatile device they smuggle in, at once plaything and terrorist prop, may well be the bomb of deterritorialisation, a potential threat that sits quietly on the fireplace or the carpet or close to a cat, finally replacing identity and homeliness with intimation, or what a scholar calls the 'diasporic of melancholy'[30] and what a curator depicts as the 'beauty of distance.'[31] It may well also be an incendiary imminence, the postcolonial polytrope of immanent critique, that proverbial blast from the past, nothing less than the horror and catastrophe as well as the thrill and fearlessness of belonging in a world that refuses the hospitality, migrancy, and rights of others whenever the latter threaten the privileges of settlement. In 2013, the highest court in Hong Kong ruled that a foreign domestic worker, a restrictive category of migrant, can never be granted permanent residency.

---

30 See Sarah Brophy, 'Angels in Antigua: Diasporic of Melancholy in Jamaica Kincaid's *My Brother*', *PMLA* 117, no. 2 (2002): 265–77.
31 This is from the title of the 17th Biennale of Sydney: *The Beauty of Distance: Songs of Survival in a Precarious Age*, curated by David Elliott, 2010.

2. The Worlding of the Asian Modern

John Clark

This paper reconsiders the historical depth and global range of art works and practices that we might call the 'Asian Modern'.[1] It will not rehearse the copious arguments for,[2] and some against,[3] the notion of a modernity in Asian art emerging parallel to and, at the same time, in concert with, modernity in Euramerica. Suffice it to reiterate that the Asian Modern is an hermeneutic construct for interpreting multiple art discourses; an empirical field for understanding and ordering the minutiae of data about art practice and interpretation; and, a periodisation that can be culturally and historically denoted in a particular set of geographically defined entities, which became the modern state system in Asia from the onset of late Euramerican colonialism in the eighteenth century until the end of colonial rule in the mid-twentieth century. To facilitate discussion, there is no harm in putting indicative dates on this period and location; i.e., from the Battle of Plassey in 1757 in India, up to the end of the Third Vietnam War in 1976. This may be taken notionally to slightly extend up to the fall of Soviet communism in 1989/1990, which was roughly contemporary with the tensions that reached brief but bloody resolution in China in the 1989 massacre in Beijing's Tian'anmen Square.

In practice in art and in the still largely absent discourse of a worlded art history that takes account of Asia, the Asian Modern denotes a broad period with slightly different empirical artistic delineations to the political. It varies from a threshold marked by, say, the foundation of Damián Domingo's art school in Manila in 1821; by the first exhibition of a major Asian artist, Raden Saleh, at a European salon, in Amsterdam in 1834, or by his exhibition in the French salon in 1847; or, by the first counter-colonial appropriation of academy style for a history painting in Saleh's 1857 *The Arrest of Prince Diponegoro*. The overall period of the Asian Modern, which offers much to be subdivided by further

---

1 This paper adapts sections and ideas from papers in which I have previously explored similar themes: 'The Changing Nature of Paris as a World Art Capital for Chinese (and Some other Asian) Artists', in *Artistes chinois à Paris*, ed. & cur. Eric Lefebvre (Paris: Musée Cernuschi, 2011); 'The Southeast Asian Modern: Three Artists', in *Modern and Contemporary Southeast Asian Art: An Anthology*, ed. Nora Taylor (Ithaca: Cornell University Press, 2011), 15–32; 'The Asian Modern, Approaches in Defining the Contemporary in Asian Art', *Journal of the History of Modern Art* 30 (December 2011): 145–66.
2 In my book *Modern Asian Art* (Sydney: Craftsman House & Honolulu: University of Hawai'i, Press, 1998), I argue for a constructed 'Asian Modernity', not that of Euramerica. See also, Jonathan Hay, 'Double Modernity, Para Modernity', in *Antimonies of Art and Culture: Modernity, Postmodernity, Contemporaneity*, eds Terry Smith, Okwui Enwezor, Nancy Condee (Durham, N.C.: Duke University Press, 2008), 113–32.
3 The Marxist determinism of Fredric Jameson leads him to consign all the difficult cases of pre-modernity to a reactionary past defined against Euramerica. See, Fredric Jameson, *A Singular Modernity: Essay on the Ontology of the Present* (London: Verso, 2002), 53.

micro analyses, lasts up to the first exhibition of Chinese artists on any scale at the Venice Biennale in 1993, which can be seen as a globalised stage and not merely one covered by an immanent Euramerican hegemony. It is capped, symbolically, by the first acquisition of a work from a modern Asian artist by the canon-keeper at the Euramerican art centre: the 1997 acquisition by the Museum of Modern Art, New York, of Zhang Peili's video *Eating* [or *Ingesting*].

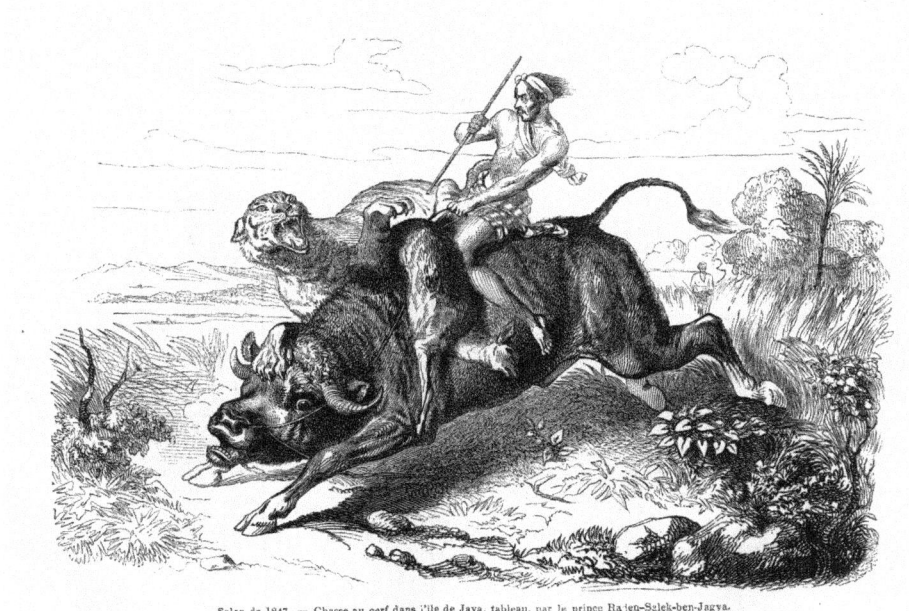

Raden Saleh, *Hunt on Buffalo* Salon de 1847; wood engraving from *L'Illustration* vol. IX, no 0217, Samedi, 24 Avril 1847, p. 117.

Photograph from the journal

Speaking periodically, one may of course take the Asian Modern forward, or back, from the mid-1990s, but most observers would consider that the empirical nature of art practice, its pragmatic interlinking and its hermeneutic positioning changed after that point, in Euramerica, worldwide, and in Asia. The mid-1990s saw the advent of the 'postmodern'—some would say 'post-postmodern'—'postcolonial', 'global' or 'transnational' as bounding concepts for art practice and interpretation. These are articulated top-down to a set of upwardly and laterally articulated local discourses, many of which exist inside the global, but to which some local discourses also pay scant attention. One indeed sees the 'worlding' of phenomena—the application of interpretive frames to art discourses that are visible in a global perspective across cultural and temporal zones—that have been occluded, by Euramerican domination, as derivative or different from those in Euramerica. This occlusion did not mean these discourses, which include parallel or alternative modernities made possible by that worlding, had not been there already, however difficult to view they might have been from a Euramerican position.

'Worlding', from the outset, meant making local interpretive frames visible in a global perspective across cultural and temporal zones because, from the early nineteenth century, there was the potential for local discourses to penetrate the non-local. In a sense, this is counterintuitive to a simple view of colonial processes as the imposition of a hegemony, rather than the collaboration with it. Such access had, at least theoretically, to include kinds of articulation of the local into the non-local and vice versa. 'Worlding' is a notion which implies a coherence other than that provided by internal discourses: it posits an outside, and this depends on how the nature and extent of the outside were reciprocally conceived. The problem for later nationalist, anti-colonial conceptions of art discourses was the level at which the inclusive was to be conceived. Or, what is that which includes, inclusive of? If it includes the pre-colonial it is, in this perspective, a domination of the culturally other by the colonial hegemony. If it excludes the pre-colonial, it is also a hegemony of exclusion where assimilation of art discourses is to the colonial order, and only on its terms.

'Worlding' posits a spatial and temporal discontinuity with innerness, but it is, in the colonial and nationalist anti-colonial conceptions, mobilised by outerness. 'Worlding' is marked, sometimes temporarily, by the period when a discourse is supposed to have overcome its inwardness or closure, or it is spatially designated as in distant, regional, provincial styles within an art culture.[4] These relations depend on types of inheritance of the pre-modern, or transitional modern, and their relation to later formation of domestic discourses.

'Worlding' means that these continua are given an externally constructed presence in the formulation and attribution of authority to art discourses now, whatever they carry forward internally or intrinsically. External, objectivist interpretations, as much as internal subjectivist ones, are equally and necessarily ideological.

Modern Asian art discourses have arisen in conditions where there have been internal or endogenous forces at play, with external or exogenous demands and provision of models. It is important now, in postcolonial times, to reconsider more carefully the ways of conceiving the distinction between exogenous and

---

4   On closure and openness, see my essay, 'Open and Closed Discourses of Modernity in Asian Art', [1991] in *Modernity in Asian Art*, ed. John Clark (Sydney: Wild Peony, 1993); reprinted in *Contemporary Art in Asia: A Critical Reader*, eds Melissa Chiu & Benjamin Genocchio (Cambridge, Mass.: MIT Press, 2011), 27–45.

endogenous art discourses since the resulting works have become the originary works for long-term and, in most cases, almost wholly endogenous genealogies of the modern.

The task of understanding the Asian Modern is first of all to know what the artists did to map their work and times, and then to compare them. The Asian Modern had its inception in the early to mid-nineteenth century and I have divided it by marking five generational artistic cohorts, since the empirical materials fall into five rough chronological groupings with corresponding patterns of artistic practice. One of the features of artistic generational cohorts is that they fall into very rough correspondences between artists active at the same time, but may be in different stylistic trajectories. This loose empirical correlation also produces a sense of chronological divisions which are more like domains or clouds of influence and interference rather than rigid analytical categories or temporal boxes. Based on empirical research and comparative historical categorisation, for me these cohorts are:

- I Transitions to Modernity, 1850s–1890s
- II Academy Realism, Salon Art and the National, 1880s–1910s
- III Early Modernism, 1920s–1930s
- IV Abstractionism and Conceptualism, 1940s–1960s
- V The Contemporary, 1980s to the Present.

Cohorts have the feature of viewing the 'worlding' of the Asian Modern as both an inward or exogenous process and, at the same time, an outward and endogenous one. They take art history away from seeing change as dependent on external or hegemony-down origination, and as a more complex intermediate zone that is in part isolated from the forces of modernity they also manifest. Despite its apparently broad temporal and geographical scale, my project is small and initial in this direction. This essay represents the summary of work in progress that I have undertaken up to 2010, and its conclusions are therefore tentative.

Types of Siting of Artists in Art Discourses

It pays to consider in detail where artists are sited, and the range of situations for artists, both domestically and internationally. What does the domestic, interior, or endogenous siting of artists in art discourses mean? There were not one, but multiple, types of these discourses, which later critics, historians and nationalist aestheticians called 'traditional' in apposition, and often opposition, to the 'modern'.

In *Type One*, artists who never go abroad have contact with foreign discourses via exemplars that are locally designated as such by a patron.

We may take as an example the Siamese muralist Khrua In Khong, who was active in the 1850s and 1860s, but of whom little is directly known. Much may, however, also be deduced from works by him, or attributed to him. It is important that he is nameable and known, since even if he was the subordinate painter of a king, his reputation exceeded his social subordination. Indeed, there are anecdotes that indicate Khrua In Khong was assured of his own *métier*, and this changed self-consciousness of the artist as a professional is certainly one index of modernity in art.[5]

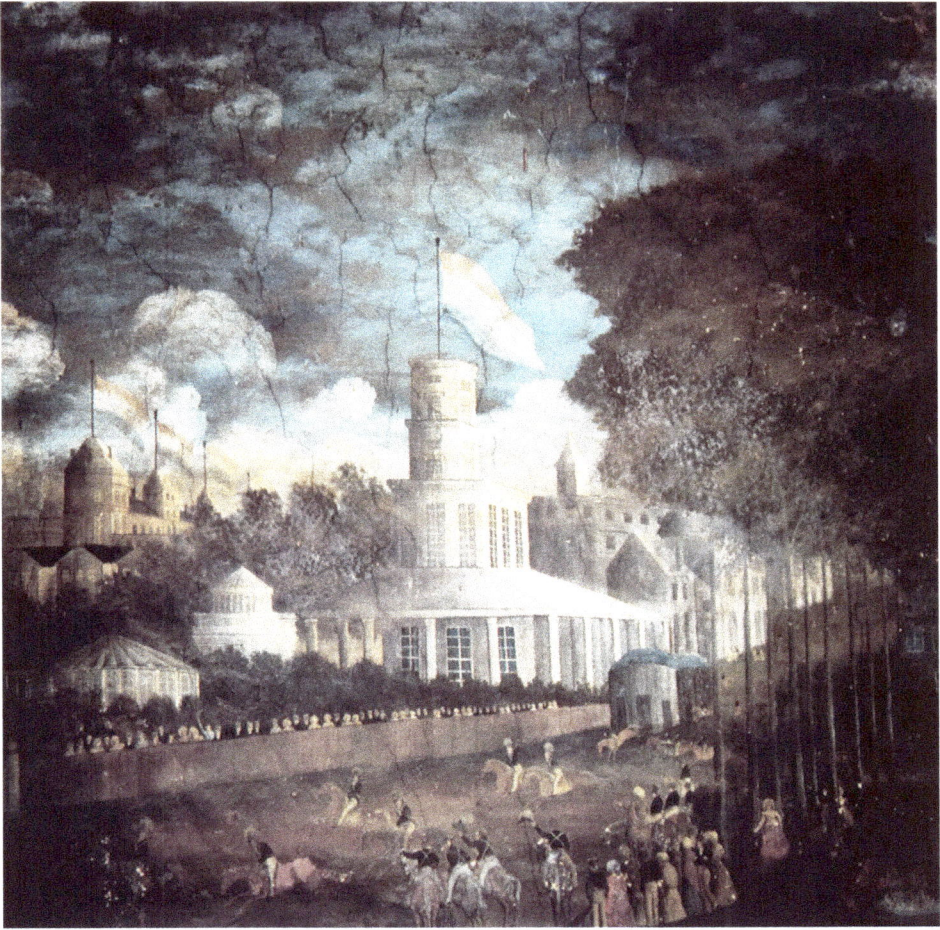

Khrua In Khong, *Horsemen training* c. 1850s; Wat Borom Niwat, Bangkok.

Photograph from Wiyada Thongmitr, *Khrua In Khong's Westernized School of Thai Painting*, Thai Painting Series No. 1, Bangkok: Muang Boran, 1979

---

5   See Wiyada Thongmitr, *Khrua In Khong's Westernized School of Thai Painting* (Bangkok: Thai Cultural Data Centre, 1979), 110; quoting *Saan Somdet* (Princes' Correspondence) III & XII (Bangkok: Khurusapha, 1962).

The art world he inhabited was one hierarchically governed by royal, aristocratic and sometimes merchant patronage for mural decorative schemes in temples and palaces.[6] Khrua In Khong was aware of a rich, iconographically and stylistically variegated temple painting discourse, and also of the reputation of previous masters. His work's claim to mastery over a new pictorial discourse thereby relativised the customary works of the past, which would be reassessed by his own work, and is thus pre-eminently a modern assertion.[7] It happens that the mastery claimed by his works rests in an external, or exogenous, visual discourse. This discourse represents the pressure to absorb Euramerican visual styles that existed under the various threats of cultural domination, and opportunities to counter-appropriate the art styles and forms received from nineteenth century colonialism. Since these were found widely across South-East Asian art, Khrua In Khong is an interesting example of an artist emerging from a hitherto craftsman substratum.[8]

As an artist he was embedded as a monk–painter in the religious mission to produce paintings as narrative or allegorical expostulation and, in a society where incorporation of new visual discourses was only possible if they were ideologically sanctioned by an abbot or an aristocrat; in his case this would have certainly been directly ordered by the king.[9] Yet, his work is largely the application of drawing techniques, pictorial composition, spatial construction and painting technique, which given the apparent explicitness of his use of Euramerican cityscapes for Jataka scenes, was derived from Euramerican art. These influences can be dated, with some precision, from reviewing the 1855 list of images presented to the king by the US envoy Townsend Harris.[10] But it is almost certain, given the early life of Khrua In Khong's patron, King Mongkut, from 1836–1850 as a monk at Wat Bowon Niwet, a major teaching monastery where the king came to know the French Abbé Pallegoix,[11] Khrua In Khong moved in circles that had access to late eighteenth and early nineteenth century illustrated books from Europe, particularly France.

---

6   See Saran Thongpan, 'Chiwit thang sangkhom khong chang nay sangkhom thaay phaak klang samay ratanakhosin kon P.S. 2448' ('The social life of craftsmen in Central Thailand society of the Ratanakhosin era before 1905') (master's thesis, Thammasat University, P.S. 2534 (1991)); Akin Rabibhandana, *The Organization of Thai Society in the Early Bangkok Period, 1782–1873* (Bangkok: Wisdom of the Land Foundation & Thai Association of Qualitative Researchers, 1996).
7   See also, John Listopad, 'The Process of Change in Thai Mural Painting: Khrua In Khong and the Murals in the Ubosot of Wat Somanasa Vihāra' (master's thesis, University of Utah, 1984).
8   See Thongpan, 'Chiwit thang sangkhom khong chang nay sangkhom thaay phaak klang samay ratanakosin kon P.S. 2448'.
9   In a January 2008 conversation with me, the specialist on Thai mural painting, Professor Santi Lekhsukhum, averred that the use of elements from Western pictorial discourses by Khrua In Khong was inconceivable without the direct intervention of King Mongkut, Rama IV, given the social subordination of painters at that time.
10 Townsend Harris's list of American printed material among gifts to King Mongkut, Rama IV, is found in Abbot Low Moffat, *Mongkut, King of Siam* (Ithaca: Cornell University Press, 1961).
11 Jean-Baptiste Pallegoix (1805–1862) was the author of the dictionary *Sappha phachana phāsā Thai = Dictionarium linguæ Thai: sive Siamensis interpretatione Latina, Gallica et Anglica* (Paris, 1854), and also of

The habitual Euramerican interpretive position of assessing the 'inadequate copy', which so denigrates endogenous discourse and how it nests the exogenous, does not mean that Khrua In Khong would not have benefited from knowing more accurately how to generate his own images within the Euramerican tendencies that he chose. Indeed, instrumental drawing of a medical kind was certainly known in his lifetime. We can assume it was a Thai artist who illustrated the midwifery manual produced in 1843 by the American medical missionary Dr Bradley, for use by royal midwives. We may also speculate that technical drawing was known to the architectural technicians who created a kind of neo-Georgian style for certain buildings ordered by King Mongkut in the 1850s and 1860s. King Mongkut had sent a diplomatic mission to London and Paris in 1857.

Khrua In Khong would probably have known something of this in his larger perspective constructions, but even more so in his technique for getting chiaroscuro effects. These clearly fascinated him. He tried to go against the zonal red grounds on white distempered walls that was practised by previous Thai muralists in the 1830s. These grounds created a vibrating and complementary contrast effect on green or mixed hues that were used elsewhere in the quite unconnected Venetian oil painting. Khrua In Khong seems to have deliberately chosen dark and, in some cases, very dark grounds against which to set bright contrasts through the addition of white.

In *Type Two*, the artist never goes abroad, but has contact with foreign art discourses that are currently in favour among resident expatriate foreigners. This artist is found frequently among Chinese treaty port painters in service to make largely topographical paintings for foreign merchants from the 1780s to the 1860s, or in Yokohama in the 1860s and early 1870s. The type may be thought to characterise many craftsmen who were active across a variety of visual discourses, including those used in printing industries, at many entrepôts.

In *Type Three*, the artist never goes abroad and has contact with foreign discourses via educational institutions and often resident foreign teachers. In the Philippines, Simon Flores (1839–1902) typifies that type of artist who did not travel abroad and yet whose discourse has a nested exogenous component. To understand this we need to consider the longevity and particular structures of Spanish colonial art in the Philippines.

---

the *Description du Royaume Thai ou Siam* (Paris: Mission de Siam, 1854), which was widely used by Sir John Bowring in his *The Kingdom and People of Siam* (1857), and translated by Walter E.J. Tips, as *Description of the Thai Kingdom or Siam: Thailand under King Mongkut*(Bangkok: White Lotus Press, 2000).

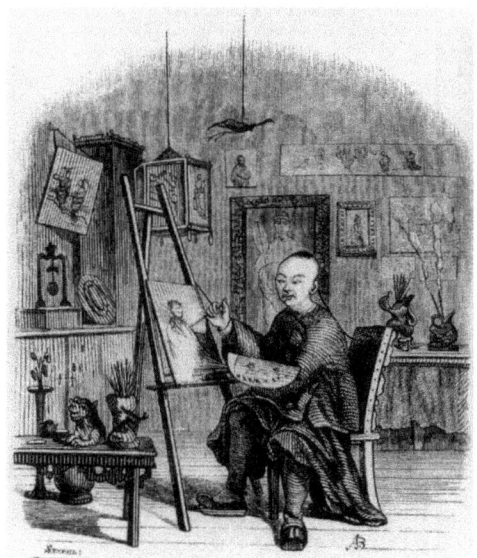

August Borget, 'Lamqua in his Canton studio', *La Chine Ouverte* 1845.

Photograph from the journal

An art school was founded in the Philippines by local worthies and functioned from 1821–1834 under Domingo (ca. 1790–1833/1834), and an art academy was authorised in 1845, regulated in 1848 and opened from 1850–1898. It was followed by the School of Fine Arts of the University of the Philippines from 1908 to the present day, whose first director, Rafael Enríquez, was significantly a Spaniard born in the Philippines and a former student of the Manila Academy.

The Chinese relationship with Philippines' art is deep and longstanding, particularly via paintings and glass paintings done in Chinese treaty ports and which, from these ports, spread to the Philippines,[12] and via *tipos del pais*, sets of images of typical occupations having reached Manila from Canton in the 1790s, which were a staple element in the production of Domingo and some of his students from the late 1820s.[13]

There is very little early Philippine history painting. That which exists seems largely to have been produced by late nineteenth century academy-trained artists.

---

12 On glass painting in Asia, see Seiichi Sasaki et al., 'Yooroppa Yûsaiga no Nihon dotchaku katei no kenkyû—Doro-e, Garasu-e kenkyû' ('The settling-down process of European coloured painting in Japan—research on gouache, glass painting'), *Tama Bijutsu Daigaku Zairyôgaku Kenkyûshitsu Kiyô* 1 (1976), 2 (1978), 3 (1982), 4 (1985).
13 On *tipos del pais*, see Francisco de Santos Moro, *La Vida en papel de arroz* (Madrid: Museo Nacional de Antropología, 2007). On Damián Domingo's works, see Jose-Maria Cariño & Sonia Pinto Ner, *Álbum Islas Filipinas 1663–1888* (Manila: Ars Mundi, Philippinae, 2004); Nick Joaquin & Luciano P.R. Santiago, *The World of Damian Domingo* (Metropolitan Museum of Manila, 1990); Stephen Ongpin, *Filipino Master: Damian Domingo* (Manila: Intramuros Administration, 1983).

There are records of *The Conquest of Batanes* having been painted by an anonymous *naturales* and adorning the Palacio Real in Intramuros, but this was destroyed by earthquake in 1863. The only other example, which fortunately survives, is an important 1821 regional painting by Esteban Villanueva (1798–1878)—a regional painter about whom little is known—that is held in Vigan in Ilocos Norte and which records an uprising and its relentless suppression.[14]

Flores' *Woman with a Religious Image* (undated, but possibly the late 1870s to mid-1880s), is close to the Spanish notion of portrait realism, in the manner of Velasquez and Murillo, possibly via copies which had been ordered from Spain for the Manila Academy from the 1850s–1860s.[15] It is likely that Flores, therefore, had several styles, one being the realism in the manner sanctioned by the Spanish academy and, the other, a kind of informal genre painting for intimate themes. This can be regarded as an articulation of a distance between an elaborately decorated surface, putatively that required by the patron, and the raw incarnation of the human body which carried it. To date, interpretation has been restricted by there being no surviving image or illustration of Flores's 1875/1876 *La Orquesta del Pueblo* (Musicians of the Town), which was exhibited by Spain at the Centennial Exhibition in Philadelphia in 1876, where it is said to have won a silver medal.[16]

Type Four artists only go abroad to sojourn, and take up temporary residence in a foreign country, such as Yoshimatsu Goseda (Period I), Juan Luna (Period II), Amrita Sher-Gil (Period III), Abdul Latif Mohidin (Period IV), and Zhang Peili (Period V).

In *Type Five*, temporary sojourners become long-term residents by dint of circumstance, such as Pan Yuliang (Period III) in Paris, who wanted to return to China later in life, but was prevented from doing so by the Cultural Revolution.

---

14 See Patrick D. Flores, *Painting History: Revisions in Philippine Colonial Art* (Manila: National Commission for Culture and the Arts, 1998), 288–93; Santiago Albano Pilar, 'The Basi Warriors', *Archipelago* (May 1976). Pilar's essay was seen by Roberto Feleo and became the inspiration for new works exhibited in 2007 at the National Museum, Manila. Images of the Basi Revolt paintings and Feleo's works can be viewed online: http://hugzone.multiply.com/photos/album/90/BASI_REVOLT_IN_ART.
15 See Flores (*Painting History*, 247), for a list of these works. There is no surviving evidence that such copies arrived; but, the Dr Eleuterio Pascual collection includes early copies by Juan Luna, executed before he went to Spain in 1876 and which I have seen, of portraits of Phillip IV of Spain after Velasquez (Museo Nacional del Prado P–1185, ca. 1653) and purportedly of Cervantes (but more likely to be *Pablo de Valladolid*, Museo Nacional del Prado p–1198, ca. 1635). See Javier Portús Pérez et al., *El retrato español, del Greco a Picasso* (Madrid: Museo del Prado, 2004), 117, 226.
16 Some sources have yet to be examined, but the retrospective catalogue (Francis A. Walker, *International Exhibition 1876 Reports and Awards Vol VII Group XXVII* (Washington: Government Printing Office, 1880)) neither mentions the Philippine exhibits nor illustrates them. It does, however, include an illustration of the general hang in the Spanish section, and lists the Spanish artists, as opposed to those from Cuba, the Philippines and Puerto Rico. Other Philadelphia Centennial Exhibition records to be investigated further indicate the title of a work by Flores, that was exhibited in 1876, to be *A Village in the Province of Pampanga*.

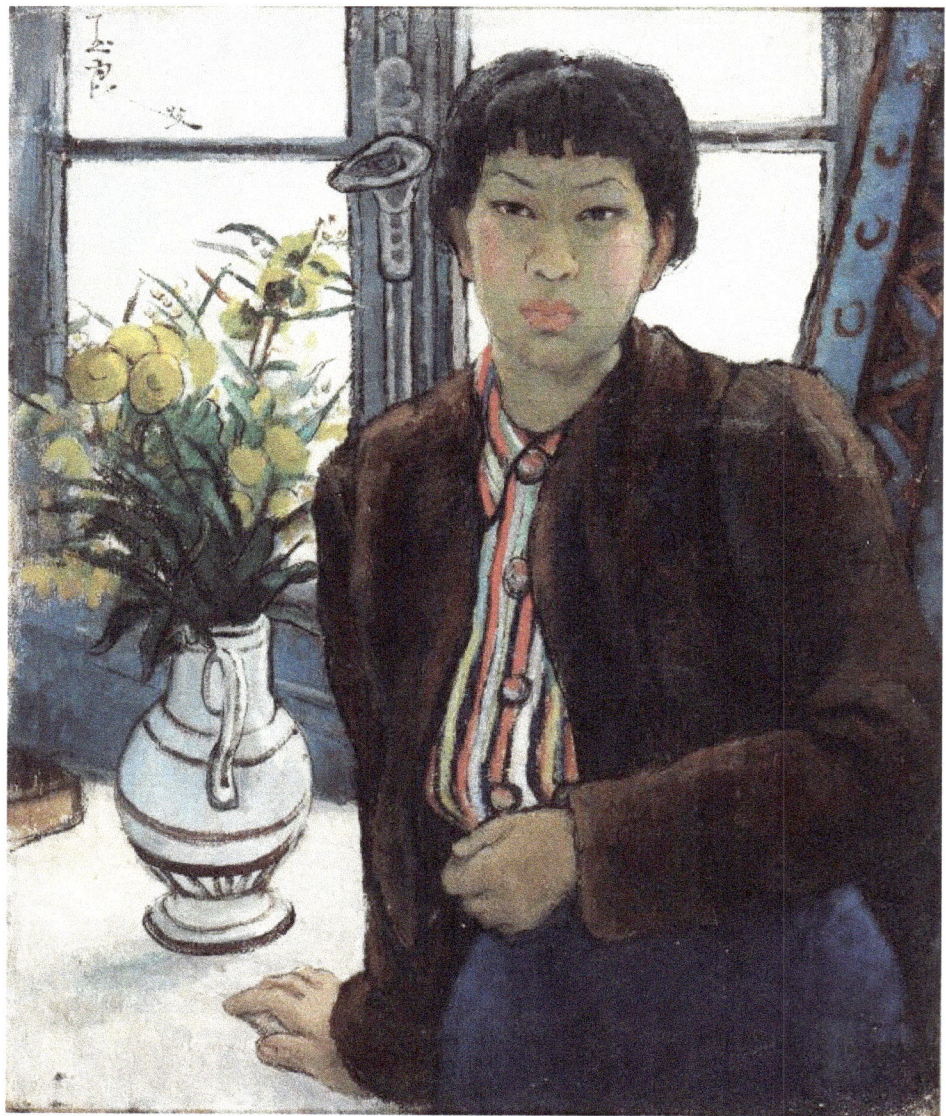

Pan Yuliang, *Self-Portrait* **1945; oil on canvas; 60 x 73.5 cm.**

National Art Museum of China, Beijing; photograph provided by the Museum

Artists in *Type Six* engage in intermittent returns to their home countries; that is, they can temporarily return home, but become long-term residents by choice of artistic affiliation. For instance, Zhao Wuji or Yan Peiming in France, who often return to China, but for much of their active life remain resident in one country, such as France, or centre, such as Paris. Some, such as S.H. Raza or Yang Jiechang, become permanent residents and acquire various signs of acculturation: a local spouse, a domicile, a studio, a gallery, a *côterie* of local or other resident foreigner friends.

Type Seven is usually constituted by artists who have left home for reasons of political or artistic exile; a circumstance that may become one of intermittent return if the situation that forced them to go abroad is resolved, such as Chinese Wang Keping, Ai Weiwei and Huang Rui from The Stars group in 1979–1982.

Type Eight is the site of transhumant cosmopolitans. In a last (but by no means *the* last) type of siting for an artist, such as Wang Du in France and Paris, or Cai Guo-Qiang in the United States and New York, the artist comes to regard an overseas country or city as a regular port of call.[17] It becomes a stopping-off point or base for studio and family in a style of living that is between sites and basically globalised, to whose cultural specificities the artist might be relatively unattached. This type is a kind of artistic transhumance, which depends on the quality of local mediation and acceptance, as well as access to art markets or sites of primary cultural appraisal. These do not have to be stationary and are, in the main, not in a given overseas country.

Type Eight is also a kind of siting by a self-awarded prerogative, perhaps like the *apanage* or prerogative claimed by French aristocrats, where there is a quasi-feudal claim to ownership of certain cultural characteristics, which may be manifested materially or virtually in a non-native place. Against the backdrop of the growing economic and cultural importance of China in the world, de-territorialised discourses of 'Chineseness' have become a kind of marker of access (often negotiated with some irony by 'Chinese' artists, especially in France),[18] and the national discourse of Chinese art has become, for a few artists, a de-localised globalised discourse of Chineseness. This type is widespread and Indian (M.F. Husain), Thai (Surasi Kusolwong), Indonesian (Heri Dono), and Malaysian (Wong Hoy Cheong) exemplars also exist. Transnational artists claim the prerogative to carry certain cultural characteristics with them, a self-declaration of rights, an *apanage* which frees them to arrogate the expression of

---

17 *Paris pour escale* (Paris as port of call) (2000), included Chen Zhen, Huang Yongping, Shen Yuan, Wang Du, Yang Jiechang (curated by Hou Hanru & Evelyne Jouanno, organised by Musée d'Art Moderne de la Ville de Paris).

18 See Chen Zhen's 'Transexperiences, A Conversation between Chen Zhen and Zhu Xian', *Kitakyushu* (1998), (reprinted in *Chen Zhen: The Discussions*, ed. Jerôme Sans (Paris: les presses du réel/ Palais du Tokyo, site de création contemporaine, 2003)). A Chinese translation of this conversation is included in Xu Min ed., *Chen Zhen* (Changchun: Jilin Meishu Chubanshe, 2006), 73–95.

culturally specified contents or subjects at a transnational site, such as overseas commercial or biennale exhibitions. Such artists have deployed (and sometimes deliberately traduced) signs of specific cultural derivation. This discourse does not have to be sited in the claimed culture of origin, such as 'China', or in just one localised and culturally specific site of reception 'outside China'.

If, in this last type, artists have carried the notion of their access to culturally defined experiences or forms outside their culture, what has been that outside for modern Asian artists, and has it changed in nature over time?

Transitions to Modernity, 1850s–1890s: Appropriation and Counter- Appropriation [I]

The styles and practices of art under what I will call transitional or proto-modernity were much more than mere counter-appropriations adopted under the constraints of colonialism or neocolonialism.

One can begin briefly with a progenitor who can be recognised as an international cosmopolitan, the Indonesian artist, Raden Saleh (ca. 1811–1880), who worked with natural history, familial and individual portraits, and rarely with historical subjects. If he had not spent so much time abroad in the Netherlands, Saxony and France, it would be easier to locate Saleh within the general context of modern Asian discourses. The discrimination of modern South-East Asian art discourses occurred later, and on multiple grounds, but Saleh stands at the head of a long line of Asian artists whose relationship with exogenous discourses—the function of which was to relativise endogenous discourses—started with deep, and colonially constructed, contact with European art centres and dominant art styles.[19]

Sir Thomas Raffles, British colonial administrator, noted that, despite there being no traces of an extensive pictorial discourse, the Javanese could be well trained and he mentions 2,000 natural history drawings he selected to take home, but which were lost to fire in 1824.[20] Javanese and Java-based Chinese artists did

---

19   For Raden Saleh in general, see the works of Werner Kraus: 'Raden Saleh's Interpretation of *The Arrest of Diponegoro*: An Example of Indonesian "Proto-nationalist" Modernism', *Archipel* 69 (2005): 259–94 (also published in *Eye of the Beholder*, eds John Clark, Maurizio Peleggi & T.K. Sabapathy (Sydney: Wild Peony, 2006), 29–55; and, his catalogue of the Saleh exhibition in Jakarta in 2012, *Raden Saleh: The Beginnings of Modern Indonesian Painting*, eds Werner Kraus, Irina Vogelsang; trans Chris Cave, Werner Kraus (Jakarta: Goethe-Institut Indonesien, 2012). See also work by Marie-Odette Scalliet: 'Raden Saleh et les Hollandais: artiste protégé ou otage politique', *Archipel* 69 (2005): 151–258 (includes list of paintings done in Holland 1831–1839); and, *Antoine Payen, peintre des Indes orientales: Vie et écrits d'un artiste due XIXe siècle (1792–1853)* (Leiden: Research School CNWS, 1995).
20   Cited in Anthony Forge, 'Raffles and Daniell: Making the Image Fit', in *Recovering the Orient: Artists, Scholars, Appropriations*, eds Andrew Gerstle & Anthony Milner (Chur: Harwood Academic Publishers, 1994), 112, citing from *Memoir of the Life and Public Services of Sir Thomas Stamford Raffles, by his Widow*, vol. 2 (London, 1830), 329–30.

some of the original drawings which illustrated the three major English texts of the 1810s and 1820s about Java.[21] Raffles also brought with him an Anglo-Indian artist whose hand, or whose atelier, must have been responsible for a screen depicting Javanese noble attendants; the screen, later in a Danish collection and now in the Rijksmuseum, Amsterdam, bears some similarity with earlier North Indian, so-called 'Company' paintings.[22]

Unlike the hybrid application of a 'Company Painting' manner to the subject of Javanese nobles, it is clear from surviving drawings that, for Saleh, his visual discourse was, from the outset, European. He received early training in drawing, during 1819–1820, from the then Dutch, later Belgian, artist Antoine Payen.[23] He must also have been present when Payen did some of his in situ oil sketches of natural scenes, which he later worked up in Europe into formal compositions. In fact, Payen's early oil sketches should be seen as the originator of landscape painting in Java[24] and, by implication, of the whole later tendency, which was disparagingly called *Mooi Indie* (Pretty Indies).

Saleh is the first artist of Asian origin to have received training in European studios and to have exhibited at a European salon.[25] From 1845 to 1848 he was largely in Paris, where he was visited in his studio by a linguist of Malay, Auguste Dozon, who was accompanied by his friend the, then unknown, poet Charles Baudelaire. This was probably the first encounter of a major figure in the European artistic avant-garde with an Asian painter. Saleh exhibited *Chasse au Tigre* at the Salon in 1846, a work in the manner of Horace Vernet (whom he had met), and which was subsequently purchased by Louis-Philippe, who was known as 'King of the French'. His work in the Salon of 1847, *Chasse au cerf dans l'isle de Java*, was noticed by Théophile Gautier, and an image was reproduced in *L'Illustration*.

---

21   Forge indicates that the illustrations are in three texts: William Marsden's *History of Sumatra* (1811); those depicted in Raffles's 1811–1816 *History of Java*, and subsequent variations; and, those by Adi Warna, who illustrated 11 of 34 plates in John Crawfurd's *History of the Indian Archipelago* (1820). See also, Annabel Teh Gallup, *Early Views of Indonesia: Drawings from the British Library* (Honolulu: University of Hawai'i Press, 1995).
22   For an illustration, see John Clark, 'Presenting the Self', *Ars Orientalis* 43 (December, 2013): 67–81.
23   On Payen, see Scalliet, *Antoine Payen*. I am also grateful for the opportunity to see and photograph Payen's oil sketches, which were done in situ in Java, at the Ethnology Museum in Leiden.
24   See Tony Day, '"Landscape" in Early Java', in Gerstle & Milner, 198.
25   Earlier, see David Clarke, 'Chitqua's English Adventure: An Eighteenth Century Source for the Study of China Coast Pidgin and Early Chinese Use of English', *Hong Kong Journal of Applied Linguistics* 10, no. 1 (2005): 49.

Academy Realism, Salon Art and the National, 1880s–1910s: [II]

Modern Asian art discourses have arisen in conditions where there have been internal or endogenous forces at play, with external or exogenous demands and provision of models. It is important now, in postcolonial times, to reconsider more carefully the ways of conceiving the distinction between exogenous and endogenous art discourses since the resulting works have become the originary works for long-term and, in most cases, almost wholly endogenous genealogies of the modern. The scope of this essay does not allow me to pursue all of these issues for the artists of Period II. It is important to point out, however, that in the era of formation of 'national' art discourses—which in Australia, India, and Japan corresponds to the decades from 1880 to 1914, with China following similar patterns under different historical constraints in the 1920s and 1930s—what could be seen as an appropriation or assimilation of Euramerican art styles by successful artists from outside, is also to be seen as a counter-appropriation of those styles and practices. This can be regarded as having been given its space—its room for domestic siting—by the continuation of customary aesthetic modes which are non-Euramerican.

Many more Japanese artists in Period II, among whom was Hosui Yamamoto, were to come to Paris in 1878–1888. Soon after his arrival in Paris he provided illustrations for the *Poèmes de la Libellule* by Judith Gautier and Kinmochi Saionji. After his return to Japan he was known for a theatrical visualisation of Japanese myths. An artist of lesser social origin from the marginal samurai and Meiji craftsman class, Goseda, lived and worked in Paris from 1881–1886. He was the first Japanese artist to exhibit at a French salon in 1881 and 1883.

But, among the grandest Asian artists was Juan Luna from the Philippines, a member of the *illustrado* class, who was later intimately involved in the liberation war against Spain. He was in Europe from 1877–1894, and in Paris, 1885–1893, where he changed from the academy grand manner, which had won him the gold medal at Madrid in 1884, to a lighter, impressionist and more spontaneous style. Even though Luna was relatively well-off, and married into a wealthy family, he had attended the 1882 funeral of the Italian general and politician Giuseppe Garibaldi, who may have provided Luna with a model of a nationalist hero, and some of Luna's Parisian works were depictions of the working-class life of Italian labourers in the district of Paris where he lived.

Among remarkable similarities, several Australians, who did not identify themselves as 'Asians', were Tom Roberts and Margaret Preston. Roberts was in Europe for several periods (1881–1885, 1903–1919, 1921–1923), and in Paris in 1883. On his return he directed light-toned *pleinairisme* towards allegories of heroic figures of settlers who embody the values of developing the bush or harvesting agricultural plenty.

Roberts came to Paris just before the arrival of Seiki Kuroda, who settled there from 1884–1893. Soon after returning to Japan, Kuroda executed a celebrated and, in nationalist terms, equally allegorical portrait of an apprentice geisha. In significant institutional reinforcement of the pedagogy of French art, which Kuroda learnt in France, he took over the private art school founded by Yamamoto, and went on to become the first professor of oil painting at the Tokyo School of Fine Arts in 1896.

Preston, also from Australia, was in Europe 1904–1906 and 1912–1918, and in Paris from 1905–1906 and 1912–1913, the same period during which a second cohort of Japanese artists was studying in France. Preston first encountered Japanese prints at the Musée Guimet in Paris and redeployed their design conventions in the 1920s for scenes of Sydney Harbour.

It is perhaps too soon to clearly see how these Australian artists, who have hitherto been conventionally viewed as working in extensions of Euramerican discourses, in fact were trying to develop their own national art in ways not so dissimilar to their Asian counterparts. The difference was that the Australians found their situation within a 'tradition' thought to be European, and the Japanese thought the contents of their 'traditions' uniquely their own. Different contexts of colonial domination between a neo-colonial Japan in the 1880s and 1890s and a set of colonies in Australia dependent on a colonial metropolis, did not allow both of them to be seen in the same frame. In fact the artistic careers and travels of these Japanese and Australian artists frequently crossed and sometimes intersected. It is only the use of later mid-twentieth century nationalist blinkers which now prevents us seeing them in the same field of view.

Early Modernism, 1920s–1930s: The Formalisation of Internality and Externality (Endogeny and Exogeny), Movement and Stability, Localism and Cosmopolitanism [III]

Whether artists moved or stayed at home, the notional stability and motility of modern Asian artists and artworks seems to be a grounding feature of their existence, one that has sometimes been occluded by later nationalist ideologies. But, these were emplaced in a set of relations between domestic and overseas art centres, which made it no longer feasible to see these relations as merely those of colonial or later neo-colonial following and transfer.

Indeed the nature of art centres is so various, and changed so completely in Paris, for example, between the 1880s to 1910s and the inter-world war years. Similarly, changes in the nature of another international art capital, New York, may be observed between the 1960s, when it was a place of training and exhibition for artists from all over Asia, to the 1990s, when it had become a discretionary port of call for artists, rather like Paris had become by the 1970s.

How did the status of Paris as a world art capital for Chinese change between the two world wars? Post–World War I, there was a regular flow of Chinese artists to Paris and France, but clearly not as many as from Japan.

Lin Fengmian was in France from 1918–1923, studying in Dijon and then in Paris at École Nationale Supérieure des Beaux Arts (ENSBA) and the studio of Fernand Cormon, followed by a period in Berlin from 1923. He had significant exhibition activity in the first exhibition of Chinese contemporary art in Europe, *Exposition chinoise d'art ancien et moderne*,[26] which he organised at Strasbourg in 1924, as well as a personal exhibition at the *Salon d'Automne* in 1924 and at the *Exposition internationale des arts décoratifs et industriels modernes à Paris* in 1925. But the Chinese contribution to this exhibition did not attract much attention and, certainly, contemporary Chinese art was largely ignored by the French critics.[27]

Xu Beihong was in Paris from 1919–1927, studying with the conservative Pascal Dagnan-Bouveret at ENSBA. He had an important break in Berlin from 1921–1922 when he studied at the Hochschule für bildende künste with the painter Arthur Kampf, a nationalist who later became a Nazi (1864–1950), the implications of whose histrionic nationalist expression escaped his later followers in China.[28]

Pan Yuliang, one of the few major Chinese women modern artists, studied in Lyon and at ENSBA in Paris from 1921–1928, with an important break in Rome to learn sculpture from 1925–1928. She returned to France in 1937, visited the USSR in 1942, and died in Paris in 1977.[29]

---

26 Craig Clunas, 'Chinese Art and Chinese Artists in France, 1924–25', *Arts Asiatiques* 44 (1989): 101.
27 Ibid., 101.
28 There is absolutely no doubt about Kampf's Nazi sympathies, as for many 'Germanic' academy painters who were absorbed by Nazi culture. See Arthur Kampf, *Aus Meinem Leben* (Aachen: Verlag Museumsverein, 1950); Ernst Klee, *Das Kulturlexikon zum Dritten Reich, Wer war was vor und nach 1945* (Frankfurt: S. Fischer Verlag, 2007), 294. The most recent catalogue is *Xu Beihong in Nanyang* (Singapore Art Museum, 2008). Xu Beihong's second wife wrote a hagiography of him, see, Liao Jingwen, *Xu Beihong, Life of a Master Painter*, trans. Zhang Peiji (Beijing: Foreign Languages Press, 1987), which can be useful.
29 Pan Yuliang has a reasonably large bibliography, among which one may mention *Huahun: Pan Yuliang* (Taibei: Guoli Lishi Bowuguan, 2006), which includes texts by Lu Rongzhi, Jia Defang, Li Fuchang; and Jiang Biwei, *Jiang Biwei Huiyilu* (Taipei: Huangguan Zazhishe, 1966). There were further Chinese artists in France and an earlier list is found in Li Chu-tsing, 'Paris and the Development of Western Painting in China', which is included in Zhang Yuanjian et al., *Zhongguo-Bali, zaoqi liufa huajia huiguzhan zhuanji* [1918–1960] (Taipei Fine Arts Museum, 1988), 8, 12.

The changing nature of Paris as a world art capital is also clearly shown in the life experiences of two other visitors to Paris: Tsuguharu Fujita (the later Léonard Foujita), who was in Paris and elsewhere in France in 1913–1929 and 1939–1940; and, the Indian painter Amrita Sher-Gil who was in Paris from 1929–1933.

After World War II, and following a period in New York from 1947–1949, Fujita was in France from 1950–1968. Fujita has always been regarded as the Japanese artist who was most easily assimilated to the French art worlds, having formed friendships with artists such as Picasso, as well as a kind of niche market for his *fond blanc Japonais*. He married a French woman (like Chang Yu and, indeed, Lin Fengmian married a German woman who died in tragic circumstances before his return to China).[30] Undoubtedly there is a dimension of Chinese male erotic self-exploration through art, which, like Fujita's, involves exploring the visualisation of the non-Chinese body, but which can now in the main only be explored through the artists' works.

In the case of these artists, separation from home culture also involved a kind of distance from or relativising of the experience of French culture. Why, on Fujita's first return to Japan in 1929, did he not directly return home, but took a long, meandering trip on the way through Argentina and Mexico, made possible by the many artistic and literary contacts that he had formed in Paris? The answer can only be that, for artists like Fujita, however well integrated they became into French artistic life and its sub-society, Paris was as much a site for new kinds of international linkages and sympathies, which would not have been possible in his homeland, but which also were important beyond the site of Paris itself.[31] Whether there was anything intrinsically *Parisian* about such possibilities is debatable, as plenty of other cases of such networking and exploration exist in other cities overseas. In other words, one, if not *the* attraction of Paris was its significance as a site of lateral international connections and not only vertical connections between China or Japan and France: it was these connections which liberated the artist's imaginary from both the constraints of their domestic art world and those of France itself.

Sher-Gil was a young artist when she came to France with her family to study at ENSBA. She can more accurately be characterised as an Hungarian–Indian painter and was in Europe for several periods (1913–1921, 1924, 1929–1934, 1938). She left many photographs of herself and other young artists at ENSBA and it must have been attractive, despite the presence of her elite family and of

---

30   See the entry by Christina Wei-Szu Burke Mathison & Julia F. Andrews, 'Lin Fengmian', in *Encyclopedia of Modern China*, ed. David Pong, vol. 2 (Detroit: Gale/Charles Scribner's, 2009). Lin Fengmian's second wife was a French art student, Alice Vattant, who he married in 1925.
31   See Hayashi Yôko, *Fujita Tsuguji, sakuhin wo hiraku, tabi, teshigoto, Nihon* (Nagoya Daigaku Shuppankai, 2008).

social events organised by them, to have such a wide social network of peers prior to becoming a professional artist. Indeed, Sher-Gil's discovery of, or at least emphasis on, the Indian side of her origins followed her student period in Paris.[32] The notion of a globalised discourse of 'Indianness' or 'Chineseness', which arises much later in the 1990s, might look for its precursors in the social relations—including sexual self-exploration—of younger artists in a site such as Paris of the 1920s and 1930s. These were people from, or with access to, the wealthy classes in their countries of origin. Their relative privilege can be seen to rehearse the more easily and widely adopted privilege of the students of Period IV, which evolved after World War II, who were able to competitively obtain scholarships to study overseas, such as Abdul Latiff Mohidin or Gulammohammed Sheikh.

Abstractionism & Conceptualism, 1940s–1960s: Developments under Postcoloniality [IV]

Did the nature of 'worlding' change after the end of World War II in 1945? Or, did the change occur after the rise of postcolonial states, with their own nationalist cultural agendas and stylistic identifications? Across the cohort of artists throughout Asia in this period, there can be identified a drive for the local and essential, and for a locally conceptualised generality. This went in two directions, sometimes at the same time, sometimes in the work of the same artist.

One direction taken was towards a new narration of 'our people', a subject in storied representation, which was considered to go beyond the constraints of the colonial or external hegemony.

Other attempts were made to concretise 'our national' aesthetic tastes or sensibilities. These are seen clearly in the work of Korean Park Seobo, which switched from a burgeoning figurative narrative, towards an *art informel*, that was first manifested in the meaningless chaos of the civil war years, in the 1960s. This transformation ceased following the armistice and the resulting hopes for economic development. The shift then went further, however, to a new kind of line writing in pigment, or over differently pigmented grounds. The debt to the late work of the French artist Jean Fautrier was not always acknowledged, given the existing cultural space that sought a national 'Korean'

---

32 On Sher-Gil see Geeta Kapur, ed., with Vivan Sundaram, Gulammohammed Sheikh, K.G. Subramanyam, Special issue on Amrita Sher-Gil, *Marg* 25, no. 2 (1972); Yashodhara Dalmia, *Amrita Sher-Gil: A Life* (New Delhi: Viking/Penguin, 2006); Vivan Sundaram, *Amrita Sher-Gil: An Indian Artist Family of the Twentieth Century* (New Delhi: Photoink & Munich: Schirmer/Mosel, 2007).

aesthetic. If abstraction and conceptualism carried the possibility for this kind of essentialisation of national aesthetic values, they also carried the perils of repetitive factory-like production of a formal stereotype and, later, of elegant, but obvious, redeployments of form types, which could claim national affiliation.

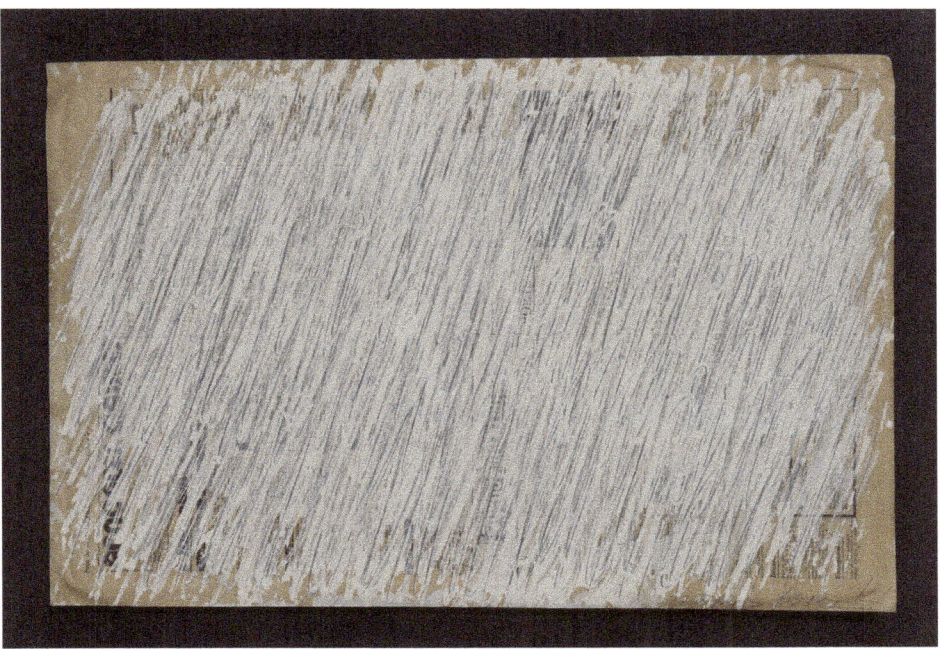

Park Seobo, *Écriture no. 45–77* 1977; pencil and oil on *Le Monde* newspaper; 33.5 cm x 50 cm.

Collection of the artist, Seoul; photograph provided by the artist

The Contemporary, 1980s to the Present: Locality and Contemporaneity, the Global Transnational Emerges [V]

The ability of local discourses to rediscover their own 'tradition' or 'national subjects' and wrap them in approved narratives, combined with the changing nature of exogenous art centres through their pluralisation and volatile shifting through the multiple temporary centres of the biennales of the 1990s, has meant that exogenous art centres can no longer be opposed, tritely, as representative of 'neo-colonialist' hegemony. Endogeneity in local art discourses, which we now associate with particular Asian nations, also shifted in that the eclecticism that is one feature of the postmodernity found in international and transnational discourses was a freedom hitherto claimed by local discourses in their nesting of the exogenous. It is now no longer a preserve that has been taken away from them; such eclecticism is now only definable against transnational conceptions of the postmodern.

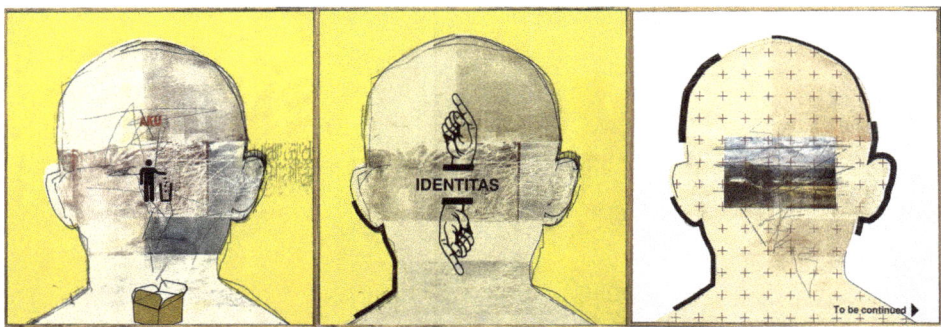

FX Harsono, *Identity* 2003; screenprint on canvas; 3 panels, each 93.5 x 90 cm.

Photograph provided by the artist

Postmodernity in the international and transnational domains has forced the joining of the local to other-worlded modernism, to exogenously and hegemonically directed dissolution and reconstitution of binaries, like 'the West' and 'the East', Orientalism and Counter-Orientalism, however much these binaries and their dissolution might appear liberatory from a global position. This situation was in some ways a reinstitution of a lack of freedom, since these decomposing binaries or their oppositions, were frames which the local had to adopt in order to appear worlded to others. Many artists necessarily fought against this, but did not have the vocabulary, the economic resources, or the theoretical imperative to fully overcome them.

Two other phenomena, which can be observed in Paris and other Euramerican art capitals, such as Amsterdam and London, should be mentioned.

The first was the massive expansion of multicultural backgrounds required of artists in thematic exhibitions. These were in some cases organised by Chinese independent curators, some resident in France, such as Fei Dawei and Hou Hanru.[33] In France, in particular, non-French curators intersected with a parallel universe of French curators and thinkers, such as Jean-Hubert Martin,

---

33 See the catalogues *Art Chinois 1990 Demain pour Hier*, which include the work of Cai Guo-Qiang, Yang Jiechang, Yan Peiming, Gu Wenda, Huang Yongping, Chen Zhen, Chen Qigang (curated by Fei Dawei, organised by Association Française d'Action Artistique & Les Domaines de l'Art at Pourrières); and, *Paris pour escale* (2000), note 17 above.

Jerôme Sans, and Nicolas Bourriaud, who were interested in relativising the status of Euramerican art practices and also in seeing art objects through paradigms of relationality co-created by artist and audience. Art was mobilised for exhibition that referred to global issues, such as flows of information or environment, but where, I would argue, the 'Chinese' reference was incidental. Paris/France was simply one site among others, and official reports indicated its earlier status had been lost or was in sway to unsurmountable forces in the international art world.[34] The new biennales, several of which were held in Asia, were a further loop in this process of de-culturalisation of specific discursive references. But paradoxically, for the receiving Euramerican art cultures, they were a simultaneous cultural broadening of general exhibition context in which the works were shown.

In the middle of this change, only acknowledged by the presence of new exhibition spaces, such as the Palais du Tokyo, and the collection role assigned to new regional art centres in France, were the tendencies to spectacularisation evident in the creation of gargantuan art works to fill huge spaces.

A second phenomenon, which was evident by the 1990s, was that international houses of luxury consumer goods, many of which were French-owned or based in Paris, began to recognise a new trend in the way cultural references could be attached to objects, particularly high-end consumer goods, and engaged in cultural marketing through their foundations. These cemented the cultural aura and brand power of their associated houses to new, fashionable icons of cross-nationality. Paris and France became a host body for the launch of cultural goods, in some ways similar to the way *haute couture* figured for *prêt-à-porter* in the clothing industry in the second half of the twentieth century. Chinese objects and artists were prominent in these changes from the early 1990s. The tendency, which has shown no sign of abating, has expanded from China to include art and artists from other Asian countries, such as Sudarshan Shetty and his *House of Shades*, which was made for Louis Vuitton in 2009/2010 and displayed in a galleria in Milan, or Eko Nugroho from Indonesia, whose mural installation *Republic of Lost and Found* was exhibited at Espace Culturel Louis Vuitton in June 2011, as part of the exhibition *Trans-Figurations: Indonesian Mythologies*.[35]

---

34   See Alain Quemin, *L'art contemporain international: entre les institutions et le marché (le rapport disparu)* (Nîmes: Éditions Jacqueline Chambon / Artprice, 2002).
35   Among prominent cases are the Fondation Cartier exhibitions of Huang Yongping in 1994 and 1997, Louis Vuitton Chinese pre-modern luxury object exhibitions 2004, the activities of Chanel in its Mobile art campaign in 2008 including the work of Yang Fudong, and Eko Nugroho's projects were also at Espace Culturel Louis Vuitton in June 2011.

Conclusion

I suggested in the introduction to this essay that the task of understanding the Asian Modern is first of all to know what the artists did, to map their work and times, and then to compare them; that cohorts have the feature of viewing the 'worlding of the Asian Modern' as both an inward or exogenous process and, at the same time, an outward and endogenous one. They take art history away from seeing change as dependent on external or hegemony-down origination, and as a much more complex intermediate zone in part isolated from the very forces of modernity they also manifest.

It is a feature of the generational cohorts of artists that they represent in many cases also a periodisation. This marks simultaneously an overlapping absorption of Euramerican art techniques and institutions with their local repositioning against other and prior art discourses. These processes took place in Asia, as state units so differently and variegatedly constituted from semi-colonies (littoral China), full colonies (India and French Indo-China), settler colonies (Australia and New Zealand) and two relatively free states (Siam and Japan). It happened in cultural zones with both extensive discourses of two-dimensional art and their histories and ideas (China, Korea and Japan) as well as including those where two-dimensional representation was relatively tabooed (the courts of Sumatra and Java, the Malay States). As I proposed at the beginning of this essay, it is important now, in postcolonial times, to reconsider more carefully the ways of conceiving the distinction between exogenous and endogenous art discourses since the resulting works have become the originary works for long-term and, in most cases, almost wholly endogenous genealogies of the Asian Modern.

3. An Experiment in Connectivity: From the 'West Heavens' to the 'Middle Kingdom'

Chaitanya Sambrani

This essay is based on my curatorial work for the exhibition *Place.Time.Play: Contemporary Art from the 'West Heavens' to the 'Middle Kingdom'* (various venues in Shanghai, October–December 2010). The first instance of contemporary art collaboration between artists from India and China, this exhibition resulted from unprecedented opportunities and challenges for artists, curators and scholars from the two countries. In addition to the exhibition, this project involved fieldwork and dialogue for participants from both countries, and fed into the ongoing 'West Heavens' platform that has grown to encompass Sino-Indian dialogue across art, architecture, political theory and film.[1] A major bilingual (Mandarin and English) publication was produced that recorded the exhibition and the process of dialogue through edited and footnoted transcriptions of conversations between Indian and Chinese participants.[2] The following text represents a retrospective consideration of the 2010 exhibition, intended to highlight questions relevant to the theme of Asian connectivities and intra-Asia regional connections.

It is an enduring irony of contemporary Asian art as a discursive field that most intra-Asian conversations have been mediated via non-Asian locations such as Australia and the United States. As a postgraduate student of art history in India, I gained only limited awareness of modernist art in 'Asia'.[3] This limited awareness came via the pan-Asianist adventure launched in Calcutta and Santiniketan (Bengal) in the first decades of the twentieth century, primarily between Indian and Japanese actors. The Japanese scholar Kakuzo Okakura Kakuzo (1862–1913) visited India in 1901–1902 at the invitation of Indian poet and philosopher Rabindranath Tagore (1861–1941). This visit led to the publication of *Ideals of*

---

1 See http://westheavens.net/en for descriptions, forums and announcements about this ongoing project. 'West Heavens is an integrated cross-cultural exchange programme. It aims to untangle and compare the different paths of modernity taken by India and China, to facilitate high-level communication between the two countries' intellectual and art circles, and to promote interaction and cross-references between the two countries through social thoughts and contemporary art. Since 2010, the project has organized more than 100 events including forums, exhibitions, film screenings and workshops, as well as publishing more than 10 books.'
2 Chang Tsong-Zung, Chen Yun & Chaitanya Sambrani, eds, *Place, Time, Play: Contemporary Art from the 'West Heavens' to the 'Middle Kingdom'* (Hong Kong: Hanart TZ Gallery, 2012).
3 I was an MA student in the Department of Art History and Aesthetics, Faculty of Fine Arts, MS University, Baroda, India, over 1992–1995.

the East, a manifesto that propounded the essential unity of Asian art from India to Japan.[4] Okakura's book begins with the singular claim: 'Asia is one!', which could be seen as part of the cultural logic for the development of the pan-Asianist foreign and military policy of Taisho (1912–1926) and Showa (1926–1989) Japan. Okakura was not alone in propounding the unity of Asian art; Rabindranath Tagore and A.K. Coomaraswamy (1877–1941) also supported a pan-Asian internationalism as an alternative to the cultural hegemony of Europe. Coomaraswamy asserted that Okakura was the first to emphatically argue the fundamental unity of Asian art, essentially that of Indian with Far Eastern art.[5] Okakura's ideals of a pan-Asian cultural unity found sympathetic ears among Abanindranath Tagore's (1871–1951) circle of artists, which sought a revival of 'Indian' art. Okakura placed India and China as the two fountainheads of Asian culture,[6] arguing, however, that India had lost its 'capacity to give ... its sublime attainments [having been] almost effaced ... by the rough-handedness of the Hunas, the fanatical iconoclasm of the Mussulmân, and the unconscious vandalism of mercenary Europe, leaving us to seek only a past glory in the mouldy walls of Ajanta, the tortured sculptures of Ellora, the silent protests of rock-cut Orissa ...'.[7]

The pan-Asianist experiment in revivalist art across India and Japan resulted in Japanese *nihonga* artists (Yokoyama Taikan (1868–1958), Kanpo Arai (1878–1945), and Katayama Nanpu (1887–1980)) travelling to India during the first two decades of the twentieth century, as well as Indian artists, notably Nandalal Bose (1882–1966) and Benodebehari Mukherjee (1904–1980) travelling to Japan, China and Nepal during the 1920s until the 1940s. Kala Bhavana, the Visva-Bharati University's school of art at Santiniketan ('abode of peace'), founded by Rabindranath Tagore in rural West Bengal, became a location for an eclectic intra-Asian dialogue. This did not, however, mean the exclusion of European influence, as R. Siva Kumar has shown.[8] The study of European modernist developments was complemented by a growing interest in 'Far Eastern' art. Nirmalendu Das notes that Bose's 1924 visit to Japan resulted in the arrival into Santiniketan of 'an authentic collection of Chinese rubbings and Japanese colour woodcut prints with him.'[9] Mukherjee embarked on a self-funded trip to

---

4 Okakura Kakuso [sic], *The Ideals of the East* (London: John Murray, 1903).
5 AK Coomaraswamy, *Fundamentals of Indian Art* (Jaipur: Historical Research Documentation Programme, 1985), 21.
6 Recent art historical writing has rightly contested the assumption that these two fountainhead cultures dominated the art of Asia.
7 Okakura, *Ideals of the East*, 6.
8 R. Siva Kumar, 'Benodebehari Mukherjee: Life, Context, Work', in *Benodebehari Mukherjee (1904–1980): Centenary Retrospective*, curated by Gulammohammed Sheikh and R. Siva Kumar (exhibition catalogue) (New Delhi: Vadehra Art Gallery in collaboration with the National Gallery of Modern Art, 2006), 73–75.
9 Nirmalendu Das, 'A Brief History of Printmaking at Santiniketan', *Art Etc. News and Views*, August 2011, http://www.artnewsnviews.com/view-article.php?article=a-brief-history-of-printmaking-at-santiniketan&iid=23&articleid=593#sthash.Rv1d7SEz.dpuf.

Japan and China over nine months in 1936–1937. Even though his trip to China was necessarily short and restricted by the Japanese invasion, Kumar argues that the influence of a Chinese aesthetic sensibility remained paramount for Mukherjee, his most admired Japanese artists—Toba Sojo, Sesshu and Tawaraya Sotatsu—being 'considered Chinese in spirit, or more accurately, eclectics, combining Chinese sublimity with the dramatic force and decorative rigour of Japan.'[10] Chinese artist Xu Beihong (1895–1953) spent several months in 1940 at Santiniketan, marking a 40-year engagement between modern art in India and the 'Far East'.[11]

The legacy of the Santiniketan experiment in Asian internationalism has been translated variously in diverse locations across India.[12] In Baroda, for instance, the syllabus in modern art covered the history of Indian and Euro-American modernism, but remained largely devoid of modernist art in other parts of Asia, or of modernism in Latin America (save for figures such as Diego Rivera and Frida Kahlo), or Africa. I first encountered modern and contemporary 'Asian' art in locations outside Asia proper, particularly in Australia. Institutionalised opacities continue to attend art historical scholarship and pedagogy in many parts of Asia, and indeed the world, where a biennalised world order of a reified 'contemporary' seems to offer redemption from Euramerican dominance.[13] The dream of Asian (or other) connectivity continues to be beset by the limits of knowledge. The spectre of mutual ignorance haunts the cosmopolitan imagination.

Underlying this 'inequality of ignorance' is the problem of the 'hyperreality' of Asia, as argued by Dipesh Chakrabarty.[14] Anthony Milner and Deborah Johnson have demonstrated historical dimensions and modern constructions of the 'idea of Asia' in political and cultural dimensions, as well as the limits of such constructions.[15] Historical constructions of Asia originate in ancient Greek thought and, while these constructions have changed over time, it is significant that they have almost always originated in non-Asian contexts. In other words, the definitions of 'Asia' and 'Asian' have primarily come from outside Asia, particularly Europe. The exhibitionary and scholarly field of contemporary Asian art is of relatively recent origin, emerging almost simultaneously in Australia and the United States in the late 1980s and early 1990s, with a slightly earlier Japanese precedent noted below. The Artists' Regional Exchange project was

---

10 R. Siva Kumar, 'Benodebehari Mukherjee', 76. There is an underlying argument here regarding the differences between *Kara-e* (Chinese manner) and *Yamato-e* (Japanese manner) in Japanese art history.
11 Ibid.
12 This translation could be the subject for another study in its own right and cannot be addressed here.
13 Terry Smith, 'Worlds Pictured in Contemporary Art: Planes and Connectivities', *Humanities Research* 19, no. 2. 2013, eds Caroline Turner, Michelle Antoinette & Zara Stanhope.
14 Dipesh Chakrabarty, 'Postcoloniality and the Artifice of History: Who Speaks for 'Indian' Pasts?', in *A Subaltern Studies Reader 1986–1995*, ed. Ranajit Guha (Delhi: Oxford University Press, 1998), 263–93.
15 Anthony Milner and Deborah Johnson, 'The Idea of Asia', https://digitalcollections.anu.edu.au/handle/1885/41891.

initiated in Perth, Western Australia, in 1987 and ran until 1999, inaugurating exchanges between Australian, South-East Asian and New Zealand artists. In 1989, the Queensland Art Gallery, Brisbane, organised an exhibition of Japanese art of the preceding decade. In 1990, the Asialink Arts program at the University of Melbourne was established with Alison Carroll as founding director. In 1991, John Clark (then at The Australian National University, Canberra) convened a conference on modernity in Asian art.[16] In 1992, Vishakha Desai (then vice-president and director of the Asia Society Museum, New York) convened a roundtable comprising eminent curators from Asia. Participants included T.K. Sabapathy, Singapore; Gulammohammed Sheikh, India; Apinan Poshyananda, Thailand; Jim Supangkat, Indonesia; and Redza Piyadasa, Malaysia.[17] In 1993, subscribers to *Art and Australia* were supplied with a small supplement, *Art and Asia Pacific*, which has since become the major international art journal, *Art Asia Pacific*.[18] In the same year, the Queensland Art Gallery launched the first of its Asia-Pacific Triennials of Contemporary Art, an ongoing series of influential exhibitions and publications. It would seem that, at the beginning of the 1990s, a number of locations at the margins of the Asian mainland simultaneously started paying attention to contemporary art in their neighbourhoods.[19]

In making these observations, I do not seek to imply that art historical scholarship is of recent origin in Asia. Sophisticated traditions of scholarship on modern and contemporary art within national boundaries exist in many Asian art cultures, but they are largely restriced to national boundaries. With the exception of the Fukuoka Art Museum's exhibitions of modern and contemporary Asian art initiated in 1979,[20] the 'invention' of contemporary Asian art, however, took place outside Asia.

Recent years have seen an amelioration of this situation via commercial exhibitions and museum projects involving intra-Asian relationships. Here again, Japanese organisations have taken the lead: witness the Japan Foundation-initiated project *Under Construction: New Dimensions of Asian Art* (2001–2003) that involved 'a new type of collaborative project initiated in Asia, [with] 9 young curators in their twenties and thirties from 7 Asian countries (China, India, Indonesia,

---

16   The edited proceedings were published as John Clark, ed., *Modernity in Asian Art* (Sydney: Wild Peony Press, 1993).
17   It is significant to note that of these, three (Sheikh, Supangkat and Piyadasa) had trained primarily as artists.
18   *Art Asia Pacific* is now a quarterly journal of some 200 pages, with global distribution. It has been based in Sydney, Hong Kong and New York and is currently in Hong Kong.
19   For an analysis of this phenomenon, even as it was being born, see Apinan Poshyananda, 'The Future: Post-Cold War, Postmodernism, Postmarginalia (Playing with Slippery Lubricants)', in *Tradition and Change: Contemporary Art of Asia and the Pacific*, ed. Caroline Turner (Brisbane: Queensland University Press, 1993), 3–24.
20   See http://faam.city.fukuoka.lg.jp/eng/about/abt_history.html#b. The Fukuoka Art Museum is the parent organisation of the Fukuoka Asian Art Museum (which opened in 1999 with the *1st Fukuoka Asian Art Triennale* (The 5th Asian Art Show).

Japan, Korea, the Philippines, Thailand)' being invited to to engage in fieldwork 'to produce one integrated exhibition as the result of their collaborative effort.'[21] In 2006, Arario Beijing (a branch of the Seoul-based gallery) hosted a major exhibition of contemporary Indian art. To my knowledge, this was the first substantial exhibition of contemporary Indian art to be held in China.[22] The Museum of Contemporary Art Shanghai, a private space adjoining the Shanghai Art Museum, hosted exhibitions of contemporary Indian art in 2009, and of contemporary Indonesian art in 2010.[23] Apparently, commerce in contemporary 'Asian' art was no longer a matter of selling works domestically, or else in Euro-American venues: intra-Asian transactions in contemporary art were emerging as a financially viable proposition for the international art market.

The 'West Heavens' Project

Johnson Chang (Chang Tsong-Zung) and I first met at the Asia Art Archive, Hong Kong, in 2008.[24] Chang was keen to explore how contemporary Chinese artistic and academic cultures might benefit from interactions with their Indian counterparts. He wanted to present an exhibition of Indian contemporary art in China accompanied by an ongoing intellectual dialogue. We corresponded over the course of the following year leading to the inception of the 'West Heavens' project. While Chang was inclined to organise an exhibition of Indian work in China, I was keen that the works of contemporary Indian artists be seen in dialogue with those of their Chinese colleagues. We agreed to invite Indian and Chinese artists to travel to each other's countries, to engage in dialogue, and to produce work as a result of these interactions. The project title came from the ancient Chinese name for India, as the heavenly realm lying to the west; heavenly because it was the place where the historical Buddha was born, lived and attained enlightenment.

---

21 An introduction to this project can be seen at http://www.jpf.go.jp/e/culture/new/old/0210/10_07.html. See also, Mami Kataoka, ed., *Under Construction: New Dimensions of Asian Art* (Tokyo: Japan Foundation Asia Center; Tokyo Opera City Art Gallery, 2002).
22 Hungry God: Indian Contemporary Art, Arario Gallery, Beijing, 3 September – 15 October 2006. See Chaitanya Sambrani, 'Ways of Belonging: Post-national Art in India', in *Hungry God: Indian Contemporary Art* (Beijing, Arario, 2007), 32–46.
23 See www.mocashanghai.org for details.
24 Chang co-founded the Asia Art Archive and, as gallerist, curator and scholar, has made a major contribution to raising international awareness of contemporary Chinese art. I was visiting the archive to give a presentation on my curatorial project *Edge of Desire: Recent Art in India*, which was exhibited in Australia, the United States, Mexico and India over 2004–2007.

Since then, the 'West Heavens' project has developed into an ongoing series of individual yet related projects incorporating art exchanges, social theory, publications, independent cinema, performance and video, as well as dialogues on urbanism and architecture across India and China.[25]

Place.Time.Play: The Making of an Exhibition

The process of making the exhibition *Place.Time.Play: Contemporary Art from the 'West Heavens' to the 'Middle Kingdom'* involved a series of contacts, reciprocal visits and discussions involving artists, curators and scholars from India and China. The title of the exhibition was designed to signal the invitation to encounter locations (place) and histories (time) across old and new borders, and to engage with them critically and creatively. *Place* signals geography, *time* speaks of history, while *play* invokes a potential for artists to work with, or subvert, established structures. Reckonings with place imply an understanding of contextual difference, and an attempt to enter another location. Taking time is both a requirement of this process, and an opportunity to encounter a different sense of history, and to work with legacies of tradition as well as current economic and political conditions. The invitation to play was extended on the premise that the *ludic* instinct is a fundamentally life-affirming gesture, which is too often lost in the pursuit of representations of topical issues.[26] The project hoped to inaugurate continuing relationships between artist communities across the two nations.

In the course of fieldwork, we travelled to locations in India (Delhi, Baroda, Ahmedabad, Bombay) with a group of Chinese artists and curators in March 2010. In April 2010 we travelled with a group of Indian artists to Shanghai, Hangzhou, Yiwu and other places in the Yangtze Delta, including waterside villages, a Buddhist monastery and a Literati poets' retreat. In both countries, we convened 'moving forums' that brought the travellers together with local artists for conversations and reciprocal presentations of work.[27] In addition to these collective trips, the project enabled several artists to visit specific locations of interest to their individual practice.

---

25 As part of the 'West Heavens' project, Gao Shiming and Chen Kuan-Hsing were invited to convene a series of lectures by Indian intellectuals of different nationalities (Sarat Maharaj, Partha Chatterjee, Prasenjit Duara, Ashis Nandy, Tejaswini Niranjana, Dipesh Chakrabarty, Homi Bhabha and Geeta Kapur). Significant publications from the oeuvre of each individual were published in a series of bilingual readers under the series *Readers of Current Indian Thought*, Nanfang Daily Press.
26 I am thinking of the general tendency for exhibited works from less privileged contexts to highlight issues considered relevant to recent history. It is relatively rare to find a valorisation of 'Third World' abstractionists. Nasreen Mohamedi (1937–1990) is a case in point in that her international acclaim has been posthumous.
27 The model of the 'moving forum' was an adaptation of the discursive structure devised during the 2008 Guangzhou Triennial *Farewell to Post-Colonialism*, curated by Johnson Chang, Gao Shiming and Sarat Maharaj, at the Guangdong Art Museum, Guangzhou, 6 September – 16 November 2008.

3. An Experiment in Connectivity: From the 'West Heavens' to the 'Middle Kingdom'

In choosing which artists to invite, we first considered ongoing concerns within the artists' work. We were especially interested in work that crossed boundaries and aspired to speak to audiences beyond the familiar binary of local self and Euro-American other. We considered which artists would be willing and able to accommodate within their practice the challenges of interaction with a parallel civilisation: one that appears to be historically inextricably linked with one's own and, yet, so far removed in modern experience, except in an adversarial role.[28] What kind of artistic internationalism could be imagined without the international being routed via Western Europe, North America or Australia? Equally, we were keen to steer clear of revivalist practice that would involve a nostalgic return to the traditional, but to seek contemporary re-activations of the traditional in a politics of the present.

The impatience we felt with the East/West binary could be mapped on to the growing ambitions and strengths of Chinese and Indian art cultures and economies. Certainly, we were responding to the aspirations of artists who straddle continents and cultures in their work, confounding inherited structures of belonging and address. A major point of discussion was the display of specific national or regional characteristics that marked an artist's work as being an authentic representation of an originary culture. Who would this display be for? Was a display of 'Indian' or 'Chinese' authenticity more valid when it appealed to the exhibitionary desires of the West? What characteristics would the work display if it were aimed at a Chinese (or Indian) audience? As an exhibition *Place.Time.Play* sought to address the possibilities and limits of artistic conversation within Asian contexts without recourse to Euro-American forums.

A concern with national histories and traditions, especially in their authorised guises, was a frequent feature of the conversations. In what was constituted an 'Indian' view of Indian tradition, given the inheritance of British colonialism and more than 60 years of the existence of the Indian nation state? How did contemporary Chinese artists situate their tradition, considering an ancient history of learning and international contact, and the tumultuous events of the twentieth century with Euro-American colonisation and Japanese imperialism, followed by the establishment of the Peoples' Republic and the destructive events of the Cultural Revolution? India and China came to realise their republic at the same time, but with marked differences. With similar challenges, they chose different paths to modernisation. What might be the gains and losses in understanding modern historical parallels and divergences between these two nations? In addition to being considered major economic growth regions, India and China are participants in long-running border disputes and, in an ironic reprise of neo-colonialism, competitors over the resources of poorer Asian and

---

28   India and China fought a war over territory in 1962. At the time of writing, there are ongoing disputes over the boundaries that are shared between the Republic of India and the Peoples' Republic of China.

African nations. Meanwhile, the cash registers of dealers and auction houses regularly ring with the next big sale achieved for the work of one or more of the superstar artists from India or China.

What, then, might it mean for artists from these countries to address each other, and what would be the terms of that address, acknowledging that both sides were increasingly implicated and imbricated within the post-conceptualist framework of an international contemporary art world mediated via biennials and art fairs? What did Indian and Chinese artists, curators and academics have to learn from each other? Would the process of a single art event adequately address the entire range of possible conversations between the two art cultures? In retrospect, I do not hold that all the works in the exhibition lent themselves to this range of speculation or aspiration. In a process-driven and exploratory exhibition, it would be futile to expect every work to address the, sometimes intractable, issues of inter-cultural communication, especially between countries such as China and India, and within the time frame in which we worked. Language was a formidable barrier, despite the efforts of Chen Yun, our project manager, and Chang, both of whom functioned as interpreters and intermediaries in most of the Sino-Indian conversations.

That the exhibition took place at all was remarkable in view of the challenges we faced. Not only were we embarking on an exception to established practice in international exchanges, we were exploring a way of communicating with a cognate art culture, which defied the existing framework of such exchanges being routed via non-Asian academic and exhibition venues. Leaving aside the Santiniketan experiment at the beginning of the twentieth century, there was no history of collegial interaction on which we could rely. That we did not have the support of a major museum placed logistical and infrastructural limitations on the exhibition. This limitation, however, could be seen as an asset in view of the artists' works discussed below, several of which undertook experimental forms that deviated from conventional museum formats. For instance, the project enabled artists to undertake projects that, due to legal issues, would have been impossible for a museum administration to support.

Despite this, the production and installation process did present a range of difficulties associated with bureaucratic and infrastructural conditions. The exhibition sites comprised the foyer of a 22-storey bank building on Nanjing Xi Lu (Nanjing West Road, opposite the Shanghai Art Museum, site of the Shanghai Biennale), and a pair of nineteenth century heritage-listed monastery and chapel buildings (South Suzhou Road, adjoining the Bund). After many bureaucratic delays, the crates containing works from India were delivered only three hours before the scheduled exhibition opening on 23 October 2010, in the midst of a torrential downpour associated with Tropical Cyclone Megi. The 2010 World Expo in Shanghai had already altered timelines for customs clearance.

The audience was met by an exhibition team and artists frantically unpacking crates, with only the locally made (Chinese and Indian) works ready for display. As a consequence, the formal opening was rescheduled to 30 October.

Place.Time.Play: Crossings and Conversations

The routine censorship of work in the Peoples' Republic of China played a role in the process of installing the exhibition and a work by Wu Shanzhuan (b. 1960) and Inga Svala Thorsdöttir (b. 1966) was affected by state intervention. Wu and Inga (as they call themselves) had proposed a reworking of their text-based *Things' Rights*, which idiosyncratically reinterprets the Universal Declaration of Human Rights by replacing each instance of the word 'human' with 'thing'. That Wu Shanzhuan's family name (Wu) also equates to 'thing' was something the artists exploited in the work. Wu and Inga proposed a series of texts for the exhibition that represented the 'manifesto' of thing's rights in three languages: Mandarin, Sanskrit and Hindi. In the context of the (then) recent award of the 2010 Nobel Peace Prize to the dissident Liu Xiaobo (who is a political prisoner in China), Chinese censors took a dim view of any work that invoked, no matter how obliquely, the idea of human rights. The work was refused a license for exhibition. As a compromise, small booklets with the Sanskrit and Hindi text were available for the audience to take away, the vast majority of whom (including the officials) could not read the text in those languages.

Atul Bhalla's (b. 1964) work was another casualty of Chinese censorship. His location-specific series *The Listener from the West Heavens* addressed his ongoing concern with water and its cultural meanings. Bhalla's practice has involved an investigation of the values associated with water in all its forms: as drink and irrigation; as rivers, canals and reservoirs; as an object of value and a precious resource to be controlled and administered; and, as carrier of refuse. In a series of choreographed photo-performances, Bhalla assumed the role of a stranger listening intently to the underground streetscape of Shanghai. For him, the spectacular growth of Shanghai conceals a buried history: the many streams, lakes and canals that once constituted a waterside economy might still be audible below the concrete. Vestiges of the past, haunting the pursuit of hyper-modernity, are perhaps discernible to the ears of strangers from afar. Bhalla subtitled his back-lit images with modified texts from Chang Jung's novel *Wild Swans* (1991), which recall slogans from the Cultural Revolution. Bhalla modified these slogans to appear as consumerist exhortations and some of these re-alignments—especially those that mentioned the words 'communist' or 'democracy'—were refused an exhibition permit. Our token protest in response to this refusal was to display the works as blacked-out light-boxes, coupled with a stop-motion video of Bhalla 'listening' in a number of Shanghai locations.

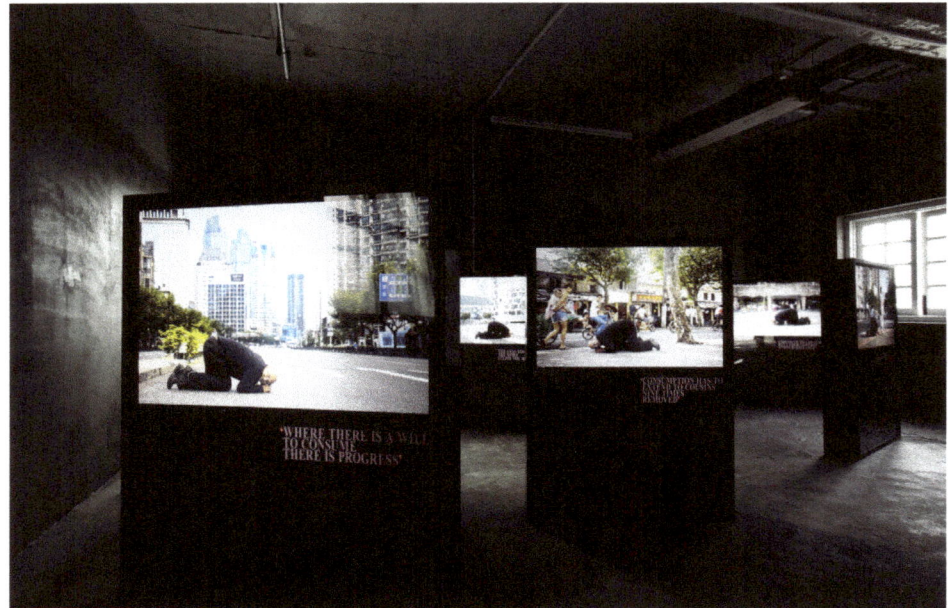

Atul Bhalla, *The Listener from the West Heavens* 2010 (detail); light boxes and video; 9 pieces, 135 x 95 x 20 cm each.

Photograph: Thomas Fuesser; courtesy of West Heavens

The idea of entering another location, or of intruding into another territory, was also exemplified in Qiu Zhijie's (b. 1969) *Railway from Lhasa to Katmandu* [sic] (2006–2010). In 2006–2007 Qiu Zhijie walked from Lhasa (Tibet) to Kathmandu (Nepal). The trigger for this project was the inauguration in July 2006 of the Golmud–Lhasa railway line, complete with pressurised passenger cars to facilitate high-altitude travel. For Qiu Zhijie, this represented the latest in a series of entries into the mythical Shangri-La that Tibet represents: a hermetic realm of spirituality and peace, but also a geopolitical prize vied over by European as well as Chinese imperial interests.[29] His research into the 'discovery' of Tibet led him to the character of Nain Singh (Nain Singh Rawat, 1830–1895) an Indian employee of the (British) Geometrical Survey of India who mapped the route from Nepal to Tibet in 1866.[30] Qiu Zhijie set about replicating Nain Singh's journey in reverse, using as much as possible of the same technology for navigation and measurement (including wearing shackles to mimic Nain Singh's

---

29 As part of the work, Qiu Zhijie presented an annotated map insinuating his own journey among the routes and dates of the various nineteenth century European expeditions into the north-west of China.

30 Nain Singh Rawat was one of the first explorers of the Himalayan territory working for the British Government. His 1865–1866 journey from Kathmandu to Lhasa was characterised by intrigue and impersonation. Having been trained to take equidistant steps regardless of terrain, he posed as a monk, but with a modified prayer rosary of 100 instead of 108 beads to keep track of distance, and a compass and thermometer camouflaged in his monastic equipment.

3. An Experiment in Connectivity: From the 'West Heavens' to the 'Middle Kingdom'

measured footsteps of precisely 33 inches. The idea of Tibet as an object of desire, sandwiched between British India and Imperial China, and its conflicted history in the twentieth and twenty-first centuries was presented in the exhibition through a series of photographs, video and *thang-ka* paintings. In an ironic comment on Tibetan identity and destiny, Qiu Zhijie also included three lengths of rail tracks reconstituted from an alloy of objects of ritual, musical and religious purpose that he collected, via barter, on his journey.

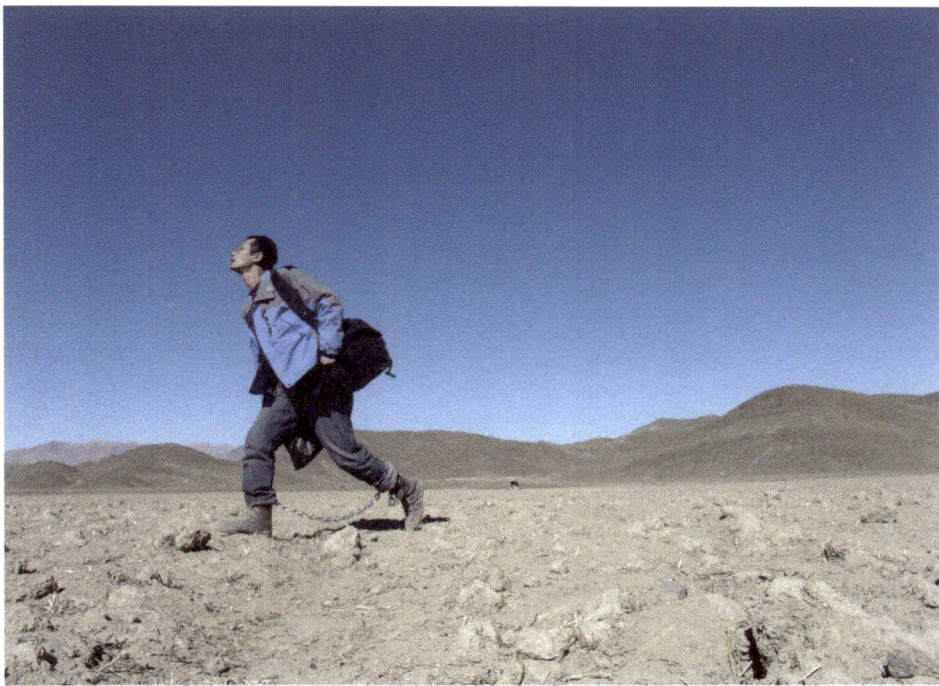

Qiu Zhijie, *Railway from Lhasa to Katmandu* 2010 (detail); performance, photographs, installation.

Photograph: Thomas Fuesser; courtesy of West Heavens

Throughout history, wanderers, explorers and colonisers have been seduced by the promise of crossing culture: of discovering the unknown and thereby oneself. Such trespass might uncover the unknown within the intimate, and reveal the familiar within the seemingly foreign. The travels of Sun Wukong in the Chinese classic *Journey to the West* are evocative and revelatory in respect of Qiu Zhijie's experimental walk. This journey of self-discovery was echoed in Tushar Joag's (b. 1966) motorcycle odyssey from Bombay, India, to Shanghai, China. On his unassisted ride between these two financial capitals, Joag made strategic stops among communities affected by India's Sardar Sarovar complex of dams on the river Narmada, and the Three Gorges complex on the Yangtze. Both governments have represented the projects as major landmarks in nation-building, and both projects have resulted in large scale dispossession of indigenous tribes and farmers in service of the presumed greater ideal of modernisation. Crossing diverse terrain and experiencing extreme temperatures, landslides and storms, Joag undertook a feat of endurance in *Riding Rocinante from Bombay to Shanghai via Sardar Sarovar and the Three Gorges*[31] astride a 1950s-designed, 350 cc Enfield 'Bullet' motorcycle with sidecar. Joag's journey to Shanghai followed earlier journeys in reverse, such as that of the Buddhist monk Xuanzang (seventh century CE) who travelled to India in search of original Buddhist scriptures. It also made reference to the Buddha's journey of renunciation on his horse Kanthaka, and Ernesto 'Che' Guevara's travels of self-discovery in Latin America. On reaching Shanghai, Joag dismantled his motorcycle, which was presented as a sculptural installation, *The Realisation of Kanthaka*, using water from the Yangtze, Joag's battered equipment, a copy of his blog entries, maps used on the journey[32] and other ephemera.

Crossing boundaries was a repeated refrain in the artists' responses to the exhibition theme. Having undertaken a research trip to Beijing, Anant Joshi was fascinated by the imposing gateways that he observed in many cities, including Beijing (the gates to the Forbidden City) and his home city of Bombay (the Gateway of India). Associated with imperial might, these gateways function as proclamations of authority; at once welcoming portals and forbidding bulwarks. In his *Musical Chairs*, Joshi manipulated the form and function of gateways to create a sculpture that functions as a closed gateway from one side, and a series of hospitable thrones from the other. His ongoing concern with games and play was represented by a tongue-in-cheek comment on thrones and the jostling for power that goes on in the backrooms of government. Joshi's installation and accompanying flipbook presented a playful critique of how civilisations and empires construct parameters of permissibility and prohibition.

The idiosyncratic paintings, intended as a trilogy/triptych, of Liu Dahong (b. 1962) gestured towards a series of improbable syntheses between Indian, Chinese and European histories. *Travelling Worldwide* presented a seemingly wanton series of leaps across European, Indian and Chinese sources. The artist's intentions, however, were more complex than syncretism for its own sake. He sought a radical revision of art historical narratives, potentially rewriting them from within, to construct an alternative vision of that which *was*, and that *might have been* in terms of art historical representation. Liu Dahong constructed an amalgam of historical material that presented reinvented histories of India and China. The drama of this fantasy was enacted under the poetic penumbrae of the reclining figures of Leo Tolstoy and Rabindranath Tagore, and of an allegorical and heavily pregnant nude mother figure, perhaps about to give birth to a new,

---

31 Joag chose to name his motorcycle Rocinante after the horse on which Spanish writer Miguel de Cervantes's delusional character Don Quixote famously tilted at windmills.
32 Joag's blog *Riding Rocinante* can be accessed at http://riding-d-rocinante.blogspot.com/.

reconfigured world. This comedic and cosmic drama encompassed a gamut of historical characters ranging from long-dead emperors of the past to political figures of the twentieth century. The work asked the viewer to 'think otherwise', to contemplate the nature of political and cultural relationships in an altered articulation of history.

Nilima Sheikh (b. 1945) also chose to work with historical realignments in her *Over Land* series of 14, free-hanging, tempera-on-paper scrolls (mounted on silk in Hangzhou). Installed in the chapel at 107 South Suzhou Road, her work originated in her commitment to working with elements of Asian tradition. Her engagement with the poetic and the lyrical has traversed visual and literary traditions across India, Pakistan and China. Having first visited China in 1991, and several times since, she studied Chinese traditions and their intersections, via the Himalayan regions, with Indian traditions. Her constellation of works included abbreviated notations and motifs that encompassed various forms of trans-culturality. Her poetic and pictorial references included legends from the Jatakas (the previous lives of the Buddha in Indian Buddhist traditions), and poetic works from Chinese, Kashmiri and Punjabi poets: amongst them Sung Chih-Wen (*Crossing the Han River*), Yuan Mei (*The Tree Planter Laughs at Himself*), Shah Husain (Punjab, Shaalu and Heer) and Lal Ded (Kashmir).

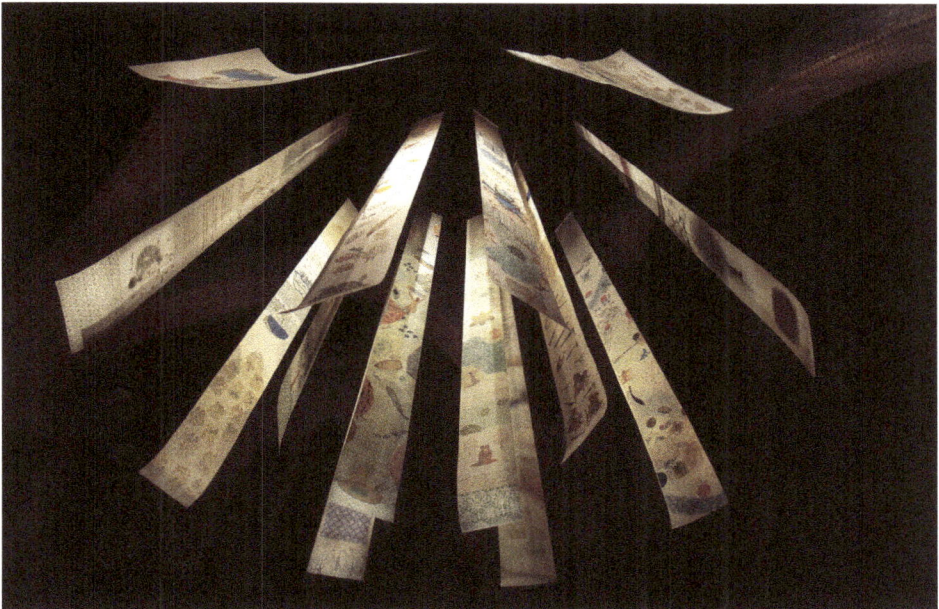

Nilima Sheikh, *Over Land* 2010; casein tempera on rice paper mounted on silk; 14 scrolls, 366 x 30 cm each.

Photograph: Mao Xingyu; courtesy of West Heavens

In the same space was installed Hema Upadhyay's (b. 1972) motorised installation *Twin Souls* comprising 40 mechanical birds whirling in a cage-like structure. Upadhyay's birds spoke of the troubled experience of migration and (re)settlement, exploring the interstices between belonging and alienation. Upadhyay used Chinese-made, mass-produced toys to construct a cacophony of caged birds circling endlessly, trapped between destinations and forever unable to reach home. The birds' erratic behaviour as a flock hinted at a state of anxiety driven to violence, invoking a mob in place of a community. Where a confluence of cultures might have been imagined, Upadhyay presented a collection of imprisoned beings driven to desperation.

Sonia Khurana's (b. 1968) work was concerned with embodying a private ethics of being in the world, and the complications attendant to the meeting between this private realm and that of the public. She produced for the exhibition a (work-in-progress) project, *An Imprecise Portrait*, which resulted from the chance discovery of a scrapbook belonging to an anonymous person (a Chinese woman?) containing in addition to 'authorised' images from the Cultural Revolution, various interpolations that had presumably been made by the owner/occupier of this book. Khurana also presented in the exhibition the ongoing work *Lying Down on the Ground* in which she variously enacted temporary inhabitations in the public space, where the human presence (the artist's body) temporarily assumed the role of dereliction, dispossession, and abandonment. Khurana presented herself as standing, or more precisely, lying, outside the boundaries of the permissible in society.[33] Khurana's work was connected to its exhibitionary context in Shanghai through a discreet subversion: an everyday practice subtly undermining the conceits of supervised society.

Place.Time.Play: Legacies

Contemporary accounts represent India and China as areas of extraordinary commercial and industrial growth in this century. As arenas of unsurpassed opportunity for enterprise, they are also characterised by extreme inequalities in income distribution. Ethical modernisation and social equity are ongoing concerns and challenges in both countries. As many artists in this exhibition highlighted in their work, the incomplete legacies of nationalist modernisation remain relevant to the future.

---

33 Khurana's artist's statement asks, 'Can the critical possibilities offered by small acts of transgression—or trespass—be considered beyond their value as individual acts, for the potential of their accumulation? Could these acts be seen as perpetual rehearsal, of being into becoming? Can the dynamic build-up of infinitely small disturbances change structure into movement, a thing into a current?'

3. An Experiment in Connectivity: From the 'West Heavens' to the 'Middle Kingdom'

Highlighting an ethics of everyday life, Hu Xiangcheng's (b. 1950) work was animated by an admiration for Gandhian principles and concerns with sustainability in the context of rapid modernisation. That Hu Xiangcheng had worked in Africa as well as China underlined his investment in these issues. His work in this exhibition addressed food security in the developing world in the context of the rapid growth in genetically modified and artificially fertilised food crops. His installation consisted of replicas of architectural monuments from historical and contemporary periods in India and China, constructed from (potentially) edible material, using Chinese reinterpretations of Indian dairy-based sweets suspended on an armature that alluded to agrarian origins. Underneath these superstructures, Hu Xiangcheng installed a mass of silhouettes of restless figures: images of turmoil against a background dominated by fertiliser in plastic bags.

L.N. Tallur (b. 1971) based his work on his decade-long engagement with monetary and cultural values of specific objects. His work involved subjecting currency and objects of reverence to the eroding scrutiny of the artist's mechanical contrivances. In his interactive *Coin Polisher*, coins were mechanically brushed into devaluation in the search for polish/civilisation, rendering them into certified 'clean' money that was manifestly 'civilised' and useless at the same time. In the process, claims of sovereignty associated with the coinage were made irrelevant, and ultimately transferable, as every coin could be made to look like every other, regardless of the issuing authority. With *Enlightenment Machine (Beta Version)* Tallur made the audience implicit in humour-laced transcultural erasure, by offering them a chance to contribute to the gradual effacement of 'heritage' in the form of iconic images from India and China.

Having researched and performed over a decade the intermissions between dreams of modernisation, governmental fantasies of control and the illusion of redemption, the Raqs Media Collective (founded 1992) produced an interactive work for a street-side audience. In *Revolutionary Forces (The Three Tasters)*, Raqs 'delegated' their agency to a group of volunteer actors who performed a script written by Raqs. The performances took place intermittently over two months on a tableau designed by Raqs. Viewed as a companion/counterpoint to Raqs' work in the Shanghai Biennale 2010, *Revolutionary Forces* sought to insinuate 'new' mythology into the midst of existing Confucian, Taoist and Buddhist lore. While the narratives, all of which began with 'There was once a …', seemed to belong to the time of legend, they also conveyed an underlying current of revolutionary transformation, an uncoiling of certainties yielding a pliable twine to be woven anew.

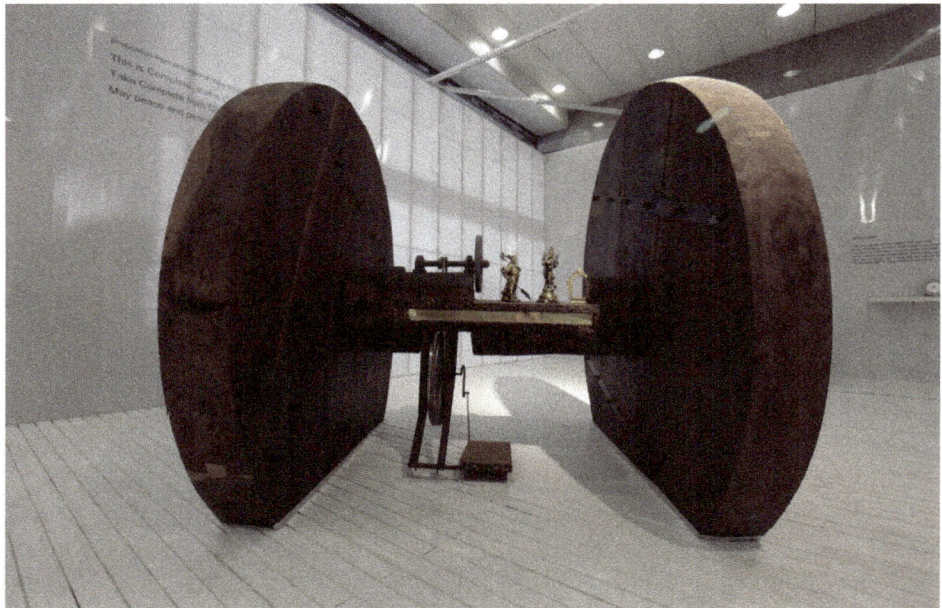

Tallur L.N., *Enlightenment Machine (Beta Version)* 2010; wood, bronze, steel, grinding stone; 180 x 200 x 220 cm.

Photograph: Thomas Fuesser; courtesy of West Heavens

In a different register, Gigi Scaria's (b. 1973) works *No Parallel* and *Raise your hands those who spoke to him* also unwound authorised histories of revolution and social transformation. In these works Scaria's concern with the successes and failures of physical and philosophical modernisation extended to an investigation of the meanings associated with iconic historical figures. *No Parallels* highlighted the incongruent careers of two national giants, Gandhi and Mao. Scaria was struck by the commonalities in their status as national icons and symbols of liberation who committed their lives to the emancipation of their peoples, and the distinct positions that they occupy in terms of their political philosophies. The portrait of Mao that gradually emerges in *Raise your hands …* moves between nostalgia and propaganda. In every case though, there is a sense of a fleeting essence being resuscitated on the screen, even as the flipping panels of the animation in *No Parallels* reveal sometimes touching and, often, conflicting juxtapositions between the careers of the Mahatma and the Chairman.

Gulammohammed Sheikh's (b. 1937) monumental installation *City: Memory, Dreams, Desire, Statues and Ghosts: Return of Hiuen Tsang* asked a number of historical questions. Sheikh was interested in what Huien Tsang (Xuanzang) might experience if he were to return to India (and to Sheikh's home city of Baroda) in 2010. In his career as artist, poet and teacher, Sheikh has engaged with diverse artistic and literary traditions and his interest in Indian, Chinese, Persian and European art history dates back four decades or more. The installation combined these ongoing streams in his oeuvre, mapping the art historical onto the contemporary, teasing out the interstices between tradition and contemporaneity and collapsing place and time into an amalgam that can speak in diverse registers. The world view of this work was rooted in the welter of contact, exchange and influence that has given rise to contemporary cultures. Sheikh's re-visioning of the world is capacious and his inclusive imagination makes it possible to integrate the anguish of contemporary events, such as episodes of sectarian violence that have occurred in his native state of Gujarat (most recently in 2002), with historical phenomena, such as the spread of Buddhism (the creed of non-violence) from India to China, as symbolised by the figure of Huien Tsang.

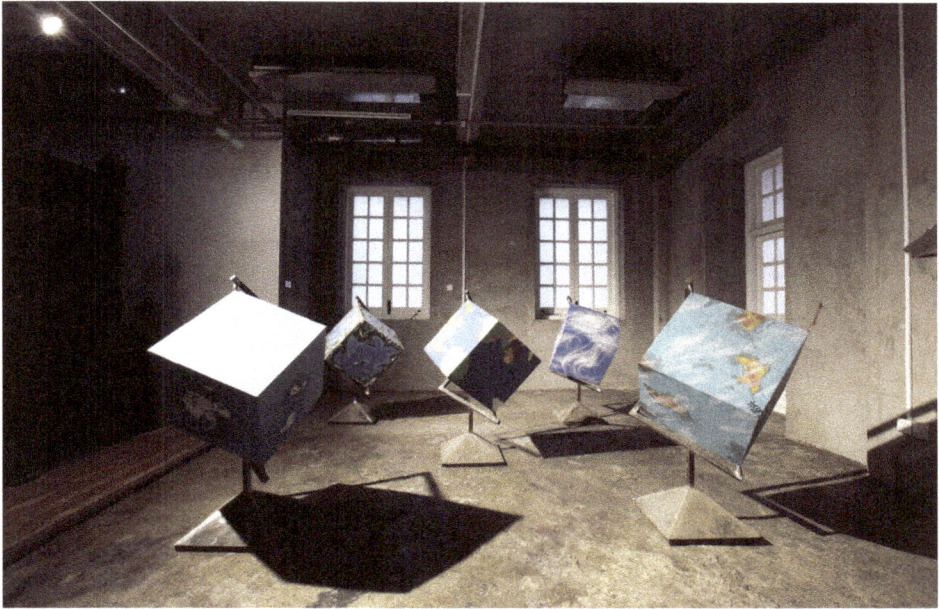

Qiu Anxiong, *Cubic Globe* 2010; wood and steel; 5 pieces, 120 x 60 x 60 cm each.

Photograph: Thomas Fuesser; courtesy of West Heavens

In *Cubic Globes*, Qiu Anxiong (b. 1972) revisioned contemporary geopolitics by invoking ancient Chinese understandings of the cosmos (a round Heaven and a square Earth). Each of the five cubical works elaborated on topographical, geological, climatic and political ramifications of an alternate configuration of the world as cube rather than sphere. The most significant manifestation of these cubical earths lay in the relations of power and marginality between and within nations. Qiu Anxiong's flat-faced earths proposed their own theory of distance, spatial relationships, centrality and the peripheral and tied into the adventurous traversals represented in many of the works exhibited in *Place.Time.Play*. What might be the spatial and political experience of seekers, migrants, refugees, traders (or artists), on this radically reconfigured earth? As realignments of power re-draw the political and economic landscape of the world, Qiu Anxiong's work encouraged a reflection on these matters from an always-marginal position situated on a pointed corner of his new worlds, looking anxiously towards one of the three facets visible, a position doomed to perpetual anticipation of being flung into space as the cube made its clumsy rotations.

In Conclusion: Relief and Return

A central consideration of many works in the exhibition was responses to ongoing rehearsals/re-inscriptions of history—and the need to critically re-historicise what they represent. Such responses are critical if we are to remain interested in the idea of connectivity, intra-Asian or otherwise. Contemporary connectivity across the two so-called 'fountainhead cultures' of Asia is, we discovered, fraught not only with linguistic and political barriers, but with entrenched institutional conditions involving logistics and reception. What did a Chinese audience expect Indian contemporary art to look like? Producing work that was intended for neither domestic commercial gallery spaces or mainstream international venues (biennials, art fairs, country specific museum exhibitions) was also a factor in the artists' processes, and perhaps a liberating one. Not being aligned with any major institutional structure perhaps offered artists participating in this project a sense of relief and return: relief in that there was no expectation to represent their national art cultures, and return in that there was an opportunity to consider historical recursions as they impact on contemporary practice.

The exhibition, despite its acknowledged limitations, can be seen as part of a larger and ongoing project in Sino-Indian conversation, one that continues to build, but is yet in its initial stages. No single event can adequately address the entire range of potential conversations between two art cultures. Mainstream institutional and political conditions remain hostile to connectivities between China and India. The survival and continuance of a platform such as 'West Heavens' demonstrates the potential for flexible and adaptive practices that intend to address entrenched 'inequalities of ignorance'.[34] This acknowledgement of unequal ignorance is a necessary first step. Transcultural exchanges in an inter-Asian context need, however, to remain attentive to the combination of

---

34 Chakrabarty, 'Postcoloniality and the Artifice of History'.

blindness and super-vision that comes out of shared inheritance: an inheritance that always needs to be claimed, whether by members of the originary culture or by others that aspire to expanded forms of belonging. Only through adventurous—and sometimes faltering—claims can connectivity grow.

4. The Irreverent Contemporary and Radical Tradition

Pat Hoffie

The Asia-Pacific Triennial of Contemporary Art (APT), an exhibition with an explicitly regional focus that presents art from Asia, the Pacific and Australia, is held at Queensland's QAGOMA.[1] There have been seven iterations in its 20-year history. This essay traces how the theme of the first triennial held at the Queensland Art Gallery (QAG) in 1993—*Tradition and Change*—sought from the outset to establish an interpretation of the 'contemporary' in the region as emerging from a series of critically responsive, historically and geographically specific discursive spaces. Drawing from an anthology of critical writing focused on the 20-year history of the APT in *Broadsheet* 41 (no. 4), the essay argues that this premise continued throughout the first three iterations of the exhibition, after which, as the parameters of the exhibition have grown wider, it moved towards a less critical, although more inclusive space. The essay examines the changing understandings of the terms 'tradition' and 'change' and poses questions about how a productive model for an 'irreverent contemporary' can be fostered within the region. The essay may therefore be positioned within current debates about what defines 'the contemporary' in art, particularly when viewed against non-Western contexts such as Asia. Ultimately, the essay argues that what is needed is a renewed attention to the particular conditions and contexts of art's differentiated production.

As Philippine historian, critic and curator Patrick Flores observed in his essay in *Broadsheet*, 'Revisiting Tradition and the Incommensurate Contemporary',[2] the first APT established traditional practices as an important focus from which to observe, analyse and interpret the contemporary cultural production of the region. If this exhibition did not claim to undertake a 'world view' of contemporary art, then it certainly aimed to cover a fair slice of how it had unfolded in the region and, more importantly, it sought to challenge the

---

[1] Editor's note: The Asia-Pacific Triennial of Contemporary Art is a series of exhibitions that have been held every three years since 1993 at the Queensland Art Gallery and also since 2006 at the Gallery of Modern Art in Brisbane, Australia (since 2006, the gallery's institutional spaces have been collectively labelled as QAGOMA). For a discussion of the project, see Part 1 of the Introduction by Caroline Turner, which explains that the purpose was to exhibit and collect contemporary art from Asia and the Pacific, including Polynesian and Melanesian Pacific art. The first APT concentrated on East Asia, South-East Asia and, to a small extent, the Pacific (New Zealand and Papua New Guinea), but the project now covers all of Asia (including, most recently, West Asia) and a wider selection of art from islands in the Pacific (http://www.qagoma.qld.gov.au/exhibitions/apt).
[2] Patrick Flores, 'Revisiting Tradition and the Incommensurate Contemporary', *Broadsheet* 41, no. 4 (December 2012): 234–39.

fundamental assumptions of an uncritical contemporary that had grown as the fabled 'natural' inheritor of international modernism. The title of that exhibition—*Tradition and Change*—flagged this up-front, as if the very parameters for considering the art of the present time—what is inferred in the latter part of the APT's title as the 'contemporary'—might best be made through an assessment of the *changes* in and to traditional forms and practices. In this essay Flores returns to the understanding of the term 'contemporary' in a way that sets it apart from the assimilative all-inclusive term that is critiqued in other essays in the publication.

At that time of the first APT, contemporary expressions from the cultures of the region were largely unknown to Australian audiences. Indeed, this was equally true outside Australia: according to many APT observers, including many of the writers in the 2012 edition of *Broadsheet*, a broad knowledge of the diverse cultural practices of the region had not yet been established in the work of writers, curators, gallery directors and artists right across the region, let alone beyond it. Any knowledge that did exist had been garnered, generally speaking, through a vague sense of the artefactual production of the region via anthropological work collected in museums and/or through first-hand experiences of tourism.

As Flores points out, the publication that accompanied APT1 was in part an invitation to consider the work of the region within, and in terms of, an imaginary space that might sit somewhere beyond the parameters of the 'globalised' international art realm that had been created by the impact of 'economic, technological and information changes'.[3] Although, after 20 years, the possibility that any zone of 'beyond-ness' might exist seems barely credible, at that time, the option of an alternative reading to a homogenising sequential development of modernism into globalism still seemed possible from south of the equator, where glitches and blips in the history of modernism and postmodernism surfaced repeatedly in cultural expressions and histories that could not be easily accounted, translated and absorbed within mainstream historical accounts. For 'the south' harboured abundant evidence of modernism's failure to account for the wilful mistranslations that had produced a diversity of vital, critical and locally responsive cultural expressions engaging with colonisation and internationalisation in a range of ways.

A second important factor that rendered the possibility of the emergence of other understandings of 'the contemporary' lay in the fact that, by 1993 and even up to APT3 in 1999, the technological grip of ubiquitous personal computers and instant messaging had not yet taken hold across a great expanse of the globe. In the early 1990s it still seemed likely that not all zones of the earth's surface would

---

3   Caroline Turner, quoted in Flores, 'Revisiting Tradition', 235.

4. The Irreverent Contemporary and Radical Tradition

be culturally as well as cartographically google-mapped. The third factor that underpinned the emergence of this (some might say naively) optimistic premise came about through QAG's awareness of the critical response of Indigenous Australians to historical accounts of cultural development in this country. The gallery's engagement with local Indigenous people in establishing cultural agency was focused on the contemporary during a critical project *Mandjad* or *Balance 1991: Views, Visions, Influences*.[4] The aims, the process, the exhibition and the forum for this project prepared a fertile trough of scepticism about singular interpretations of, among other things, the development of modernism. This in turn produced fallow ground for the seeding of new possibilities for reassessing the development of non-Indigenous Australian art within the region.

None of the first three triennials, however, attempted to elaborate a definition of what that imaginary space might encompass. In fact, it could be argued that the early triennials conscientiously maintained an approach that avoided the limitations of theoretically predetermined parameters and definitions, in order instead to coax any interpretations that might emerge from interpretations of the work in the exhibitions, rather than being imposed by institutional or curatorial imperatives.

The curatorial overview for the first of the triennials created a discursive space within an imprecisely defined region where two impulses—that of tradition and of change—collided and morphed. Within this implied sphere, one bounded by indistinctly described geographies and imprecise and complex historical accounts, the concept of '*tradition*' was, to a large extent, uncritically associated with memory, history and place. And it was also generally associated, by implication, with reflective expressions of an amorphous understanding of 'the past'. By default, the '*change*' part of the dichotomy was associated with the here and the now—with the tempo of movement and the blur of shape-shifting. In the first exhibition—and in the two that followed—the contemporary production of artists was presented as having emerged from both aspects of these two contested areas: that of '*tradition*' and that of '*change*'. The 'contemporary' in the region, therefore, was presented and understood as having emerged as a result of this collision or chemistry.

This offered a purview that, although broad, was delineated in terms of significant differences from the art-historical assumptions that associated the term 'contemporary' with a category that absorbed modernism as an unproblematic and un-resisted inheritance. And, as such, this interpretation in turn signalled a shift in the understanding of the term 'contemporary' as it was understood within the many accounts of the post-postmodern/postcolonial world of 'international' art theory that was emerging from north of the equator.

---

4   *Balance 1990: Views, Visions, Influences* (Queensland Art Gallery, 1 March 1990).

In these accounts the term 'contemporary' signified cooler shifts into newness; a term that was not tied to any of the messy, resistant (often wilfully resistant) ballast of the past. Even though Jean-Hubert Martin's controversial exhibition *Magicienes de la terre*, which was held at the Centre Pompidou and Parc de la Villette in 1989, proposed an interface between contemporary art and that produced by tribal 'Others', the underlying inference, according to a number of critics at the time, was that the exhibition foregrounded an understanding of 'traditional' with notions of 'primitive', spiritual and the past. Fredric Jameson criticised the way modernist impulses underscored the enterprise of the exhibition through a post-modern/post-colonial approach that conflated the art into a single, simplistic and non-contextually specific overview.[5] Other critics described the exhibition as signalling a 'post-ethnic and post-historic' world order. Freed from the weight of having to consider the nuances implied by the myriad ways that understandings and interpretations of the 'modern' might have unfolded in particular regions, unleashed from the burden of having to consider the precise parameters of the 'colonial' in particular annexed territories, the term 'contemporary' offered a giddy limitlessness to possibilities for describing all work produced in all places as having emerged from a spaceless, ageless, non-contextually specific state of newness.

And this is the very point at which—from the inaugural exhibition in 1993—the first of the three triennials made the potentially radical proposal by suggesting, in this region at least, the 'contemporary' had not emerged mysteriously as a weightless and shadowless ghost of the eternal now, but as a force that had developed through different forms in accordance with different circumstances and in relation to particular contexts. Rather, it was presented as an active, contested zone of conflict, contrapuntals, contradictions, productive confusions, contrarieties and contrasts. Wherever there was a fixed site, opinion, point of view, approach, idea, or assumed imaginary associated with the region, the first three APTs, and their associated forums, made room for an active engagement that teased, refuted or refused, augmented or opened up, fixed cultural assumptions about the development of modern art history and, alongside this, contemporary art.

As has been described for the first three iterations of the APT, for the general audience, the fact that the region was home to a range of disparate 'traditions' had already been established as an a priori, but non-specific 'given'; an expectation of generalised 'difference' held sway. This was also, in no small way, a drawcard to other players from the region. Quoting the response of Imelda Cajipe Endaya, an artist involved in APT1, Eileen Legaspi-Ramirez describes how the artists involved felt empowered in their role to effectively shape this nascent understanding:

---

5 Fredric Jameson, *Postmodernism, or, the Cultural Logic of Late Capitalism* (Durham, NC: Duke University Press, 1991).

I felt rather privileged that my advice and comments were properly responded to and synthesised into the body of discussions and plans.[6]

And Iftikhar Dadi describes his experience of the APT as having taken place in a decade during which 'the idea of multiculturalism in contemporary art was just beginning to emerge as a significant issue globally' via a number of exhibitions. Among these, he says, the APT offered an important opportunity to map 'emergent currents in contemporary art'. He writes,

> nevertheless, in its scale, criticality and its timing during the critical decade of the 1990's, the APT emerged as a key force formulating an understanding of the emerging practices in much of the Asian region.[7]

At that time, the role of giving form to a new understanding of the emerging contemporary practices in the region, and to tracing and describing the synergies and differences between them, was as much in the hands of the artists involved as it was in those of the curators, critics and writers.

Beyond the potential emergence of all such interpretations, however, the interpretive framework of the APT's curatorial position had already established an understanding that the cultural production it had selected from the region was avowedly 'contemporary'. Concomitantly, a great deal of the work selected and produced for the exhibition reflected the shared concerns, issues, subject matter and media of the 'contemporary', while simultaneously bearing traces of the 'traditions' from which it had emerged. That is, as with the exhibition itself, much of the work was expected to play a kind of double-dealing where at least two 'master' narratives were concurrently acknowledged. Alison Carroll, one of the curators of the first three APTs, recalls how the commitment to highlight the 'contemporary' made curators 'very cautious about choosing work that did not appear to relate to the contemporary world.' She remembers that curators were

> cautious about choosing work that reinforced the audience's assumptions about Asian art being either unchangingly traditional or second-rate European. The emphasis was on work that was exciting, relevant, often personal, often political, visually strong and intellectually convincing, and if that was possible, it would carry the audience with it, which is indeed what did happen.[8]

Nevertheless, the first three triennials included evidence of the use of materials and themes that were 'indigenous' to their particular part of the region. For example, by 1993, the insistence on indigenous materials and themes in the work practice of a number of artists from the Philippines had, for at least a decade, been embraced as part of a resistance to the aesthetic and economic demands of

---

6   Eileen Legaspi-Ramirez, 'Largesse', *Broadsheet* 41, no. 4 (December 2012): 274–75, 275.
7   Iftikhar Dadi, 'Reflections on the First Decade', *Broadsheet* 41, no. 4 (December 2012): 266–69, 267.
8   Author's conversation with Alison Carroll (15 February 2013).

an international art world dominated by Western values. To some, the first APT provided a kind of 'market place of ideas' through which they could flag their difference to broader audiences. Filipino artist Santiago Bose used this as the subject of his installation in APT1, for which he constructed a floor-based work that reflected the humble, makeshift, but nevertheless global, ambitions of a 'third world marketplace' within the more grandiose schemes and bravado of the international exhibition. In a much-quoted statement, the artist described what he believed to be central to the role of the artist in the region:

> The artist cannot but be affected by his society. It is hard to ignore the pressing needs of the nation while making art that serves the nation's elite .... We struggled to change society, which is difficult and dangerous, and we also sought to preserve communal aspects of life .... The artist takes a stand through the practice of creating art. The artist articulates the Filipino subconscious so that we may be able to show a true picture of ourselves and our world.[9]

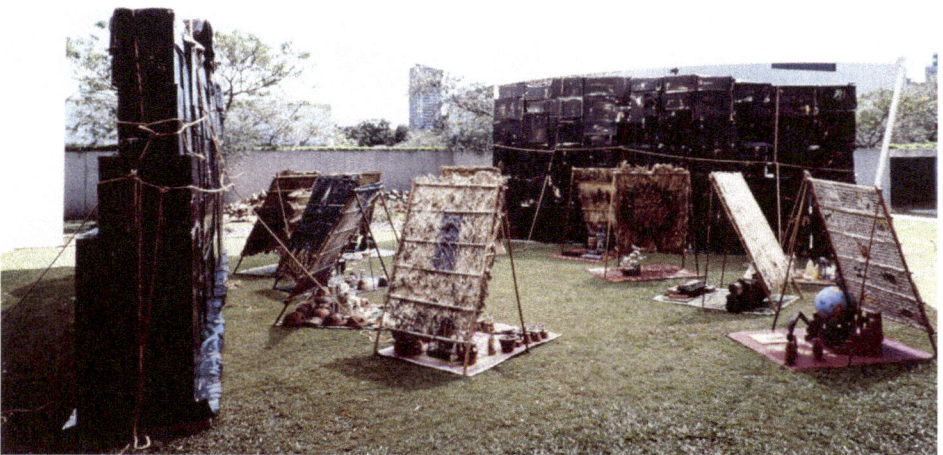

Santiago Bose, The Philippines, *Talipapa (Marketplace)* 1993 (exterior installation); installation comprising wooden boxes, organic materials, handcrafted and found objects; dimensions variable; installation view at the '1st Asia Pacific Triennial of Contemporary Art', Queensland Art Gallery, Brisbane, 1993.

© Estate of the artist; image courtesy: Queensland Art Gallery | Gallery of Modern Art (QAGOMA)

9   http://en.wikipedia.org/wiki/Santiago_Bose.

4. The Irreverent Contemporary and Radical Tradition

A number of other artists produced work that incorporated aspects of 'indigeneity', 'nativism', 'traditions' in ways that were provocative and challenging, and that made it difficult to see where the boundaries between the category of 'tradition' and that of the 'contemporary' might lie. That year Roberto Villanueva, also from the Philippines, drew from indigenous ritualistic practices from the Cordillera region of northern Luzon for his performative installation *Ego's Grave*, for which he fired a clay pit in the outside courtyard of the water mall on the opening night. The water, smoke and fire were used to dramatic effect in a work that combined Cordillera cultural references with elements of Kabuki theatre and aspects of a Greek chorus. Audience involvement on the opening night metamorphosed into deeper and more significant personal concerns when the artist was diagnosed some days later as suffering from acute myeloblastic leukaemia. The artist's four-month stay in Brisbane, where he was hospitalised while he continued to fight the cancer, was marked by ongoing rituals of various kinds, including an Indigenous Australian smoking ceremony on the site of the installation. In the face of great concern and sadness, the principles of shamanism and Western medicine came together in ways that members of the local art community, who rallied in support of the artist, had not experienced before.

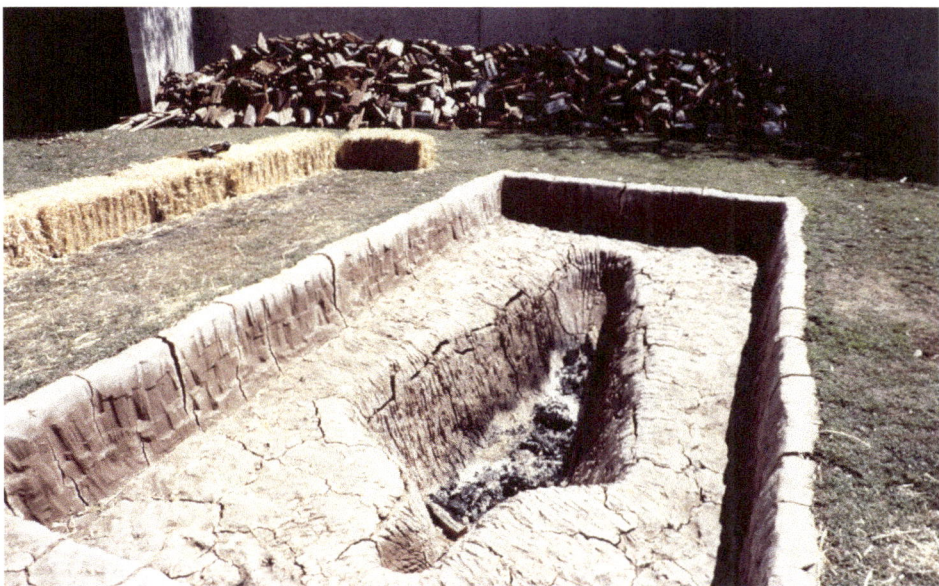

Robert Villanueva, *Ego's grave* 1993; installation and associated performance; carved earth figure in outdoor pit; glazed terracotta; installation view at the '1st Asia Pacific Triennial of Contemporary Art', Queensland Art Gallery, Brisbane, September 1993.

© Estate of the artist; image courtesy: Queensland Art Gallery | Gallery of Modern Art (QAGOMA)

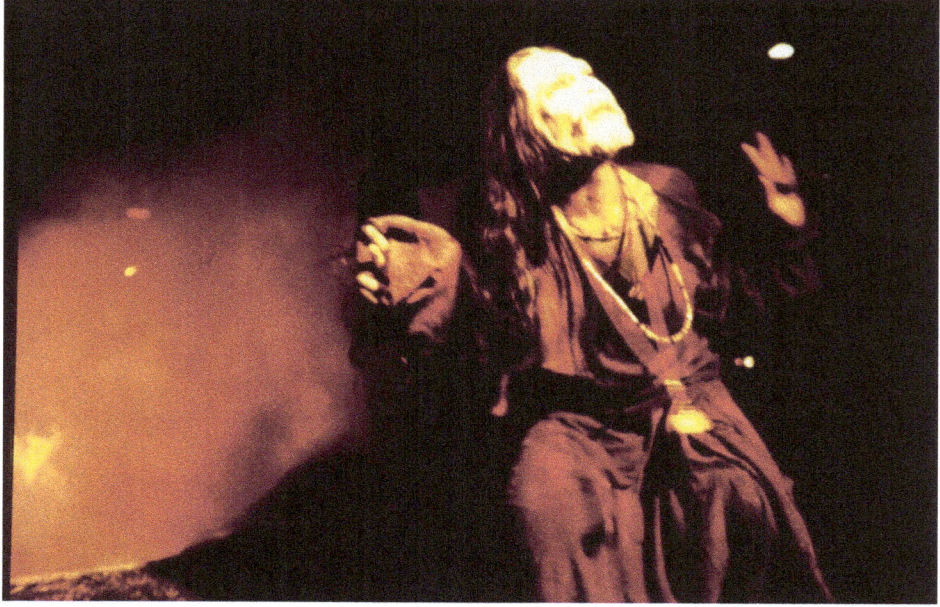

Roberto Villaneuva, The Philippines, performance in association with *Ego's Grave* 1993 at the '1st Asia Pacific Triennial of Contemporary Art', Queensland Art Gallery, Brisbane, 1993.

© Estate of the artist; photograph: Andrea Higgins; image courtesy: Queensland Art Gallery | Gallery of Modern Art (QAGOMA)

Other local responses to traditional expressions of marking and mourning that were included in the exhibition continued in personal and often moving ways—the audience response to Indonesian artist Dadang Christanto's installation *For those …* was evident on a daily basis through floral tributes, letters and notes to loved ones 'who had suffered'. The form of Christanto's bamboo and wood sculptures became appreciated as much for their capacity to act as a site for affective engagement as they were for their aesthetic strength, especially alongside the artist's related performance.

From the beginning, audiences were aware that there were surprises in store—the anticipated was not going to be delivered in terms set down by the institutions or the expectations of the West. But, perhaps surprisingly, local audiences were quick to embrace the differences offered in responsive and participatory ways. There was a preparedness to engage with 'Other' approaches and traditional practices, for audience members to respond in ways that were tentative but responsive and, at times, interactive.

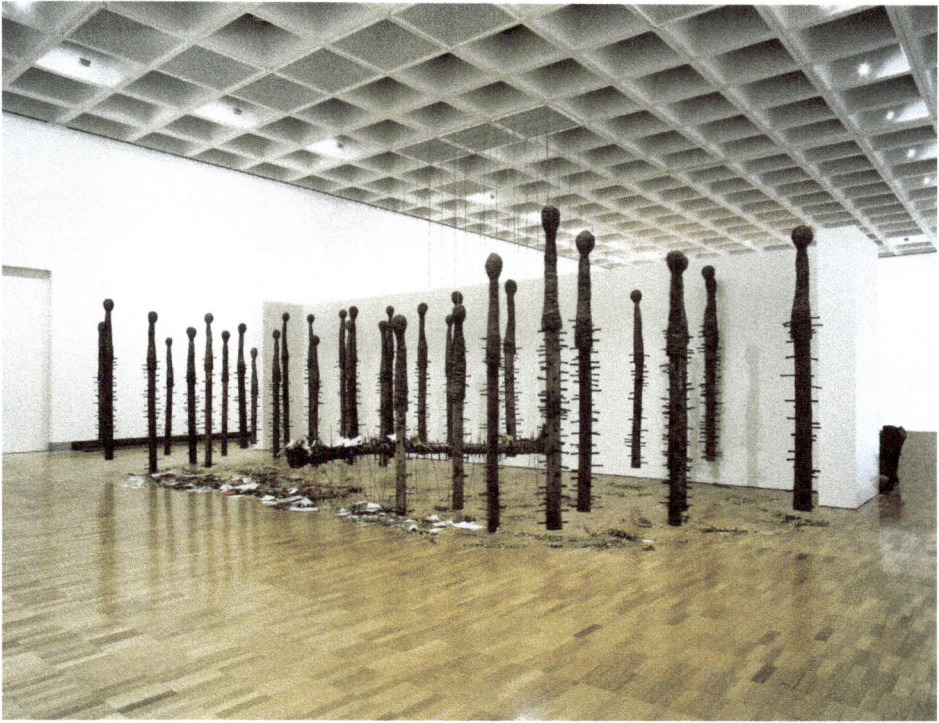

**Dadang Christanto, Indonesia, b. 1957, *For those who have been killed*
1992; bamboo, metal; 110 x 80 x 335 cm (irreg., approx.); installed at the
'1st Asia Pacific Triennial of Contemporary Art', Queensland Art Gallery,
Brisbane, 1993.**

The Kenneth and Yasuko Myer Collection of Contemporary Asian Art; purchased 1993 with funds from The Myer Foundation and Michael Sidney Myer through the Queensland Art Gallery Foundation; collection: Queensland Art Gallery; © Dadang Christanto; image courtesy: Queensland Art Gallery | Gallery of Modern Art (QAGOMA)

Twenty years on, in APT7, the installation at the entry to the Queensland Gallery of Modern Art (GOMA) suggested that there has been a radical change in what is considered to be 'contemporary'. Here, the architectural details of a Papua New Guinean spirit house or *haus tambaran* were part of the first artwork to greet visitors. And from there, down the high-ceilinged central hallway of GOMA, the featured works were predominantly those of the Kwoma, the Asmat[10] and the Abelam people from Papua and New Guinea. Even so, the extent to which the inclusion of such works might be affected by, or affect, the notion

---

10 Editor's note. The Asmat people live in south-western New Guinea, an area that is part of Indonesia, along a river system flowing into the Arafura Sea. The Metropolitan Museum, New York, has a major Asmat collection, most of which was collected by Michael C. Rockefeller in 1961; see, http://www.metmuseum.org/toah/hd/asma/hd_asma.htm.

of 'contemporary' hovers in the exhibiting rooms like the proverbial elephant. Responses from some visitors from other countries noted that such work would be better included in exhibitions that were not featuring contemporary art. Other writers have claimed that, in terms of the comprehensive nature of the exhibition, the notion of 'contemporary' as an active, critical and contested site has lapsed into an all-inclusive lassitude.

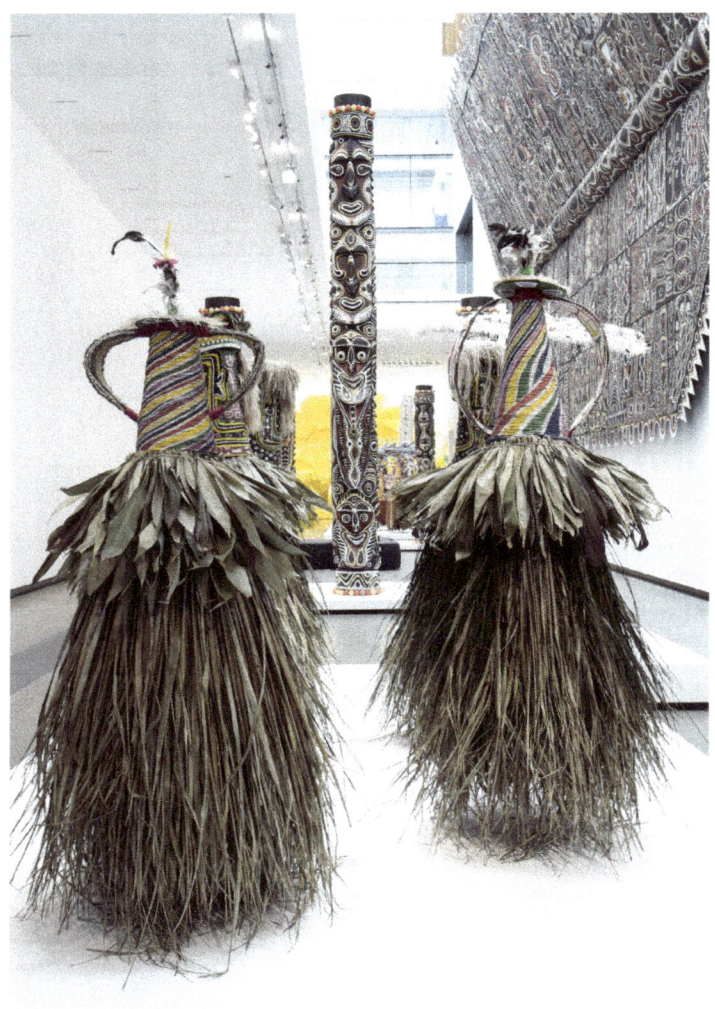

Kwoma Arts, Papua New Guinea, *Koromb (Spirit House)*; installation view at the '7th Asia Pacific Triennial of Contemporary Art', Queensland Art Gallery | Gallery of Modern Art, Brisbane, 2012.

Purchased 2012; collection: Queensland Art Gallery; © the artists; photograph: Natasha Harth, QAGOMA; image courtesy: Queensland Art Gallery | Gallery of Modern Art (QAGOMA)

According to some of these critics, the context of the current APT is evidence that the 'contemporary' is now fixed as a state of non-specific change—a place of incessant movement and change for the sake of change, leached of the potential for productive critical friction. Rex Butler describes his understanding of the contemporary as a yawning chasm of empty potential:

> There is no positive centre from which the work comes, there is no tendency that is dominant, everything and everywhere is of equal interest and merit. And it is this that the exhibition must seek to capture: contemporary art's all-inclusiveness, scale, unclassifiability and incomprehensibility. The only principle, the only selection allowed is that which does not allow selection, that is contemporary in the sense of being post-stylistic, post-national and post-historical.[11]

According to this point of view, the productive contentiousness of the subject of the 'contemporary'—about what can or should not be included within its descriptors—has been exhausted, and what we are left with is a rule-less, context-free, historically bereft vacuousness, not unlike the flat pristine wasteland of a wealthy man's cultural trophy room.

Some artists in the exhibition, however, used this as the subject matter of their work: Graham Fletcher's *Lounge Room Tribalism* series offers a brilliant and pithy critical reflection on the museum's role as an ersatz cultural trophy room, one that presents indigenous art as a decorative addendum to the ongoing project of modernism. Fletcher's moderately sized canvases stand out as almost anachronistically modest in scale, execution and subject matter, presented as they are within the belly of an exhibition that has increasingly tended to feature the grand statement. Within this context, the paintings make a humble salute to the modest power of silence and simplicity. Yet, something about the subject matter of the work, and the way in which the pieces resonate with and within the broader context of the exhibition, offer pertinent insight into the ongoing role of international modernism and the appropriation of the indigenous and the traditional.

Fletcher's series features scenes from domestic interiors from the 1950s and 1960s—around the time, according to the artist, when there was 'a point of intersection of Western and non-Western cultures within the homes of many collectors and consumers'.[12] With skeins of paint that seem to have been effortlessly applied, the works make more than a cursory nod to a DIY clunkiness. This in turn evokes a light, deceptively throwaway spirit in works that are pregnant with criticality. The initial response to these images is that

---

11 Rex Butler, 'All or Anything at All', *Broadsheet* 41, no. 4 (December 2012): 277–79, 279.
12 Graham Fletcher, interviewed by Ruth McDougall (July 2012) in *The 7th Asia-Pacific Triennial of Contemporary Art* (Queensland Art Gallery/Gallery of Modern Art), 114.

we are witnessing the origins of an all-too-familiar obsession with the details of lifestyle and 'good living' that are the nascent ancestors of our contemporary IKEA internationalism. As Ella Mudie has pointed out,[13] however, Fletcher's interiors belie the 'inherent instability of the domestic'. Poised amidst the 'form follows function' design style of the objects in the room, the artefacts and items of indigenous cultural production are mutely brooding inclusions. Fletcher is well aware of the contradictions of his own position—as a New Zealand artist of Samoan and European ancestry, his fascination with the Oceanic collection of Surrealist Andre Breton is one fraught with productive incongruities. He writes of the tribal artefacts featured in his *Lounge Room Tribalism* images:

> For me these objects no longer emanate the power of the Old World, but are historically aestheticised as objects of the New, thereby raising questions of context, assimilation, ownership and authenticity. In a broader sense, what I try to suggest is the complex relationship between Western and non-Western cultures and how many indigenous artists today are subject to influence and transformation in the advent of globalisation.[14]

As sites of tension where items of 'the incorporated indigenous' quiver and quake with indignant potency, Fletcher's work is a microcosm of the exhibition in which they are included. It carefully poses the rifts, fissures and frictions of inclusion of traditional forms of cultural production as positive problems worthy of further reflection and enquiry. The mute, bland and impassive artefacts of modernity that inhabit the empty rooms of Fletcher's imaginary world become implicitly destabilised by the silent challenges of traditional artefacts.

Within the larger, all-inclusive zone of the contemporary exhibition, a benign inclusiveness is at play; one that admits all, but which simultaneously gives all-too-scant attention to the details of context. This is not dissimilar to the bland inclusiveness of Fletcher's 'contemporary modernist' interiors. It is an easy jump to see Fletcher's world as having re-emerged in the post-postmodernist modernism of APT7.

Instead of including traditional work as primitive inclusions, however, a generalised acknowledgement of the contemporaneity of this work is evident throughout the didactic panels included in the exhibition, and in the exhibition catalogue. This is illustrated in curator Ruth McDougall's description of the Asmat work,

> the *bisj* poles, *wuraman* and spirit masks on display themselves derive from cross-cultural encounters. Most of these works were created

---

13   Ella Mudie, 'Graham Fletcher's *Lounge Room Tribalism*', *Art and Australia* 50, no. 2 (Summer 2012).
14   Fletcher, *The 7th Asia-Pacific Triennial of Contemporary Art*.

specifically as art works for sale; in the Asmat region, the appreciation and acquisition of carving and weaving have taken place since the first collectors visited the region in the early twentieth century.[15]

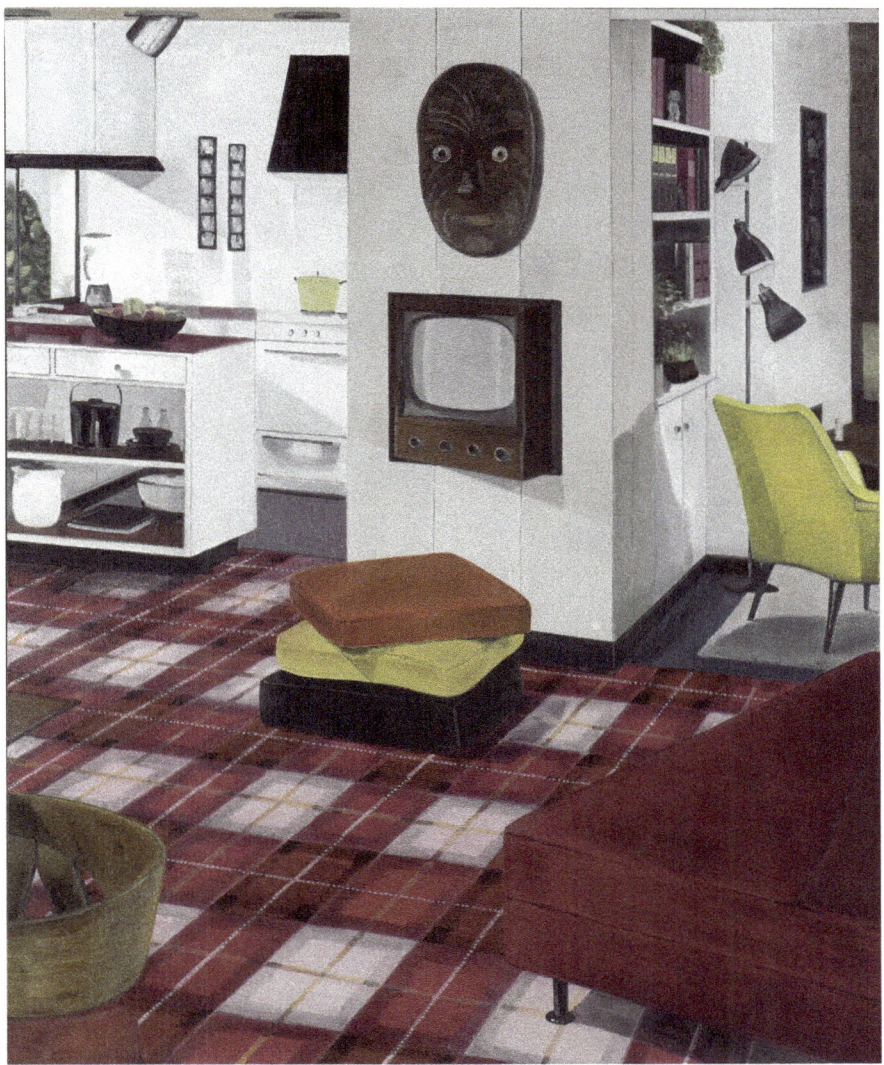

Graham Fletcher, New Zealand, b. 1969, *Untitled* (from *Lounge Room Tribalism* series) 2010; oil on canvas; 162 x 130 cm.

Acc. 2010.632; purchased 2010 with funds from the Estate of Lawrence F King in memory of the late Mr and Mrs SW King through the Queensland Art Gallery Foundation; image courtesy Queensland Art Gallery | Gallery of Modern Art (QAGOMA)

---

15   McDougall, 'Asmat; The Eloquence of Wood', in *The 7th Asia-Pacific Triennial of Contemporary Art*, 89.

Even so, more comprehensive and detailed descriptions of the way in which these works have come to be understood as 'contemporary' would have affected a deeper understanding of them, their content, the artists and their relationship to their own community and the potential relationship of that community to the viewing community. The presence of rich histories of confrontation and negotiation with the various aspects of modernity are only hinted at:

> Over the past 50 years, with the introduction of Christianity, the development of cash economies and increased cultural diversity, there has been an influx of new ideas, materials and values. This has had a considerable influence on how the Asmat view their work.[16]

This kind of generalised description of the inevitable processes of modernism somehow suggests that the details of how the work and the artists 'got here' is not as important as their inclusion; as if their entry into an exhibition of contemporary art can be paid for by a no-questions-asked-no-answers-given ticket. New Zealand writer Peter Brunt draws attention to this anomaly of Western international exhibition practice:

> We members of the 'art cult' know next to nothing about the art history of the Kwoma—or that of the Asmat, the Iatmul, the Abelam or any of the other tribes from Papua New Guinea and the Indonesian province of Papua, who are making a splash at APT7. It is not that they don't have one; the art they have made for the exhibition bears complex histories in which it has had to negotiate its survival and transformation in relation to the impacts of missionaries, colonial administrators, collectors, national bureaucracies, the tribal art market and more. Those histories can be framed as projects of colonial resistance, cultural survival, empire and decolonisation, modernism and nationhood, religion and secularisation, the global diaspora of material culture and cultural memory, tribalism and the global art world—the list goes on. But those are stories barely told or understood in the consciousness of the contemporary art world.[17]

And, in another statement, Brunt describes the extent to which this stands in contrast to those late-admissions to recognition as art of the 'international contemporary' who have long been aware of the shapes and parameters of a range of Western cultural structures and the expectations that go with them:

> There is no tribal artist in New Guinea or its surrounding archipelegos who has not pondered his or her relationship to either the 'State'

---

16 Ibid.
17 Peter Brunt, 'Transcultural Space and Art Historical Consciousness', in *The 7th Asia-Pacific Triennial of Contemporary Art*, 72–75, 72.

(Indonesia, Papua New Guinea, Australia, Germany, the Netherlands, Britain), Christianity, anthropologists, the tribal art market, the museum world, expatriate kin, urban relatives or the past or future …[18]

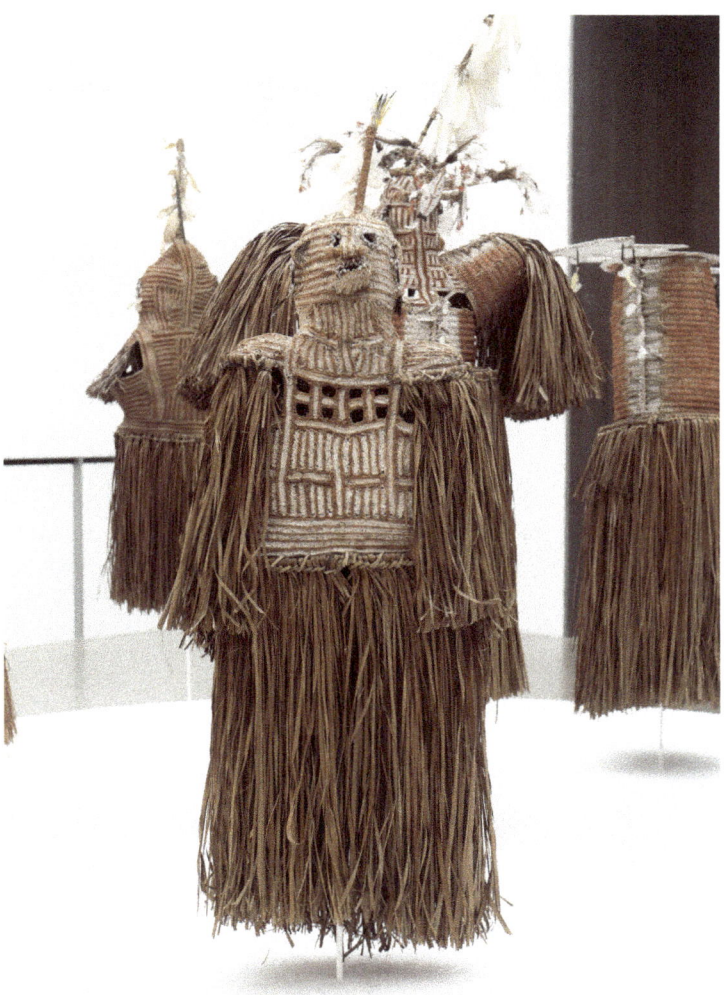

Installation view of Asmat artists, Yakobus Serambi, Primus Isimin and Amatus Ahmak, *Bi jumbo, Manimar and Doreo (Spirit masks)* 2012; '7th Asia Pacific Triennial of Contemporary Art', Queensland Art Gallery | Gallery of Modern Art, Brisbane, 2012.

Purchased 2012; collection: Queensland Art Gallery; © the artists; photograph: Mark Sherwood, QAGOMA; image courtesy: Queensland Art Gallery | Gallery of Modern Art (QAGOMA)

---

18 Ibid.

For those authorities—historians, critics, curators, writers—who might assume knowledge of the 'international art world', this is startling stuff. Brunt's statement makes it clear that, for a significant period of time, these 'tribal artists' have been in possession of an historical depth of knowledge and an understanding of cultural complexity that is not evident in the presentation of overviews of 'international contemporary art'. As Brunt says, the legacy of our 'knowing too much' about Western art stands in the way of our capacity to engage with a range of others in our region, who may have a different world view, or who—perhaps surprisingly—might seek to 'not fit' within the flawed monologue of global modernism that has pre-assigned them a particular role. That single-voice narrative has stood in the way of what might have been a more polyfluent interpretation of the emergence of the 'contemporary' in the region, obscuring the specific contexts in which contemporary art develops outside of the West.

The kind of awkwardness and, at times, shambolic ruptures that characterised the presentation and language of the first three APTs, as artists, critics and writers stumbled in search for the words and forms to describe the synergies and continuities they were witnessing around them, has been supplanted by the glitch-free, blooper-reduced purity of an international, globalised account of the 'contemporary'. According to some critics, the burgeoning growth of international biennales throughout the first decade of this century represented a steady move towards the 'contextless contemporary'. Although APT4 made an attempt to reconnect regional tendencies with those of the senior artists of the region who had gained international recognition, by APT6 the critical potential of the exhibition to follow through with its original premise to rethink the contemporary had lapsed. Andrew Maerkle writes,

> In this sense I have to admit that when I finally made it to see the Triennial, the most disorienting aspect of APT6 was not any juxtaposition of 'traditional' with 'contemporary', but rather the juxtaposition between the 'contemporary' and the 'contemporary'.[19]

The extent of the ground lost, and the degree to which this kind of enervated, reductive account is at odds with the region's history of critically engaged confrontations, contextualisations, appropriations and renegotiations of the international influences of Western modernism throughout the twentieth century is apparent within even the most cursory historical point of view. Here, Maerkle's synopsis reminds us that, throughout the previous century, the art of the region continuously developed in a spirit of informed critical responsiveness between the 'traditional' and the 'change' resulting from external influences:

---

19 Andrew Maerkle, 'Lable/Babel', *Broadsheet* 41, no. 4 (December 2012): 251–52, 252.

Entering the twentieth century, artists returned from study in Europe with experience in movements from Cubism and Futurism to Dada and Surrealism, upon which they elaborated and shared with their peers, creating an avant-garde that operated in distinction to the 'traditional' and the conventionally 'Western'.[20]

What, if anything, has been lost in this quick transition to everything being contemporary? Not all critics lament the passing of the more definitive categories of cultural definition. Ranjit Hoskote writes,

> We have put behind us the essentialist, static characteristics of people, regions, cultural practices and artistic production on the basis of such entities as 'civilisations', 'traditions', 'blocs', and 'identities'. Instead, we attend to the dynamics of the intensely networked, migratory, layered global present. We grapple with it, in the atlas-resistant, lexicon-eluding fullness of its unexpected adjacencies and interstitial hybridities; we probe its unsought intimacies and unexpected estrangements: its circulatory paths along which economic migrants, proscribed refugees, technocratic itinerants and cultural pilgrims travel; and the continuous renegotiations between people and places, between interpretation and location, between position and predicament, between citizenship and alienation, that it demands.[21]

But Hoskote's exhortation to drop categories such as 'civilisations', 'traditions', 'blocs', and 'identities' does not, ipso facto, vouch for the adoption of an homogenised account of the contemporary; rather, it demands an energetic enquiry that searches and re-searches the global present, not as a thing that is presumed, assumed, expected to be an immediately recognisable hereditary entity. Hoskote calls for attention to the 'unexpected adjacencies'; he invites unwavering discrimination in responding to the subtleties of place ('location'), 'position and predicament', context and purpose: it is doubtful that the 'lexicon-eluding fullness' that Hoskote alludes to could be crammed into any pre-packaged understanding of a de-limited 'contemporary.'

But, it is not the intention of this argument to lay the blame for any lapse in the critical potential of the 'contemporary' on the shoulders of the APTs alone; as Hoskote argues, since the first three APTs, there has been a major strategic shift in international survey exhibitions that has moved the discursive parameters for presenting and considering the work from the 'intercultural' to the 'transcultural', rendering approaches that emphasise identity through markers such as nation-states outmoded. In his critical response to this

---

20 Ibid.
21 Ranjit Hoskote, 'Wager on Cosmopolitanism. On the 7th Asia-Pacific Triennial', *Broadsheet* 41, no. 4 (December 2012): 258–60, 258.

trend, he calls for curatorial approaches that move away from the impulses of 'representation' (of cultures, nations and regions) to those of 'translation', and draws upon curator Kathryn Weir's words to describe ways of thinking 'in terms of changing, generative relationships rather than established identities.'[22] Although respectful curatorial humility in the face of identity-interpretation is always essential in zones of either cross-cultural and inter-cultural (if not trans-cultural) endeavours, there may, however, be a case for arguing that any jettisoning of understandings of geo-cultural histories of the region, at this stage, is pre-emptory. The presentation of the work of the Kwoma, Asmat and Abelam is a case in point; the lack of a deeper historical and cultural understanding of the development of their 'traditional' forms, as they have been confronted by the successive changes to their context and understanding of the world, prevent audiences from acquiring a comprehensive, nuanced appreciation of the work that is currently being celebrated as a 'contemporary' manifestation of past traditions.

The term 'tradition' is itself fraught; but, it is fraught in exciting, potentially radical ways. In his essay in *Broadsheet*, Flores problematises the term 'tradition', analysing it through three vectors: its association with (1) 'civilisation'; (2) 'folklore'; and, (3) 'culture'. This analysis explores the parameters of the term, and reconsiders the extent to which 'interpretation' might be utilised as a term with continuing validity in considering, understanding and interpreting the development of artwork in the region. He writes,

> It is through the meditations of Roces on the term 'culture' that we are able to revaluate the consequences of the theory of tradition and co-extensively of the constantly re-negotiated and re-appropriated neo-traditional and the neo-ethnic, a subject that deserves separate discussion …. To a significant extent, this revisit to tradition gives us the opportunity to reconsider a theory of transculturality or equivalence, or the exasperating problematic of a contemporary 'cross culturality'.[23]

Flores shares Weir and Hoskote's conviction that the 'local' has an 'ever elusive address' and, again like Weir and Hoskote, he advocates 'an ethical responsibility' towards remaining wary of the folklores of nationalisms and identity. Flores goes one step further, however, when he advocates an understanding of the traditional as a 'critical inheritance' that is 'always present'; and, in turn, he steps away from the position shared by Weir and Hoskote when he warns against any collapse into a transculturality or cross-culturality that might become bland equivalence. Furthermore, Flores warns about the way the demand for 'contemporary equivalence' fosters a particular predicament for artists working

---

22   Kathryn Weir quoted in Hoskote, 'Wager on Cosmopolitanism', 259.
23   Flores, 'Revisiting Tradition', 239.

in a postcolonial context, who are faced with the double bind of experiencing 'a latecoming both to their own traditions and to the foreign one'.[24] Lost in limbo, caught between a diminished sense of tradition and a contextless contemporary, their art seems doomed to resonate hollowly only within the brittle veneer walls of 'the new'.

In his interview for the APT7 catalogue, Fletcher describes a passage from Robert Louis Stevenson's novella *The Beach of Falesa* (1892) in which a colonial trader sets up a 'haunted cave' filled with wondrous items from both Western and non-Western sources in an attempt to awe and control the indigenous people. Fletcher speaks of his own images of modernist interiors, haunted by the presence of indigenous artefacts or cultural productions, as the inheritors of that magical cave. The 'pleasure domes' of contemporary art spaces are effortlessly interpretable as the offspring of such colonial appropriation and control. Fletcher's metaphor and the images he produces open the way towards a less authoritarian, more open and playful analysis of the emergence of the contemporary. If there is a haunting at hand, then surely part of that lingering melancholy has to do with the failure of negotiation, with misinterpretations, with the sheer stupidity of not taking time to listen, look and think about the differences that contextually responsive traditions have worked with over time. The 'indigenous objects' in Fletcher's otherwise ethnically cleansed interiors glower and thrum with the indignity of having been included in a space to which they never requested entry. We look at these images and we are simultaneously caught in the potential of understanding what those objects might tell us, if only they could speak, and of also considering how their presence threatens to shatter the ordered elegance of the modernist design chic. As viewers, we are left almost willing that to happen.

And what if it did? What if the rooms were blasted apart with the intensity of that built-up tension? What if all the bits and pieces had to be reconfigured? What if we had to stop and slowly, carefully, start asking questions about pasts and places, allegiances and alliances, and enmities before we put it together again in another (temporary) iteration? Who would we ask to help us do it so that it didn't happen again? What might the real costs of that consultation be? How much time might that take? What if it looked a little messy? What if it didn't look like the all those catalogues of beautiful rooms before it?

Natasha Conland's term, the 'irreverent contemporary' may be adequate to the task of encompassing that possibility:

> The irreverent contemporary might however embrace the possibility of failed dialectics, disagreement, a less majestic turn of phrase and

---

24 Ibid., 238.

conflict might be there at least as a possibility. In the first three APTs the symposia were widely felt to own this position, but in the absence of a more sustained formal dialogue, how does an exhibition hold this state while assuredly celebrating and owning its outcome to provide the world a location for viewing art of the Asia Pacific?[25]

The APT's specific regional distinction among biennales/triennales of the world, namely its mission to address the geo-cultural specificity of the Asia-Pacific, is clearly indicated in its title. It is therefore uniquely placed, as it has always been, to lead and advance the critical frames and debates on the contemporary as a necessarily context specific project. One of the hopes of the first three APTs was that the region might be able to offer an understanding of the emergence of the contemporary in a way that was not as conclusive as that presented in exhibitions north of the equator; in a way that sought for a gradual, slow, collaborative and consultative understanding that made way for disagreements and 'failed dialectics'. Not all of that potential might yet be lost: the APT's unique structure offers both the pedagogy of a growing archive and a growing collection, offering both a major recurring exhibition and the steadily amassing research of a museum, prepares the ground for the possibility that an 'irreverent contemporary', based on an acknowledgement of the fundamentally radical nature of many traditions in the region, might still be recognised and articulated.

---

25 Natasha Conland, 'I Fell in the Pacific Rim. I Fall in the Pacific Rim. I Will Be in the Pacific Rim', *Broadsheet* 41, no. 4 (December 2012): 262–63, 263.

5. Future Imaginaries

Charles Merewether

> 'natural history' has no actual existence other than through the process of human history, the only part which recaptures this historical totality, like the modern telescope whose sight captures, in time, the retreat of nebulae at the periphery of the universe.[1]

The governance, if not control, of water has become an increasingly critical subject. The subject of water—of seas and rivers—as integral to the sustenance and sustainability of the land, demands urgent attention.[2] Over the past century this has become a major issue that requires an understanding both across and between national boundaries, giving consideration to the increasing needs of individual countries, especially as attempts to address the adequate supply of water has driven some countries to take what can only be described as drastic measures. These measures are not an issue of territorial or national sovereignty, such as the ongoing disputes in the South China Sea involving China, Japan, Korea and the Philippines. And, while there is truth to the idea of a growing openness of borders and access to and between countries, there are other concerns and solutions that involve the control, use and future of river systems or of the seas that directly effect the sustainability of countries and their peoples.

This essay focuses on a series of projects undertaken by artists who have made visible and evident through their work the plight of people whose lives have been changed by the state's attempt to resolve issues relating to water. These solutions affect not only access to the land and the resource of water, but the sustainability of the land itself. Such issues have produced a new consciousness amongst artists about their art practice and the kind of issues they wish or feel necessary to address through their practice. I will refer to China and Singapore in regard to rivers and the sea.

My essay focuses on three Chinese artists whose projects address the Three Gorges Dam in China. I also consider the work of Debbie Ding and Charles Lim, who have been exploring the fate of the rivers and the sea, together with that of land reclamation in and around Singapore.

---

1   Guy Debord, *La société du spectacle* (Paris: Buchet-Chastel, 1967).
2   In 2010, Campbelltown Arts Centre in Sydney held the exhibition, *The River Project*, that included artists from Australia, China, India, Korea, Papua New Guinea, the Philippines and Vietnam. This project is an important example of the increasing recognition of the importance of water as a subject recognising the very concept of 'nature' as having become the subject of social forces.

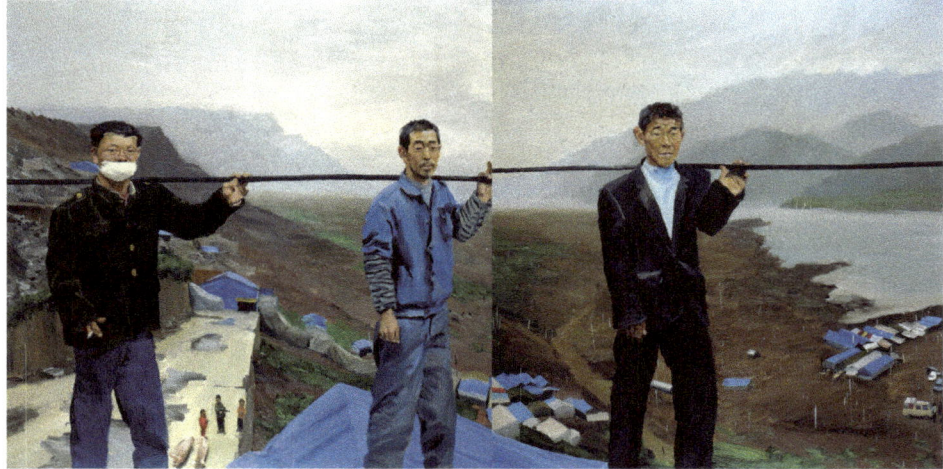

Liu Xiaodong, *Three Gorges: Displaced Population* 2003 (detail); oil on canvas; 200 x 800 cm (4 panels).

© Xiaodong Studio; image courtesy of the artist

The subjects represented by these artists have become more prominent due to their artistic practice and their ability to capture public attention by virtue of participating in and, in effect, validating the importance of a public sphere. Their practices constitute forms of articulation that sharpen our focus on the subject at hand. They avoid political rhetoric and other forms of expression that are shaped by political exigencies and interests. Moreover, the subject of this essay is about the connectivities that water makes between people across countries. The idea of connectivities is significant, not in the overt manner of networks or mutual alliances, but rather, as aligned subjects across the artists' practice. Once understood in these terms, the concept of the public sphere also expands beyond national boundaries to that of a transnational issue.

Part One

In the histories of modernism, the subjects of water and the land are important, but without any sharply defined distinction between the two, or overtly directed social significance. Art critic John Berger, amongst others, eloquently argued the link between landscape painting and eighteenth century aristocratic claims over the land. In counterpoint to this history, the contemporary artist William Kentridge has shown how the landscape is in fact the burial ground for a people, especially in South Africa under apartheid rule. In the 1960s the traditional subject of landscape merged into that of land. Artists began to immerse themselves in the land and to engage directly with it in regard to its physical materiality. We may note here artists in North America, such as Robert Smithson and his *Spiral Jetty*, and *The Lightning Field* by Walter de Maria, or Richard Long and Hamish Fulton in England, the Arte Povera movement in Italy, or others, such as Christo and the Japanese Mono-ha group, including Nobuo Sekine, Lee Ufan, Koji Enokura and Kishio Suga. All of these artists, in different ways, used commonplace materials and challenged the logic of rationalism and technology as evident in the modernist abstraction of the postwar years, most notably in American minimalism. In different ways they immersed themselves in the land, sometimes with a sense of its sheer power and physicality, while in others, it was more a sense of essence, a spiritual almost animistic homage to nature.

While contemporary art may pay due homage to these artists of the 1960s and 1970s, the orientation and consciousness of the practice of contemporary artists, and their engagement with the land and with water (albeit the sea or rivers) is far more directly informed by the social consciousness of the profoundly irreversible and damaging effect on them of the state's shaping of the land. One of the contributing factors enabling this orientation has been the influence of Conceptual art. Since its advent in the 1970s, Conceptual art proposed a more direct engagement and critique of the social domain. That is, artists explored the use of language and institutions as informing, if not determining, the way in which art and visual language was framed and received. Art critic Boris Groys argues that:

> from today's perspective, the biggest change that conceptualism brought about is this: after conceptualism we can no longer see art primarily as the production and exhibition of individual things—even readymades. However, this does not mean that conceptual or post-conceptual art became somehow 'immaterial'. Conceptual artists shifted the emphasis of art-making away from static, individual objects toward the presentation of new relationships in space and time. These relationships could be purely spatial, but also logical and political. They could be relationships among things, texts, and photo-documents, but could also involve performances, happenings, films, and videos—all of which were shown inside the same installation space. In other words, conceptual art can be characterized as installation art—as a shift from the exhibition space presenting individual, disconnected objects to a holistic exhibition space in which the relations between objects are the basis of the artwork.[3]

The exhibition *Global Conceptualism: Points of Origin, 1950s–1980s*, went a long way to considering more specifically the breadth and significance of conceptual

---

3   Boris Groys, 'Introduction—Global Conceptualism Revisited', *e-flux* 29, no. 11 (2011), accessed 18 October 2013, http://www.e-flux.com/journal/introduction%E2%80%94global-conceptualism-revisited/.

practice.[4] The organisers argued that there were two waves of conceptual practice between the 1950s and 1980s. These activities took place in various parts of the world as the postwar social and political upheaval prompted artists to re-examine traditional forms of representation and question art's social utility. Much of the art in the exhibition, which took the form of photographs, documentation, films, videos, postcards, posters, drawings, as well as paintings, mixed media objects and installations, was made to provoke the viewer by disturbing previously accepted ideas about social, political, and cultural systems.[5] The inclusiveness of 'global conceptualism' was made possible by a distinction between Conceptual art as 'an essentially formalist practice developed in the wake of Minimalism' and Conceptualism, 'which broke decisively from the historical dependence of art on physical form and its visual appreciation' and was characterised by the de-emphasis of the object in favour of the 'idea' (a largely unexamined term in the discourse on Conceptual/ist art) and the conduct of art.[6] If, as the exhibition demonstrated, many socially/politically active artists have taken approaches that look similar to conceptual strategies—that is, to the act of de-materialisation, engagement with institutional contexts, emphasis on relations between language and perception—those artists have also, clearly, been concerned with the form of their acts.

The legacy of this diverse body of work is fundamental, while not necessarily directly related to understanding the character of contemporary practice. While the *Global Conceptualism* exhibition included Asia, the focus was Japan, South Korea, mainland China, Taiwan, and Hong Kong. There was no artwork from elsewhere in Asia; for example, Indonesia, Singapore, or the Philippines, where there was a strong engagement and redefinition of Conceptualism within the local context. Of course, one may argue that there were limits resulting from the availability of the necessary and substantial documentation as well as secondary research. The category of 'conceptualism' itself, however, was so expanded across Asia that there were no substantive grounds for this exclusion.[7]

---

4   The exhibition was held at the Queens Museum of Art, New York, in 1999, followed by a national tour. The curatorial team of Jane Farver, Luis Camnitzer and Rachel Weiss invited a group of 11 international curators to contribute to the exhibition and the work was grouped into regional sections and two chronological sections: the 1950s through until approximately 1973 (Japan, Western Europe, Eastern Europe, Latin America, North America, Australia and New Zealand), and 1973 through to the end of the 1980s (the Soviet Union [Russia], Africa, South Korea, and mainland China, Taiwan, and Hong Kong).
5   Frazer Ward notes that the exhibition might be seen as a 'riposte' to the Los Angeles Museum of Contemporary Art's exhibition of 1995–1996, *Reconsidering the Object of Art, 1965–1975*. See Ward, 'Global Conceptualism: Points of Origin, 1950s–1980s', *Frieze 48*, September–October (1999), accessed 18 October 2013, http://www.frieze.com/issue/review/global_conceptualism_points_of_origin_1950s_1980s/.
6   Luis Camnitzer, Jane Farver and Rachel Weiss, 'Foreword', in *Global Conceptualism: Points of Origin, 1950s–1980s* (Minneapolis: Walker Art Center & New York: Queens Museum of Art, 1999), viii.
7   The exhibition publication, however, attempted to address this omission by including an essay on Conceptual art in South-East Asia by Thai curator Apinan Poshyananda. See Poshyananda, '"Con Art" Seen from the Edge: The Meaning of Conceptual Art in South and Southeast Asia', in Camnitzer, Farver and Weiss, *Global Conceptualism*, 143–48.

Moreover, the development of a conceptual practice in these countries has been vital to socio-political debate across the art world and within those countries. This engagement has occurred within the broader cultural and social spheres, making visible what was otherwise obscured by city and national authorities as their regulatory mandate.

Since the 1970s, the lessons of Conceptualism have been received and developed in a variety of forms in Asia. If there are 'connectivities' they are drawn from the legacy of what is characterised as the 'global conceptual' art movement and from the legacy of 'land art'. This has included the revision of land art to include the subject of water and to become a more reflexive practice as to the socio-political context and agencies of change. This focus has been sharpened by the degree to which the process of modernisation has led to the rhetoric of globalisation and an almost exclusive focus on the city as a metropolitan and transnational centre of exchange economies. In some cases, the practice has been developed by individual artists, in other cases by groups who have come to the practice of art as a powerful means of articulation and dissemination.

In the process of its elaboration, my essay shows the connectivities between practices in these countries and other parts of the world. As suggested, these connectivities can be in part located in the way in which Conceptual art has helped to inform the practice of some of these artists. While there are parallels to be found between their practices with regard to their subject, there are, however, no direct connections between them as artists. The idea of transnational artistic movements seems to have virtually disappeared following the advent of Conceptual art movements. This is in part due to the strong growth of galleries and the lack of institutions or organisations to advance transnational artistic movements or other similar interests.

Part Two

In China a number of artists have explored the subject of the hydroelectric Three Gorges Dam in Central China. The project began in 1994, costing an estimated US$24 billion, and the question that has emerged is in weighing the economic gains produced through generating a clean energy resource (as opposed to coal), and the control, if not elimination, of flooding in the Three Gorges area. Against this is the long-term environmental and social costs, including the displacement of over 1 million people, submergence or disappearance of 1,200 towns and loss of some 8,000 archaeological sites. Over the past four years the damming of the Yangtze River has caught people's attention, not simply due to the massive scale of the project, but also the destruction of villages and towns and the enormous displacement of people and the loss of their livelihood. Even government official

Wang Xiaofeng, who oversees the project for China's State Council, admitted the potential for disaster at a meeting of Chinese scientists and government representatives in Chongqing:[8]

> We can't lower our guard ... We simply cannot sacrifice the environment in exchange for temporary economic gain.[9]

In 2008 an exhibition exploring the dam project was held at the Smart Museum of Art, Chicago, and included the work of Chen Qiulin, Yun-Fei Ji, Liu Xiaodong and Zhuang Hui.[10]

Zhuang Hui, who is known for his conceptually based photography, began his engagement with the subject of the Three Gorges Dam with his work *Longitude 109.88° E and Latitude 31.09° N* (1995–2008), which he initiated in April 1995 four months after the start of the dam project. He visited three sites affected by the construction of the dam—Hubei province in the Xiling Gorge area, the meeting point of the Yangtze and Daning rivers in Wu Gorge, and White Emperor City at the entrance of the Qutang Gorge. The artist then created several site-specific works in which he bored holes in the ground to mark sites that would be buried under water. He used a Luoyang shovel—a long-poled drill invented by tomb robbers in traditional China—to make configurations of holes at each site and then took photographs. Ten years later, Zhuang sent a photographer to document each site underwater, the treasures that had once been the subject of tomb robbers activities having disappeared under the rising water.

In 2005 Liu Xiaodong had begun to visit the area where the dam was being constructed. Towns were beginning to be destroyed and Liu Xiaodong went to the city of Fengjie where he painted 11 peasant labourers on the site. He portrayed them relaxing, sitting together on old mattresses on a rooftop, stripped half naked in the warm sun and looking down as if in thought. During this time, the artist also travelled to Thailand where he painted what he envisaged as a companion work. Reminiscent of the post-impressionist paintings of Paul Gauguin in Tahiti, he chose a group of Thai women, also sitting together on a mattress, surrounded by papaya, coconuts, melons and bananas, looking out towards the viewer. In subsequent exhibitions, the artist brought these two paintings together in a work entitled *Hot Bed*.[11] As the Chinese curator Pi Li has suggested, the repeated iconography of the mattress in both paintings symbolically unites these separate people. The tacit implications are made overt.

---

8   Chongqing is a municipality of around 31 million people abutting the dam. Mara Hvistendahl, 'China's Three Gorges Dam: An Environmental Catastrophe?', *Scientific American*, 25 March 2008, http://www.scientificamerican.com/article/chinas-three-gorges-dam-disaster/.
9   Wang Xiaofeng, quoted in Hvistendahl, 'China's Three Gorges Dam'.
10 The exhibition *Displacement: The Three Gorges Dam and Contemporary Chinese Art* opened in Chicago on 2 October 2008 and at the Nasher Museum of Art, Duke University, in 2010.
11 In *Zones of Contact*, Biennale of Sydney 2006, the two paintings were shown facing one another with a mattress and television monitor between them.

5. Future Imaginaries

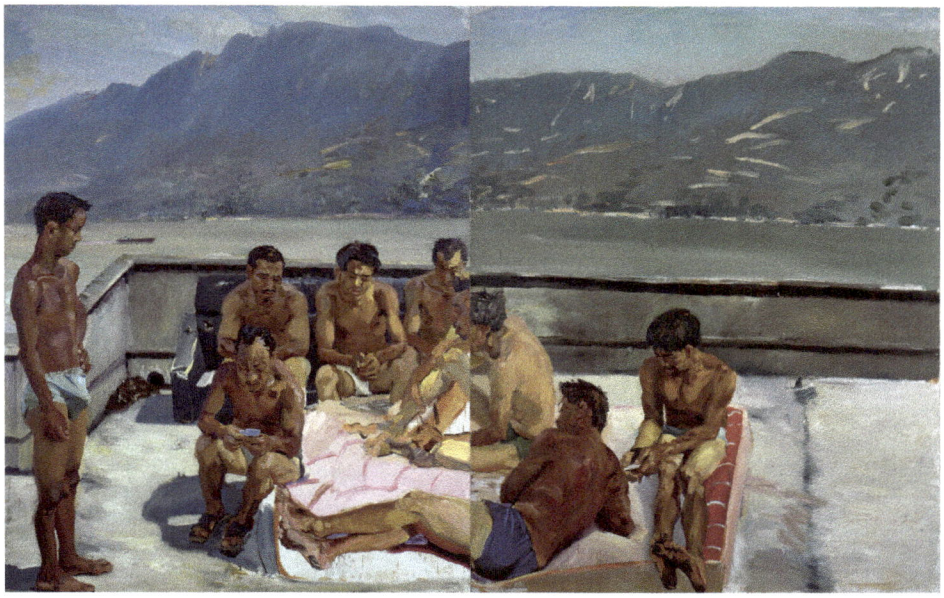

Liu Xiaodong, *Hot Bed I* 2005; oil on canvas, 260 x 1,000 cm.

© Xiaodong Studio; image courtesy of the artist

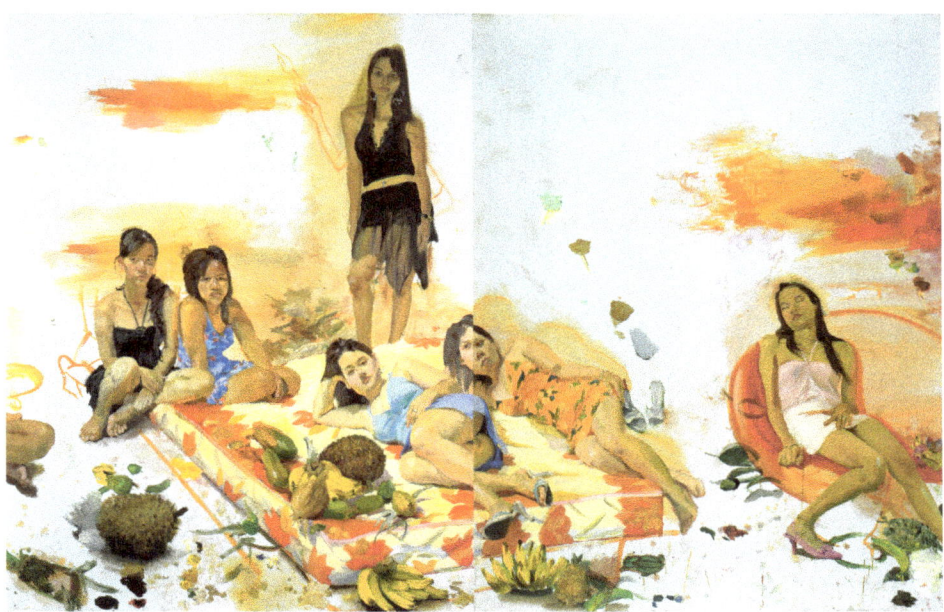

Liu Xiaodong, *Hot Bed II* 2006; oil on canvas; 260 x 1,000 cm.

© Xiaodong Studio; image courtesy of the artist

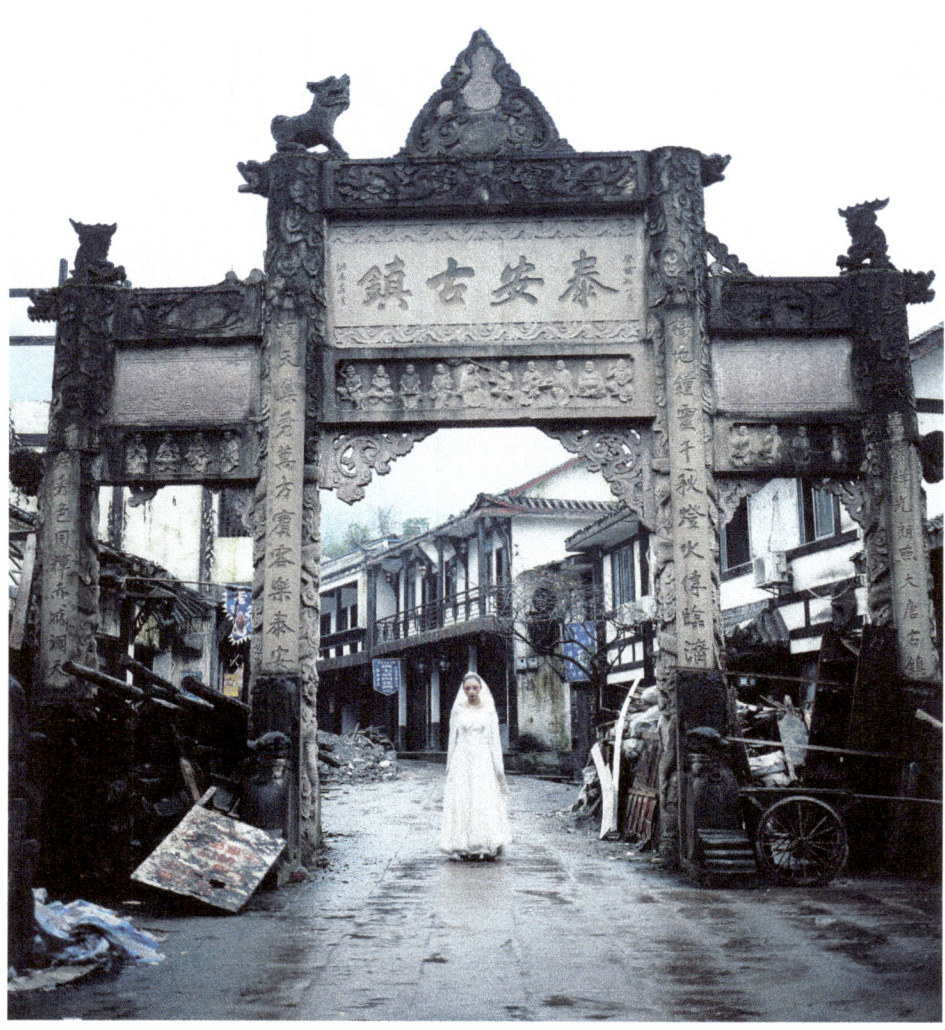

Chen Qiulin, *Old Archway* (from 桃花 *Peach Blossom*) 2009; 录像 video; 16 min, 37 sec; photograph, 154 x 124 cm.

Courtesy of the artist and Beam Contemporary Art, New York and London

In an unrelated project, the artist Chen Qiulin responds to the demolition of homes in the Three Gorges area. Covering both the Three Gorges Dam and the Sichuan earthquake, her work anticipates the paintings of Liu Xiaodong. Using video, one of the key subjects of Chen Qiulin's art practice has been the transformation of Sichuan, the province where she was born and lives. In May 2008, three months before the Beijing Olympics were scheduled to open, Sichuan province experienced the worst earthquake in its history. Hundreds of thousands of people lost their lives, friends and homes. Less than a year later, Chen Qiulin released the video work *Peach Blossom* (*Tao Hua*) 2009. Her research for this film led her to discover that her hometown of Wanxian, lying next to the Yangtze River, was destined to be submerged beneath rising water as a result of the dam construction. She made three video works *Farewell Poem* (*Bie Fu*) 2002, followed by *River, River* (*Jiang He Shui*) 2005, and *The Garden* (*Hua Yuan*) 2007, each of which corresponds to the successive stages of the flooding of her city.[12]

Unlike many, Chen Qiulin seeks to be optimistic in her exploration of how people adapt to traumatic change and what the future holds. The result is often fragmented and disjointed, as in Chen Qiulin's *Farewell Poem*, which is constructed from memories of her childhood and the ruins of the city. In *River, River* she captures images of the new city as it rises out of the ruins and, using operatic scenes, she portrays the contrast of the old and the new. *The Garden* shows the disappearance of part of Wanxian as the dam water rose, and the appearance of a new city and daily life shaped by the demands of change.

Together, these Chinese artists show distinct approaches that seriously engage with the subject. The work of Zhuang Hui extends the power of a conceptual practice to abstract the essence of the issues. In a sense his work offers a serious parody that refers to both the history of the Three Gorges and the futility of any action that can now be taken to reverse the course of what has happened. Liu Xiaodong's paintings refer to the subject of the dam, but create an imaginary relation to another world that relieves the affected communities from the pressing immediacy of the situation. While offering a personal reflection on what has happened to her city and the people of the region, Chen Qiulin seeks to invent a new future by engaging young residents to perform a mock Chinese opera and imagine the future.

Artists have been at the forefront of raising social awareness of pressing issues as they impact upon communities. They have collaborated with others who have different forms of expertise and skills. This phenomenon has developed in

---

12 Chen was commissioned to produce the first work *Farewell Poem (Bie Fu)* for the exhibition *Harvest: Contemporary Art* at the Agricultural Museum in Beijing, 2002, organised by the Chinese curator and art historian Gao Minglu.

South Korea in relation to the Four Rivers Restoration Project, a plan begun in 2009 to further develop Korea's four major river systems—the Han, Nakdong, Geum and Yeongsan. This has involved building 16 dams on those rivers and rebuilding 87 old dams, alongside dredging 520 million cubic metres of mud from the riverbeds in a bid to simplify flood prevention. The stated objectives of the project are flood control, prevention of water shortages, improvement of water quality, and the creation of parks for tourism. One of many groups to have developed in response to the project is the Seoul-based organisation Listen to the City.[13] For this group, and others active in opposition to a project that has cost, to date, some US$19.3 billion, the project is destroying the natural environment and ruining the habitat of multitudes of migratory birds.

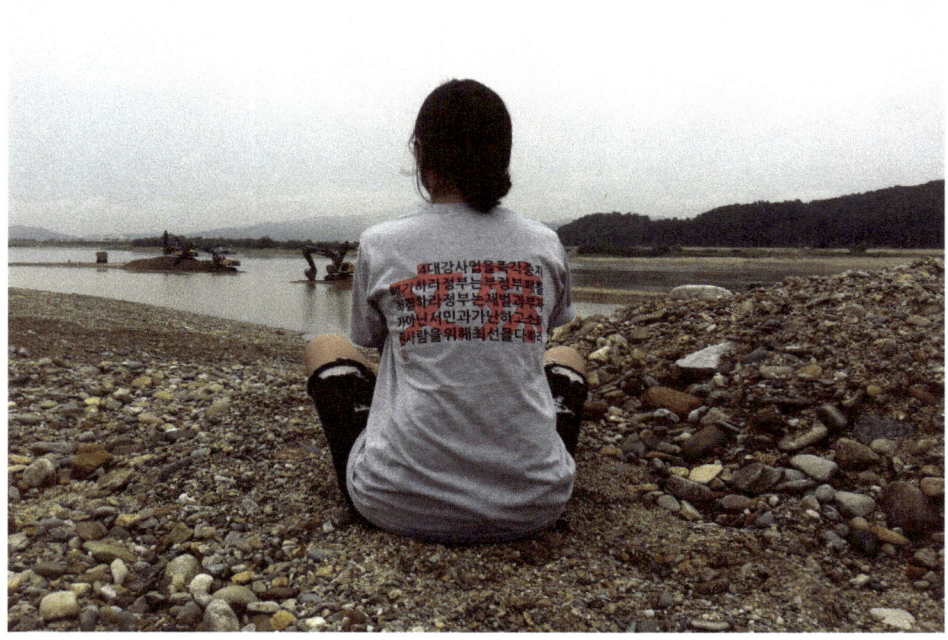

Eunseon Park—Listen to the City, *A Monument for Buddhist Monk Munsu who Self-immolated Against 4 River Construction 2010* 2011; C-print.

Image courtesy Eunseon Park

In Singapore the issue of water has never stopped being a subject of concern, as has land. The exploration and transformation, if not destruction, of the land has exposed its history, as if laid bare in the moment prior to its disappearance.

---

13 See 'Listen to the City', accessed 18 October 2013, http://listentothecity.org/; http://urbandrawings.blogspot.com; http://www.eunseonpark.com.

The coincidence of such forces has encouraged greater exploration and research of its history, both in its telling and as a point around which to defend its existing value. And yet, arguably, its present condition and future have become increasingly fragile, even precarious under the impact of urban development. This has affected the availability of land for sustainable natural resources: namely, of food and water.

Debbie Ding is an artist, designer/programmer and cartographer who maps and visualises spaces—whether they be real or imaginary. She develops touchscreen applications, interactive installations and teaches the website development and software technology of Actionscript (AS3). Her personal interest is in map-making, documenting and researching local histories, and reconstructing local narratives. She facilitates the Singapore Psychogeographical Society, referring to one of her works, discussed below, as an 'interactive and generative art piece depicting the Singapore River as a "psychogeographical faultline"'. Ding notes:

> I believe that most people living in Singapore are unaware of the shape or precise location of the Singapore River, despite it being Singapore's eponymous river and arguably its most historically important river. This may be because the name is not geographically precise, or because the river itself is relatively small and resembles nothing more than a large canal at some points. ...
>
> I would like to create an interactive installation of a generative 'Map of the Singapore River', that will redraw itself according to different variables marked out on a map on a table. It may be viewed as an act of speculative archeology—staring into the great big crack in the earth, taking a peek through the geological layers of the city underneath.[14]

Describing the Singapore River as a 'psychogeographical faultline', Ding writes of it as a site at which memories of spaces, fictional (imagined) spaces, and dream spaces interact, merge, or drift apart—like a series of tectonic plates. In using the term 'psychogeographical', Ding pays tacit homage to the French writer Guy Debord who was a key figure in founding the social revolutionary organisation Situationist International in the 1950s. Debord wrote a major critique of consumer culture and commodity fetishism in *The Society of the Spectacle* (1967). In *The Naked City* (1957), he defined psychogeography as the study of the specific effects of the geographical environment, consciously organised or not, on the emotions and behaviour of individuals and the need for *dérive*, which was a technique of transient passage to disrupt an increasingly commodified and organised society.

---

14   Debbie Ding, *The Singapore River as a Psychogeographical Faultline I* (2010), accessed 18 October 2013, http://dreamsyntax.org/dbbd/portfolio/psychogeographicalfaultline/.

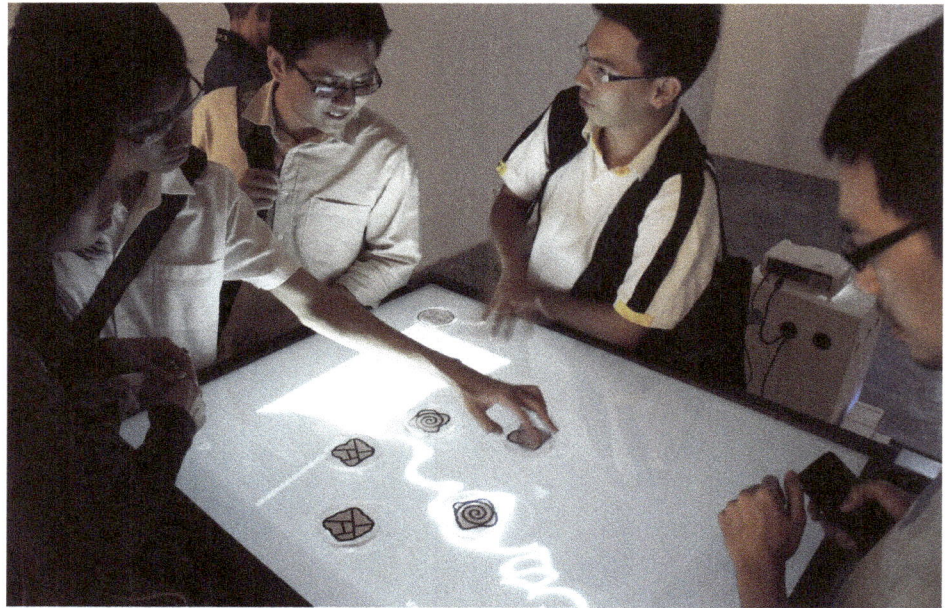

**Debbie Ding, \\ *(The Singapore River as a Psychogeographical Faultline)*
2010; Substation Gallery, Singapore.**

Photograph by Kevin Lim; image courtesy Creative Commons (http://www.flickr.com/photos/inju/)

For Ding, the Singapore River is a site where residents congregate to socialise, create memories, or dream of things to come—yet, when prompted, very few know where it is or what it looks like. Just as people struggle to pin down an image of it in their minds, it is also a site constantly in construction and in motion, as the water ebbs out to sea, and as people struggle to give meaning to their geography.

In distinct ways, artists who share Ding's interests look at the constitution of a country through land reclamation. In terms of the percentage of land reclaims, Singapore is said to exceed the Netherlands. Water is integral to this process and Ding, along with other Singapore artists such as Charles Lim and Zhao Renhui, have each in different ways, explored the growth of Singapore as a land mass. As Zhao Renhui shows, we can trace this development back to the nineteenth century, when the hills of Singapore were slowly levelled in order to provide the sides of rivers.[15]

At face value it is possible to link such practices to those of land art in the late 1960s and 1970s. But, while there are links that can be drawn, the differences

---

15 See the photo essay by The Land Archive and Zhang Renhui, 'The Lost Hills of Singapore', *ISSUE 1: Land* (Singapore, 2012): 25–33.

are greater. These differences can be characterised by Lim's practice. In 2011 Lim produced a 20-minute video, *all lines flow out*, which follows the journey of a mysterious figure who walks along the '*longkangs*'—a local term for drains—that create a vast network across the city state of Singapore. He is searching for a way home. Recalling the mysterious, almost science fiction, landscape of Andrei Tarkovsky, Lim creates a mysterious latter-day world of the French poet Charles Baudelaire's flâneur. And yet, these *longkangs* have slowly been subsumed to the dictates of Singapore's almost compulsive obsession to construct itself as a modern cityscape. This construction ignores the boundless force of nature, evident when the city is immobilised by the monsoon period, which causes flash flooding that can strike at the heart of its shopping district.

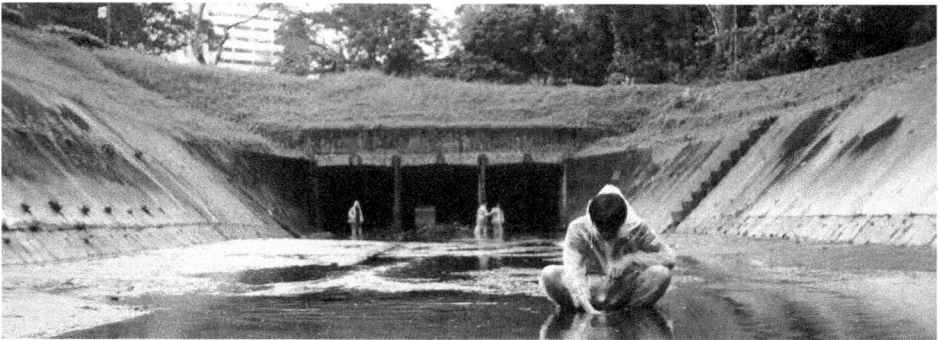

Charles Lim, *all lines flow out* 2011 (still); video installation, 21 min.

Image courtesy the artist

Lim has expanded his view of Singapore to look at its topographical character, discovering that even this is not immune to the governmental logic of instrumentality and its ambition. Lim has explored the nation's physical growth through the addition of sand to its shores—land 'reclamation' projects—which has involved the dredging of sand from small islands belonging to neighbouring countries.[16] This has resulted in Singapore being at the top of the list of countries that have grown in physical size. As the curator David Teh has suggested, Lim's *Sea State* project captures how the 'maritime geography' has been 'all but erased from the national imaginary and everyday experience', replaced by land-based urban visions.[17]

---

16   See Charles Lim, 'Sea State 2: As Evil Disappears', and interview with Jessica Anne Rahardjo, in *ISSUE 1: Land* (Singapore, 2012): 34–45.
17   David Teh, 'Charles Lim's Informatic Naturalism: Notes on *Sea State 2*', in *'Sea State 2: As Evil Disappears'* (Singapore, 2012).

The work of Lim, as with other artists discussed here, points to a national imaginary that will never cease to disturb the future of the nation's people, that will inexorably draw together the residual connectivities between countries and the fate of their folly.

Conclusion

Most significantly, the work of these contemporary Asia-based artists is grounded on considerable research of their subject and its realisation as an artwork. Their work draws from research and documentation to offer an exploratory form, a 'work in progress' that extends the subject into the world of the imaginary. This move is critical to an appreciation of the way in which the idea of the archive is not a fixed repository or evidence of an inalienable truth. Rather, the archive becomes a means of locating the past, what was and is no longer and to detect the passage of fictive elaborations surrounding, often obscuring this past. This practice is not something closed, belonging simply to the past, but as the German intellectual Walter Benjamin aptly stated, it is a history of the present. This is how it is but equally, this is how it was!

Let me also return, however, to the naming of this practice as artwork. The work is exhibited in art museums and galleries, in the domain of the art world. It is made principally as art. Both Ding and Lim explore a world made opaque by the silence surrounding their subjects, which are steadily having a profound effect on the well-being of people's lives and their country. The three Chinese artists offer radically different approaches and, at the least, attest to the power of art to not only document but lead the way to creating an imaginary future.

Art becomes an operative, a means of conveying histories of ourselves. It offers an imaginary future, a creative solution, if not resolution, of the crisis of the present. Although these practices vary between themselves in this regard, they are nevertheless connected in the belief that through art, a deeper logic is shaped about the rapidly changing urbanscapes of Asia, about the subjection of nature to the dictates of progress: a logic which defies understanding as to its effects on human lives.

6. Response and Responsibility: On the Cosmo-politics of Generosity in Contemporary Asian Art

Marsha Meskimmon

Responding | Giving

Between 1996 and 1997, Indonesian artist Dadang Christanto produced the sculptural installation *They Give Evidence* (*Mereka Memberi Kesaksian*). The work, funded through a grant from the Japanese Government, was first shown at the Museum of Contemporary Art in Tokyo and then travelled to the Hiroshima City Museum of Contemporary Art. In Japan, the installation consisted of 20 sculpted male and female figures arranged facing forward in four rows of five,[1] each bearing in their outstretched arms the traces of bodies, rendered palpable in, and by, the folds and contours of clothing. The figures that comprise this work are eloquent in their simplified rendering: their eyes look straight ahead, their mouths are held as if ready to speak and their arms gently bear the weight of absent bodies while they stand unwavering, present with us, in the space. The striking bodily gesture that is made by these figures as they give evidence can be described as an offering, an open gesture toward those who may respond. The figures neither raise their hands to threaten, avenge or admonish, nor fold their arms to protect or exclude. They offer, they *give*.

This open and generous bodily signal is a fitting gesture with which to begin this essay, linking as it does the possibility of ethical generosity with the double play of *response* as both the sensory result of bodily perception and as a reply or answer to another. Responding is a key concept in relation to Christanto's practice and one that is frequently noted in criticisms of his work. Christanto's performances and sculptural installations are themselves understood as a response to trauma and, significantly, to have an unusual capacity to elicit explicit and immediate responses from their audience, without seeking these in a direct or, more to the point, *directed* way. That is, while Christanto does not see his work as complete without participation from viewers, the work does not include 'instructions' to participant–spectators telling them how to respond, nor is his practice 'participatory' in the sense of requiring the audience to undertake an action or set of actions to complete the work of art.

---

[1] Four figures were acquired for the permanent collection in Tokyo. The remaining 16 figures were acquired by the Art Gallery of New South Wales in 2003 as a central focus of their Asian Galleries.

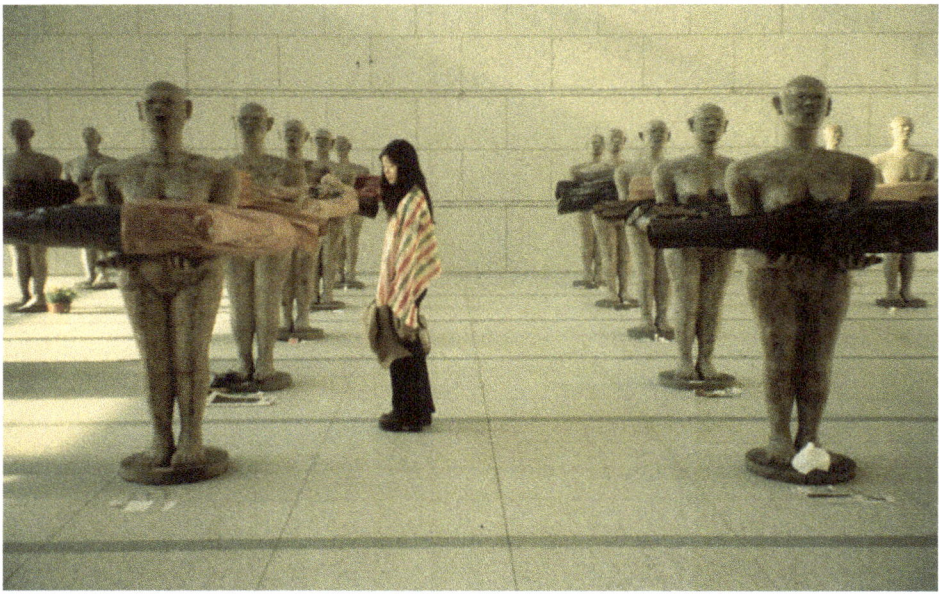

**Dadang Christanto, *Mereka Memberi Kesaksian (They Give Evidence)*
1996–1997; installation view; exhibited at Museum of Contemporary Art,
Tokyo and Hiroshima City Museum of Contemporary Art, 1997; standing
figures holding clothes; terracotta powder mixed with resin/fibreglass,
cloth and resin; height 200 cm (male), 190 cm (female), width and depth
c. 100 x 150 cm, weight c. 90 kgs each.**

Collection: Museum of Contemporary Art, Tokyo and the Art Gallery of New South Wales, Sydney; reproduced by courtesy of the artist

Yet, the effect that Christanto's performances and sculptural installations have on their audiences is remarkable, especially the extent to which the works engender a vibrant, visceral and spontaneous response that often includes what can only be called 'offerings'. As Caroline Turner and Glen Barclay wrote of *They Give Evidence*: 'It had a major effect … on Japanese audiences, who spontaneously left flowers and poems about universal suffering …'.[2] Turner and Barclay further note that responses to Christanto's work are international in their scope—they are not limited to this specific installation, or to Japanese audiences—and they describe a similar response from Australian viewers to an installation from 1993.[3] In their astute reading of such international responses, Turner and Barclay argue for the works' ability to link specific, regional events with universal experiences of human suffering, loss and grief.

---

2 Caroline Turner & Glen Barclay, 'Dadang Christanto: Wounds in Our Heart', in *Dadang Christanto—Wounds in Our Heart*, ed. Caroline Turner & Nancy Sever (Canberra: The Australian National University, Drill Hall Gallery, 2010), 12. I would like to thank Turner for first making me aware of Christanto's work.
3 Ibid., 11.

Christanto himself appears to concur with this understanding of the effect of his work on audiences internationally, suggesting, for example, that the response to *They Give Evidence* by individuals in Japan was to do with personal contexts of loss and with a wider sense of collective, national guilt in relation to the Japanese occupation of Indonesia during the Second World War.[4]

I am indebted to these insights concerning the imbrication of the regional and the global in the responses of spectators to Christanto's practice, and I seek here to develop these ideas in a different, but related, exploration of the twofold sense of *response* described above. To do so, it is important to think critically about the elements of the work to which participant–spectators have responded and the nature of that response. I want to suggest that it is significant that the responses to *They Give Evidence* have emerged across cultural and linguistic divides, that they connect the micro-stories of individuals with the macro-histories of global geopolitics, and that they find their most compelling form through unbidden giving. Arguably, these features constitute what might be described as a 'cosmopolitan' mode of responsibility, in which subjects simultaneously acknowledge the difference and specificity of others' experiences, yet respond generously to them.

Christanto makes no secret of the fact that a central impetus for his practice resides in a personal experience of traumatic loss; as an eight-year-old child in 1965, Christanto's father 'disappeared' during the violent anti-communist political struggles in Indonesia. His father never returned—he is one of the many 'disappeared' whose absence is mourned without resolution. *They Give Evidence* is but one of many works that Christanto has made in the wake of his personal experience of political violence, yet it is not a representation of particular events, nor in any sense directly illustrative of the Indonesian political context.

Significantly, when *They Give Evidence* was shown in Japan in 1997, and later, in the 24th Bienal de São Paulo in 1998 (where just six of the sculptural figures were shown) and from 2003, in the Art Gallery of New South Wales (where 16 figures form part of the gallery's permanent collection), audiences approaching the work have been made aware of the artist's biography. In other words, there is a narrative that accompanies *They Give Evidence*, however lateral its connection to the work may be. The narrative exemplifies the interweaving of the local and the global; its detail is specific to a particular time and place, but the overarching tale is not—a child losing his beloved parent in an act of unspeakable and unnameable[5] violence has a universal resonance.

---

4   Sue Ingham, 'Witnesses from Indonesia', *TAASA Review* 12, no. 4 (December 2003): 22.
5   See Charles Merewether, 'Naming Violence in the Work of Doris Salcedo', *Third Text* 24 (Autumn 1993): 35–44; and, Griselda Pollock, *After-Affects, After-Images: Trauma and Aesthetic Transformation in the Virtual Feminist Museum* (Manchester University Press, 2013).

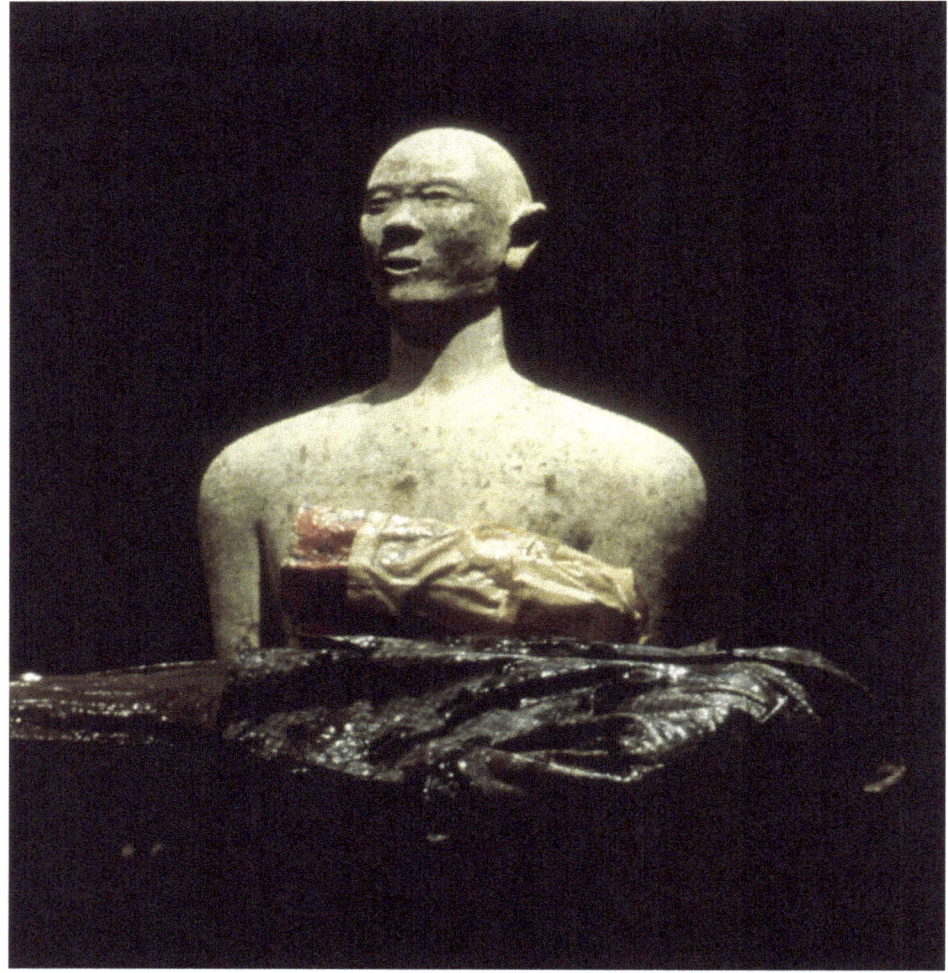

**Dadang Christanto, *Mereka Memberi Kesaksian (They Give Evidence)*
1996–1997; installation view; exhibited at Museum of Contemporary Art,
Tokyo and Hiroshima City Museum of Contemporary Art, 1997; standing
figures holding clothes; terracotta powder mixed with resin/fibreglass,
cloth and resin; height 200 cm (male), 190 cm (female), width and depth
c. 100 x 150 cm, weight c. 90 kgs each.**

Collection: Museum of Contemporary Art, Tokyo and the Art Gallery of New South Wales, Sydney; reproduced by courtesy of the artist

Arguably, the audiences for this work in major metropolitan centres from Tokyo and Hiroshima to São Paulo and Sydney, daily hear tales of political violence, poverty and suffering on a global scale through televised news, print media and the tireless fundraising of charitable organisations. And while some news stories and charity 'infomercials' certainly hit their mark, producing an epiphanic moment of empathy, many do not. Thus, the unanticipated and spontaneous responses evoked by *They Give Evidence* cannot merely be attributed to the translation of a moving narrative in the gallery space, though this micro-story does form one part of the experience of the work. I want to suggest that responding to *They Give Evidence* is, rather, at once a form of multi-sensory, kinaesthetic response to the transformation of grief and trauma into the affective aesthetic registers of art, and a compelling ethical response to the entreaty of another. It is at the level of these dual economies of response that art offers a potential crossing between cultural, linguistic and social boundaries—and a place in which we can imagine and respond to other people who are different from ourselves. It is here that the cosmo-politics of response can emerge.

If responding to *They Give Evidence* does not require a shared language, history or cultural tradition on the part of its international audience, the evidence of its ability to evoke such demonstrative responses begs further analysis. At what point and in what sense does the work provide conditions sufficient to engender collective engagement and a willing, proactive, display of emotion? As I see it, the start of the answer resides in the concept of bodily empathy, the operation of our proprioceptive capacities in an organised and orchestrated space. The figures in *They Give Evidence* are, literally, *compelling*; the rows of monumental human forms, both male and female, unique and yet collective in their orientation and gesture, beckon to us bodily, seeking a corporeal recognition. Our bodies come to understand the spatial dimensions of the work by moving around these other *bodies*, both absent and very present, and we are obliged to orient ourselves in connection with them, to understand and locate ourselves, proprioceptively, in relation to this collective act of corporeal witnessing, of giving evidence, of standing in an attitude of openness and entreaty. A proprioceptive engagement with the work brings us to our senses, resonates kinaesthetically, such that our bodies *make sense* of the work through gestural empathy; if we engage with the work (kin)aesthetically, we are compelled imaginatively to entertain an open gesture of offering in and through our own bodies. *We* give evidence, *we* entreat, *we* offer.

As Barbara Stafford has argued, kinaesthesia can be a compelling sensory state in that it connects sensation with cognition: 'We become aware of thinking only in those kinaesthetic moments when we actively bind the sights, savours, sounds, tastes and textures swirling around us to our inmost, feeling flesh.'[6] With our bodily empathy in play in the space of *They Give Evidence*, we become responsive to the entreaty of the other, we can hear the evidence we are given, and we can be moved to respond in the second sense: we can offer our answer.

---

6   Barbara Stafford, *Visual Analogy: Consciousness as the Art of Connecting* (Cambridge, MA: MIT Press, 1999), 58.

But, what is asked by *They Give Evidence*? Whom do we answer and how? The dual nature of response is again useful in thinking critically about this question. In addition to indicating a sensory awareness of our embodiment and our connections with other subjects and objects in the world, response implies an ethical or moral obligation to others. Response comes from the French, where the root retains the sense of a reply as an oath or obligation, an answering back that entangles us with the one who seeks our response.

If the premise of *They Give Evidence* is an aesthetic transformation of trauma into testimony, then these witnesses, amongst whom we may find ourselves located through kinaesthetic empathy, are not simply asking a question to which there is a definitive answer. Their entreaty operates instead as an open call to others for recognition. In this gesture, we are invited to *bear witness*, to share responsibility for the weight of the evidence that they offer. This does not entail accounting *for* or *to* (an 'answering back' that closes the generosity of the ethical relation), but impels a further giving. This is the nature of the response that has arisen spontaneously across divides of language, history and culture, by those who have engaged, bodily, with this work—and this response speaks volumes.

I am proposing here that both ethical responsibility and generosity are underpinned by an affective ability to respond, in the double sense, to the needs and demands of others. This interpretation accords with Kelly Oliver, who eloquently described the inter-relationship between response and responsibility in her book, *Witnessing: Beyond Recognition*, thus:

> There is a direct connection between the response-ability of subjectivity and ethical and political responsibility. … The responsibility inherent in subjectivity has the double sense of the condition of possibility of response, response-ability, on the one hand, and the ethical obligation to respond and to enable response-ability from others born out of that founding possibility, on the other.[7]

Neither response-ability, nor responsibility can be obliged, but they can be engendered, fostered and compellingly performed in and through the sensory registers of art. And if generosity and responsibility are necessary corollaries to justice, hospitality and forgiveness, then politics and ethics here converge at the point of an embodied, engaged and affective cosmopolitan subject.

---

7 Kelly Oliver, *Witnessing: Beyond Recognition* (Minneapolis, MN and London: Minnesota University Press, 2001), 15.

6. Response and Responsibility: On the Cosmo-politics of Generosity in Contemporary Asian Art

Giving | Imagining

How might we understand the progression from response to generosity, or from responding to giving, and what role might an imaginative engagement with art play in this unfolding? To begin to address this question, it is useful to turn to another work that has elicited strong responses across cultural boundaries: Araya Rasdjarmrearnsook's *Reading for One Female Corpse* from 1998.[8]

The work consists of a single-channel video showing the artist, seated in the Chiang Mai Hospital morgue in Thailand, reading passages from the classical Thai text, the *Inau*, over the corpse of a young woman. The body of the unnamed young woman lies in a clear perspex container, covered from head to knee by white cloths. The intimate and visceral presence of the corpse is central to the piece, but her body is not rendered as an object of grotesque fascination. For most of the duration of the work, we watch the scene of the seated artist reading to the covered body at a slight distance, as a witness or fellow mourner might, rather than as a voyeur. And, even when the video pans along the length of the body, revealing the mottled skin surface of the woman's arms and legs, we are never privy to a fetishised, forensic visual dissection of the dead woman. The camera, accompanied by the low tones of the artist's reading, is gentle to this body; searching, but not probing.

Reading for One Female Corpse is one of a number of video works that Rasdjarmrearnsook made during the late 1990s and early years of the present century, for which she read, spoke, sang to or dressed corpses in the Chang Mai Hospital morgue. This complex and multifaceted body of work has been shown extensively throughout the world, in solo shows and major group exhibitions, such as the Venice, Sydney and São Paulo biennales and the Carnegie International. Sometimes the videos are shown individually and, at other times, they are configured as themed clusters. Tellingly, *Reading for One Female Corpse* has been grouped with other work under the title of *Lament*,[9] placing the emphasis on the recitation for the dead woman rather than the representation of her body as an object within the work.

The act of recitation, the artist's solitary lament for the young woman whose body lies alone in the morgue, is central to the piece and critical to the argument being developed here concerning the complex imbrication between responding and giving that is articulated by *Reading for One Female Corpse*. The *Inau* is not a traditional Thai funeral lamentation, but a classical literary work of the

---

8   There are discrepancies in the dating of this piece; in some sources it appears as 2001, though it is clear that it was shown as early as 2000. For this reason, I am using the earlier date.
9   The collective title *Lament* was used, for example, when the work was shown in Sweden, at the Edsvik Museum in Stockholm, in 2000.

eighteenth century originating in Java and having been brought to Thailand via Malaya. It is the story of a prince and his courtship of three women and includes long passages in which the women's longing and sexual desires are voiced. These are elements of the *Inau*, which are well known to Thai audiences, that Rasdjarmrearnsook reads as her lament to the young woman. *Reading for One Female Corpse* thus makes an explicit link between female sexuality, subjectivity, desire and death.

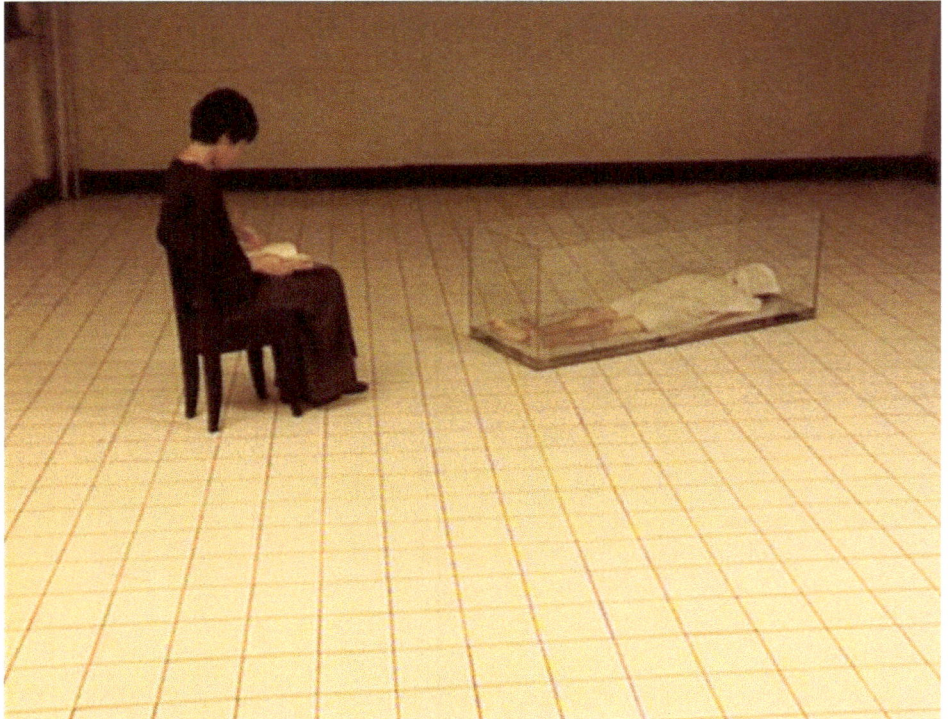

Araya Rasdjarmrearnsook, *Reading Inaow for Female Corpse (Lament Series)* **1997; video.**

Work and image courtesy: Araya Rasdjarmrearnsook, with kind assistance of 100 Tonson Gallery, Bangkok

Arnika Fuhrmann has argued convincingly that Rasdjarmrearnsook's lamentations over anonymous corpses in the Chiang Mai Hospital morgue not only raise the question of sexual difference in the textual sources, some of which are the artist's own writings, but in the highly resonant act of female lamentation.[10] Historically, the lengthy duties of public lamentation, which were central to Thai funeral traditions, were undertaken by women. Only in

---

10   Arnika Fuhrmann, 'Ghostly Desires: Sexual Subjectivity in Thai Cinema and Politics after 1997' (PhD thesis, University of Chicago, 2008), 234.

recent times has an established male Buddhist hierarchy dislocated female voices from their active participation in the processes of mourning, rendering women members of the unseen and silent labour force that prepares bodies (cleans and dresses them) but does not sing their desires through the rituals of death. *Reading for One Female Corpse* thus enacts a double sense of voice. Acknowledgement is key to the Thai concept of a 'good death'; the anonymous, unclaimed body over whom Rasdjarmrearnsook recites from the *Inau*, is, in this generous act, reclaimed, voiced and acknowledged in her full, desirous, sexed subjecthood. And, likewise, the mourner's female voice is heard, and recognised, through this intonation of unbidden generosity.

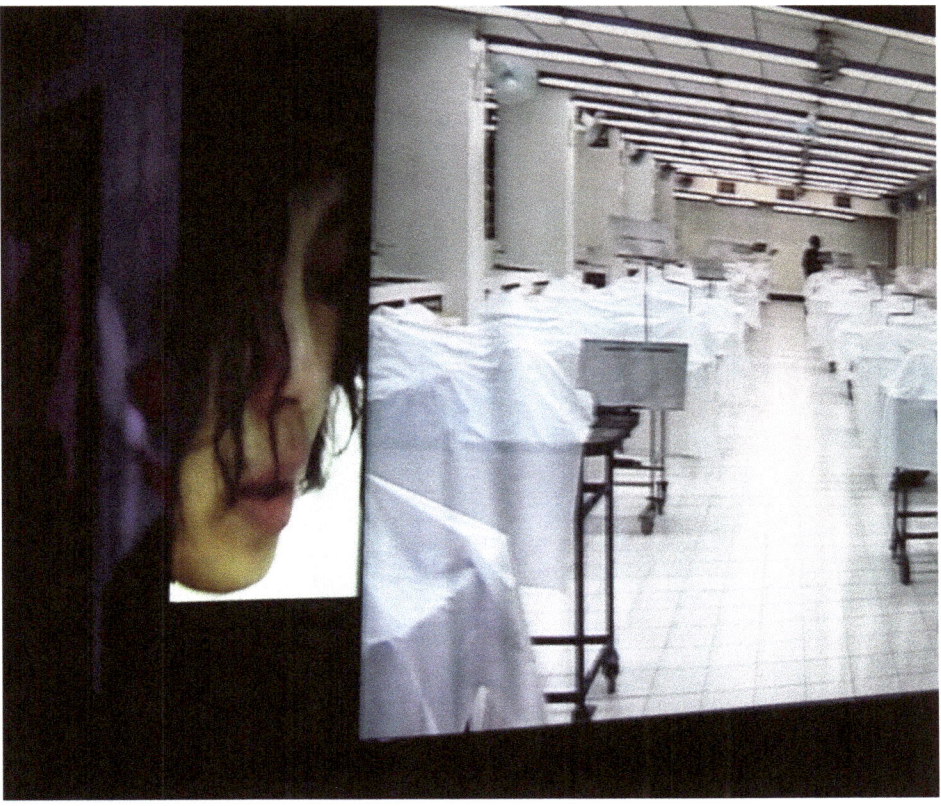

Araya Rasdjarmrearnsook, *Lament* 1998; 3 single screens / video installation.

Work and image courtesy: Araya Rasdjarmrearnsook, with kind assistance of 100 Tonson Gallery, Bangkok

As one might anticipate, Rasdjarmrearnsook's readings for corpses have engendered strong responses from audiences globally, but the strength of the response does not render it uniform. On occasion, within Thailand particularly, the works have been met with derision;[11] the subject has been said to be too feminine, too personal and too local to give the artwork an appropriate gravity. As many international critics (and Rasdjarmrearnsook herself) have noted, much of this criticism has come from a male art establishment and professional jealousy may well play a part in this response. I want to suggest, however, that there is a more complex failure of response at the core of these critiques, such that the failure to respond to the work perceptually negates its potential to engender a response to its entreaty.

Reading for One Female Corpse has been problematic for those viewers at a local level[12] who cannot, or will not, move beyond its literal subject matter, to engage with it as a work of art, a space in which we might reimagine the impact of everyday violence and destitution on others who are not, in fact, so distant or different from ourselves. For some viewers, a woman artist sitting in a morgue reading to the body of a young woman who, in life, was so insignificant as to be anonymous and unclaimed on her death, is too base a material from which to make 'art'. Thus read, the work engenders negative criticism for what it represents.

Remaining at the level of representation in encountering this work (where 'representation' is understood as the mirror of an external 'reality') renders an aesthetic response—an embodied and multi-sensory response—to what the work materialises as *art*, all but impossible. Yet, *Reading for One Female Corpse* is an artwork, not a documentary exposition of a particular social problem; the artist stages, films and edits a performance, constructing an aesthetic event with attention to the visual, sonic and spatial qualities of the work. This point is significant because it sustains the logic of the analysis of *Reading for One Female Corpse* as *art*, so as to critically evaluate the move from imaginative response-ability to ethical responsibility and subjective generosity.

Notwithstanding these few negative responses, Rasdjarmrearnsook's video works in which she read for corpses have been lauded by international critics and have been included in curatorial projects globally. Across national, cultural and linguistic divides, viewers have frequently expressed a profound sense of being moved by Rasdjarmrearnsook's video lamentations—the works provoke positive responses in different geopolitical contexts.

---

11 Fuhrmann uses the word 'derision' in a discussion of Rasdjarmrearnsook's satirical response to her critics between 2003–2004; Ibid., 247.

12 The issue of local interpretation is important: as discussed earlier, the Indonesian political context of Christanto's *They Give Evidence* yields with relative ease to more universally applicable interpretations. But it is significant that *They Give Evidence* was difficult to show in Indonesia where, in 2002, the figures' nudity had to be shrouded before an exhibition of the work, and the work was subsequently removed altogether before the event opened. In the context of a growing political accommodation of Islamic fundamentalism in Indonesia since 1998, the work took on a differently 'politicised' cast.

Two viewers' responses to the installation of *Reading Inaow*[13] *for Female Corpse* at the 54th Carnegie International (2004–2005) in Pittsburgh are suggestive:

> Araya Rasdjarmrearnsook's (born in Trad, Thailand) *Reading Inaow for Female Corpse* is a disturbingly moving installation that includes a single chair facing a video projection of the artist reading *Inaow* (an ancient Thai text on female desire) to a decomposing female corpse. ... Rasdjarmrearnsook's melodic reading of the text is mesmerizing and comforting ... [the artist] forces individual viewers to contemplate death by making them a part of her ceremony ...[14]

> Araya Rasdjarmrearnsook's *Reading Inaow for Female Corpse* was just beautiful in a very touching way ...[15]

These responses are not 'professional', in the sense of commissioned critical writing for art journals, exhibition catalogues or academic publications; rather, these writers have felt compelled by their experiences of the work to commit to writing to speak to others about being moved by *Reading for One Female Corpse*. In terms of their experience, the language they use is striking in its sensory resonance: 'disturbingly moving', 'mesmerizing and comforting', 'in a very touching way'.

How does this work of art touch viewers and to what effect? Arguably, the perceptual play of proximity and distance evoked by the work is critical to its ability to touch/move viewers and this play operates kinaesthetically, engaging subjects through their embodied responses to the piece. These responses are powerfully motivated by the multi-sensory qualities of the installed work as it combines immersive and resonant sound with haptic visuality in an intimate spatial configuration. Responding to the work in this sense moves beyond representation, toward an imaginative and intercorporeal form of response-ability.

Installed in Pittsburgh, *Reading Inaow for Female Corpse* was projected onto a wall in a small, darkened space. Facing the screen was a single chair, over which hung the translucent bell of the audio speaker; seated alone in the space, on the chair, the 'viewer' became a 'participant' in the recitation, not simply watching the performance, but being immersed in the sound of the reading. The sonorous incantation of the lament as it articulated women's desirous, corporeal subjectivity, acknowledged within the space of the performance both the reader, who came to voice, and the subject who came, in death, to be recognised.

---

13   In the Carnegie International, curated by Laura Hoptman, the work's title included a direct reference to the *Inau*, transliterated as *Inaow*.
14   Lyz Bly, 'Feeling the Zeitgeist: The 54th "Carnegie International" is Worth the Drive to Pittsburgh' (5 January 2005), http://www.newsenseonline.com/l_FT_2005_01_05.html.
15   gwenix, 'A Bit of Cotton Doesn't Equate Fluff. - International Art Exhibit @Carnegie' (12 February 2005), http://gwenix.livejournal.com/373741.html.

Seated in a mirror image of the position of the artist reading from the *Inau*, enveloped by the concentrated sound and visually focused on the brightly lit projection, participant–spectators were kinaesthetically positioned by the work, such that the wall of the gallery perceptually yielded to the space of the Chiang Mai Hospital morgue, and participant–spectators were left sitting with Rasdjarmrearnsook as she intoned her lament over the body of the young woman.

The treatment of the body of the anonymous woman, within the artist's performance and within the frame of the video, is significant to the work's ability to engender a kinaesthetic empathy among viewers; more strongly, I would propose that it is first in the haptic visuality of the video that we are 'touched' by the work, and that this touching establishes the subjects who are articulated through the piece (including the artist, the dead woman and the viewers) as permeable and interconnected with others: response-able and responsible.

Rasdjarmrearnsook's readings for corpses were produced in the wake of more than one artworld controversy concerning the deployment of human corpses within lens-based practices; as early as 1992–1993, Joel-Peter Witkin's still-life compositions using human body parts, and Andres Serrano's *Morgue* series were at the centre of heated debates concerning the ethical implications of making art with unclaimed, anonymous corpses. Without rehearsing those arguments again here, and without suggesting that the projects undertaken by Witkin and Serrano were in any sense alike,[16] the visual strategies they employed provide a useful point of comparison with those deployed by Rasdjarmrearnsook. In addition, it is likely that a proportion of the viewers of *Reading for One Female Corpse*, when it was shown in international biennials and group exhibitions, would have been familiar with these projects and/or the controversies that attended them. Moreover, international viewers aware of contemporary Asian art would likely have been reminded of the controversy caused in 2000 by Chinese artist Zhu Yu when he exhibited documentary photographs from his 'foetus-eating' performance *Eating People* in the Shanghai show *Fuck Off*. Zhu Yu was subject to investigations by both the FBI and Scotland Yard when images from this work circulated on the internet and were shown in a Channel 4 (United Kingdom) documentary on Chinese art.[17] While Zhu's work tested the limits of

---

16 Witkin's works with corpses form part of a much larger body of images centred on the visual excess of the histories of the exhibition of 'monsters' and the 'freak show'; the ethical questions raised by his access to corpses in Mexico, not to mention the treatment of the bodies and body parts by the artist in the staging of the compositions, have been discussed elsewhere (see Ann Millett, 'Performing Amputation: The Photographs of Joel-Peter Witkin', *Text and Performance Quarterly* 28, nos 1–2 (January 2008): 8–42). Serrano's *Morgue* series does not locate the anonymous bodies within the context of the display of 'monsters', and there are not the same ethical issues involved in his access to the corpses. The question of the aestheticisation and objectification of the dead (many of whom met violent ends), however, still meant that his series courted controversy. See Anna Blume's interview with Serrano in *BOMB* 43 (Spring 1993), http://bombsite.com/issues/43/articles/1631.

17 I would like to thank Michelle Antoinette for pointing out to me the relevance of Zhu Yu's work to contemporary viewers.

conventional morality and law at the point of the foetal hinterland between human cells/flesh and 'personhood', the use of corpses by Witkin, Serrano and Rasdjarmrearnsook operated at the other end of the spectrum, exploring personhood (our own and others') *post-mortem*.

There are three central differences between the visual treatment of the dead body in *Reading for One Female Corpse* and the works of Witkin and Serrano that are critical to our potential response, as viewers, to Rasdjarmrearnsook's video: the absence of visual fragmentation of the body, the absence of a fixed, disembodied viewpoint or frame, and the presence, in the space of the performance and video, of the artist. One of the most shocking elements of Witkin's photographic use of corpses is his consistent emphasis on the dismemberment of the body; the works are frequently composed of pieces of bodies, severed roughly and juxtaposed so as to reinforce our sense of estrangement from these corporeal, yet *inhuman* objects. Serrano's morgue compositions fragment the bodies with the lens of the camera; through close focus and framing, we are given just blackened fingertips, or bruised cheeks, or a long abdominal scar.

The body fragments, which are central to the work of Witkin and Serrano, produce a distanced and disembodied viewpoint, even when the lens brings the viewer astonishingly close to the corporeal remains. We are able to look, voyeuristically, or be turned away, uncomfortably, from the abject fragments of others that are presented to us as aesthetic objects. By contrast, the corpse we encounter in *Reading for One Female Corpse* is seen first as whole, covered by clean, white cloths; when the camera pans across the skin of the woman's body, it is *moving*, the frame of any particular view of the flesh is constructed as a detail of the whole. It alights gently upon the skin, touches the surface, renders it palpable. This visual structure embodies the eye of the lens, gives it a location from which it encounters this body from *within* the same space, rather than from a fictional, distanced, objectifying beyond. And this is all the more strongly materialised through the unconditional presence of the artist, maintained audibly even when the camera places her body out of spectatorial view.

As a work of art, *Reading for One Female Corpse* mobilises sound, light, image and space to bridge objectifying visual distance and bring participant–spectators into a proximate, haptic relationship with the bodies of the artist and the dead woman. Responding to the work perceptually, through a form of heightened kinaesthetic resonance, opens us to respond, ethically, to the entreaty of the other—in this instance, to recognise the woman who has died, not as a gruesome and abject object to be kept at a safe distance from us, but as a subject whose death implicates each of us in life. Indeed, the bodies brought viscerally and vitally together by the work—the artist, the dead woman and the viewer(s)—are positioned as *intercorporeal* subjects through this work and its pivotal gift of the lament. Our response-ability to this unrecognised other generates a corporeal responsibility to recognise her; the generosity of the artist's reading becomes an act of reclamation in our space.

This sense of generosity is materialised within the work as the condition by which subjectivity emerges in and through its fundamental interconnectedness with others. And such generosity is premised upon our embodiment and ethical entanglement, or 'response-ability' to and 'responsibility' for, other subjects in the world. Such giving is not easy, as Rasdjarmrearnsook wrote in a poetic accompaniment to her readings for corpses, and requires an effort, the assumption of the weight of responsibility: 'The air perfumed by death was so sad. Forcing herself, the weak one made the effort to be Giver. She then voiced a melodic strain …'.[18]

Reading for One Female Corpse establishes aesthetically the interrelationship between subjectivity, affect and generosity that Rosalyn Diprose has described so eloquently as the premise of ethical social relations. Diprose speaks of 'being given to others without deliberation in a field of intercorporeality, a being given that constitutes the self as affective and being affected, that constitutes social relations and that which is given in relation.'[19] This is, in the artwork, materialised as the gift of recognition in and through difference. The logic of the gift is maintained in the haptic touch of the camera and the immersive song of the lament, which neither objectify the dead woman nor assimilate her to our experience; we recognise her and ourselves as connected, yet not the 'same'. Intercorporeal generosity unfolds from responding, from answering the call of the other. Our subjectivity is premised upon the response-able and responsible relationship we maintain with others in the world and, in this, we see the potential of a cosmopolitan ethical subjectivity.

The unnamed woman for whom no one laments touches us—through the artwork—and this touching constitutes us as embodied and permeable. As an abject object of representation, she is unrecognisable, unable to be articulated, a Jane Doe to whom we can give nothing but our voyeuristic attention. When we are touched, however, we are moved, compelled differently in our subjecthood. Here subjectivity responds to the entreaty of the other; we can recognise, we can give.

This giving establishes social bonds, but it is not synonymous with legislative or political action in the conventional sense. I am interested here in the effects that the affective economies of art can have at the level of the subject, and how these can compel action, but I am not confusing this with artworks being used, for

---

18   Rama IX Art Museum, 'Araya Rasdjarmrearnsook, Thai Artists', http://rama9art.org/araya/index.html.
19   Rosalyn Diprose, *Corporeal Generosity: On Giving with Nietzsche, Merleau-Ponty and Levinas* (Albany, NY: State University of New York Press, 2002), 5.

example, to campaign for specific political purposes. My propositions are both more limited in their scope and more demanding in their critique. Rather than propose that artworks can change the world for the better if they follow certain strategies in their production, formal means and consumption, this exploration of the relationship between response, responsibility and generosity seeks to identify how our embodied and perceptual engagement with art can position us as subjects, open and responsive to encounters with people in the world who are very different to ourselves.

Engendering such an attitude, subjectively, has important ethical and political ramifications at a micro-level. I see these as being akin to the practices of 'critical responsiveness' that Stephen K. White has argued may underpin a more generous geopolitical pluralism:

> And it is the practice of such a micropolitics of critical responsiveness that is necessary to engender a pluralism more generous than one operating only with more traditional liberal understandings of tolerance and justice.[20]

It is not insignificant that feminists who have sought to explore a critical ethics of care in the field of international relations, such as Fiona Robinson, have pointed to 'responsibility and responsiveness' as *practices*—modes of subjective engagement that can be fostered, but not forced.[21] Nor is it surprising to find that feminist philosophers, exploring the possibility of an ethics of (sexual) difference, also focus on generosity, affect and imagination.[22] Practices of response-ability configure our identities through forms of imaginative empathy and generosity that connect us, bodily, with others. Or, as Moira Gatens and Genevieve Lloyd have argued:

> Our identities become determinate through processes of sympathetic and imaginative identification which respond to our present; these responses happen in a context set by our consciousness of our past, still present to us in bodily awareness. The ongoing forging of identities involves integrating past and present as we move into the indeterminate future; and the determining of identities is at the same time the constitution of new sites of responsibility.[23]

---

20 Stephen K. White, *Sustaining Affirmation: The Strength of Weak Ontology in Political Theory* (Princeton and Oxford: Oxford UP, 2000), 124.
21 Fiona Robinson, *Globalizing Care: Ethics, Feminist Theory and International Relations* (Boulder, CO and Oxford: Westview Press, 1999), 38, 39.
22 *Cf.* Diprose, op.cit. and Luce Irigaray, *An Ethics of Sexual Difference* (London: Continuum, 2004).
23 Moira Gatens & Genevieve Lloyd, *Collective Imaginings: Spinoza Past and Present* (London & New York: Routledge, 1999), 80.

The ability to respond is connected to political and ethical responsibility, and generosity emerges at the point where our kinaesthetic response compels us to answer the entreaty of another. Arguably, both *They Give Evidence* and *Reading for One Female Corpse* can be understood to have materialised this dual sense of response, such that participant–spectators, in different cultural contexts, are moved by the works and compelled to respond generously to their entreaty. The affective qualities produced by the works as *art*, enable spectators to engage with embodied others, different from themselves, through forms of kinaesthetic empathy and imaginative identification. These works have crossed worlds, eloquently articulating local, Asian experiences of loss, mourning and reclamation while, at the same time, communicating fluently with global audiences. Responding to difference by recognising others in their specificity acknowledges our permeability as embodied subjects, interdependent and interconnected with others. We are embedded in multiple forms of sociability and share multiple forms of responsibility. Cosmopolitanism is predicated on response and responsibility, as well as on corporeal generosity and the significance of imaginative identification. It is my contention that art can foster just such generous and imaginative forms of intersubjective sociability, and thus move some way toward the hopeful position of Gatens and Lloyd:

> On this view 'world citizenship' does not involve an 'idealistic', or unattainable, transcendence of embodied being, but rather an immanent, embodied and ongoing negotiation between multiple forms of sociability.[24]

---

24   Ibid., 149.

7. The Unexpected Guest: Food and Hospitality in Contemporary Asian Art

Francis Maravillas

In recent times, there has been a growing critical and curatorial interest in the conjunction of food and art. This renewed interest in the alimentary has coincided with a heightened awareness of the ethics and poetics of hospitality that underlie the cosmopolitan imaginings of home and belonging in contemporary art. This paper explores the potential of contemporary art in and from Asia to engender new ways of imagining, engaging and becoming at home in the world through distinctly alimentary practices of 'world-making' that are predicated upon acts of hospitality and dialogue within and across specific geographical locales. In particular, it considers how the recent manifestations of food in contemporary Asian art might evoke alternative and more extensively relational frameworks for understanding home and hospitality in ways that intimate new forms of cosmopolitanism and foreground the tensile connections between the aesthetic, the ethical and the political in an increasingly globalised world.

Alimentary Tracts

In her account of the alimentary economy of colonial and postcolonial South Asia and its diaspora, the literary theorist Parama Roy describes the 'alimentary tract' as a bodily passage encompassing not just the mouth but also 'skin, sinew and gut', 'olfactory organs and nerve endings', and as a corporeal disposition or 'habitus' that functions as a contact zone wherein questions of identity, difference, desire and responsibility are staged.[1] Significantly, by figuring the alimentary tract as a somatic circuit and gastro-poetic agent that incorporates as much as differentiates, she implicitly refutes the oft-repeated trope of 'eating the Other' that informs the alimentary order of colonial and postcolonial narratives.[2] For Roy, the alimentary tract is both a *boundary* and *portal* that at once feeds and confounds any neat distinction between self and other. Significantly, it does so by engendering appetites and aversions through a recurrent performance

---

1 Parama Roy, *Alimentary Tracts: Appetites, Aversions and the Postcolonial* (Durham: Duke University Press, 2010), 7.
2 See bell hooks, 'Eating the Other', *Black Looks: Race and Representation* (Boston: South End Press, 1992), 21–39.

of ethics wherein the terms of encounter with otherness are negotiated. In this context, the alimentary tract may also be viewed as an ethical terrain and fertile metaphor for the sensuous and gustatory passageways that traverse the territories of food and art, and which potentially enable responsible and imaginative forms of connection with others in the world.

The history of food in art is varied and integral, encompassing numerous embodiments of alimentary practice while inhabiting its tracts in the manner of a symbiotic parasite. One may locate these alimentary tracts within a certain arc of vanguard art, one that extends beyond the representational imagery of food (in traditional still-life tableaux, composite portraits or paintings of aristocratic feasts) towards its non-mimetic (ritualistic, metaphorical and performative) uses by experimental and contemporary artists over the past half century. The landmark survey exhibition, *Feast: Radical Hospitality in Contemporary Art* (2012), for instance, set out to chronicle the emergence of the artist-orchestrated meal, tracing its roots in the iconoclasms and provocations of the European avant-garde of the early twentieth century (through the art movements of Futurism, Dada and Surrealism), its re-emergence in the conceptual and performance-based work of the 1960s and 1970s (by artists such as Daniel Spoerri, Gordon Matta-Clark, and Suzanne Lacy) and its increasingly ubiquitous appearance in the socially engaged or relational practices of the 1990s through to the present (by artists such as Michael Rakowitz and Rirkrit Tiravanija).[3] Within such a trajectory, tropes of incorporation, digestion, aversion and purgation abound amidst the evocations of commensality and conviviality, revealing a shared investment in a utopian impulse, a desire to constantly test the limits of the body, and an antipathy towards idealist notions of art and the reified habits of modern living.[4] These conjunctions of food and art, moreover, enact a radical questioning of the pre-eminence of vision in the hierarchical ordering of the senses, while foregrounding the permeability of the boundaries between subject and object, self and other, art and everyday life.

---

3   *Feast: Radical Hospitality in Contemporary Art*, was held at the Smart Museum of Art, Chicago, from February to June 2012. It surveyed the emergence of the artist-orchestrated meal through documentary material and newly commissioned public art projects by over 30 artists and art collectives. Having billed itself as the first comprehensive survey of the history of the artist-orchestrated meal, one may question not just the selectiveness of its scope and the particularity of the trajectory that it chronicles, but also its efforts to canonise—partly via archival documentation—a diverse body of work that has its roots within the discourse of institutional critique, and which is intimately tied to the performative spaces and moments of inter-subjective encounter outside the museum. Other, less ambitious, but no less insightful, explorations of the conjuncture of food and art that extend beyond the representation of comestibles in painting can be found in the *Pot Luck: Food and Art* exhibition held at the New Art Gallery, Walsall, in 2009, and *FEAST! Food in Art* exhibition held at the Singapore Art Museum in 2000.

4   See Cecilia Novero, *Antidiets of the Avant Garde: From Futurist Cooking to Eat Art* (University of Minnesota Press, 2010).

Significantly, the revival of the alimentary in contemporary art has coincided with the globalisation of both food and art, along with a growing recognition of the confluence of epicurean concerns in the culinary and artistic world.[5] The emergence of contemporary Asian art onto the global stage has, moreover, expanded the range of alimentary practice across new sensory and semiotic terrains, as well as cultural and geographic territories. Indeed, it is more than just a passing coincidence that food has been a recurring motif in contemporary Asian art, one anchored in the popular valorisation of the alimentary as a vital ingredient of sociality and a quotidian index of identity (variously coded in cultural, gendered and religious ways) in a region deeply marked by multiple colonial and postcolonial histories, and by contemporary processes of globalisation.

The alimentary tracts that course through the art of the region are expansive and manifold. At the most basic level, food is used as a *raw material* for art-making. Here, the substance, materiality and sensory qualities of food are amplified, as in the aromatic spices and herbs in the late Thai artist Montien Boonma's installations, the edible sculptural landscapes of Chinese artist Song Dong, and the rotting apples and bananas in the installation work of his compatriot Gu Dexin. Moreover, given its prosaic association with the everyday within particular cultural contexts, it is perhaps not surprising that food is also often figured as a *trope of identity and difference*, as evinced by the symbolic use of rice as a national staple, commodity and spiritual offering in Singaporean artist Zai Kuning's installations and New York-based Malaysian artist Chee Wang Ng's photography, and by the gendered coding of Thai artist Pinaree Sanpitak's multi-flavoured, breast-shaped desserts. Other alimentary explorations of identity and difference include Singaporean artist Tang Da Wu's *Tapioca Friendship Project* (1995), comprising a series of workshops on the cassava root as a source of sustenance in Singapore during the Japanese occupation in the Second World War, and Sydney-based Singapore-born artist Simryn Gill's *Forking Tongues* (1992), which features dried red chillies and silver cutlery as indices of particular histories of passage and migration.

---

5   For an account of the globalisation of food, via its circulation as a commodity in transnational supply chains, and the rise of culinary cosmopolitanism, see David Inglis & Debra Gimlim, eds, *The Globalization of Food* (Oxford: Berg, 2009). The globalisation of the artworld—arising from the decentring of metropolitan discourses of art and the emergence of contemporary art from outside Euro-America onto the global stage—is now well-documented. See Charlotte Bydler, *Global Artworld, Inc: On the Globalization of Contemporary Art*, Figura Nova Series, no. 32 (Uppsala University Press, 2004); and, Hans Belting & Andreas Buddensieg, eds, *The Global Art World: Audiences, Markets, Museums* (Karlsruhe: Hatje Cantz, 2009). In this context, the participation of Michelin-star chef Ferran Adrià of *El Bulli* in Roger Buergel's *Documenta 12* in 2007—involving the consumption of Adrià's conceptual meals by randomly selected guests who were flown from Kassel to his restaurant in Spain (designated as the offsite Pavilion G)—is perhaps an index of the art world's recognition not just of the role of food in mediating aesthetic experience, but also of the artful innovations of avant-garde cuisine. See Roger M. Buergel & Ruth Noack, 'One Artist', in *Food for Thought, Thought for Food*, eds Richard Hamilton & Vincent Todoli (New York: Actar, 2009), 77.

The evocation of identity and difference closely intertwine with the use of food as a *site of place-making*. The Melbourne-based Thai artist Vipoo Srivilasa's community-oriented sculptural workshops that were held in Sydney and Bangkok, and Montreal-based Chinese artist Karen Tam's kitsch-like replica of a Chinese-Canadian restaurant are notable examples, tapping into transnational and diasporic vectors of connection to an imagined 'home'. On another level, food and its trappings are elevated to the status of *utopian ideals* and *metaphors of social, political and economic change*. Here, the pastoral ideals of communal living and socio-ecological sustainability, as explored in the rice paddies of The Land Foundation in Chiang Mai, Thailand, and Thai artist Sakarin Krue-On's *Terraced Rice Fields* (2007) in *Documenta 12*, along with the fantastical images of alimentary excess and decay in London-based Chinese artist Gayle Chong Kwan's *Cockaigne* (2004) series, are exemplary, as are the cooking utensils and domestic wares in the sculptural installations of Indian artist Subodh Gupta and Chinese artist Zhan Wang.

Significantly, it is the use of food as a *site and medium of sociality* geared towards interaction and participation that facilitates the enactment of artful modes of hospitality predicated upon dialogue with differently situated others in the world. Notable in this regard are Singaporean artist Amanda Heng's performance *Let's Chat* (1996) and the interactive installation of her compatriot Matthew Ngui entitled *You can order and eat delicious poh-piah* (1997), both of which involve the preparation, cooking and eating of food in participatory settings within community and gallery contexts. Here, the use of food as a performance medium orients our attention to the way the act of shared communion or commensality dramatises the already *artful* and performative qualities of the alimentary. As performance studies scholar Barbara Kirshenblatt-Gimblett has demonstrated, cooking techniques, dining rituals and culinary codes are already highly elaborated and theatrical, 'already larger than life ... already highly charged with meaning and affect.'[6] Food, like performance, is 'an *art* of the concrete ... alive, fugitive and sensory'.[7] In this way, food and its trappings may be viewed as performance art *avant la lettre*[8]—which, like performance-based works, engages the senses through their relationship to the body and to others in the world. As we shall see, it is precisely these performative, relational and sensuous processes of the alimentary that sets the table and the stage for the enactment of an artful hospitality and connectivity through generous and responsible acts of 'world-making'.

---

6   Barbara Kirshenblatt-Gimblett, 'Playing to the Senses: Food as a Performance Medium', *Performance Research* 4, no. 1 (1999): 1.
7   Ibid.
8   Ibid., 11.

Eating Pad Thai and Swikee

In the early 1990s, *pad Thai* made its celebrated appearance on the international stage of contemporary art, featuring as *le plat du jour* in the performance installations of aforementioned Thai artist Tiravanija, for which the dish was cooked and served in makeshift, semi-official exhibition spaces or architectural 'non-spaces' of various galleries.[9] His cooking performances, however, were less about food as substance and sensuous materiality (such as the amber sheen, fulsome flavour and unmistakably aromatic quality of *pad Thai*) than occasions aiming to prompt—via the forms of sociality and conviviality they conjure—reflection on a series of displacements: the displacement of the sites of art-making, of the identity of the artist and the public, and of the locations in which art is staged and encountered. Nevertheless, it is worth dwelling on the fact that *pad Thai* (or more accurately, *kway teow pad Thai* or Thai-style stir-fried rice noodles) has only come to symbolise a quintessential form of 'Thai' cooking in the West—despite its Indo-Chinese origins—largely thanks to the ongoing efforts of the Thai Government to promote the country's food to the rest of the world.[10] These official efforts to promote what is now a renowned signifier of 'Thai' cuisine in the foodscapes of global cities, belie the nationalist investments in the notion of 'Thai-ness' as a powerful solvent that not only absorbs the ethnic heterogeneity of the nation as its mythical essence, but also renders diversity as such, promoting a no-less mythical plurality.[11]

And yet, it is precisely this entangled social and ethno-culinary history of *pad Thai* that was elided or displaced in Tiravanija's work in the galleries of SoHo and elsewhere, potentially reducing the work to a readily digestible form of culinary cosmopolitanism wherein the 'exchange and communication about "good living" erases the politics of difference'.[12] Such an elision thus highlights the need to be more attentive to not just the historical embeddedness of hospitality in modes and relations of power, but also to the question of how the artful enactment of hospitable relations with others involves the translation (as opposed to the mere transfer) of the meaning, valence and sensory order of the alimentary across local and transnational contexts.[13] This process of translation entails being attuned to the specificities of taste and alimentation as much as the

---

9   Tiravanija uses the term 'non-space' to refer to the in-between space that is neither in the gallery nor in the street, but suspended between art and everyday life. See Laura Trippi, '"Untitled Artists" Projects by Janine Antoni, Ben Kinmont, Rirkrit Tiravanija', in *Eating Culture*, eds Ron Schapp & Brian Seitz (Albany: State University of New York Press, 1998), 132–60.
10 See Alexandra Greeley, 'Finding Pad Thai', *Gastronomica: The Journal of Food and Culture* 9, no. 1 (2009): 78–82.
11 David Teh, 'Hoong khao blachot maa', in *Feast: Radical Hospitality in Contemporary Art*, ed. Stephanie Smith (Smart Museum of Art, University of Chicago, 2012), 377–84.
12 Novero, *Antidiets of the Avant Garde*, 268.
13 For an account of hospitality as historically embedded in relations of power between host and guest, see Stuart Hall & David Scott, 'Hospitality's Others: A Conversation', in *The Unexpected Guest: Art, Writing and*

particular contexts in which commensality takes place. In particular, one needs to be attentive to how the question of not just *what* one eats, but also *how*, *with whom* and *where* one eats, may bear upon the relational acts of generosity and responsibility towards others in the world.

Whereas Tiravanija's performance installations thematise the site and location of art, without addressing its concrete socio-political and historical determinations, Dutch-born, Indonesian resident artist Mella Jaarsma situates her food performances in relation to the complex history of colonialism in Indonesia and the struggles over identity, culture and belonging that it has spawned so as to highlight both the differences and connectivity they engender. In particular, Jaarsma's work seeks to transform the ways in which audiences and participants view and interact with one another by encouraging them to inhabit the 'skin of the other' so as to experience the discomfort and anxiety, as well as pleasure and intimacy, of that role. Her 1998 performance, *Pribumi* (meaning 'son of the soil' or indigenous person),[14] for instance, featured stir-fried frog legs or *swikee*—a Chinese delicacy considered unclean (*haram*) by local Javanese Muslims—that were cooked and served to passers-by on the street outside the Presidential Palace in Yogyakarta as a way of engendering dialogue about race and identity with differently embodied others. Along with referencing Jaarsma's own complex diasporic relation to the Netherlands[15] (whose sobriquet is 'Kinkerland', or land of the frogs) and the entanglement of Dutch and Indonesian histories, the cooking and consumption of frog legs highlights the process of incorporating the abject and unfamiliar as a way of inhabiting the 'skin of the other' across lines of racial and religious difference. Hence, by provoking moments of discomfort and dialogue in the presence of the other, Jaarsma's performative interventions provide concrete polemical grounds for reconfiguring one's relationship to others in the world, as well as rethinking the representation of identity in local and transnational contexts inflected by relations of power and hierarchy.

Thinking on Hospitality, eds Sally Tallant & Paul Domela (London: Art Books, 2012), 291–304. For an account of the processes of transfer and translation of food in cross-cultural contexts, see John Clark, 'Food Stories', *Gastronomica: The Journal of Food and Culture* 4, no. 2 (2004): 43–50.

14   Staged in the wake of riots that took place in May 1998, during which numerous ethnic Chinese were raped and killed, the performance's title—*Pribumi*—also refers to the declarations of indigeneity in notes that ethnic Chinese placed on the doors of their homes.

15   For an account of how Jaarsma's complex diasporic position—as a Dutch artist residing in Indonesia—has informed her practice, see Michelle Antoinette, 'Deterritorializing Aesthetics: International Art and its New Cosmopolitanisms, from an Indonesian Perspective', in *Cosmopatriots: On Distant Belongings and Close Encounters*, eds Edwin Jurriëns & Jeroen de Kloet (Amsterdam: Rodopi, 2007), 217–26.

7. The Unexpected Guest: Food and Hospitality in Contemporary Asian Art

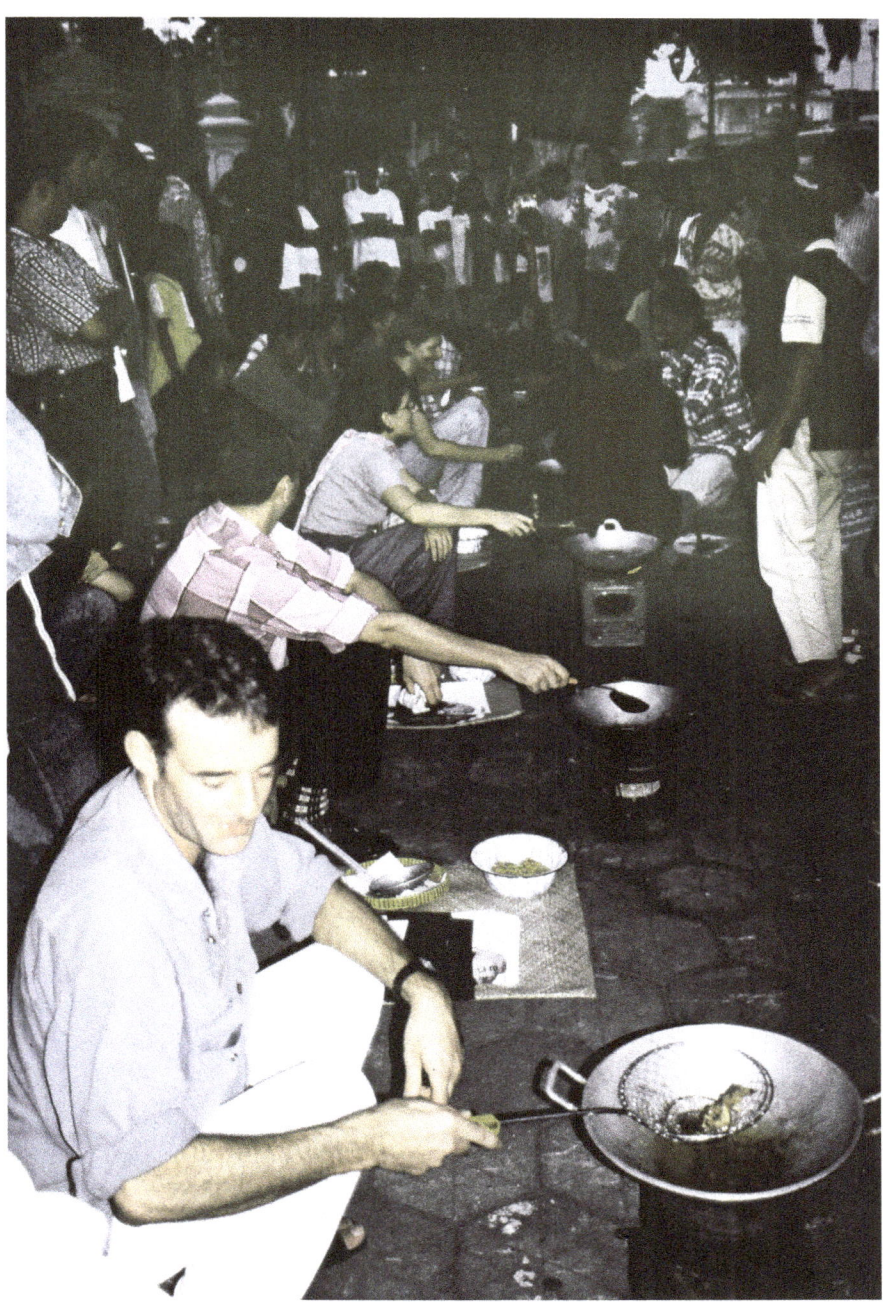

Mella Jaarsma, *Pribumi-pribumi* 3 July 1998 (performance) Malioboro Street, Yogyakarta; frying frog legs, a Chinese food, by seven Westerners, opening up a dialogue about the racial riots, 1998.

Courtesy of the artist

Significantly, the experience of inhabiting the 'skin of the other' through the exchange and ingestion of food, in Jaarsma's work, renders one's body open to the orchestration of affective intensities, that range from the affordances of vulnerability, discomfort and anxiety to those of carnality and intimacy. Her food performances thus open up a consideration of the body less as a bounded substance or essence, but as an 'interface' that is 'affected, meaning "effectuated," moved, put into motion by other entities, humans or nonhumans'.[16] The corporeal economy of affect that undergirds Jaarsma's alimentary performance of hospitality is thus not only defined by relations of difference and connectivity to others in the world, but is also shaped by 'encounters with forces and passages of intensity that bear out … folds of belonging (or non-belonging) to a world'.[17] Her performances can thus be understood as enacting a mode of hospitality that is predicated upon the making of deeply sensuous and affective worlds across often politically charged and socially conflicted contexts that are at once local and transnational.

The contrasting conditions of relationality and exchange in Tiravanija's and Jaarsma's food performances highlights some of the tensions in the debates around relational aesthetics. In his seminal text, *Relational Aesthetics* (1998), the French curator Nicolas Bourriaud sought to register a shift away from the autonomy of the art object toward notions of process and participatory agency as key to understanding not so much what art means, but what it *does*.[18] He defines relational art as those practices where 'the figures of reference of the sphere of human relations have now become fully-fledged artistic "forms"'.[19] Significantly, Bourriaud contends that relational art nurtures inter-subjective relations that are properly democratic, predicated upon 'negotiations, bonds and co-existences' that are sociable, open-ended and non-hierarchical.[20] Advocating a more critically engaged account of the politics of participatory art, the art theorist and critic Claire Bishop questions Bourriaud's implicit privileging of a harmonious or emphatic connectivity as the basis of democratic relations over artistic autonomy, antagonism and complexity.[21] By contrast, Grant Kester and other art theorists argue that ethical engagement is an integral part of collaborative art, wherein the artist must overcome his/her privileged status in order to create an equal dialogue with participants.[22] At stake in this

---

16 Bruno Latour, 'How to Talk About the Body? The Normative Dimension of Science Studies', *Body and Society* 10, no. 2–3 (June 2004): 205.
17 Gregory J. Seigworth & Melissa Gregg, 'An Inventory of Shimmers', in *The Affect Theory Reader*, eds M. Gregg & G.J. Seigworth (Durham and London, Duke University Press, 2010), 3.
18 Nicolas Bourriaud, *Relational Aesthetics*, trans. Simon Pleasance & Fronza Woods with M. Copeland (Dijon: Les presses du réel, 2002).
19 Ibid., 28.
20 Ibid., 31, 109.
21 Claire Bishop, 'Antagonism and Relational Aesthetics', *October* 110 (Fall 2004): 68.
22 Grant Kester, *Conversation Pieces: Community and Communication in Modern Art* (Berkeley & Los Angeles: University of California Press, 2004).

debate, then, are precisely the kinds of interaction, connectivity and exchange that make up the relational worlds imagined and conjured by art. Moreover, as we shall see, the artful and alimentary practices of 'world-making', borne out of relational acts of commensality and hospitality, not only turn on the question of both ethics and aesthetics; they are also—just like Tiravanija's and Jaarsma's food performances—already embedded within worlds that resonate in different ways across transnational networks of meaning and connection. Indeed, *pad Thai*, cooked and served in the backroom of a SoHo gallery, is apt to have a markedly different resonance to the same dish cooked and served on the streets of downtown Bangkok. Likewise, *swikee* cooked and served on the streets of Yogyakarta signifies differently to the same dish consumed as part of a performance enacted during the vernissage of a major international art exhibition in Brisbane.[23] In this way, both Tiravanija's and Jaarsma's food performances also open up a horizon for thinking about the meaning and intensities of the alimentary within the manifold permutations of commensality and hospitality across non-proximate locales.

Indeed, what tends to be overlooked in the debates about 'relational art' is precisely the *scalar* dimension of relational connections. How then can we gauge the ways in which such art is generative at different scales, able to produce new modalities of relationality and connectivity—that are imaginative, affective and resonant—in and through the tangle of differences between locales that may be far distant from each other? What are the frameworks for understanding the ligatures of meaning and connection in art which are at once local and transnational? In short, how do we understand art's complex and dynamic relationship with the world at and across a variety of scales?

World-making, Cosmopolitanism and Hospitality

In his account of contemporary art and the world in which it is made, the art historian and theorist Terry Smith argues that the condition of contemporaneity compels us to grapple with the question of '[h]ow might we think difference and connection at once? [and h]ow might they be conceived so as to capture the complexities of the relationships between them?'[24] Smith's concern with the complexity and dynamism of relationality and connectivity within and across difference derives from his contention that the act of 'world-making'

---

23 As part of the *Third Asia-Pacific Triennial of Contemporary Art* in Brisbane in 1999, Jaarsma enacted her *Hi Inlander* performance, which featured people wearing different cloaks made of frog's legs, chicken feet, kangaroo skins or fish skins. Meat from each animal was cooked and served to an international audience as part of the performance.
24 Terry Smith, 'World Picturing in Contemporary Art; Iconogeographic Turning', *Australian and New Zealand Journal of Art* 6, no. 2 (2005) & 7, no. 1 (2006): 27.

is constituted by the 'passages of differencing and connecting'.[25] Crucially, this claim rides on a key proposition: that contemporary art is 'essentially, definitively and distinctively *worldly*'; it is '*from* the world' and may well become '*for* the world … the world as it is now and as it might be'.[26] In this way, the worldliness of contemporary art is not only constituted by the condition of contemporaneity in which it is embedded; it also indexes alternative ways of inhabiting and remaking the world through both difference and connectivity.

Indeed, as key ingredients of the 'contemporary', the condition of worldliness and the agency of 'world-making' can, as art theorist Marsha Meskimmon astutely observes, have a significant role to play in imagining the world *otherwise*, opening up an ethico-political horizon that seeks to evoke new ways of inhabiting the world, of making worlds within the world.[27] For Meskimmon, the ethical potential of contemporary art resides in neither a predetermined teleology nor in a set of contractual relations, but rather within an imaginative and affective register 'where the future can be made anew and opened to difference'.[28] Moreover, she locates the ethical agency of art in its capacity to mobilise 'sensory forms of engagement' and tap into 'affective economies of meaning', thereby enabling the emergence of responsible encounters with others in ways that '*makes worlds*, rather than mirror them'.[29] Crucially, for Meskimmon, the ethical agency of world-making in art is engendered through a 'cosmopolitan imagination' that is premised upon 'an embodied, embedded, generous and affective form of subjectivity in conversation with others in and through difference'.[30]

It is in the context of the potential conjuncture of art, ethical agency and world-making in an open-ended cosmopolitan future that one may fully grasp the ways in which the conjugation of food and art can potentially lay the groundwork for an ethics of the alimentary oriented towards the making of worlds through the enactment of artful modes of hospitality. In an interview in *Le Monde*, Jacques Derrida evocatively suggests that hospitality is ultimately 'an art and a poetics', even if 'a whole politics depends on it and a whole ethics is determined through it'.[31] At the heart of Derrida's thinking is the paradox of absolute hospitality, wherein the imperative to offer hospitality to others unreservedly is locked in a

---

25   Ibid., 26.
26   Smith, 'Currents of World-Making in Contemporary Art', *World Art* 1, no. 2 (September 2011): 175.
27   Marsha Meskimmon, 'Making Worlds, Making Subjects: Contemporary Art and the Affective Dimension of Global Ethics', *World Art* 1, no. 2 (2011): 189–96.
28   Ibid., 191, 193.
29   Ibid., 193–94.
30   Marsha Meskimmon, *Contemporary Art and the Cosmopolitan Imagination* (London: Routledge, 2010), 6.
31   Jacques Derrida, 'Il n'y a pas de culture ni de lien social sans un principe d'hospitalité', *Le Monde*, 2 December 1997.

tensile relationship with its conditional form, thereby marking its threshold.[32] Hospitality cannot thus be defined by a horizon of expectation (as a right or duty regulated by law); rather, it remains an event that arrives unexpectedly from the future: it is a 'hospitality-to-come' (*à venir*)[33] and, as such, it must be struggled for inventively and imaginatively. In this context, the art and poetics of hospitality may be understood as one that is enacted in ways that imagine the world *anew*, opening up an ethico-political horizon that is distinctly cosmopolitan in its diverse and unforeseen encounters with others in the world.

Significantly, the question of hospitality as an artful way of relating to others, of poetically welcoming an unexpected guest (*arrivant*), is both a condition and an effect of the question of eating and the sharing of food. In an interview with Jean-Luc Nancy, Derrida undertakes to recast the theatre of hospitality by dwelling on the question of 'eating well' (*bien manger*) as communion, sharing and commensality—for 'one never eats entirely on one's own'.[34] Eating well is a matter of '*learning* and *giving* to eat, learning-to-give-to-the-other-to-eat', for 'one eats [the other] regardless and lets oneself be eaten by him'.[35] The question, then, of hospitality turns on the question of what it means to eat well, and to remain responsible to the other *with* and *on* whom one dines and *to* whom one submits to being eaten. In a similar vein, Emmanuel Levinas—to whom Derrida is deeply indebted—restages the question of the alimentary as a profoundly ethical question that lies at the very core of one's being—for 'only the subject that eats can be for-the-other'.[36] For Levinas, the act of eating forms the basis of ethics precisely because our complex alimentary relationship to the world prepares us for an acknowledgement of, and responsibility to, others in the world.[37] Within this lineage of philosophical thought, the visceral, multi-sensorial processes of alimentation, gustation and digestion appear as ethical frontiers, as sites for the negotiation of our relation to diverse others in the

---

32 For Derrida, absolute hospitality is one given by a host to a guest, whoever the guest may be, without question and with no expectation of reciprocity. To be the perfect host is to offer hospitality unconditionally and unreservedly. This idealised form of hospitality is impossible because, in practice, hospitality is conditioned or rendered conditional via a calculus of obligation and reciprocity. Absolute or pure hospitality is thus locked in a paradoxical tension with its conditional form, which is offered out of duty or by law, and involves making choices about whom to host, how much to offer or accept, and how long to allow a guest to stay. See Jacques Derrida, *Of Hospitality*, trans. Rachel Bowlby (Stanford University Press, 2000).
33 Derrida, 'Hospitality', trans. Barry Stocker with Forbes Morlock, *Angelaki: Journal of the Theoretical Humanities* 5, no. 3 (2000): 14.
34 Derrida, 'Eating Well', in *Points: Interviews 1974–1994*, ed. Elisabeth Weber and trans. Peggy Kamuf et. al (Stanford University Press, 1995), 282.
35 Ibid.
36 Emmanuel Levinas, *Otherwise than Being: Or, Beyond Essence*, trans. Alphonso Lingis (Pittsburgh: Duquesne University Press, 1998), 74.
37 According to Levinas, 'To recognise the other is to recognise a hunger. To recognise the other is to give'. Emmanuel Levinas, *Totality and Infinity: An Essay on Exteriority*, trans. Alphonso Lingis (Pittsburgh: Duquesne University Press, 1969), 75.

world through our relations with food.[38] In this way, eating with whom one has welcomed into one's home is the condition for the performative enactment of an artful hospitality, one that opens up a distinctly cosmopolitan space of encounter, signifying the deferment of definite belongings and partaking in the making of responsible worlds.

Making Alimentary Worlds

Lee Mingwei's *The Dining Project*

First presented in 1998 at the Whitney Museum of American Art, New York, as part of the solo exhibition *Way Stations*, Lee Mingwei's performance installation *The Dining Project* has since been staged around the world, including as part of the 2012 *Feast* exhibition in Chicago. In this work, Lee selects individuals by lottery to visit the museum to share a private repast with him, one at a time, after the museum has closed. He then shops for the food and prepares the menu, tailoring it to include his guest's favorite dish. Over dinner the artist engages in conversation with his guest, which is recorded by a video camera placed at table level and played back to museum visitors the next day, so they can gain a sense of what this private meal might be like should they choose to volunteer. In order to ensure the anonymity of his subjects, Lee combines the audiovisual recording of the dialogue with his guests with excerpts of conversations conducted with other people, playing the mixed recording back at a barely audible level during the museum's opening hours. At the Whitney Museum, Lee's guests included a 12-year old girl, a grandmother in her 70s, a tourist from Milwaukee, an editor of pornographic magazines, a Pakistani taxi driver who had been an art historian before coming to New York, and a bulimic who wanted to participate in the work in order to confront her illness.[39] Notably, many of Lee's dinner companions expressed bewilderment at the ease with which they were able to confide in the artist.[40]

These acts of intimate self-disclosure based on trust highlight the way conversation is an integral part of *The Dining Project*. This dialogical component is consistent with Lee's longstanding interest in communicative interaction, as

---

38 For a sustained account of Derrida and Levinas' exploration of eating as the frame of reference of ethics, see Sara Guyer, 'Buccal Reading', *CR: The New Centennial Review* 7, no. 2 (2007): 71–87 and David Goldstein, 'Emmanuel Levinas and the Ontology of Eating', *Gastronomica: The Journal of Food and Culture* 10, no. 3 (2010): 33–44.
39 Chinese Information and Cultural Centre, 'Service with a Wink at the Whitney', *CICC Currents* (New York (July/August), 1998), 2, http://web.mit.edu/allanmc/www/leemingwei3.pdf.
40 Charles Yannopoulos, 'Guess Who's Coming to Dinner?', *Scene Magazine*, 3 June 1999, http://www.clevescene.com/cleveland/guess-whos-coming-to-dinner/Content?oid=1472228.

evinced by his other 'relational' works including *The Letter Writing Project* (1998), *The Sleeping Project* (2000), *The Living Room Project* (2000) and *The Mending Project* (2009). In *The Dining Project*, the conversation occurs in the context of the presentation and eating of food, wherein the host and guest enter into a shared communion, performatively enacting hospitality through dialogue and commensality. On one level, Lee's work may be understood as exemplifying the form of practice that Kester refers to as 'dialogical aesthetics'.[41] For Kester, dialogical practices are participatory and interactive, involving conversational exchanges through situational encounters between the artist and the participant that are often performative.[42] On this basis, he argues that art needs to be viewed as a 'process of communicative exchange rather than a physical object'. And yet, while Lee's work may be viewed as sharing some of the features of 'dialogical aesthetics' through the communicative interactions it stages between the artist and the participant, the *quality* of these conversations and reciprocal exchanges hinges on the multi-sensorial, material and affective aesthetic of Lee's performance installation.

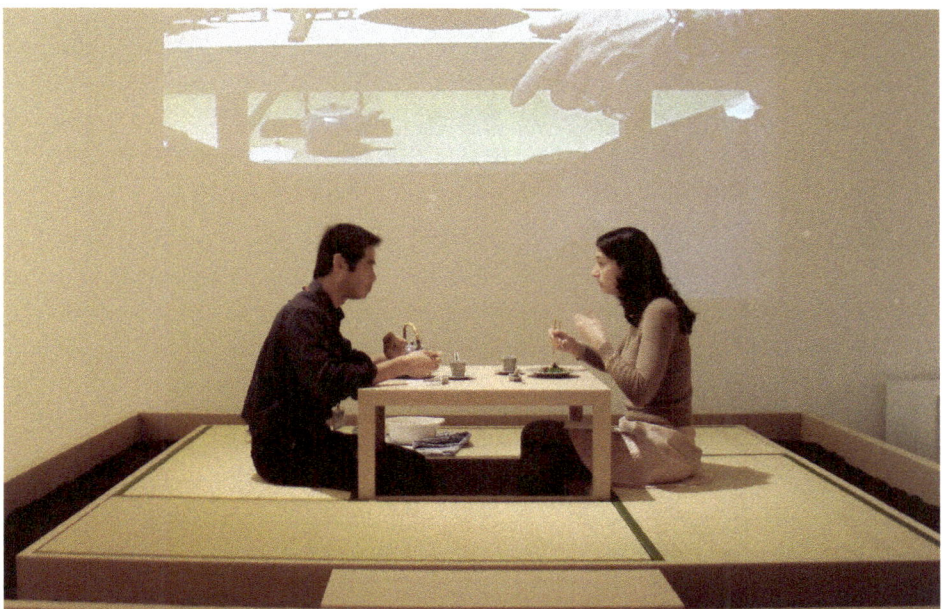

Lee Mingwei, *The Dining Project* 1997–present; installation view at Mori Art Museum, Tokyo, Japan, 2005; mixed media interactive installation; wood, tatami mats, tableware, beans, projection; 323 x 323 x 85 cm.

Courtesy of the artist and Lombard Freid Gallery, New York (commissioned by Whitney Museum of American Art, New York, 1998); photograph: Lee Studio

---

41 Kester, *Conversation Pieces*, 90.
42 Ibid.

A key component of *The Dining Project* is the minimalist design and sensuous materiality of the installation itself. Each meal is consumed on a table for two built inside a raised platform consisting of an inner rim of four *tatamis* (which exude the aroma of the rice straws that form their core), and a hollowed outer rim that is filled with black beans (seeds which signify the start of a conversation and a relationship). The simple yet multi-sensorial design of Lee's installation alludes to the spatiality and sensuality that accompanies the consumption of a meal, and is in keeping with the Zen Buddhist principle that emphasises the paramount importance of the present moment.[43] Indeed, the quiet apposition of form and substance in the performance of commensality in Lee's work is suggestive of the 'secret architecture of food'.[44] For, like the elegant minimalist platform itself, food and its exchange moves towards the theatrical, enacting a performance on the table and the stage, and thereby becoming an architecture that inhabits the body. In this way Lee's work engenders a gustatory aesthetics marked by the convergence of taste as sensory experience and taste as an aesthetic faculty. As one of his dinner guests observed:

> [Lee] had also filled the 'courtyard' with black beans, which provided a massage for our socked feet when we sat at the table. I thought the beans were a lighthearted and fanciful touch, which provided a constant sensory experience throughout the course of the meal. We are so used to the idea of hospitality through our sense of taste, but people rarely think of how hosts attend to the other senses of their guests.[45]

Significantly, for Lee, the sensuous materiality and design of the installation has a bearing on the quality of the conversation over dinner. As he puts it, 'I really could not imagine myself eating on an office table. The conversation would be so different'.[46] In Lee's work then, food and its trappings—the physical and spatial setting of the installation, the occasion and experience of sociality, the presentation of the meal and the dining ritual—engages the senses through their relationship to the body and to the various others with whom an alimentary world is shared. These sensuous, performative and relational processes of the alimentary—along with the architecture of food and commensality—enables Lee to enact an artful hospitality through communion and generosity, one that partakes in the making of shared worlds across difference.

---

43 Lee's installation also recalls the work of the Japanese filmmaker Yasujiro Ozu wherein space, void and stillness are irrevocably tied to form and movement. For an account of the way space defines and instructs form in Ozu's films, see Mark Freeman, 'Kitano's Hana-bi and the Spatial Traditions of Yasujiro Ozu', *Senses of Cinema* 7 (2000), accessed 15 December 2012, http://sensesofcinema.com/2000/7/asian-cinema/kitano-2/.
44 Jamie Horwitz & Paulette Singley, eds, *Eating Architecture* (Massachusetts: MIT Press, 2004), 5.
45 Dory Fox, 'My Dinner with Lee Mingwei', *Feast: Radical Hospitality in Contemporary Art* (2012), accessed 10 December 2012, https://blogs.uchicago.edu/feast/2012/02/my_dinner_with_lee_mingwei.html
46 Lee Mingwei, *The Dining Project*, Smart Museum of Art Chicago, accessed 10 December 2012, http://vimeo.com/36285834.

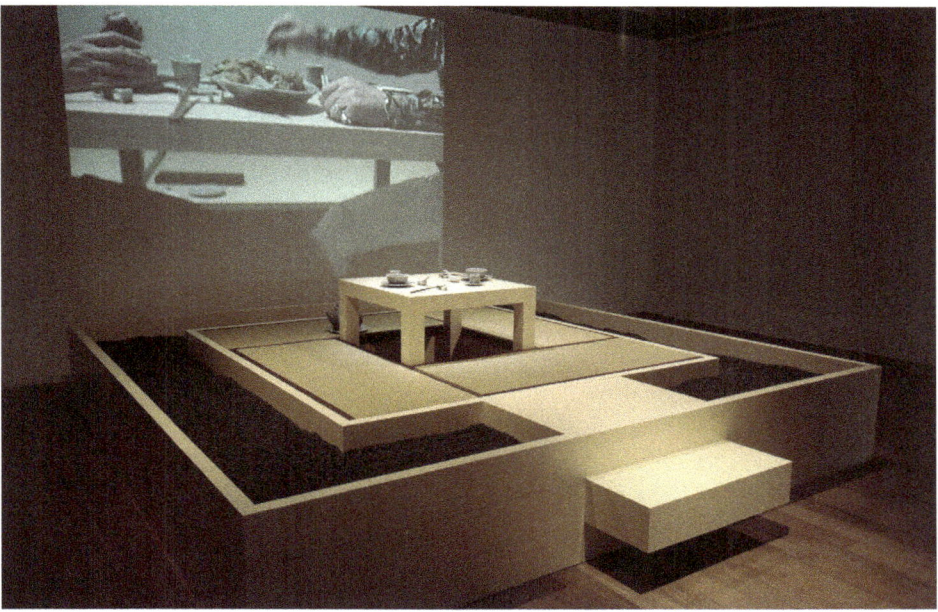

Lee Mingwei, *The Dining Project* 2007; installation view at Museum of Contemporary Art Taipei (from *The Dining Project*, 1997–present); mixed media installation; wood, tatami mats, tableware, beans, projection; 323 x 323 x 85 cm.

Courtesy of the artist and Lombard-Freid Projects, New York (commissioned by Whitney Museum of American Art, New York, 1998)

Roslisham Ismail's (a.k.a. Ise) *Langkasuka Cooking Project*

Commissioned as part of the *7th Asia-Pacific Triennial of Contemporary Art* exhibition (2012–2013) at the Queensland Art Gallery and Gallery of Modern Art (QAGOMA) in Brisbane, the Malaysian artist Roslisham Ismail's (a.k.a. Ise) *Langkasuka Cooking Project* is a collaborative and socially engaged project comprising a cookbook illustrated by the artist, a multimedia installation and a participatory cooking performance. The project was inspired by the artist's travels and interaction with communities across his home state of Kelantan, a culturally rich and politically dynamic region north-east of Malaysia that is renowned for its unique cuisine, one which is strongly influenced by neighbouring Thailand.

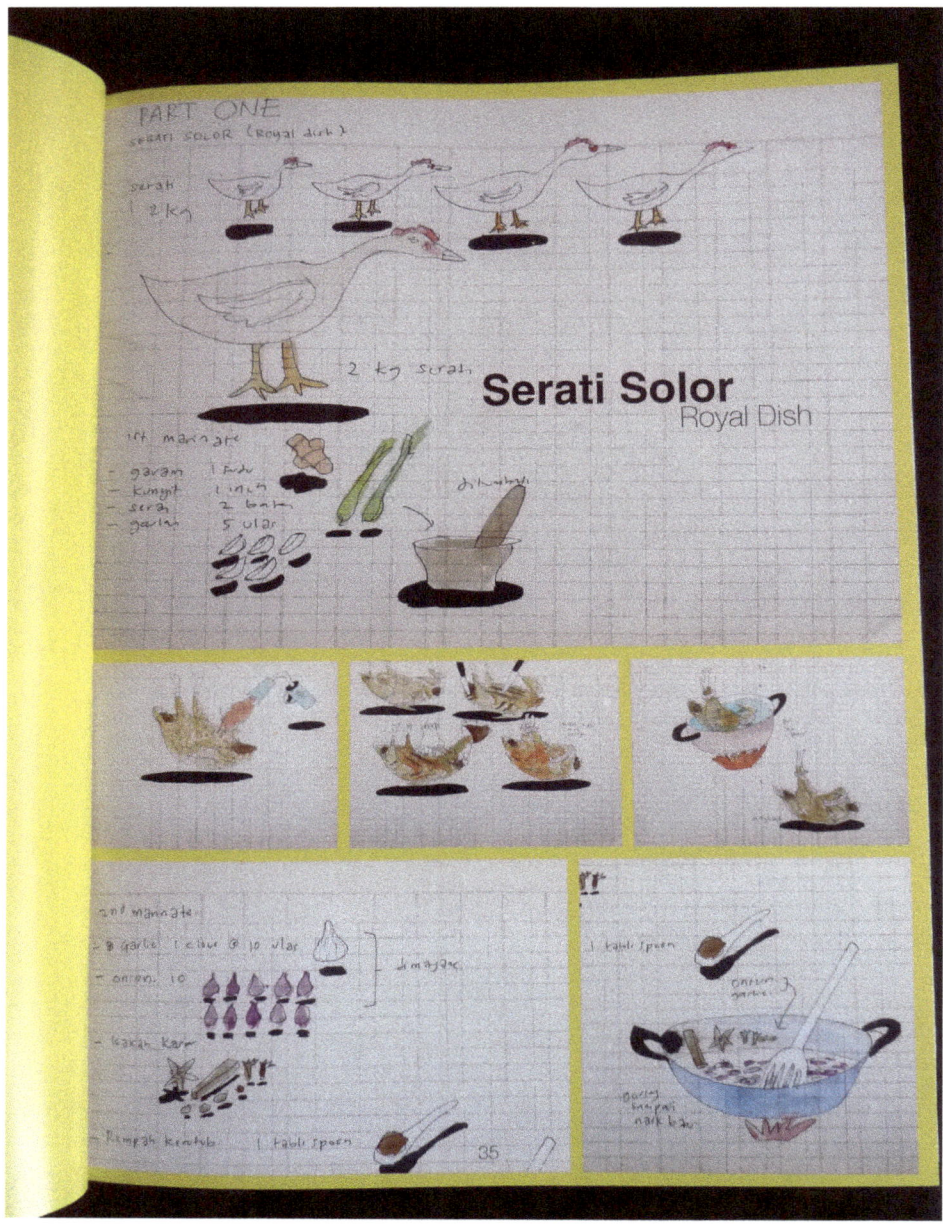

Rolisham Ismail (aka Ise), *Langkasuka Cookbook Project* 2012–2013; multi-media installation, cookbook and participatory cooking performance commissioned for the '7th Asia-Pacific Triennial of Contemporary Art', Queensland Art Gallery | Gallery of Modern Art (QAGOMA), Brisbane.

Photograph: Francis Maravillas

Produced as a limited edition publication that is also accessible online,[47] the *Langkasuka Cookbook* features vividly illustrated cooking techniques, photographs of local produce markets, stallholders and regional specialties, short essays on the history of Langkasuka as well as recipes from the region's diverse gastronomic heritage that have been drawn from the diverse communities of Kelantan with the help of various collaborators whom Ise refers to as 'superfriends'. Gleaned from Ise's observations and interactions with masterchefs and expert home cooks, including his grandmother and aunt, these recipes include simple popular offerings, such as *nasi kerabu* (blue rice with salad) and *sigang limpa* (cow spleen soup), as well as fine cuisine, such as *serati solor* (a traditional Langkasukan royal dish featuring duck or goose). As both a compendium and a cultural memoir, the significance of Ise's *Langkasuka Cookbook* stems from both its archival and performative qualities.

In his seminal essay 'An Archival Impulse', art theorist Hal Foster argues that the most notable function of archival art is to 'make historical information, often lost or displaced, physically present'.[48] Significantly, for Foster, the archival impulse in art is not only documentary but also generative in ways that underscore the nature of all archival materials as 'found yet constructed, factual and fictive, public yet private'.[49] As a repository of embodied memories, Ise's *Langkasuka Cookbook* stands as a physical document that records a particular version of the taste, textures, smells and flavors of both rare and popular dishes that comprise the region's shared gustatory legacy. As such, the *Langkasuka Cookbook* is not just a didactic or practical culinary guide; rather, it functions as a sensory archive whose epistemological value stems from its evocation of personal, cultural and historical memories—of places lived, foods eaten, worlds shared and identities formed—through textual and visual devices. In this way, it articulates what cultural anthropologist Jon Holtzman calls a form of 'gustatory nostalgia', whereby the region's diverse food and culinary practice 'offers a potential window into forms of memory that are more heteroglossic, ambivalent, layered and textured'.[50] Such a nostalgia conveys less a desire to return to a lost home through the memories encoded in food; rather, the sensuous presentation of the region's traditional food is used to connect the past with the present so as to 'go deeper into the layers of who people are'.[51]

---

47 https://www.qagoma.qld.gov.au/exhibitions/past/2012/apt7_asia_pacific_triennial_of_contemporary_art/artists/roslisham_ismail_ise
48 Hal Foster, 'An Archival Impulse', *October* 110 (Fall 2004): 4.
49 Ibid., 5.
50 Jon D. Holtzman, 'Food and Memory', *Annual Review of Anthropology* 35 (2006): 361–78.
51 Roslisham Ismail (Ise), 'An Interview', *The 7th Asia-Pacific Triennial of Contemporary Art*, exhibition catalogue (Brisbane: Queensland Art Gallery | Gallery of Modern Art, 2012).

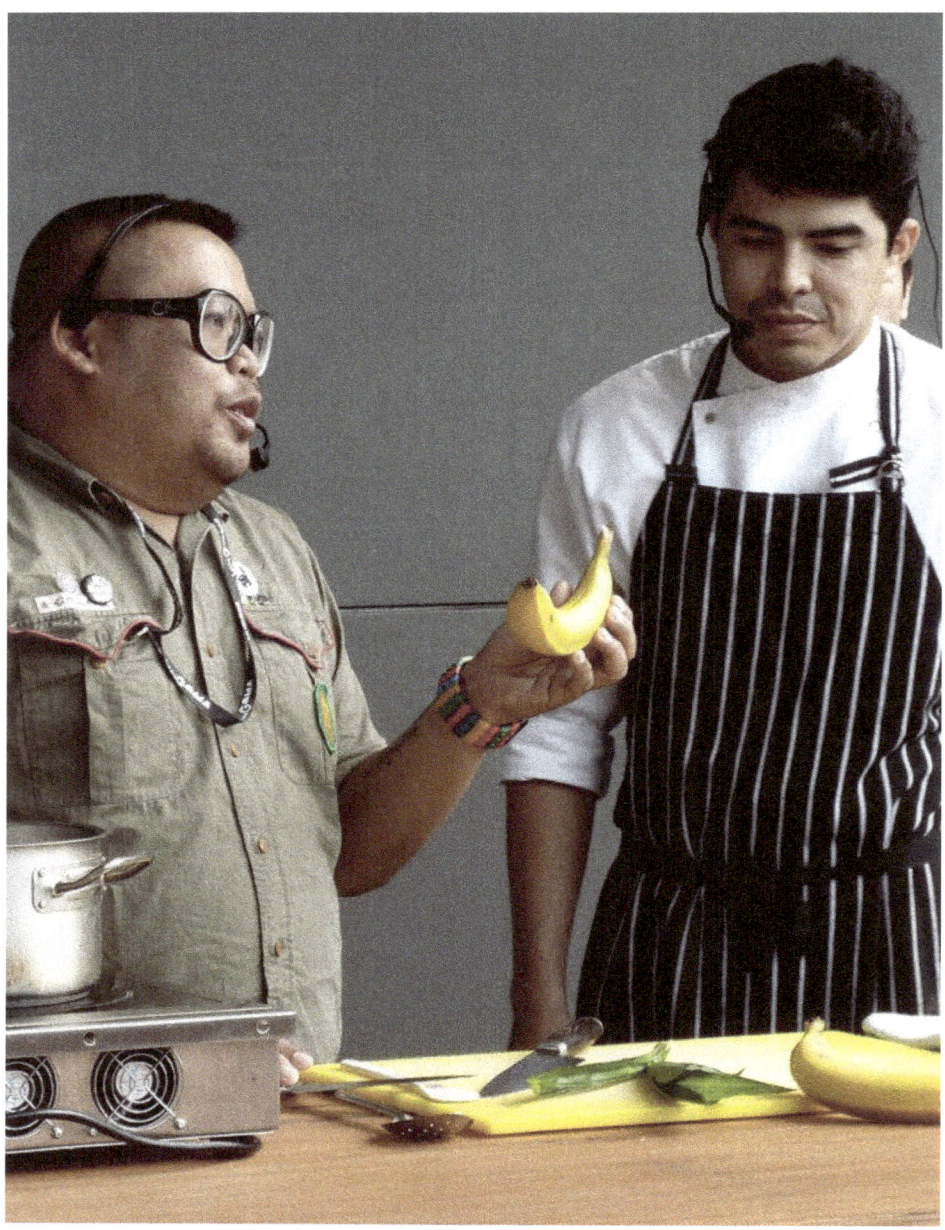

Rolisham Ismail (aka Ise), *Langkasuka Cookbook Project*, 2012–2013; multi-media installation, cookbook and participatory cooking performance commissioned for the '7th Asia-Pacific Triennial of Contemporary Art', Queensland Art Gallery | Gallery of Modern Art (QAGOMA), Brisbane.

Photograph: Francis Maravillas

At the same time, the *Langkasuka Cookbook* may also be understood as exhibiting a performative quality through Ise's simple yet vivid illustrations of the cooking techniques that accompany each recipe. These graphic, comic-like illustrations impart a fictive and actively rhetorical quality that eschews the representational rules of classical mimesis and destabilises the boundaries of art and everyday life, presenting the making and eating of food as an effect of a desire to reconnect with memories of 'home' by creatively re-encoding it in the present. The performative quality of these illustrations is thus reflected in its active and dynamic process of archive-making, one that unsettles the stability of memories encoded within the food documented by the cookbook, while affirming the gaps and openings of the physical document as it enters into circulation and use in a contemporary transnational context. Indeed, while cookbooks provide signposts for cultural reproduction, they cannot contain the embodied practice and experience of what Luce Giard calls 'doing-cooking',[52] whereby the body, memory and the senses work to link past and present, here and elsewhere. The *Langkasuka Cookbook*'s performativity, therefore, also stems from the actual, 'hands-on' preparation, making and consumption of the food it records, which takes places in the public cooking demonstrations performed by Ise as a key component of the project. At QAGOMA, Ise worked alongside staff from GOMA's café, either in the kitchen or outside the gallery, during the Triennial's vernissage, to make, serve and tell stories about *sira pisang* (sweet glazed bananas with pandan leaves), one of Ise's favourite childhood dishes. While the making of the dish reproduces the taste and textures of 'home', Ise's public demonstrations enact a form of hospitality through the sharing and cultural transmission of embodied memories, thereby engendering a form of sensuous and sensory connectivity with others in the world.

The Ethics and Aesthetics of the Alimentary

Across these diverse conjunctions of the alimentary and artistic realms, food and its trappings appear as variously sensuous, affective and semiotically charged in ways that confound the boundaries of art's territory, thereby acting as portals for ethico-political engagement with the wider world. In this context, an ethics of the alimentary demands an expanded notion of the senses that encompasses the affective structures of pleasure, intimacy and sociality as much as those of anxiety, discomfort and disdain. As Roy has observed, the grammar of an 'alimentary ethics' orients our attention to the sensuous appetites and aversions

---

52 Luce Giard, 'Doing Cooking', in *The Practice of Everyday Life*, vol. 2. *Cooking and Living*, ed. Michel de Certeau, Luce Giard & Pierre Mayol (Minneapolis: University of Minnesota Press, 1998). See also Simon Choo, 'Eating *Satay Babi*: Sensory Perception of Transnational Movement', *Journal of Intercultural Studies* 25, no. 3 (2004): 210.

that precede and set the terms for encounters with otherness.[53] It is an ethics that is predicated on economies of hospitality that confound the boundaries between self and other. It is one, moreover, that is attuned to the 'complex moral structure of embodiment' and is grounded in a somatic engagement with others that is both sensuous and affective.[54] Significantly, as an affective pedagogy of encounters with others in the world that 'disturbs, opens up and rearranges parts of ourselves',[55] the ethics of the alimentary is a key locus for the 'precarious' making and remaking of the world in and through art.[56] The ethical world-making agency of art is thus defined by the horizon of what Jill Bennett refers to as a 'practical aesthetics', one that 'apprehend[s] the world via sense-based and affective processes—processes that touch bodies intimately and directly but that also underpin the emotions, sentiments and passions of public life'.[57] In this context, the sensuous, performative and relational process of the alimentary in contemporary Asian art may be understood as a precondition for the enactment of an artful hospitality through acts of generosity and responsibility that partake in the making of affective and sensuous worlds across difference in a region shaped by the legacy of multiple and overlapping (post-)colonial histories.

---

53 Roy, *Alimentary Tracts*, 29.
54 Ibid.
55 Elspeth Probyn, *Carnal Appetites: Food Sex Identities* (New York: Routledge 2000), 70.
56 Marsha Meskimmon, 'The Precarious Ecologies of Cosmopolitanism', *Humanities Research* XIX, no. 2 (2013): 39.
57 Jill Bennett, *Practical Aesthetics: Events, Affects and Art after 9/11* (London: I.B Tauris 2012), 3.

8. Under the Shadow: Problems in Museum Development in Asia

Oscar Ho

Introduction

In May 2012 the office of Museum Plus (M+), the art space to be opened in 2017 at Hong Kong's West Kowloon Cultural District (WKCD), held their inaugural exhibition of contemporary art entitled *Mobile M+: Yau Ma Tei*. The multi-sited exhibition was presented across various sites in the working-class neighbourhood of Yau Ma Tei at West Kowloon. Local artists were commissioned to create installations and video art on the streets with the intention of bringing art closer to the people. Lee Chun Fung, artist and director of the nearby artists' space Wufarten[1] went to the *Mobile M+* opening ceremony in a small local park. Wearing the typical neighbourhood attire of shabby singlet, shorts and slippers, he was, however, refused entry by event security for being improperly dressed for the event.

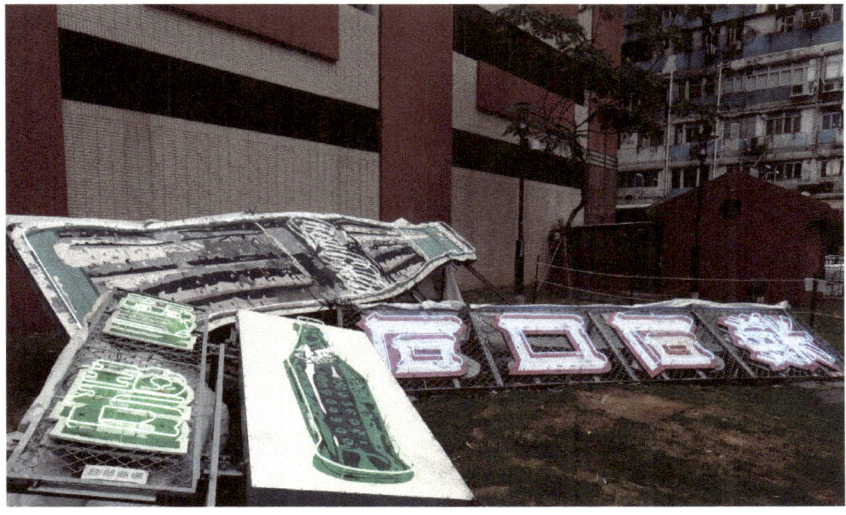

Leung Mee-ping, *I Miss Fanta* at *Mobile M+: Yau Ma Tei* 2012.

Courtesy of M+, West Kowloon Cultural District

---

1   Recently closed, Wufarten was a community-focused nonprofit art organisation and space, funded by the Hong Kong Art Development Council. See http://woofer10.blogspot.hk/.

Suddenly Cultured

Lured by the economic possibilities of the new 'cultural industries', and the desire to build national/regional pride through cultural expression, the last decade has seen Asia engage in unprecedented investment in arts and culture. New cultural venues and museums are popping up throughout Asia faster than the spread of the Starbucks global coffee chain. The rapid establishment of ambitious cultural projects has resulted in the region becoming 'suddenly cultured', and this has made clear some of the problems that have long existed within Asia's cultural infrastructure. With reference to the different objectives and outcomes of independent curatorial practices in Asia, this essay compares the original and ambitious mission for the government-supported M+ project at WKCD against the reality of the project's implementation. The essay explores the difficulties and hindrances in museum development in Asia which, I will argue, suffers internally from infrastructural weakness and externally from Western-dominated thinking.

Asia's fast-growing cultural projects are often ambitious attempts to turn a city into a 'cultural hub' and build regional or national pride through grand displays of rich local or regional cultures. During the implementation of these projects, however, there is heavy reliance on Western 'experts', who play dominant roles in shaping the content and format of the projects.

Making reference to independent curatorial projects presented at the inaugural forum of the Asian Curatorial Network (ACN), which was held in 2011 in Hong Kong,[2] and examining the process of planning and building M+, the essay argues that underdeveloped infrastructure, conservative administrative cultures, prolongation of the colonial mindset, and Western cultural domination arising from the continuing imbalance of power and influence of curatorial practices that are led by Western thinking, continue to influence cultural development in Asia and hinder the region's ability to build a unique, locally driven language of cultural practice. It argues the necessity for curatorial practices underscored by respectful sensitivity toward the local that support efforts to seek alternative modes of operation, and that evince open-minded approaches which are attentive to local, Hong Kong cultural contexts and needs.

---

2   The inaugural ACN forum, *Curatorial Critique: An Asian Context*, was funded by the Asian Cultural Council and held at the Hong Kong Academy for Performing Arts on 24 May 2011 (organised by the Chinese University of Hong Kong's Department of Cultural and Religious Studies in association with the University of Hong Kong's Centre for Culture and Development). The event showcased curatorial practices from the perspective of independent art spaces and curators. Principal speakers at the forum included Mizuki Endo (Japan), Ringo Bunoan (Philippines), Erin Gleeson (Cambodia), Yao Jui-Chung (Taiwan), Agung Hujatnikajennong (Indonesia) and Siu King Chung (Hong Kong), with Oscar Ho as moderator and David Elliott as commentator.

History: Real Estate Project in Disguise

In 2004 the Hong Kong Government announced its grand plan to build the WKCD on 40 acres of reclaimed land in the western part of Kowloon. The development plan proposed three theatres, four museums (ink, contemporary art, design and moving image), and business, hotel and residential developments. The entire district, including the cultural institutions, would be designed, built and administered by a single real estate developer—the UK architectural firm Foster + Partners, headed by the internationally famous British architect Norman Foster.

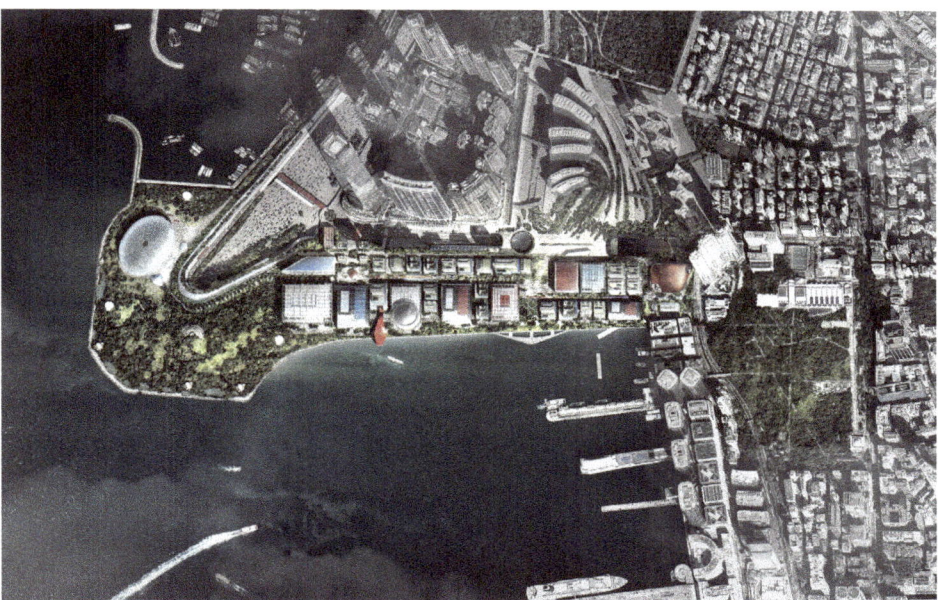

Proposed plan of the future West Kowloon Cultural District.

Courtesy of West Kowloon Cultural District Authority

Like many cultural projects in Asia (China in particular), cultural districts are frequently real estate developments in disguise. In a paper submitted to the Legislative Council in 2006, the Hong Kong Alternatives, an advocacy group of architects, solicitors and other professionals, asserted that 'WKCD is not for Sale! Not for commercial property development!'[3] As evidence of the real purpose

---

3   Hong Kong Alternatives, 'An Appeal to Develop WKCD as West Kowloon Cultural Green Park as a Legacy for Hong Kong' (2006), accessed 11 April 2014, http://www.hkalternatives.com/Eng/downloads/Position_Papers/LEGCO-2006-0918-HKA-Position-Paper-Eng.pdf.

of the development, social activist Chu Hoi Dick collected news clippings recording the enthusiastic responses of developers to the commercial potential of the project, which was clearly their sole interest.[4]

A survey conducted by the University of Hong Kong in 2005 revealed that over 60 per cent of interviewees felt that allocating 60 per cent of the district for residential and commercial use was too high, and 85 per cent opposed the proposal to only allow real estate developers to bid on the land.[5]

The proposal was also criticised by the arts and professional communities as hypocritical, lacking interest in professional considerations, and deficient in its vision, as well as for not being open to smaller real estate developers that lacked the finances to participate in such a grand project. In the face of this public outcry, the government withdrew the original proposal and invited professionals and representatives from the community to rework the plan.

A revised plan was presented in 2009 and officially approved in 2011. With a budget of HK$21.6 billion (US$2.8 billion), the new plan proposed the building of 14 theatres/music halls, one exhibition centre and the M+ art space.

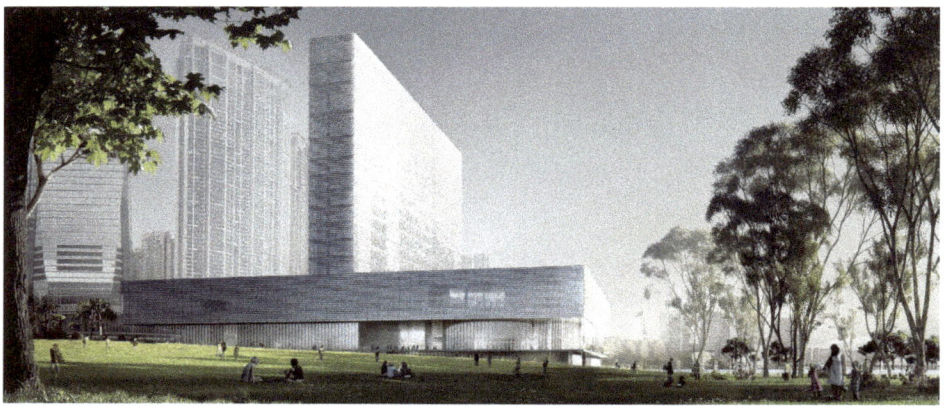

View of M+ from the Park at WKCD—next to a tree-lined avenue along the waterfront [Proposal].

Courtesy of Herzog & de Meuron and West Kowloon Cultural District Authority

---

4 Chu Hoi Dick, '西九文化區報摘之果然係地產項目' ('West Kowloon is in Fact a Real Estate Development'), *Independent Media*, 15 September 2007, http://www.inmediahk.net/node/257529.
5 Robert Ting-Yiu Chung, Karie Ka-Lai Pang & Kitty Suet-Lai Chan, 'Planning for West Kowloon and the Harbour Front Opinion Survey: Summary of Findings', The University of Hong Kong Public Opinion Program (University of Hong Kong, 21 January 2006), 14–16, accessed 1 April 2014, http://www.harbourdistrict.com.hk/enews/20060123/Summary_of_Survey_Findings.pdf.

Occupying 60,000 square metres with a budget of HK$4.7 billion (US$600 million), M+ is an unprecedented undertaking for Hong Kong. More significant is that, in its original plan, M+ sought to introduce a new mode of 'museum' curation and presentation informed by a wider field of interdisciplinary visual culture practice, reflective of not just local Hong Kong cultural experience, but also new thinking about museums.

Before discussing the curatorial directions of M+, I would like to shift the discussion to the 2011 inaugural forum of the Asian Curatorial Network (ACN), referred to earlier. The forum focused on curatorial approaches employed by independent Asia-based curators. The presentations revealed interesting curatorial adaptations of and reactions to the particular cultural ecologies of Asia that, in many ways, resonated with the initial guiding principles in the planning of M+.

Supply and control of resources shapes and dictates curatorial approaches and modes of operation. In Asia, where there is substantial government involvement in the arts, but no strong philanthropic tradition supporting creative endeavours, the government holds substantial control over resource allocation for cultural development. Curators working outside the official establishment survive with extremely limited resources. This situation often gives rise to small-scale alternative spaces that seek autonomy from government-defined cultural programs. Such spaces have become important forces in shaping the region's cultural development.

At the ACN forum, the Filipino artist/curator Ringo Bunoan used Shop 6, an artist-run space created in 1974 by Filipino conceptual artist Roberto Chabet, as an example of an attempt to address the problem of 'lack of alternative spaces and support for alternative art'. Bunoan demonstrated the influence of alternative spaces and the continuous dynamic they generate in the Philippines art scene. Similarly in Indonesia, the absence of state-run spaces for the exhibition of alternative art has led to the establishment of an array of independent artist spaces, such as the Cemeti Art House in Yogyakarta.

These independent, humble spaces are usually located in urban, frequently working-class, neighbourhoods where they often interact with and respond to their local community.[6] A typical example of this kind of engagement in Hong Kong is the recently closed artist space Wufarten at Yau Ma Tei, mentioned at the outset of this essay, which focused on the presentation of art and crafts that were made by people living within its surrounding working-class neighbourhood. The Wufarten art space aimed to 'introduce a lively conception of contemporary art engaging the community'. As their blog explains in describing their mission,

---

6   There are always exceptions, such as Hong Kong's Para Site, which although an independent art space, focuses on contemporary Hong Kong and international artists rather than its immediate local community.

'instead of attempting an out-of-place, arty white-cube gallery, Woofer Ten [Wufarten] mold[ed] itself more like a community center, a platform for art projects to explore new approaches in bridging the community and art making'.[7]

According to Indonesian curator Agung Hujatnikajennong, small independent art spaces are beginning to proliferate across Indonesia, operating like urban 'guerrilla' headquarters with 'guerilla' art tactics; they are capable of a flexible, mobile, and adaptable integration of art into the community.

Although alternative spaces offer room for creative practice outside the official sphere, they are not usually equipped to provide staff with professional development opportunities to increase their skills and operational knowledge. Given such spaces often rely on limited resources, temporary infrastructure and provisional funding, they are often disestablished as quickly as they are founded.

As I earlier mentioned, the phenomenon of Asia becoming 'suddenly cultured' describes the region's rushed response to capitalise on the new cultural industries: imperfectly developed art communities leap into staging a host of grand cultural spectacles. The proposal for M+ resulted in suspicion of the government's motives, but also its ability to accomplish such a large-scale project given the lack of bureaucractic flexibility, open-mindedness, and understanding of contemporary art and museum practices. Unease over such unprecedented ambition led some community groups to lobby that the plan be abandoned and a huge park be developed instead.[8]

For an art community suffering from decades of indifference and poverty, however, the sudden investment in art seemed worth pursuing, even at the risk of the project becoming a proverbial white elephant.

The Rich and the Poor

The WKCD is located on a prime piece of land adjacent to the famous Victoria Harbour. Its location is so outstanding that the developer community believed 'If one gets WKCD, one gets the world'. Situated next to one of the most expensive residential districts of Kowloon, with its beautiful harbour view, the value of this piece of land had already increased by its proximity to wealth—all the cultural facilities of WKCD, as some argued, would surely become the front yards or recreation clubs of the rich.[9]

---

7   http://woofer10.blogspot.hk/.
8   Hong Kong Alternatives, 'An Appeal'.
9   Oscar Ho, 'One Road, Two Very Different Worlds: The Poor and the Rich of West Kowloon', first published in Chinese in *Ming Pao*, 4 December 2012, http://www.aicahk.org/chi/reviews.asp?id=213.

Separated by a series of carefully designed roads, on the other side of the luxury apartments of Kowloon, is the Yau Ma Tei district, one of the poorest districts of Hong Kong with a population of aged and ethnic Asian minorities. It is a colourful and culturally diverse neighbourhood where grassroots folk cultures survive precisely because of the absence of opportunities for property development.

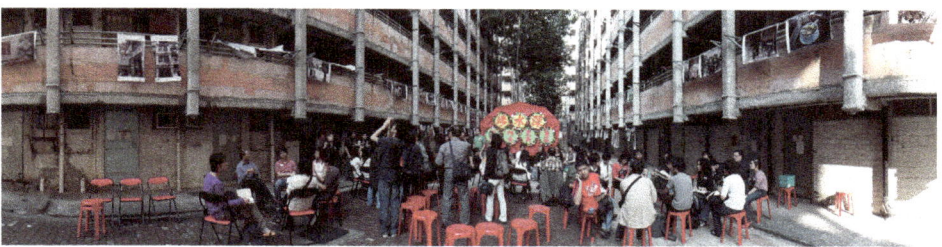

'In Search of Marginalized Wisdom' exhibition seminar, Community Museum Project, Hong Kong, March 2007.

Image courtesy Siu King Chung

For Hong Kong curator Siu King Chung, the streets of the old district are culturally rich in that they provide unlimited sources of curatorial inspiration. Siu King Chung and his friends have collaborated in organising the Community Museum Project art initiative that does not require a permanent venue; they like to see 'the street as a museum'.[10] A small, flexible space—or even the absence of space—runs contrary to the new obsession with grand, brand name architecture that is presently favoured by Asian governments. For Siu King Chung and his colleagues, who are charmed by the artistic genius of street culture on the poor side of West Kowloon, the streets are the site and boundless source of inspiration and artworks for their 'museum'. Many of their exhibitions focus on the generally overlooked work created by craftspeople[11] of the neighbourhood, with the intention of pushing for recognition of their artistic value.

---

10   Siu King Chung, 'Social Curating in Hong Kong', presentation to the ACN Forum *Curatorial Critique: An Asian Context*, Hong Kong, 24 May 2011. See also the 'Community Museum Project' website, the independent art initiative with which Siu King Chung is affiliated, http://www.hkcmp.org/cmp/c_001.html: 'Community Museum Project was founded in 2002 in Hong Kong by Howard Chan (art curator), Siu King Chung (design educator), Tse Pak-chai and Phoebe Wong (cultural researchers)'.
11   Some of their exhibits are new designs that have been jointly created by craftspeople and designers.

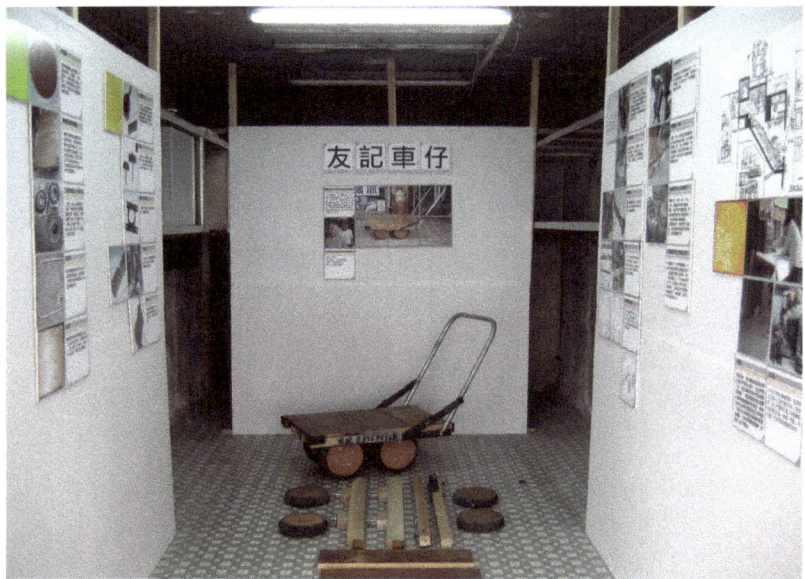

'In Search of Marginalized Wisdom' exhibition, Community Museum Project, Hong Kong, March 2007; wooden cart, crafts.

Image courtesy Siu King Chung

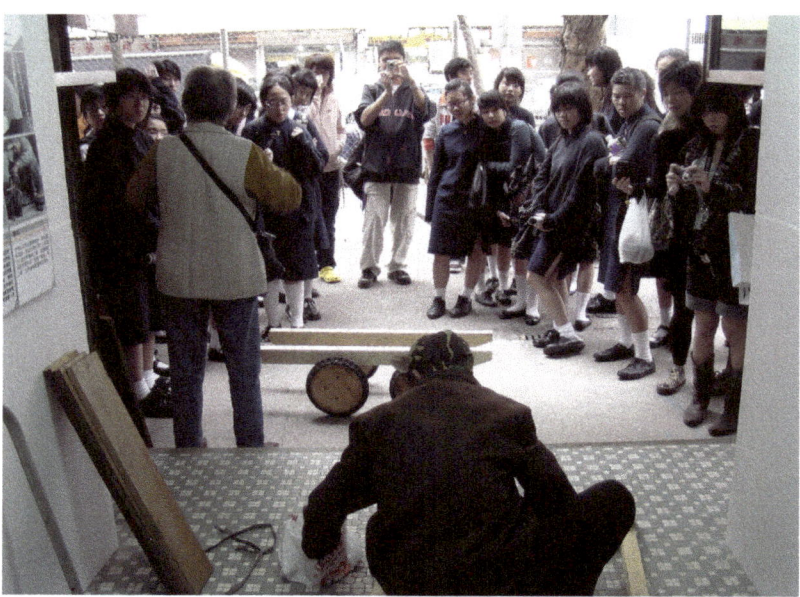

'In Search of Marginalized Wisdom' exhibition, Community Museum Project, Hong Kong, March 2007, wooden cart, crafts demonstration.

Image courtesy Siu King Chung

Local Alternative

With the intention of going beyond conventional modes of thinking about museums, M+ means 'more than a museum'. In avoiding use of the term 'museum' as part of its nomenclature, M+ seeks to address the inadequacy of museums in meeting the cultural needs of ordinary people and seeks to establish alternative languages of cultural presentation, with an orientation toward the local, not just in terms of collection, but also in terms of curatorial perspectives.

As part of its mission, M+ rejects the terms 'modern' and 'contemporary', as these concepts are yet to be, or perhaps do not even need to be, defined within the context of Hong Kong/Asia. Instead, M+ sets its mandates based on the timeframe of the twentieth and twenty-first centuries. The mission also states that M+ needs to adopt a 'Hong Kong perspective' (to be defined by the curators) with an emphasis on 'now'.[12] This mandate registers the importance of perspectives that are sensitive to and meaningful within the local Hong Kong context, and also emphasises the contemporaneity of M+'s collecting and interpretation practices.

Another outstanding feature of M+ is its expansion of the curatorial scope from fine arts to visual cultures. This broadening of definition not only recognises the increased blurring of boundaries in art, but also the strength and uniqueness of Hong Kong culture, which lies not in the narrowly defined concept of 'fine arts' but in a wider context of popular and everyday cultures. In so doing, an expanded definition of 'artistic values' is necessitated.

Hong Kong does not lack rich cultural traditions or an interested audience. The greatest obstacles to a vibrant artistic culture arise from a definition of art that is so narrow and distanced from the public that art has lost its ability to echo and respond to the cultural experience of the local community. In his community museum projects, Siu King Chung and his team discover 'a lot of interesting things from the street, such as the self-made advertisement from the plumber, the funny tools the street carpenters created to build things with'. They proudly declare that 'we do have this kind of indigenous creativity in our culture which has not been made into something prominent in our [local, Hong Kong] culture'.[13] There is a need to remap and redefine Hong Kong art and culture to uncover this cultural richness and give it the recognition it deserves. Hong Kong's rich cultural tradition is not recognised because the definition of arts and culture is often made by someone else from a distance. The local arts community expected that M+ would help deal with such ignorance.

---

12 West Kowloon Cultural District, 'M+: About M+ Museum for Visual Culture', http://www.westkowloon.hk/en/mplus/about-m.
13 Siu King Chung, 2011.

At the ACN forum, Japanese curator Mizuki Endo presented his curated exhibition of photographs tracing the history of the mass suicides of the Okinawa people following the American seizure of the island at the end of the Second World War. This tragic incident, frequently interpreted as a patriotic act of defiance against the Americans was, as Endo argued, in fact orchestrated by the Japanese army. He claimed that the exhibition was not about 'being artistic',[14] but was a process designed to arouse historical contemplation. Similarly, Cambodia-based curator Erin Gleeson's curation of work by survivors of the Khmer Rouge was also undertaken as an act of dealing with local history.[15] For both curators, artistic qualities are linked to socio-historical concerns that are generated by a specific time and context meaningful to their particular local community. In other words, these curators have found works of artistic value through a process of recognising the cultural significance of art to local communities.

Inadequate Infrastructure

Initially the WKCD charmed the arts community with its promise to operate independent of government infrastructure, which was an outstanding breakthrough in changing the mode of governance for major cultural projects. In early 2011 the M+ Advisory Group was dissolved and replaced by a museum committee under the newly established 'WKCD Authority'. The Home Affairs Bureau, the department in charge of general community affairs including recreation, culture and waste management, was assigned to support the implementation work. Following a practice adopted since colonial days, the government transferred the administration officer originally assigned to the project to another department after three years of service. Just when this officer had acquired the requisite knowledge and sensibility toward arts and cultural development, they were reassigned. Subsequently an officer from an area unfamiliar with arts and culture moved in to the leading position to work with a few members of the former group who were appointed to serve on a new museum committee.[16] The operation of M+ thus remains within a mechanism dictated by the changing terms of bureaucracies and without guarantee of sufficient and ongoing arts and culture professional expertise.

---

14 Mizuki Endo, presentation to the ACN Forum *Curatorial Critique: An Asian Context*, Hong Kong, 24 May 2011.
15 Erin Gleeson, 'Curatorial Landscape in Cambodia', presentation to the ACN Forum *Curatorial Critique: An Asian Context*, Hong Kong, 24 May 2011.
16 In 2010, when the committee hired a consultant to undertake research for M+, a member of the disbanded advisory group was recruited to explain the concept of M+ to the consultant. This demonstrated the lack of corporate knowledge passed from one administration group to the next: the newly formed administration lacked the corporate knowledge to provide such an explanation to the consultant.

The search for 'software' for M+ revealed the inadequacy of the existing infrastructure. Because civil servants run all major museums, the government apparatus plays a significant role in shaping the 'culture for conducting cultural development'. The culture of the civil service promotes rules and order, values collective decision-making, does not tolerate ambiguity and opposes risk-taking. Such a bureaucratic operational model is in fundamental opposition to artistic/creative projects, which demand experimentation, risk-taking and personal endeavour.

Another characteristic of the civil service is its 'incestuous' nature. Promotion to senior positions is an in-house practice based on seniority and length of service within the hierarchy, rather than on the knowledge or professional expertise of the individual. The exclusivity of the system offers little opportunity for anyone outside the civil service to enter public museum administration. As I mentioned earlier, independent arts organisations are, on the other hand, often unable to provide professional development training and, consequently, often struggle to nurture professionals who are capable of working at larger cultural institutions.

Conceptually, M+ is too unconventional for Hong Kong's current civil servant culture, too complex for the decision-makers unfamiliar with arts and culture, and too big for the existing cultural framework. The import of overseas support is, thus, an inevitable consequence.

Despite efforts to build an institution that reflects local cultural experiences, and to establish a language to articulate local Hong Kong culture, the cracks in the existing infrastructure, the imbalance of power between the bureaucracy and non-government cultural workers and, most significantly, the continuing prevalance of the colonial mindset, make it difficult to shape and establish the distinctive vision for M+.

Colonial Legacy

When the Hong Kong Government first presented the WKCD proposal in 2006, the inclusion of a canopy designed by Foster was a mandatory requirement in any proposal submitted. The insistence on adopting Foster's design was only abandoned after architects, engineers and cultural professionals criticised the cost and difficulties in maintaining the proposed massive canopy that would cover the 40-hectare site.[17]

---

17   Polly Hu, 'Cost May Scupper Canopy for Culture Hub', *South China Morning Post*, 28 April 2004, accessed 1 April 2014, http://www.scmp.com/article/453803/cost-may-scupper-canopy-culture-hub.

However, the desire to have Foster involved in the project persisted. After the new proposal was submitted, an open competition was held inviting proposals for an overall design of WKCD. Three finalists were selected: one local (from Hong Kong) and the others from the United Kingdom and Sweden.[18] There was no surprise in 2010 when Foster's architectural firm was announced as the final choice. Foster's landmark buildings are situated all over Hong Kong and the city can be considered as his private showroom: in addition to the HSBC headquarters there are major public buildings including Hung Hom train station, Chek Lap Kok International Airport, the recently built Kai Tak Cruise Terminal, and the upcoming WKCD which are all projects led by Foster. As the chosen architects for M+, Foster + Partners, together with the appointment of the firm Herzog & de Meuron (architects of the Tate Modern, London), proves that, culturally, the British colonial legacy lives on. Years after unification with China, the cultural or psychological affiliation with Britain persists, particularly among senior decision-makers within the bureaucracy of cultural development. Seeking support and inspiration from the former coloniser is a customary, almost instinctive act.

The first director of WKCD, Graham Sheffield, is a former director of the Barbican Centre in London. Michael Lynch, an Australian and once chief executive of the Southbank Centre in London, replaced him after five months. Swedish curator Lars Nittve was recruited in 2011 as director of M+. He is best known as the founding director of the Tate Modern at Southbank, London.

The curatorial team of M+ consists of an American-Korean, a German who worked in Hong Kong for a few years, and three Chinese from Beijing, who once worked in the United States. For nearly three years, the senior curatorial team operated without a role being played by anyone from the local Hong Kong community, or anyone capable of understanding Cantonese.[19] The museum operates, therefore, with an existing deficit in understanding local culture, particularly popular culture.

The 'import' of foreign experts is a frustrating, but inevitable, consequence of attempts to meet the needs of rapid cultural expansion.[20] The inability of outsiders to articulate local cultures can only be resolved by their willingness to understand and explore those cultures with sincerity and even humility.

The number of M+ curators from Mainland China presents another source of tension. Mounting resentment exists among the people of Hong Kong towards

---

18   The three finalist architectural firms were OMA (Sweden), Foster + Partners (United Kingdom) and Rocco Design Architects (Hong Kong).
19   In March 2014, after more than three years, a local person from Hong Kong was employed to join the senior curatorial team to look after the section focusing on Hong Kong art.
20   Chan Yuen-han, 'Change the Destiny of WKCD by Changing its Name', *AM730* (2013) accessed 7 October 2013, http://www.am730.com.hk/column-162512.CHAN Yuen-han.

what they perceive as political and cultural colonisation from Mainland China; the employment of curators from Beijing to run a cultural institution that interprets Hong Kong culture is interpreted by some as an insensitive act of provocation.

Art for the People

In addition to the geographic gap between rich and poor, the adoption of aesthetics that are familiar to foreign experts only reinforces the sense of alienation for mainstream Hong Kong audiences. The existing tendency to favour art that is based on a Western set of artistic criteria might delight a small community of local elitists, but it will only further alienate the mainstream public.

In a critique of the continuation of the colonial mode of governance, journalist Vivienne Chow states that:

> The appointment of the board members [of the WKCD Authority] closely resembles the early colonial days when the colonial government, which had troubles with dealing with the local Chinese population at the time, gave the rich Chinese the power to sort things.

She rightly points out that structural elitism contradicts the original spirit of the project:

> the majority of these figures represent the society's upper class. They obviously speak the same 'language' to the team's 'imported elites', which enjoy a great reputation in the international contemporary art world. Thus one cannot help but wonder if M+ only represents the tastes of a small circle of elites, imposing their elite ideas onto a general public of Hong Kong that lacks 'cultural capital' to understand arts and culture.[21]

Chow vividly illustrates a frustrating situation that is becoming obvious not just in Hong Kong, but also in the other 'suddenly cultured' regions of Asia.

Establishing new cultural spaces, such as M+, also poses the problem of building a collection that is meaningful to local Hong Kong people. M+ intends to introduce a perspective on art that rests outside a Western-defined aesthetic framework. Turning to the interdisciplinary field of 'visual culture', M+ broadens the definition of art and highlights the aspects of culture that are closely linked to local histories and people, such as Hong Kong's leading role in pioneering Chinese political comics during the late Qing Dynasty; its unique role as a haven of court literati culture after the collapse of the dynasty;

---

21   Vivienne Chow, 'A Series of Unfortunate Events: The Past and Present of West Kowloon Cultural District', *Cultural Vision* (May 2013).

the anti-Japanese and, later, civil war propaganda art of the 1930s and 1940s; the brief but significant Leftist Renaissance of the late 1940s, especially in the area of popular publications; the conflicting dynamic between the north (Shanghai) and south (Guangdong) of the 1950s in literature and film; and, the 'not quite East or West' pop culture of the 1960s that emerged against the background of the Cultural Revolution in China. One does not always need to look to the West for artistic excellence, as long as one is willing to take a look at what the locals already have.

Unfortunately, to this point, the M+ collection is defined mainly by the prevailing category of 'contemporary art' premised on 'global' artistic vocabularies. The curatorial team ignores, or is simply unable to understand, the histories and realities of the art and culture of Hong Kong.

The Fallacy of 'Global is Local'

While M+ recognises the coexistence of the local and global, its original plan highlights the importance of local culture. There is also a necessity to deal with the definition of the 'global', and the existing imbalance between the 'global' and the 'local'. The recently published acquisition policy of M+ states that it will 'deploy this recent and more global concept of "art"'.[22] This policy reflects an emphasis on 'contemporary' and 'global' art, a field that is familiar to the current curatorial team. The original mandate of recognising the local is downplayed and no explanation is given to justify the change.

In a defence against the criticism that M+ does not pay attention to the local, and the critique that M+ equates 'global' with 'Western', Nittve asked 'Is universal suffrage a Western idea or a global idea?'[23] Of course there are globally recognised values that are arguably generated in the West, but that does not also mean that Damien Hirst or Pablo Picasso are necessarily global. One can just as easily ask: 'Is Cantonese opera global?'

The existence of something distinctively local is an undeniable fact that cannot be obscured by wordplay. The recognition of the local and the imbalance between 'global' and 'local', which has existed in Hong Kong since colonial days, must be addressed. Until the turn of the twenty-first century, Hong Kong liked to describe itself as a 'cultural desert'. The practice of culturally degrading the locals was part of the system of colonial control. Within the academic

---

22   West Kowloon Cultural District Authority, 'M+ Acquisition Policy' (2013), accessed February 2013, http://www.wkcda.hk/filemanager/en/content_283/Mplus_Acquisition_Policy_eng.pdf.
23   Vivienne Chow, 'M+ Chief Lars Nittve Vows Museum Won't Steer Clear of Politics', *South China Morning Post*, accessed 4 May 2013, http://www.scmp.com/news/hong-kong/article/1229502/m-chief-lars-nittve-vows-museum-wont-steer-clear-politics.

establishment there was little research undertaken before the 1990s on local art and culture. A history of Hong Kong art that is acceptable to local critics has yet to be written.[24]

Gleeson rightly pointed out at the ACN forum that in Cambodia her 'curatorial practice was really a conscious effort to write and facilitate an art history that does not yet exist'.[25] In Hong Kong, as in many of its Asian counterparts, the lack of archival work and research on Hong Kong's art and culture makes it difficult to create an intellectual base for the curation of historical exhibitions and the building of collections. Instead of settling for art that has been already 'endorsed', the establishment of M+ demands ongoing research into local art and cultural history. Unfortunately there is as yet no mechanism to support such scholarship, despite the museum having begun collecting and curation. Staying within the arena of contemporary art as understood by the West continues to be the priority.

The esoteric, rarefied and indifferent attitude of M+ persists and the distance between the public and 'art' remains. According to Gleeson, getting to know the local means 'trying to bring in other conversations'.[26] The issue is not about the coexistence of the global and local; rather, it is about the struggle against the domination of one over the other. Modern curatorial practice has, arguably, been strongly shaped by the West, as in the case of Indonesia described by Hujatnikajennong. Equating 'global' with 'Western', overemphasising 'global' as an all-embracing standard, and downplaying the existence of the 'local', demonstrates a disturbing colonial mindset. In order to stand culturally on one's own, such cultural injustice must be addressed.

Chinese Art for the West

In 2012 M+ announced a major donation valued at HK$1.3 billion (US$167.5 million)[27] from the Swiss art collector Uli Sigg. The donation was in turn accompanied by M+'s obligation to purchase from the donor a further 47 works for HK$177 million (US$22.8 million). The collection includes some works from the late 1970s and 1980s, but it mainly comprises Chinese contemporary art produced after 2006. The amount spent is equivalent to one tenth of the total

---

24   Mainland Chinese historian Zhu Qi wrote a *History of Hong Kong Fine Art* (2005) that received harsh criticism from the local arts community for its academic inadequacy and political inclination. Edwin Lai Kin-keung, 'On Hong Kong Art History', *Independent Media* (2006), accessed 7 October, 2013, http://www.inmediahk.net/node/91226.
25   Gleeson, 2011.
26   Ibid.
27   Estimated by Sothebys.

budget for M+ to build its base collection. The donation plus purchase generated much debate over values and meaningfulness of arts and culture in relation to the vision and mission of M+ and the cultural experience of the locals.

The original M+ collecting plan includes a mission to collect material from outside Hong Kong, including Mainland China. The current administration must, however, clarify the reasons for such a substantial investment in art from mainland China instead of from Hong Kong, and the inclusion of these works as the core of the M+ collection.[28] The question is, what does Chinese 'contemporary art' mean to Hong Kong? In justifying the collection of Mainland Chinese contemporary art, Nittve stated that 'what happened after the Cultural Revolution is extremely important. It affects us [Hong Kong], and it's affected by what happened here'.[29] Given that practically everything that happens in China affects Hong Kong, such a general statement is essentially meaningless. In reality, the Mainland Chinese contemporary art that is favoured by the West has limited cultural impact on Hong Kong. In contrast, the pop culture of Hong Kong, for example, had and continues to have a tremendous impact on China.

It is true that, since the mid-1990s, Hong Kong has played a significant role in marketing Chinese contemporary art to the world.[30] With the exception of a small community of interested artists, collectors and dealers, however, such art does not impact on Hong Kong people. By comparison, other Chinese art movements have a profound influence, including the Lingnan School and the Woodcut Movement advocated by Lu Xun during the 1930s and 1940s. More recently, 'Chinese contemporary art' is a form of exported art that has had far less impact on the development of Hong Kong art except in terms of its influence in opening up an art market.

Submerging the Popular

Ignorant of the richness of local culture, particularly the grassroots culture evolving from Cantonese refugees, M+ has so far failed to address the aspects of local culture that are most distinctive to Hong Kong and were specifically highlighted in its original plan.

The recent decision to revoke popular culture as a distinct M+ acquisition policy area is a blatant denial of the cultures of the ordinary people, who are

---

28 M+ argues that, in terms of the number of works, the collection holds more Hong Kong artworks than works of Mainland Chinese contemporary art, but it has not revealed the amount spent on local Hong Kong arts.
29 Chow, 'M+ Chief Lars Nittve Vows Museum Won't Steer Clear of Politics'.
30 The first major exhibition of Chinese contemporary art was held at the Hong Kong Arts Centre in 1993, curated by Li Xianting, Oscar Ho and Johnson Chang.

also the richest part of Hong Kong culture.³¹ Critic Anita Tse criticised the policy, remarking that 'M+ is run by a curatorial team of foreigners who do not understand the importance of "popular culture" in Hong Kong.'³²

Responding to criticism that M+ is submerging Hong Kong's popular culture into other art forms, instead of allowing it to have its own distinctive place in the collection as M+ originally proposed, Nittve argues that 'popular culture is often represented as the flip side of fine art in the West, but this kind of differentiation is irrelevant here, as many creative works were conceived for commercial platforms. Popular culture is therefore represented in each of the three major categories'.³³ Such a statement shows a lack of understanding of the distinctive cultural history of Hong Kong.

Historically Hong Kong has experienced a separation and, thus, distinction between 'fine' and 'popular' art. Inheriting a literati tradition that was described as conservative by the progressive intellectuals of the first half of the twentieth century and, at the same time, suffering from a lack of support for such literati practice, the early generations of artists who fled to Hong Kong from Mainland China were forced to make a living from applying their skills to popular culture. The artist Lee Bing in the 1930s and 1940s lived a typical double life, consciously creating 'art' as social critique (also to generate some occasional income) on the one hand and, on the other, painting giant advertising billboards for cinemas. The dichotomy of these two art forms running parallel to each other has become a major creative topic among a generation of artists, such as Lau Yee Cheung (Liu Yichang).³⁴

Artist Law Kwun Chiu is best known across the Asian diaspora for his romantic illustrations of life in his hometown in the Guangdong *Children's Paradise* magazine. For decades since the 1950s the magazine has charmed millions of Chinese readers throughout Asia. It has not only made Law Kwun Chiu famous, but it has also extended the cultural influence of Hong Kong to its neighbouring regions. In private, the only creations that Law Kwun Chiu himself recognised as art were his traditional ink paintings of mountains and mist.³⁵ After working as a propaganda artist during the Second World War, against Japanese invasion,

---

31 Chan Yuen-han, 'Change the Destiny of WKCD by Changing its Name'.
32 Anita Tse, 'Another Discussion about Getting Rid of Popular Culture at M+', *House News*, accessed 7 October 2013, http://thehousenews.com/art.
33 Chow, 'M+ Chief Lars Nittve Vows Museum Won't Steer Clear of Politics'.
34 Lau Yee Cheung's novel *Tête-bêche* (對倒) (1975), which was about the anxiety between art and the popular, was made into the movie *In the Mood for Love* (2000) by Wong Kar-Wai.
35 I interviewed Law Kwun Chiu in preparation for an exhibition in the mid-1990s. At first, he refused to show his illustration work and only wanted to show his ink paintings, as he believed those were more dignified and artistic. Such reticence is not limited to visual arts. Another outstanding example of creativity that encompasses popular and traditional culture is the work of literary scholar and artist Jin Yong (Louis Cha Leung-yung), whose kung-fu novels have fascinated generations of Chinese all over the world since the 1950s and have been influential on many kung-fu movies.

Law Kwun Chiu found a liberating freedom in not having to make art with political or patriotic missions to fight against the Japanese or to revitalise China, as every Chinese intellectual did at that time. In Hong Kong, through paid work as a commercial artist, he was freed from the heavy burden of traditional or patriotic obligations. It was in the refugee shelter of Hong Kong that popular culture came to hold special meaning for the artist through its detachment from official culture and obligations. Artists may find creative liberation through popular culture and the opportunity to pursue a different path that results in outstanding artistic creativity.

The collection of baseball cards that is held by the Metropolitan Museum in New York is not given a distinct categorisation. M+, on the other hand, must make popular culture a unique and recognised category within its collection. Understanding the significance of popular culture in Hong Kong will ensure that it cannot be easily submerged in other art forms. Downplaying the significance of popular culture, however, will limit the opportunity for M+ to be a space devoted to visual cultures and will reduce it, rather, to a space for visual arts, which is presumably an achievable goal for the foreign experts.

A Post-Colonial Failure

WKCD marks the end of decades of indifference to the development of culture in Hong Kong. The grand undertaking, which was built around the fantasy of the economic potential of the cultural industries, was in fact a real estate project in disguise. After much controversy the project was turned back into something seemingly cultural. It is under such unusual circumstances that the idea of M+ was conceived. It signifies an attempt to move beyond the conventional, Western-based concept of art and museum.

To achieve the vision of M+, one needs to recognise the imbalance between global and local (and that the 'global' should not be synonymous with 'Western'). At the same time, an underdeveloped and imbalanced cultural ecology that is dominated by civil servants creates gaps in administration that inevitably require help and advice from external professionals. If there is no enduring engagement with local cultures, or the will or ability to understand them, these experts can retreat into their familiar vocabularies and modes of practice. This shortfall in the scope of M+ is evident when compared with the original vision and mission for the institution.

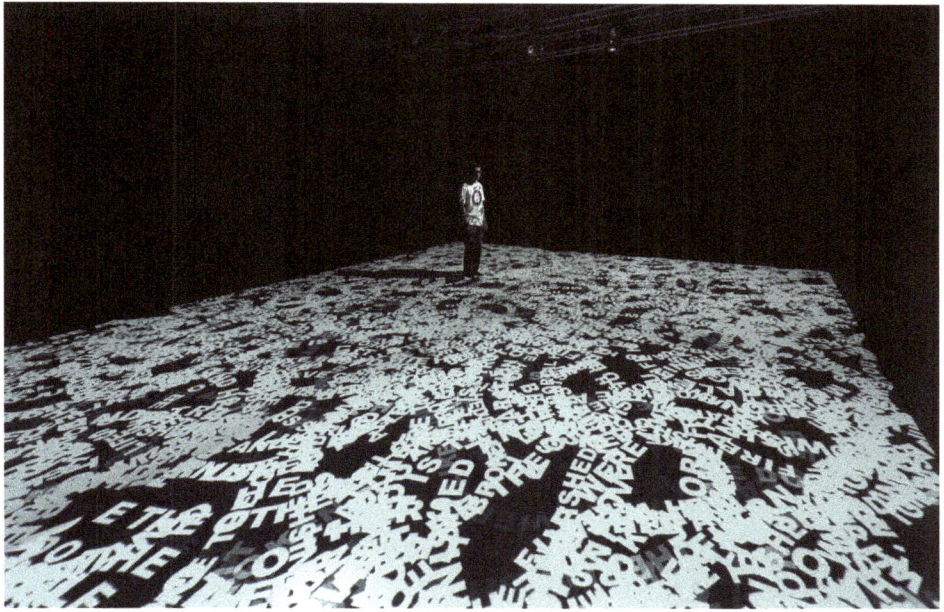

Tsang Kin-wah, *The Fourth Seal* at *Mobile M+: Yau Ma Tei* 2012.

Courtesy of M+, West Kowloon Cultural District

Underpinning the original vision and mission of M+ was the stated desire to claim cultural recognition for Hong Kong and to review and expand the conventional modes of museum operation in order to be inclusive of Hong Kong's diverse visual culture. Ultimately, however, M+ looks set to become just another museum of contemporary art, an M without a +, or even an M−. It is possible that M+ will be another example of the futility of Asia's struggle to establish its own creative languages outside a Western-dominated art world.

The editorial board of the journal *Cultural Vision* posted a question to Nittve in May 2013, asking 'M+ was set up to be a new cultural institution. How will it live up to the expectation, and distinguish itself from merely being an Asian pirated copy of MoMA or Tate Modern?'[36] So far, there has been no reply.

---

36 Editorial board, question to Dr Lars Nittve, Executive Director of M+, *Cultural Vision* (2 May 2013), 54.

9. People and Partnership: An Australian Model for International Arts Exchanges — The Asialink Arts Program, 1990–2010

Alison Carroll

'You could never have told me what it would be like.'
Australian curator, Malaysia, 1993

'It was the hardest and the best thing I have ever done.'
Australian artist in residence, China, 1996

This essay outlines how Asialink Arts, a small program evolving in Melbourne from 1990, became the main arts exchange vehicle for Australian arts engagement with Asia over the next two decades. The program was based on the principle of 'people and partnership'.

The comments at the beginning of this essay from a curator and an artist always resonated for the Asialink Arts program. They relate to the crucial role of personal experience in a different culture, and how creative people respond to this. Opening up opportunities for Australian creative people in Asia and supporting their experience was the most important role of the arts program at Asialink over the period of this essay, 1990–2010.[1] The program provided access to the variety and richness of the contemporary cultures of Asia by establishing links which artists and others could utilise and build on. It was based on the idea that artists need just a little help to take their creativity, passion and determination into new worlds, as well as on the concept of trusting them to be mature partners in this endeavour, with few checks and balances and, in reality, minimal support. This mission and focus remained consistent over time. It is remarkable, reading back over the Asialink files, how little the intention, structure and even the words changed over the period: providing opportunities, giving access, providing support and encouragement, leading to the creation of new works of meaning to the artists themselves and to their new audiences in the region.[2]

---

1 Asialink started in the late 1980s in Melbourne as a project of the Commission for the Future, with the aim of encouraging Australians to engage more closely with Asia. The early focus was on political and social issues. In 1991 the organisation became a centre at the University of Melbourne, where it remains. The Myer Foundation supported the wider Asialink program throughout this period. See www.asialink.unimelb.edu.au.
2 The first information sheet for the Artist in Residence program, written in 1991, states: 'The aim of the program is to enlarge the experience available to Australian artists in our own region, to enable a longer term involvement with the host country, and to encourage ongoing contacts between Australian and Asian artists.' None of these words—or intentions—changed over 20 years.

At Asialink we realised that the easiest path to increasing knowledge of Asian culture and to encourage direct experience was through the contemporary world: the artist of today. The premise of 'exchange' was that artists were talking to each other and to audiences, across cultures, either in person or through their work. The program was clearly about Australians and Australian work going to Asia, rather than the reverse. The reasons were many: that everyone learns by being or having their work seen by others and that we Australians had been poor at promoting our own work in the region (and much better at importing Asian work to Australia as is evidenced, for example, in the number of exhibitions invited by our museums). Also, I (and the funding was predicated on this) thought our scarce Australian arts resources should be focused on Australian artists and art, and that if people in Asia wished to come to Australia, Asialink would help with advice but they had to provide the organisational and financial backing themselves. I saw the alternative as an aid argument and did not envisage the program in this way.

Australian artists responded to Asialink with enthusiasm and, in the first 20 years of operation, the program supported some 600 artists in residence and innumerable other artists, curators, performers and writers committed to engaging with Asia. Their experiences have provided a vital resource for Australia's future.[3] It was not always easy. One of the satisfactions was in seeing artists return from an Asialink supported experience in Asia expressing not only their pride in the work they had done, but also their increased belief in their own ability to manage new and often difficult challenges.

A key element of the program, both for individuals and a variety of artist communities and institutions was the idea of partnership. As Carrillo Gantner and I have argued elsewhere:

> The critical ingredients for international exchanges in the arts are people and partnerships. Together these generate the creative product. If real partnership among the parties on both sides is built from the beginning of an exchange program, surprising results ensue. Partnerships are essential in this work so that everyone has a stake in the artistic outcome. Partnership means that new ideas and new works can be forged together, giving the greatest gift to all involved. Partnership also means that administration and costs can be shared, reducing one of the perceived barriers to engagement. Partnerships built on respect for each

---

3   Asialink has produced two publications listing the residencies: *35,000 Days in Asia* and *45,000 Days in Asia; The Asialink Arts Residency Program* in 2004 and 2007 respectively, listing all residents to those dates. An annual *Newsletter*, published since 1998, has listed each person travelling for the previous year, and these *Newsletters* continue, echoed in the Asialink website: www.asialink.unimelb.edu.au/ourwork. The Asialink Exhibition program has been documented in Alison Carroll & Sarah Bond, *Every 23 Days: 20 Years Touring Asia* (Asialink, University of Melbourne, 2010). It lists the nearly 80 exhibitions toured, including curators, artists, venues and institutional partners.

partner's creative and administrative contribution mean problems can be foreseen and overcome. In art as in life, this is the only way we can grow in a global world.[4]

Australia's relationship with Asia has changed over the nearly 25 years that Asialink Arts has been in existence. That relationship has benefited from increasing, if varied, degrees of government interest and engagement. From the focus on the region that developed under the federal Labor government of Paul Keating in the early 1990s, followed by a slowing interest in the ensuing decade, to the 2012 federal government's *Asian Century* white paper,[5] Asia remains on the political horizon in a way that was not the case prior to 1990. Relationships changed—from the few 'true believers' of the early years to the much wider, more sophisticated and intertwined engagement gained in more recent times.

The arts play a paradoxical role in Australia's relationship with Asia. Despite being central to our wellbeing and how we see ourselves, able to cross cultural boundaries, and led by curious and brave individuals, the arts have, frequently, taken a back seat to business and politics in the minds of people who care about the relationship. Equally, for many Australians the arts of Asia were, and remain, intimidating, inscrutable and 'difficult'.

Some History

The first steps towards the establishment of the Asialink Arts Program were taken as a result of my realisation, while on holiday in Sri Lanka in the early 1980s, that I had never heard the names of the ancient cultural sites in that country—wonderful, elegant and extensive as they are—despite six years of formal art history training in Australia. This realisation inspired me to curate several exhibitions; one of the largest being *East and West*, which was held in 1985 at the Art Gallery of South Australia and addressed the interaction of Asian and European (and Australian) art.[6] In working towards this exhibition, I was acutely aware of the paucity of published information on the visual art of the Asian region post 1900. I received a grant from the Visual Arts/Craft Board of the Australia Council for the Arts (VACB) to travel in South-East Asia, to explore ways of redressing this situation.[7] Everyone there said the same thing:

---

4   Alison Carroll & Carrillo Gantner, *Finding a Place on the Asian Stage*, Platform Paper 31 (Currency House, 2012), 12.
5   Department of Prime Minister and Cabinet, *Australia in the Asian Century*, White Paper (Canberra, 2012).
6   Carroll, *The State's Collections; East and West; The Meeting of Asian and European Art*, Art Gallery of South Australia, 1985. The exhibition was curated by Alison Carroll, assisted by Dick Richards, Judith Thompson and Ron Radford.
7   Australia Council Travel Grant to South-East Asia (Thailand, Indonesia, Malaysia, Singapore, Laos, Vietnam, Philippines), taken in two trips in 1988 and 1990. The Australia Council for the Arts is the Australian Government's official arts advisory and funding body and is divided into several divisions. The Visual Arts/Crafts Board was one of the key divisions at the time Asialink was establishing its Arts Program.

they wanted to see more contemporary art, from 'elsewhere'—Australia, the world, anywhere. In response I developed *Eight Views*, an exhibition of contemporary Australian art, that toured in 1990–1991, under the umbrella of AETA (Australian Exhibitions Touring Agency), to five national galleries of South-East Asia.[8] This project gave me practical experience in the methods of touring exhibitions internationally and a deeper understanding of the existing funding opportunities, the interest of audiences and the keenness of artists to take part in similar projects.

Asialink was in its early days when I approached it to support the ideas I envisaged as a follow-up to the *Eight Views* exhibition. With the agreement of Jenny McGregor (then project officer at Asialink, now CEO), I put together a program brief of exhibitions of Australian art and, after discussions with the Australia Council, the idea emerged of linking this to their existing program of artist residencies in Asia. We asked for support from both the Department of Foreign Affairs and Trade (DFAT), and the Council and, in February 1991, we received $30,000 seed funding from DFAT.[9] In May, the Council agreed to match the DFAT funds.[10] Les Rowe, assistant secretary at DFAT, later told me that he was not expecting to hear from us again. Little did he know.

The Program

Over the next 20 years, the Asialink Arts Program continued to receive strong organisational, financial and collegiate support from DFAT, via the department

---

8   Carroll, *Art from Australia; Eight Contemporary Views* (Australian Exhibitions Touring Agency, 1990). The artists were Micky Allan, John Davis, Richard Dunn, Anne Ferran, Fiona Hall, Imants Tillers, Caroline Williams and John Young. The exhibition was a large project with significant support from the Department of Foreign Affairs and Trade, the Australia Council and Westpac Banking Corporation. It travelled to the national galleries of Thailand, Indonesia, the Philippines, Malaysia and Singapore.
9   Correspondence from Leslie Rowe, assistant secretary, Cultural Relations Branch, Department of Foreign Affairs and Trade, of 19 February 1991, included the welcome words: 'We have studied the proposal carefully and I am pleased to advise you that we are prepared to offer a contribution of $30,000 as seeding funds to establish the project as outlined in your letter of 14 January 1991 to enable the project to get underway in the first half of 1991.'
10 Correspondence from Ian Were, program officer, Visual Arts/Craft Board of the Australia Council, of 22 November 1993 confirms new funding for the years 1994–1996, and includes the words: 'In making its decision the Visual Arts/Craft Board's (VACB) International Promotion Committee discussed the "Australian Art to Asia" project at length and wanted to congratulate Asialink and its visual arts coordinator, Alison Carroll on the success of the program over 1991–1993. Clearly Asialink has achieved much with the residency and exhibition programs, has gathered and exchanged information, and has been able to attract substantial support from a range of other agencies. The Committee was enthusiastic about the potential of the project to further develop and consolidate relationships through the Asian region, and has therefore agreed to a major commitment over the next three years, 1994 to 1996.'

in Canberra[11] and through its diplomatic posts in Asia. By 2010, the combined annual funding from DFAT and the Australia Council had increased from $120,000 to $760,000.[12]

While in some respects this was significant support for a small agency, it can also be regarded, conversely, as a tiny contribution to the running of the nation's main Asia–Australia arts program.

Asialink's early projects came to fruition on a wing and a prayer. I asked for practical assistance and support from people who I knew might be open to and interested in the possibility of working in Asia, such as Anne Kirker of Queensland Art Gallery (QAG) and Juliana Engberg, then a freelance curator. I also contacted those few organisations that, at the time, were expressing strong interest in Asia, such as QAG and the Royal Melbourne Institute of Technology (RMIT).

Kirker was the first to respond with an exhibition of Australian prints called *6 x 6*,[13] which toured to three venues in Thailand, including Khon Kaen in the north-east of the country. She wrote, 20 years later:

> I am working now with Thai artist Prawat Laucharoen on a collaborative print installation project with artists at his loft space in New York. Mostly we are communicating by e-mail, unlike the very slow and travel-intensive way we achieved shows in the early 1990s.
>
> With the *6x6* exhibition I worked closely with co-curator Somporn Rodboon, from Silpakorn University. She, like myself, had a special interest in printmaking. It was trial and error for us both with this show, although Ajarn Somporn had already organised international print

---

11 The key section within DFAT Canberra was the Cultural Relations Branch, led by Neil Manton at first and, at the end of my tenure, Anthony Taylor. Manton has outlined DFAT's history of sending contemporary Australian art to Asia in his book *Cultural Relations: The Other Side of the Diplomatic Coin* (Canberra: Homosapien Books, 2003), Chpt. 3. The majority of examples occurred over the period 1947–1970. Manton's experience, and support, was key to Asialink's early successful touring. The individuals within the Cultural Relations Branch were important people who had either worked in Asia or would in the future, and whose knowledge of Australian art and how it was viewed internationally was significant. Around this central culture node was the work of the 'FCIs' (foundations, councils and institutes) or bilateral agencies, like the Australia–Indonesia Institute, the Australia–Japan Foundation and so on, financially supported by DFAT, and all with culture forming part of their agenda of encouraging 'people-to-people' relationships. Again, knowledgeable arts professionals were included on their boards, co-editor of this publication Caroline Turner (then deputy director of the Queensland Art Gallery), being one of them, and they added to the pool of expertise.
12 As one measure of 'success', Asialink Arts became the largest recipient of funding from the Australia Council for the Arts. This observation was made by Australia Council staff member Andrew Donovan to the writer in 2010 and excludes the clients of the Major Performing Arts Board of the Council, which supports the main theatre companies in the country. Of course the Australia Council's support is only one part of a complex matrix of arts funding in Australia, and many other organisations would receive more substantial overall support through this combination.
13 *6 x 6: A Selection of Contemporary Australian Prints* (Asialink, University of Melbourne, in association with the Queensland Art Gallery, 1992), curator Anne Kirker; artists Ray Arnold, Diane Mantzaris, Milan Milojevic, Ann Newmarch, Graeme Pebbles and Judy Watson.

shows for the Gallery at Silpakorn. It was great that curator Roger Butler conducted the first professional practice workshop in Thailand at the time of *6x6*. We framed the works in Thailand and sent them on the road after the stint in Bangkok. I never forget walking with Robert Pound from the Australian Embassy and the Khon Kaen University gentleman in charge of organising the event there along a long veranda to get to the exhibition area, with the doors wide open to a room inside and a draped cadaver waiting for medical students to prod around.[14]

Progress involved establishing touring venues and hosts for residencies in Asia. I approached people in Asia who I knew might be willing to assist the program, particularly those that I met on the Australia Council research trip of the late 1980s and the subsequent touring of the *Eight Views* exhibition, as well as the diplomatic posts.

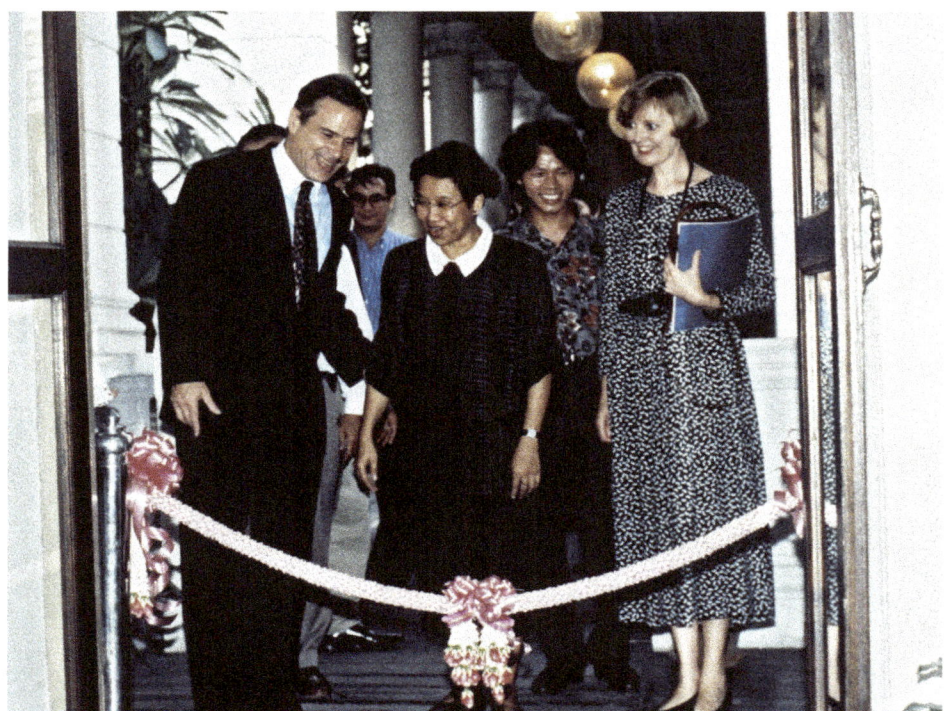

Opening ceremony, '6 x 6; A Selection of Contemporary Australian Prints', Silpakorn University, Bangkok, 1992; l–r: Ambassador John McCarthy, Somporn Rodboon, curator Anne Kirker. A partnership with Queensland Art Gallery.

Photographer unknown; image in Asialink collection; image courtesy of Asialink, University of Melbourne

---

14   Email correspondence, 9 August 2010.

For the touring exhibitions we frequently borrowed directly from artists, who were much more accepting of varying physical conditions for the display of their work than public and private collectors. The artists wanted their work to be seen and we made a point always of sending them a detailed report of their show's tour, including press coverage. Despite the varying physical conditions, Asialink made only two insurance claims:[15] a remarkable record considering that an Asialink-sponsored exhibition opened in the region every 23 days over those 20 years.[16]

The 'Background Notes' that were prepared in 1991 as guidance for possible curators are both telling in their practicality and, 20 years later, in their surprising relevance. They assert that the exhibition had to be sensitive to the audience, aware of the context, and aware of constraints, including costs, hardiness of the travelling works and physical limits of the host venues. They also outline the importance of the travelling curator as the representative of the exhibition, the need for the curator to be flexible and 'able to "go with the flow" when things go wrong', and for artists to be sensitive to the issue of the discrepancy between arts funding in Asia and Australia: 'Australia's funding for artists is sometimes seen as lavish'.[17]

Key Principles for the Program over 20 Years

The success of the Asialink Arts Program was based on the active implementation of several principles: a focus on quality programs, openness to new ideas and ventures, working in partnership, establishing excellent personal networks, and adding value to existing programs and arrangements.

The credibility of the Asialink program within the arts community was essential to its viability. The belief of arts practitioners in the quality of the program encouraged their involvement and also promoted the interest of good staff in the organisation and the development of stable partnerships. The quality of the program, in turn, led to positive and active press and public interest in Asialink's work. An instance of this was the *Sun Gazing* exhibition program in Japan of 2002–2004, which had an audience of nearly 300,000 people, and generated over 200 print media stories. It included *Patricia Piccinini; We are*

---

15 One, for wilful damage to a silver bowl in Vietnam; and another, for a dropped crate at Mumbai airport, resulting in a broken glass artwork.
16 The title of the book on the exhibition program, *Every 23 Days*, was based on the number of exhibition openings that had occurred over the 20-year period, which averaged out as 'every 23 days'.
17 Carroll, 'Some Background Notes for Curators and Artists Interested in the Asialink Exhibition Program' (Asialink, University of Melbourne, 1991).

Family which broke attendance records at the Hara Museum of Contemporary Art in Tokyo, with people queuing to get in, and there was standing-room only for the artist's lecture at the Tokyo National University of Fine Arts.[18]

Active and interested advisory committees of key people from around Australia contributed to and oversaw the program. Artists, curators, theatre practitioners, writers, arts managers, funders and musicians, male and female, of every age, kept Asialink focused on its mission. One important and always valuable criterion of Australia Council support was the inclusion of at least one person of Asian-Australian background on each Asialink advisory committee. Rather than being tokenistic, this inclusion maintained a focus on the central issue of Asialink's engagement.

DFAT and the Australia Council, as the two main funders of the program, had different agendas: the first was to support the political and economic interests of the country, and the second to support the interests of the arts community. For an arts program like Asialink's, these goals were sometimes at odds. An exhibition on golf, for example, might conform to the diplomatic interests of DFAT, but not of the arts community and, one of interest to the arts community on, for example, sexuality—an issue within those Asian countries that were predominantly Islamic—might be an issue for DFAT. Asialink's response was that some 80 per cent of the arts activity in Australia dealt with issues of pertinence and relevance between these two extremes and it was those issues that we explored. Asialink was sensitive to the criticism that its existence was based on its political and business value to DFAT and we were concerned to stress that if a program did not have value to the arts community it would not be viable.

From the beginning we looked outwards, trying to draw the ideas, projects, know-how, resources and funds of others into our work. It was clear from the outset that Asialink did not have the resources to undertake the work without relying on partnerships. Bringing in partners with their own support systems to add value to the project meant vastly increasing what was available and expanding the number of people in Australia with knowledge, contacts and interest to do the 'next' program themselves. The value of these partnerships was made starkly evident in the contrast between the internal budgets of Asialink and holistic budgets of the total projects. The *Sun Gazing* visual arts program with Japan saw the the base income of $500,000 quadrupled by income from our partners. While this is a literal way to 'value' a partnership, the financial support does translate as real commitment by all involved.[19]

---

18 See Carroll, *Sun Gazing; The Australia-Japan Art Exhibitions Touring Program 2002–04* (Asialink, University of Melbourne, 2005), 3, 18.
19 And vice versa. There were times when we regretted not achieving more support from international partners, seeing this commitment as commensurate with the commitment to the total project idea.

Asialink had to raise all its funds (and so, contrary to popular opinion, was not in a position to act as a funding body for the projects of other people). To be involved, Asialink had to add to a project a mixture of our capacity, our knowledge, our experience, and our work. Practically the program was run as leanly as possible. People were often surprised that the program did as much as it did with an arts staff of up to five people.

The Asialink Residency Program

The VACB had established the idea of a residency program in Asia in the late 1980s. True to the idea that it takes networks and commitment to get a program like this going, and despite attempting to make contact with relevant individuals and organisations in Asia, the VACB did not have the staff to follow up on its early plans. By 1990 only one artist, Joan Grounds, had travelled on the VACB program and David Castle was soon to follow. As a result of our approach to the VACB, it was agreed that Asialink would take over the residency program, in conjunction with funding for touring exhibitions.

When Asialink first mooted the idea to potential hosts of Australian artists coming to live and work in Asia, it was met with some trepidation. The idea of residencies was unfamiliar and there was concern over the cultural and language difficulties that may arise. Initially, universities, which were more accustomed to foreign engagement, were the first to agree to act as hosts. Kookmin University in South Korea, Silpakorn University in Thailand and the Jakarta Arts Institute in Indonesia were among the first to come on board. As the program continued, confidence grew and the idea of residencies became more acceptable. Gradually the arts bureaucracies in various governments started to create their own residency programs, such as Taipei Artist Village and, more recently, Tokyo Wonder Site.

From the end of 1991, when four people were scheduled to take up residencies, the program grew to 40 each year. In 2004, the arts program published a booklet on the residencies that listed all the residents to that date. The first edition was titled *35,000 Days in Asia*, the second, in 2007, amended to *45,000 Days in Asia*, reflecting the increasing number of residencies. By 2010 there had been over 600 Australians working for up to four months in the field, across 18 countries, with over 300 hosts.

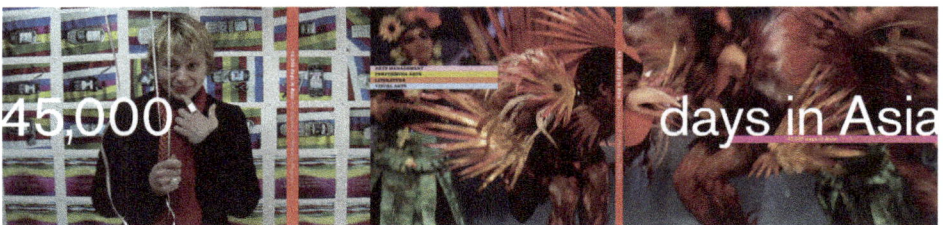

Cover of publication: *45,000 Days in Asia, the Asialink Residency Program, 2007.*

Design: Lin Tobias, LaBella Design; image courtesy of Asialink, University of Melbourne

The VACB has an international network of rented studios—of 'bricks & mortar' spaces. There is currently one studio in Asia, in Tokyo. Asialink worked on a slightly different premise: that a local host provided help securing working space and accommodation and, in return, had access to a 'foreign' artist in whatever way was of mutual benefit. This process was less secure than the studio model, but it meant there were immediate local contacts for the artist. It also meant that if something was not going well, we could change hosts the following year, and we could also respond to the interests of Australians. For example, Kookmin was a design/craft focused host, but it was clear that there was a lot of interest in Australia in other areas of work in Korea. Ssamzie Space, with its cutting edge, youth-focused new media scene proved very popular, and we were able to adapt the program to provide access to it.[20]

The residency program started with visual arts, then added performing arts and literature. An important fourth program was for arts managers, an initiative led by then chair of Asialink, Carrillo Gantner, and then head of the Ford Foundation's arts program in Jakarta, Jennifer Lindsay. Their logic was that, by introducing arts managers from Australia to regional networks, those networks would go on to develop new programs themselves—which is what happened. It also created stronger links in the then fledgling area of arts management in Asia, with the Australians frequently providing management support to new ventures there.

---

20 This example, in Seoul, is indicative of the fluid nature of institutions and organisations in Asia. Kookmin University enjoys the high respect that is common for an educational institution in a Confucian society, and our links there proved of great benefit to Asialink, through the establishment of a new Korea Program in the mid-1990s, including three exhibitions of Australian art and craft at the Seoul Arts Center in 1996. Many important Australian artists, like Carlier Makigawa, went to Kookmin and made links back into Australia. When you are starting a new program, you look back with great gratitude to the people who first accepted your overtures. Kookmin is among these. Ssamzie Space was set up as a privately supported venue for young artists to work and exhibit. It was in an area of Seoul near universities, bars, galleries and generally a 'hot' scene. Australian artists loved it, and many connections were made through their stays there. The initiating director, Kim Hong Hee, went on to work in various public art galleries and, in 2013, is the Director of the Seoul Museum of Art. Her connections to Australia have been long and very strong.

Second-Stage Programs

Each of the four 'art form' areas, including arts management, developed what we called 'second-stage' areas of action.

Arts Management

Extensions of the arts management program included internships, development of arts management how-to booklets, tours and teaching. The internship program that brought Indonesian arts managers to Australia was supported by the Ford Foundation in Jakarta. The experiences of the Indonesian participants over a ten-year period were recorded in the Asialink booklet *Jalan Jalan*.[21] The program was further extended with the creation of the Northern Territory/Nusa Tenggara Timur (NT/NTT) program, which enabled Territorians and the people of Eastern Indonesia to work together on various capacity-building projects. The manuals that were developed for Indonesian practitioners addressed issues of exhibition touring, event management and community cultural development practice. The booklets were translated into Indonesian and distributed there.[22]

Asialink had been the organiser of a number of short tours for arts managers from Asia to Australia, combining visits and lectures with workshop activity. An extension of this was Australian arts managers teaching at various seminars in the region—including on topics such as lighting, marketing, promotion, and curatorial practice. The majority of Asialink staff also gave talks and lectures in tertiary institutions in Australia about working in Asia, either to curatorial students, arts managers or artists. The core message of these presentations was the necessity of thinking a little differently when working in Asia than one might in Australia.

---

21 Georgia Sedgwick, *Jalan-Jalan: The Indonesia-Australia Arts Management Program 1999–2006* (Asialink, University of Melbourne, 2006).
22 The three booklets were: *Pameran Keliling; Sebuah Panduan Praktis untuk Galeri dan Museum Seni Indonesia* (Asialink, University of Melbourne & NETS Victoria, 2010); an edited version of Sara Kelly, *Travelling Exhibitions, A Practical Handbook for Metropolitan and Regional Galleries and Museums* (NETS Victoria, 1994), which was translated into Indonesian and with an introduction by Wulan Dirgantoro, School of Asian Languages and Studies, University of Tasmania; *Panduan Pengembangan Budaya Masyarakat* (Arts and Community Development) (Asialink, University of Melbourne and CCDNSW), Victoria Keighery, Director, Community Cultural Development, NSW, 2010, with support from Kate Ben-Tovim, Arts Manager in Residence, Yayasan Bagong Kussudiardjo, Yogyakarta, 2009, translated and with an introduction by Jeannie Park, Director, YBK, Yogyakarta; and *Perencanaan dan Pengelolaan Event dan Festival*, Asialink, University of Melbourne and UTS, an edited version of Rob Harris and Johnny Allen, eds, *Regional Event Management*, Australian Centre for Event Management, University of Technology, NSW 2002, translated and with an introduction by Amna Kusumo, Director, Yayasan Kelola, Jakarta, 2010. The three booklets were printed in runs of 5000 (as well as being available online) and all were distributed through Yayasan Kelola within one week.

Literature

The main second-stage program in literature was also a touring program. Adapted from the exhibition touring idea, then literature manager, Amanda Lawrence, devised an ambitious and successful touring program for our leading writers. With support from the Australia Council and DFAT, she initiated and managed intensive tours of up to two weeks' duration to China, India, Korea, Japan and Singapore, often focusing on a book fair, and including readings at bookshops, universities, schools and wide ranging discussions with the local literary community. Peter Carey, Tim Winton, Kate Grenville, Alex Miller, Kim Scott, Sonia Hartnett and Geraldine Brooks are among the Australian writers who took part. Brooks had just won the Pulitzer Prize for Fiction in 2006 when she put her planned Asialink trip to China ahead of all others. As a consequence of these tours, rights were sold, books bought, conversations had and, generally, the profile of Australian literature was raised as never before. The program addressed an evident need—the Asialink stand at the Beijing book fair, which was shared with Austrade, was the only stand representing Australian literature and publishing in a total of 45 countries throughout Europe and America.

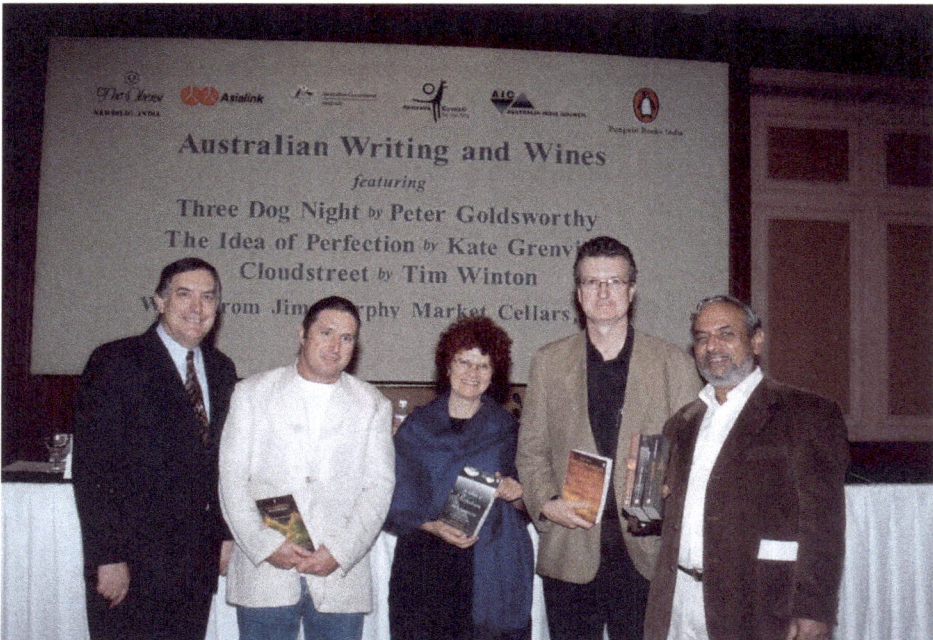

Asialink Touring Writers Program, presentation to three Australian writers; second from left: Tim Winton, Kate Grenville and Peter Goldsworthy, with other official guests, Oberoi Hotel, New Delhi, 2004.

Photographer unknown; image courtesy of Asialink, University of Melbourne

Concurrent with these tours were writers events of both Australian authors with interests in Asia as well as writers from Asia, which became a key part of Asialink's public program in Australia, mostly in Melbourne, but also at writers festivals in other states. The 'nights of stories' program, which was always popular, evolved into a Winter Writers Series. Visitors included well-known authors, such as Vikram Seth, who spoke to 500-strong audiences.

Performing Arts and Cross Media

A true 'second-stage' program was *Swimming with the Tide*, which asked for ideas from the field of community arts practice, mostly under the performing arts rubric. A small steering committee selected projects for work in Indonesia, which included theatre development in Sulawesi, performance in Java and Sydney, and politically inspired work in Jakarta's factories.[23] A second program in performing arts, which had a similar practice to *Swimming with the Tide* was *Neon Rising: Asialink Japan Dance Exchange*. Five collaborative projects were involved, with practitioners from around Australia working with Japanese colleagues to develop a wide range of programs that were shown in both countries.[24]

As a result of the increasingly cross-media practice of artists throughout the region, Asialink sought to be flexible in its programs in a way that would support artists operating outside the separate practice areas. An important annual forum was held for the first time in 2004 and focused on this area, bringing speakers from around the region to join Australian colleagues in vigorous discussion.

Visual Arts

Visual arts stands apart from the 'second-stage' programs as it was a core area from the beginning. It too, however, had components that can be discussed separately: exhibition touring, South-East Asian collaborations, and programs relating to South Asia, Korea and Japan.

Exhibition touring was the bedrock of the program, strongly supported by funders in Australia as well as partner galleries, institutions and individuals both in Australia and throughout the region. Exhibition touring began with a focus on the 'non- Foundation/Council & Institute countries', that is, those in

---

23 Zoe Dawkins, ed., *Swimming with the Tide; Australia-Indonesia Arts & Community Program* (Asialink, University of Melbourne, 2004). The committee was Robin Laurie, Andrew Donovan, Bernice Gerrand, Julia Tymukas and Alison Carroll. The introduction was by Bernice Gerrand, manager, Community Cultural Development Board, Australia Council, and the projects were: *Green Turtle Dreaming, Beyond the Factory Walls, Crocodile Hotel, West Sumatran Textile Workshop*, and *Girt by Sea*.
24 Swee Lim, *Neon Rising; Asialink Japan Dance Exchange* (Asialink, University of Melbourne, 2007). Australian dance artists and organisations included Jo Lloyd, Sue Healey and Co, Kage, Leigh Warren and Dancers, and De Quincey Co, all working with Japanese colleagues.

Asia without an associated DFAT funding organisation, such as the Australia-Japan Foundation (AJF) or the Australia India Council. So, the emphasis was on South-East Asia (excluding Indonesia) and the smaller countries of South Asia. Generally these exhibitons have been Australian shows touring to a number of venues in the region.

The South-East Asian collaborations grew out of the early touring shows. They included *Rapport*, devised by two Australian and Singaporean curators, and representing four artists from each country, which then toured to both; *Saisampan*, of four Australian and four Thai artists, curated by a Thai curator and site-specific to Chiang Mai; *Kawing*, involving four Northern Territory artists travelling to four regional venues in the Philippines and making work there; and, *Patterning*, in which a core of Australian work responding to the idea of patterns was 'answered' by local work in Pakistan, the Philippines and Indonesia. A further extension was *Foundations of Gold*, in which one artist from five Asian cities came to Melbourne to work with an Australian partner to produce new work, based on gold, resulting in a show that toured to the six (including Melbourne) cities. A more recent example was *Run Artist Run*, of work provided by artist-run initiatives in Australia, Singapore and Vietnam. These projects were more complicated to organise than traditional touring shows, but the results were frequently effective in engagement and reward.[25]

Work in South Asia led to the major show *Fire and Life*, which included five Australian and five Indian artists working together in each of their cities in Australia and India, with ten individual shows being the outcome.[26]

---

25 *Rapport: Eight Artists from Singapore and Australia*, curators Natalie King and Tay Swee-Lin; artists Hany Armanious, Carolyn Eskdale, Christopher Langton, Nicola Loder, Amanda Heng, Salleh Japar, Baet Yeok Kuan and Matthew Ngui; partners Monash University Gallery, Singapore Art Museum; tour Singapore, Melbourne, Canberra, Brisbane, 1996–1997; *Saisampan: Soul Ties—Australian and Thai Artists in Collaboration*, curator Somporn Rodboon; artists Chaiyot Chandratita, Peerapong Duangkaew, Joan Grounds, David Jensz, Noelene Lucas, Bannarak Nakbanlang, Araya Rasdjarmrearnsook and Wendy Teakel; partner Chiang Mai University, tour Chiang Mai, 2002; *Kawing: Four Regional Philippines Exhibitions*, curator Cath Bowdler; artists Dennis Bezzant, Jacki Fleet, Winsome Jobling and Techy Masero; partner 24 Hour Art, Northern Territory Centre for Contemporary Art; tour Manila, Davao, Baguio, Cebu, Negros, Puerto Princesa, Darwin, 2001–2002; *Patterning: In Contemporary Art, Layers of Meaning*, curator Merryn Gates; Australian artists Vivienne Binns, Fassih Keiso, Damon Moon and Stephen Goldate, Munupi Arts and Craft Association, David Sequeira, Jaishree Srinivasan, Wilma Tobacco and Sara Thorn; partner Canberra School of Art Gallery; tour Manila, Lahore, Canberra, Yogyakarta, Ubud, Bandung, Jakarta, 1997–1998; *Foundations of Gold*, curators Alison Carroll, Suzanne Davies, Beatrice Schlabowsky; artists Georgia Chapman, Eugene Chua Gin-Minn, Brenda V. Fajardo, Kim Ki-ra, Makiko Mitsunari, Pamela Stadus, Blanche Tilden and Caroline Williams; partners City of Melbourne, RMIT Gallery; tour Melbourne, Mumbai, Manila, Seoul, Osaka, Singapore, 2001–2002; *Run Artist Run*, curators Katie Lee and Dean Linguey, Mark Feary, David Teh, with Sarah Bond; artists Damiano Bertoli, Sue Dodd and Bianca Hester, Katie Lee and Dean Linguey, Ruark Lewis and Jonathon Jones; partners ½ doz., a little blah blah, Conical Inc., p-10, Plastique Kinetic Worms, Ryllega; tour Melbourne, Hanoi, Ho Chi Minh City, Singapore, 2007.

26 *Fire and Life*, curators Julie Ewington, Victoria Lynn, Chaitanya Sambrani and Alison Carroll; artists Jon Cattapan, David Jensz, Joan Grounds, Derek Kreckler, Judith Wright, N.S. Harsha, Surendran Nair, Jayashree Chakravarty, N.N. Rimson, Pushpamala; tour Bangalore, Baroda, Calcutta, Delhi, Mumbai, Melbourne, Sydney, Brisbane, Canberra, Perth, 1996–1997.

This, combined with our strong presence at the Bangladesh Biennale and specially prepared projects at smaller venues in Pakistan and Sri Lanka, confirmed our interest in the region.

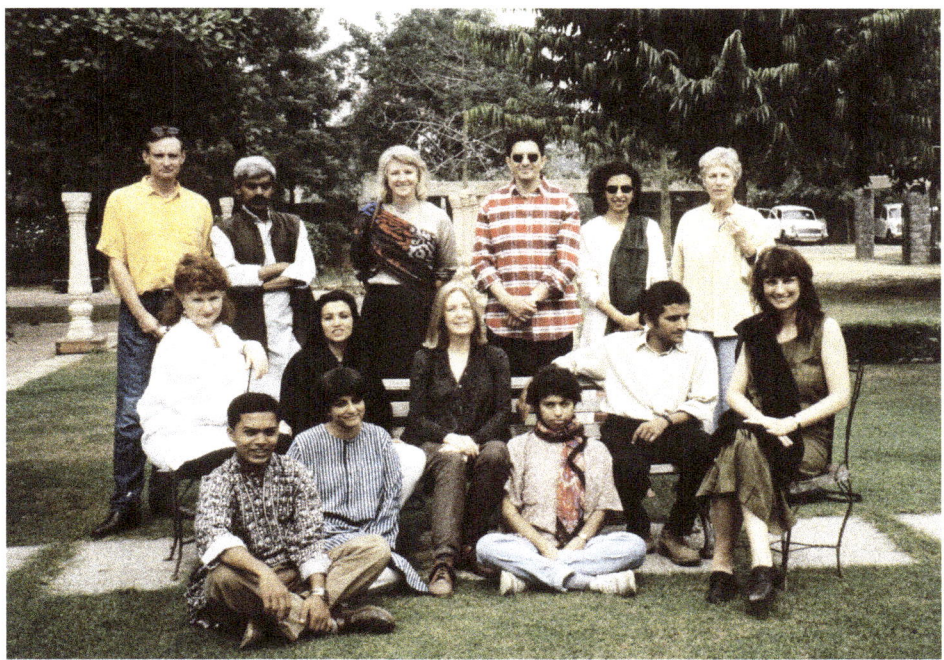

'Fire and Life' 1996–1997; l–r, top: artists and curators, Derek Kreckler, Surendran Nair, Alison Carroll, Jon Cattapan, Shireen Gandhi, Joan Grounds; middle: Julie Ewington, Suhanya Raffel, Judith Wright, N.S. Harsha, Victoria Lynn; seated on ground: Chaitanya Sambrani, Pushpamala N. and Jayshree Chakravarty, at Sanskriti Kendra, New Delhi, for exhibition 'Fire and Life', of ten exhibitions in India and Australia by five pairs of artists from both countries.

Photographer unknown; image courtesy of Asialink, University of Melbourne

The Korea program developed out of our wish to acknowledge the work occurring outside South and South-East Asia. Four Korean curators were invited to come to Australia and, out of this visit, seven visual arts projects followed in the mid-1990s, including a combined exhibition of Aboriginal art, craft and design, and general visual arts at the Seoul Arts Center in 1996. An exchange with Art Sonje saw contemporary Korean art come to the National Gallery of Victoria and the Art Gallery of New South Wales for the first time.[27]

---

27 The three exhibitions at Seoul Arts Center were *Australia: Familiar and Strange*, curator Timothy Morrell, *Voices of the Earth*, curator Gabrielle Pizzi; and, *Aurora: Australian Wood Metal Glass Fibre Ceramics*, curators Suzanne Davies, Grant Hannan, Ray Stebbins and Rachel Young. *The Slowness of Speed—Contemporary Korean Art*, shown in Melbourne and Sydney, was curated by Kim Sun Jung, Director of Art Sonje, Seoul.

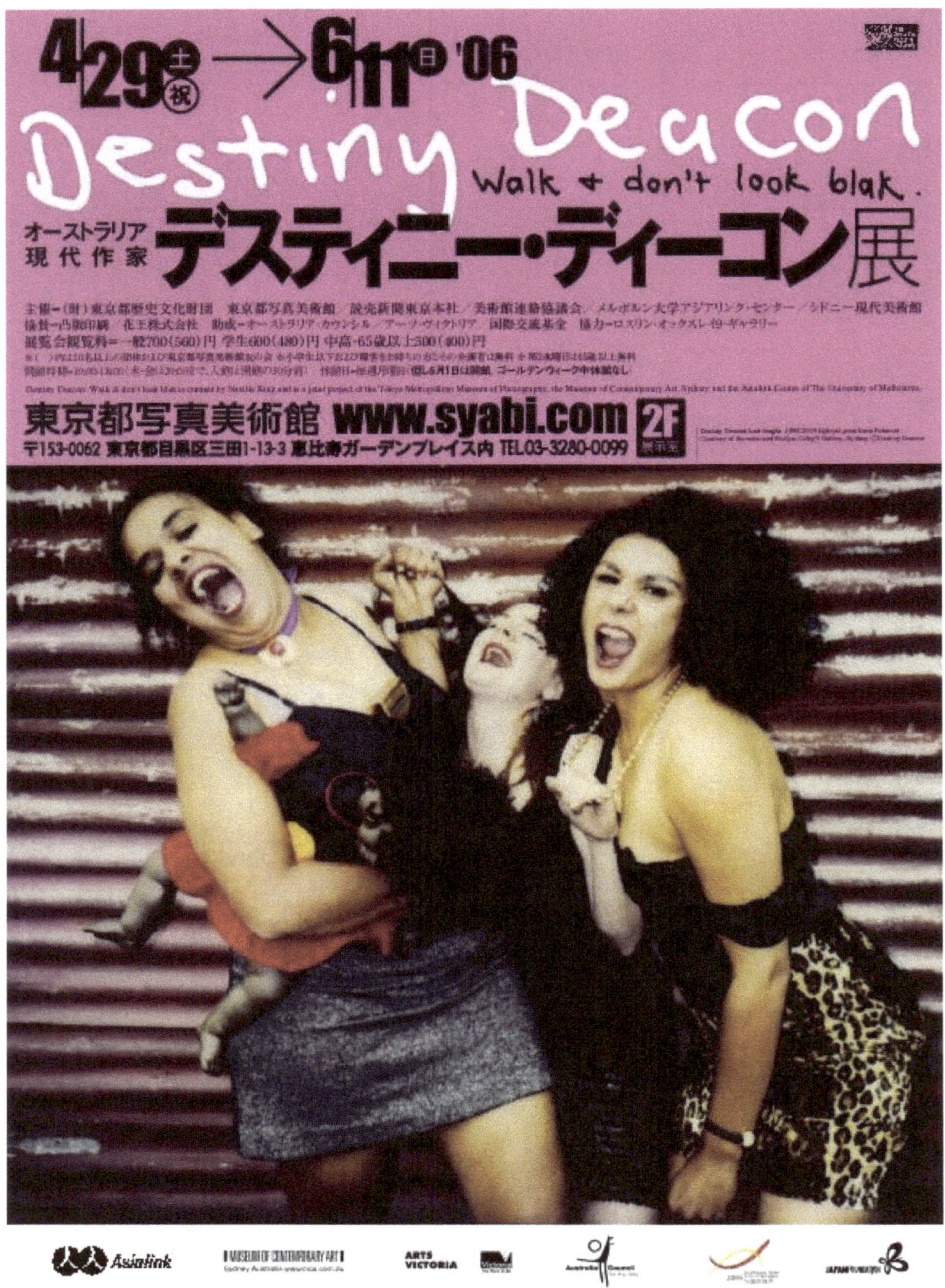

Poster from exhibition at Tokyo Metropolitan Museum of Photography, Tokyo, 'Destiny Deacon; Walk & Don't Look Blak' 2006.

Design: Tokyo Metropolitan Museum of Photography; image courtesy of Asialink, University of Melbourne

The Japan program grew out of the success of our engagement with Korea. Asialink's initial project was to lead a tour of visual arts curators in the late 1990s to Japan. As a result, the AJF and Australia Council supported a three-year program running from 2002–2004 which fostered establishing relationships in Japan with museums that were willing to host Australian art. The second iteration, running from 2005–2009, was more collaborative and involved co-curated exhibitions of Australian and Japanese work being shown in both countries. These programs also encompassed curatorial visits and two important symposia in Tokyo and Sydney.[28] An outcome has been the ongoing *Utopia@ Asialink* itinerant visual arts project.

Advocacy

In terms of advocacy for Asia–Australia arts engagement, Asialink focused on forums, publications and speaking at international events about elements of our mission, our program and our thinking. The annual Arts Forum, which started as a half-day engagement in Melbourne for the Asialink committee members representing the three art forms, evolved into a full-day public event that hosted speakers from throughout Asia. This was a highlight of the year, focusing on special issues, of community arts, residencies, and cross-cultural collaborations, and on the arts of specific countries: China, Japan, Korea and Indonesia. The arts program produced catalogues for each exhibition plus special publications on programs alluded to here, which were designed to alert local audiences to Asialink's overseas activities. The yearly *Newsletter* listed all the residents for that year. Asialinks arts staff were also required to contribute at least one article on their work to an external publication.

Challenges

There are many measurable success stories for Asialink Arts. The high (and competitive[29]) level of both individual and institutional engagement from Australia in Asialink's arts program has led to a wide dissemination of information and experience through this sector in Australia. This experience has been valued extremely highly by participants.[30] Asialink maintains that

---

28 'The Tokyo Forum 2006' and 'The Sydney Forum 2008'; see http://asialink.unimelb.edu.au/__data/assets/pdf_file/0006/421872/Asialink_SunWalking.pdf Asialink published two booklets reporting on the programs: *Sun Gazing; the Australia-Japan Art Exhibitions Touring Program 2002–04*, and *Sun Walking; Australia-Japan Visual Arts Partnerships Program 2005–9* (2009). The second volume was in English and Japanese.

29 One in ten applications for residencies were successful (based on financial capacity, not the quality of the applications), and advertised programs in other areas were always over-subscribed.

30 The 2005 survey of past residents revealed that 61 per cent of respondents found their experience 'extremely influential' to their practice, 25 per cent 'very influential', and only four per cent of 'moderate or of limited influence'. In the same survey, 68 per cent of respondents had undertaken follow-up projects (from Asialink files).

audience numbers in Asia, despite figures being hard to confirm, especially for projects with no entrance fee, have been higher for Asialink exhibitions than for any other Australian cultural program internationally. The figures noted for the Japan programs—where there are entrance fees and therefore statistics—of 300,000 for the 2005–2009 program are testament to audience hunger for such projects. The thousands of media reports in print, radio, television and through new media channels have always been greater than for similar events in Australia.

And yet, Asialink Arts, as the figures at the beginning of this chapter attest, has never had large support from any source. It was this writer's ongoing concern that there were no 'core' funds from anywhere for salaries or projects. All staff were on one-year contracts, dependent on that year's success, or not, with grant applications. This situation resulted from two main issues: the arts sector's general struggle for support, especially for offshore and avant-garde projects like ours, and for projects related to 'Asia'.

Over 20 years the general response to 'engagement with Asia' has hardly shifted. There has been wide agreement that 'Asia' is important, but the action to support engagement has been either just adequate (as in our case) or worse. As the saying goes, 'people talk the talk, but don't walk the walk'. It is well known in Australia that the number of students of Asian languages at both secondary and tertiary level has fallen over the last ten years.[31] The Currency House Policy Paper *Finding a Place on the Asian Stage* (2012), notes that *no* tertiary arts instituion in Australia offers core teaching of Asian performing arts practice. It notes the general fall in funding by the Australia Council for performing arts projects in Asia as a percentage of international engagement from around 50 per cent in the early 1990s to less than 20 per cent by 2010.[32]

This essay has outlined how Asialink Arts, a small program evolving in Melbourne from 1990, became the main arts exchange vehicle for Australian arts engagement with Asia over the next two decades and that a critical component of the exchange, as I have argued, was in forging cross-cultural dialogue. It was about more than government or business priorities. It was about experiencing something that you could 'never have been told what it would be like', and it being 'the hardest and the best thing' you have ever done. I wish this opportunity was available for us all.

---

31   *Australia in the Asian Century* (168) notes 'less than 6 per cent of Australian school students studied Indonesian, Japanese, Korean or Chinese (Mandarin) in Year 12 … Fewer Year 12 students studied Indonesian in 2009 than in 1972' and Japanese language student numbers 'fell by 16 per cent from 2000 to 2008'.
32   *Finding a Place on the Asian Stage*, 49–53, 24–25. These figures exclude the main museums of Australia, which get funding through different sources. Many, particularly QAG and, later, QAGOMA, have been very successful in a large number of important projects with Asian countries over this period.

A Postscript: 2013

The arts sector in Asia in the 20 years to 2010 developed exponentially. At the beginning of the 1990s, Australia was in a position to be a leader in the region, with arts training, models for engagement and various cultural developments, but this changed. Many cities in Asia have developed dynamic cultural centres, activities, and international engagements, increasingly importantly, within the Asian region. What is the next step that Australia can take to be part of this, to build on all the connections made over the last 20 years, and to do so strategically and with strong government backing?

Asian expert Carrillo Gantner and I have put forward the idea of an Australian international cultural agency that has the functions of creating and managing a strategic national overview, linking programs to national priorities and the national interest, establishing funding priorities, developing programs, promoting Australia internationally, and recruiting cultural staff for overseas posts.[33] Working in Asia, and extending Asialink's work onto another, stronger level, would be central to this. The arguments made against this are, first, cost—to which we say anything that is cost-effective should be a priority; second, that Australia has too small a population for such a special agency—to which we say many countries that are much smaller than Australia have very effective international bodies[34] and, third, that it is unnecessary change—to which we reply that change is needed. This is a new model that should be addressed now.

---

33 *Finding a Place on the Asian Stage*, 58–59.
34 The Dutch, Swiss and Scandinavia, for example; an alternative comparison is Britain, with three times Australia's population, spending more than three times our international arts budget.

10. Australia's Other Asia in the Asian Century

Jacqueline Lo

The recently deposed (Labor-led) Australian Government released its *Australia in the Asian Century* white paper in October 2012.[1] The document has been the subject of public and academic scrutiny both within Australia and in the region. There was praise for the document's emphasis on education to develop Australia's 'Asia-relevant capabilities', even while the issue of how the Asia-turn is to be implemented and funded remained unaddressed. The *Jakarta Post* gave an insight into the region's response to the white paper:

> [B]efore a nation can become a competitive force, it must have an accepted place in the region. On this key strategy, the white paper does little more than make a 'rally call' to Australians to come out and make it happen. … Though Australia has some deeply historical links with many parts of the region due to some heroic actions of troops during World War II, tragically these opportunities to further develop relationships were not capitalized upon … It's not about learning Asian languages but about understanding different points of view, approaches, and 'mindsets'. Austro-centrism must take a back seat in relationships around the region for Australia to be seriously considered a member of the region.[2]

At the point of writing, the new Coalition government headed by Prime Minister Tony Abbott has just been formalised. While the fate of this white paper remains uncertain, there are already signs that the new government is similarly keen to capitalise on 'Rising Asia' as the source of Australia's continuing prosperity. The *Australia in the Asian Century* white paper, for now at least, is indexical of the policy-imaginary of contemporary Australia.[3]

It should be noted that the white paper is a domestic economic policy and, as such, does not develop a nuanced approach to foreign relations, specifically through

---

1 The paper can be accessed at http://trove.nla.gov.au/version/190062879.
2 Murray Hunter, 'White Paper: "Australia in the Asian Century" or Lost in Asia?' *Jakarta Post*, 30 October 2012, accessed 25 September 2013, http://www.thejakartapost.com/news/2012/10/30/white-paper-australia-asian-century-or-lost-asia.html.
3 The *Australia in the Asian Century* white paper is, of course, not the first of its kind. The 'Asian-turn' in Australia's policy framework occurred in the late 1980s and early 1990s and is most often associated with the government of former prime minister Paul Keating, who advocated the privileging of Australia's geographic location in the region over our historical connections with Europe. The Keating years have become the yardstick for the promotion of 'Asia-literacy' and of changes introduced not only to foreign policy but also in the domestic education and cultural sectors.

the articulation of modes of relating to Asia beyond a trade and productivity-centred model founded on the notion of 'opportunity'. Nevertheless, even within this paradigm, it fails to account for the ways in which Australia is already 'Asianised'. For all the attention on Asia and Asians, there is a remarkable absence of discussion about the role of Asian Australians in the document. As Tim Soutphommasane asserts:

> Some of us seem to believe that Asia is something out there, wholly apart from us. In fact, there is already a lot of Asia in Australia. … That is because so much of our Asian-ness … is currently invisible. With one or two notable exceptions, Asian-Australians aren't in the room when it matters. Where are they represented in our ministerial cabinets, our corporate boardrooms and our editorial offices? Will they be represented in such settings soon?[4]

The economic rise of Asia has resulted in unprecedented changes to the geopolitical and economic landscape, which have necessitated a 'national blueprint for a time of national change' to rethink Australia's role and engagement with Asia. According to the then Prime Minister, Julia Gillard, at the launch of the commissioning of the white paper, 'Australia has not been here before'.[5] This assertion invoked a sense of déjà vu for many scholars of Australian history. The 'Asian century' has been both anticipated and dreaded from as early as the 1880s, and unease regarding such an eventuality contributed to the development of the so-called White Australia policy that continues to haunt Australia's profile in the region. The discourses of 'engagement' with a rising Asia and its corollary, the fear of Asian invasion, have played a critical role in the nation's political imaginary. As Carol Johnson, Pal Ahluwalia and Greg McCarthy, among others, have argued, the idea of 'Asia' has operated

> as a sign and symbol in Australian domestic politics, helping to define 'who we are' as well as the related question of what is Australia's place in the world. As such, 'Asia' has always been an ambivalent sign—one that can be both troubling and exemplify hope.[6]

A historicised approach to Australia's relations with Asia reveals that discourses about Asia–Australia relations are based on a bipolar East–West conceptual framework that continues to resonate in the present, despite the awareness of the impact of globalisation. More specifically, as Jan Jindy Pettman observed

---

4 Tim Soutphommasane, 'Australia's Asian-ness is barely visible', *Sydney Morning Herald*, 5 November 2012, accessed 25 September 2013, http://www.smh.com.au/federal-politics/political-opinion/australias-asianness-is-barely-visible-20121104-28ryq.html.
5 Julia Gillard, speech, Asialink and Asia Society, Melbourne, 28 September 2011, accessed 5 January 2012, http://www.pm.gov.au/press-office/speech-asialink-and-asia-society-lunch-melbourne.
6 Carol Johnson, Pal Ahluwalia & Greg McCarthy, 'Australia's Ambivalent Re-imagining of Asia', *Australian Journal of Political Science* 45, no. 1 (2010): 60.

some years ago, notions of engagement and regional integration are 'ideally about Australia in Asia, and not about Asia in Australia'.[7] Notwithstanding the significant progress that has been made towards a more culturally inclusive concept of the nation in the area of public education, and the growing conviction that Australia's future lies with the economic ascendancy of its Asian neighbours, there remains a significant proportion of the Australian population that is uncomfortable with the changes in cultural orientation and population demographics. The populist support for Pauline Hanson's One Nation party in the mid-to-late 1990s, the Cronulla riots in 2005 and the current growing unease about Chinese investment in Australia are indicators of anxieties about the presence of Asia and Asians in Australia, and the assumed incommensurate differences between 'Asianness' and 'Australianness'.

The emergence of Asian Australianness as fields of political action, cultural production and academic research emerged in the late 1990s in response to heightened racism against Asian and Aboriginal Australians. Asian Australianness as a category of identity was deployed in the face of exclusionary racialist politics. Drawing on concepts of hybridity and diaspora, the term was used to claim a space of critique and agency for Australians of Asian descent as both Asian *and* Australian. Asian Australianness as a platform for anti-racist political solidarity was developed to unsettle dominant expectations of an unproblematic homology between cultural, racial and national identity.[8]

More than a decade later, and with new landscapes of racism emerging, the role of Asian Australians within the national imaginary remains ambivalent. While the spectre of Asian (and especially Chinese) economic dominance invokes older fears of the yellow peril, Asian Australians are also held up as bridge-builders and cultural translators who can facilitate the country's engagement with Asia. In visual art and design, the status of Asian Australian artists has arguably risen in both esteem and currency, propelled by the growing international interest in contemporary Asian art. Interest in so-called World Literature (that is, literature that crosses the traditional cultural and national domain to reach a global audience) and diasporic literature (literature written from and about the Asian diasporas in the West) are also increasingly popular.

And yet, despite the international appeal of Australian cultural production, Asian Australian artists continue to be interpreted within a nationalist and specifically multicultural framework. This leads to a tendency to emphasise the biographical and cultural/ethnic identification of the artists as the primary means of elucidating the artworks. While some Asian Australian art is based on

---

7   Jan Jindy Pettman, 'A Feminist Perspective on "Australia in Asia"', in *Race, Colour and Identity in Australia and New Zealand*, eds John Docker & Gerhard Fischer (Sydney: University of New South Wales, 2000), 147.
8   For details see Jacqueline Lo, 'Disciplining Asian Australian Studies: Projections and Introjections', *Journal of Intercultural Studies* 27, nos 1 & 2 (2006): 11–27.

the concepts of hybridity, migrancy and diaspora, there are other works that have little to do with such matters. The danger with privileging sociological frameworks is that it risks reiterating hegemonic paradigms of racialisation. The institutionalisation of such practices within academia, as well as in the curatorial and arts marketing sectors has the unfortunate consequence of delimiting Asian Australian artworks as ethnographic testimonials of racial and ethnic difference and, thus, reinforces the location of the works at the fringes of mainstream culture.

If mainstream Australia is being encouraged to find new narratives for engaging with Asia, what roles and narratives might there be for Australians of Asian descent in this not-so-new century?

Aboriginal–Asian Intimacies

Multicultural Australia did not begin, as is generally held, in the 1970s with the official demise of the so-called White Australia policy. Northern Australia was a multicultural place where Asians and Aboriginal communities traded, coexisted and procreated prior to the British presence on the continent. Yet, within the larger context of settler Australian history, there is still the perception that Asians and Aboriginals do not have much in common. The Australian story is largely constructed in terms of black/white race relations. According to Regina Ganter, the non-British histories of Australia have 'never been unknown, but they have also never been privileged into the master narrative of domestic histories'. The histories have been conveniently forgotten because they do not extend British history and are, thus, 'not remembered very hard'.[9] The separate, but parallel, management of Asians and Aboriginals became more entrenched in the first half of the twentieth century: the former were controlled by immigration laws (most notably the *Immigration Restriction Act 1901*) that kept them outside the borders of the nation, while the latter were confined to reserves and fringe settlements. The White Australia policy and its breadth of legislative instruments prevented not only non-Europeans from entering the country, but also Asians, who were already in the country, from associating with Aboriginals.

Nonetheless, there is a long history of intimacy between Asians and Aboriginals. Peta Stephenson argues that the management of parallel communities meant that Asian men and Aboriginal women were forced to maintain

> their relationships in clandestine ways and their children remained illegitimate. Indigenous–Asian relationships were shrouded in secrecy, with many fathers reluctant to acknowledge their mixed-race children

---

9 Regina Ganter, *Mixed Relations: Asian–Aboriginal Contact in North Australia* (Perth: University of Western Australia Press, 2006), 28.

for fear of reprisal. The threat of fines, imprisonment and deportation also kept many men from publicising their relationships with their Aboriginal partners.[10]

There is no recognition of this 'Asia from within' in policy instruments, such as the *Australia in the Asian Century* document.[11] Such specific iterations of vernacular cosmopolitanism remain aporetic to the narrative of Australia's Asia-turn.

There are, however, increasing numbers of Aboriginal Asian artists, such as Jason Wing, Sandra Hill and Vernon Ah Kee, who challenge this silence and embrace their mixed-race heritage. Wing began as a street artist and has since expanded his practice to incorporate photo media, installation and painting. Despite branching into new media, his work maintains its street-art sensibility, as well as drawing on his bi-cultural heritage. Known for addressing contentious issues, Wing explores complex notions of race, the environment and politics through a graphic aesthetic.

In 2011 Wing was commissioned by the Sydney City Council to create a 200-metre-long public artwork for Kimber Lane, a service lane in Sydney's Chinatown. One of the terms of the commission was to reactivate urban spaces and to divert human traffic from congested Chinatown thoroughfares by making some of the alleyways more pedestrian-friendly. Earlier public artworks in the precinct tended to conform to traditionally recognisable and iconic representations of Han culture, such as red lanterns and pagodas. This was not just for tourism, but an important marker of identity and belonging for the local Chinese community in the area and beyond.

While sensitive to the need to respect this history of the Chinese presence in the area, the artist also wanted to make visible the hitherto absent markers of Aboriginal presence, which is part of the history of the district and Wing's biography. Wing's grandfather, born in Hong Kong, came to Australia and worked in the restaurant industry in Chinatown where he met and married Wing's grandmother, who was of Scottish descent and worked as a waitress in the same restaurant. Wing's father met his mother, who is an Aboriginal woman from the Biripi people in the Upper Hunter region of New South Wales, at school in western Sydney. When Wing's parents separated, he 'travelled between two worlds—the city and the bush—and this had a profound influence on [his] attitude to life and his artwork.'

---

10 Peta Stephenson, *The Outsiders Within: Telling Australia's Indigenous-Asian Story* (Sydney: University of New South Wales Press, 2007), 75–76.
11 There is only one brief mention of early Asian–Aboriginal contact that predated European settlement: in the document 'White Australia, industry protection, … state paternalism and imperial benevolence … had the effect of stunting the relationship with Asia', Department of the Prime Minister and Cabinet, *Australia in the Asian Century*, white paper (Canberra, 2012), 78, accessed 1 January 2013, http://asiancentury.dpmc.gov.au/white-paper.

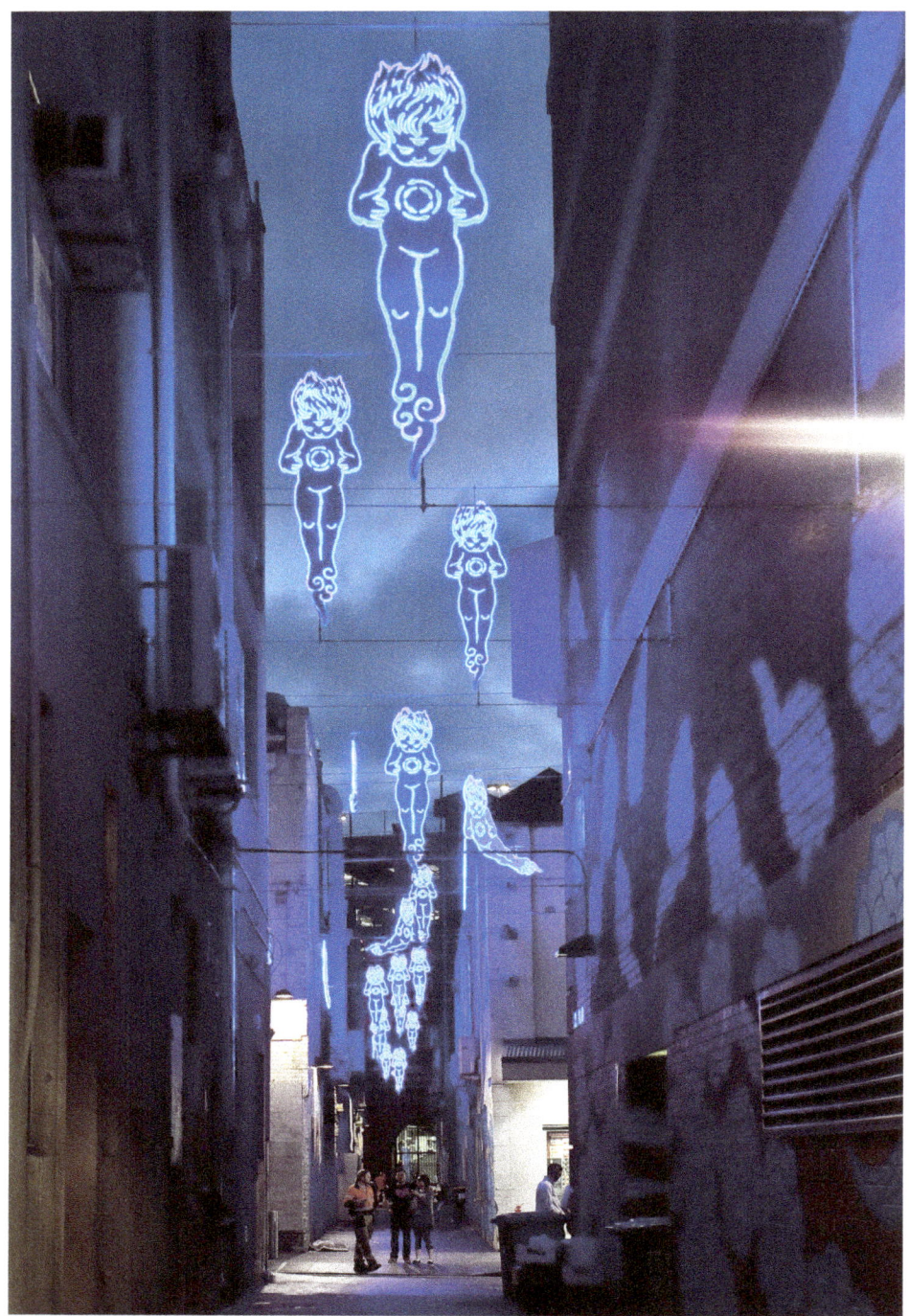

Jason Wing, *In Between Two Worlds* (entry to Kimber Lane), Sydney 2012; 200 m long x 7 m high, exterior house paint, Dibond, Perspex, LEDs.

Photograph: Paul Patterson. Special mention: Architectural Graphics. Image courtesy of the artist

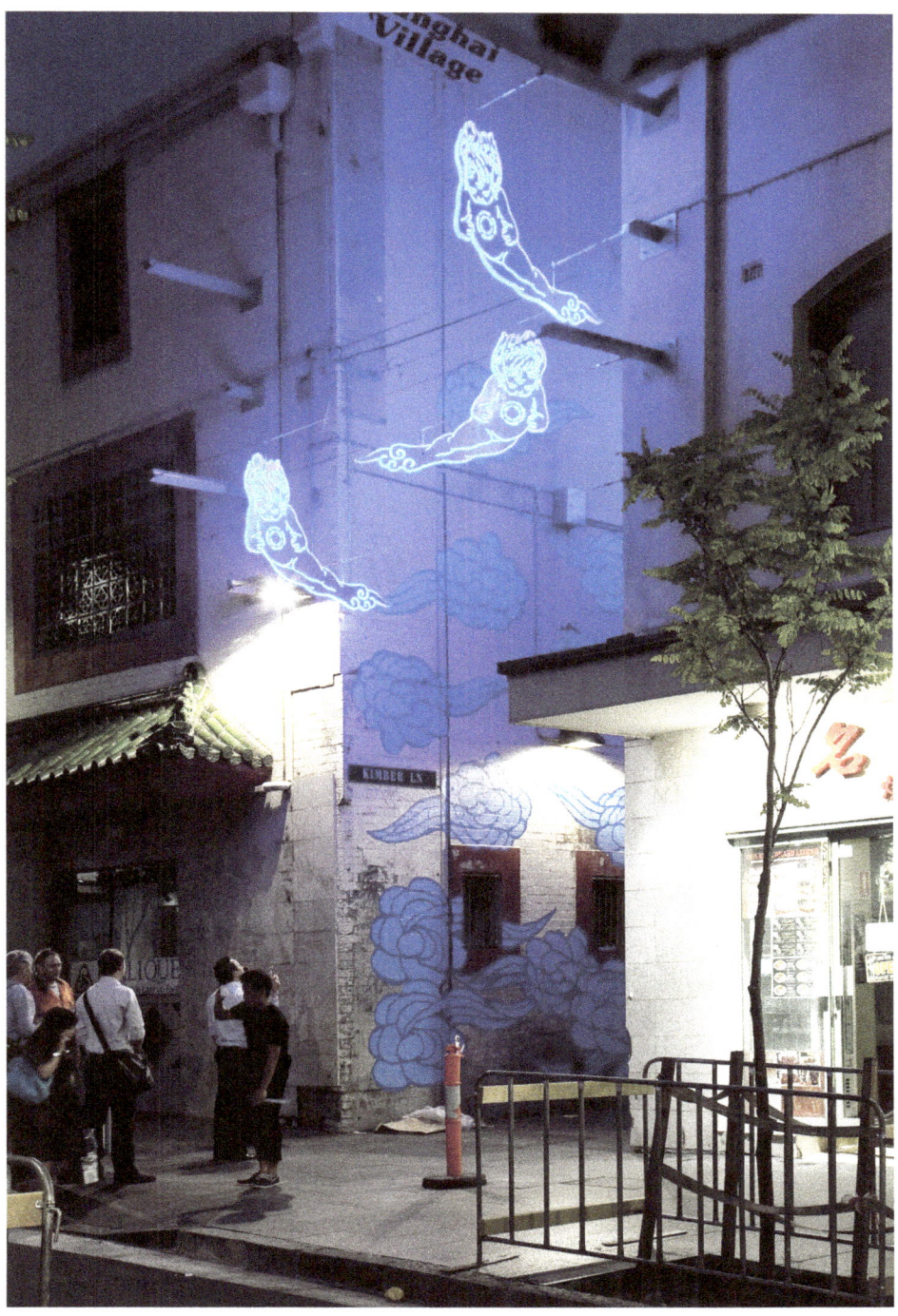

Jason Wing, *In Between Two Worlds* (lane view), Kimber Lane, Sydney 2012.

Photograph: Paul Patterson. Special mention: Architectural Graphics. Image courtesy of the artist

> I combine both traditional Chinese paper cutting and Aboriginal stencil techniques in my work. I also look for similarities in both cultures in terms of spiritual customs, teachings and detailed understanding of the human body and nature.[12]

The artwork invokes the four elements of water, wind, fire and earth, and references Indigenous Australian and Chinese cultures. Both cultures believe that these elements have their own spirits. In *In Between Two Worlds*, this spirituality is embodied in the 30 androgynous cherubic figures that represent both past and future. The spirit figures float along the alleyway (a creative interpretation of safety lighting for a public space) and entice passersby to explore the laneway. On the chest of each spirit figure is a circle, signifying that the laneway is the symbolic heartland of Chinatown. The circle also invokes the Indigenous Australian cultural symbol for a campfire, a waterhole and a place of gathering. In embodying the two cultures together in the spirit figure, Wing makes visible and material the convergence of histories that are usually represented as incommensurate.

When he was developing his plans for Kimber Lane, Wing had just returned from an arts residency in the Shanxi province in northern China. The work is partly inspired by his experience of walking through the clouds in the Taihang Mountains:

> I wanted to replicate the overwhelming oneness I felt with nature by replicating cloud murals on the walls, roads and pavement and suspending spirit figures in midair. I can only hope that this work located in the heart of an urban Chinese-Australian metropolis, evoked the same spiritual experience I had whilst walking through those misty mountains.[13]

The image of the cloud is often used in traditional Chinese imagery. In Wing's work the cloud mural invokes the four elements of wind (through the appearance of movement), water (the colour blue), earth (the cloud shape resembles mountains), and fire (the tail of the clouds look like flames). The cloud pattern is also incorporated in the granite paving of the lane, some of which is inlaid with paint to create visual continuity with the walls. Clouds represent the heavens and the Chinese word for cloud is also homophonic for 'luck' or 'fortune'. Thus, when encountering some resistance to his liberal use of the colour blue in the work (as opposed to the more conventional red), Wing was able to persuade the Chinese community elders that the laneway was presenting the community with 200 metres of good fortune.[14]

---

12   Jason Wing, 'Postcards from China', *Artlink* 32, no. 2 (2012): 91.
13   Ibid., 92.
14   Jason Wing, conversation with the author, July 2013.

Wing has returned to China since *In Between Two Worlds* opened: 'The more I travel to China the more I see similarities between Chinese and Aboriginal people struggling with the dispossession of land and traditional culture by Government policies.' During a residency in Beijing in 2012, he made a three-metre-high fibreglass red-bellied snake: 'The concept refers to the Australian status quo, promoting fear of both China and Aboriginal people. This work explores themes of power, fear and survival. Travelling overseas has made me focus more on international human issues.'

Aboriginal–Asian artists, such as Wing, activate an older subaltern narrative of contact between Asia and Australia, which in Wing's case, places the matter centrally within the space of Sydney's Chinatown. In recovering this heritage of Asian connections, our national history connects with other histories in the region in more meaningful ways than the current transactional model of engagement. As David Walker and Agnieszka Sobocinska point out:

> Acknowledging this diversity of Australia's past is not only important for our sense of self, but also for how others perceive us. Revealing the full extent of Australian Asian contacts links our past to that of our region, and supports the sense of interconnectedness vital to sustained economic, political and cultural relations.[15]

Diasporic Agency

The discourse of Rising Asia is frequently conflated with 'Rising China', which produces specific challenges as well as opportunities for Australians of Chinese descent. John Young's story illustrates the politics and poetics of diaspora. He was born in Hong Kong in 1956, the youngest child of a westernised Catholic family. His parents sent him to a Sydney boarding school in 1967 to remove him from the immediate consequences of China's Great Proletarian Cultural Revolution. Aside from annual trips back to Hong Kong, Young has made Australia his home.

Young belongs to what might be considered the first wave of Chinese Australian artists —including Lindy Lee and William Yang—who grew up and began their professional careers at a time when the White Australia policy was still in place and there was little cultural space for notions of diasporic or hybrid identities. Although the work of all three artists investigates, in different ways, their Chinese cultural heritage, this was not always the case: their early works are

---

15 David Walker & Agnieszka Sobocinska, 'Introduction: Australia's Asia', in *Australia's Asia: From Yellow Peril to Asian Century*, eds David Walker & Agnieszka Sobocinska (Perth: University of Western Australia Press, 2012), 19.

underscored by modernist and postmodernist Euro-American precepts. It was only in the 1990s, when contemporary Asian art gained increasing currency in the international arts market, that Young's work was studied through diasporic frameworks. While the dominant multicultural paradigm operating at the time created new spaces for non-Anglo artists to present their works, the interpretation of the works tended to be subsumed under simplistic identity discourses of hybridity and fusion.

Young's recent work is instructive in this respect. Rather than focusing on issues of racial or transcultural identity, his interest has turned instead to the question of how people act in cross-cultural situations. Globalisation has had a profound impact on the international arts market, opening new opportunities across national borders. There has been a surge of interest in contemporary Chinese art since the 1980s, with artists such as Cai Guo-Qiang, Gu Wenda and Xu Bing becoming major figures in festival circuits. Although the international art world is now a diffuse network of institutions and circuits of collaboration, production and exchange, Young maintains that the work of these Chinese artists is still required to perform racialised roles and deal with Chinese issues in order to maintain currency. He also sees international curators adopting a deterritorialised approach to the works themselves, specialising in the thematic manipulation of artworks drawn from diverse locations with little attention to the historical contexts that support the artworks.[16]

For Young, the speed of globalisation has exacerbated this sense of ethical indifference in the constant search for the next new commodity. He sees a role for art in linking the present to 'a world of forgotten stories, discarded objects, and memories ... Making art not only means to recollect stories, but to reawaken an intrinsic ethical impulse in the present'. This shift to 'situate ethics and moral judgment within the context of crossing from one culture to another'[17] is demonstrated in *Safety Zone*, which comprises 60 drawings and digital images organised as a panel display, three large paintings entitled *Flower Market (Nanjing 1936)*, and two vertical paintings entitled *The Crippled Tree*. The exhibition premiered at Anna Schwartz Gallery in 2010, was restaged at the University of Queensland Art Museum in 2011, and the Drill Hall Gallery at The Australian National University in 2013.

Young used a series of chalk drawings on blackboard-paint covered paper interspersed with inkjet prints from archival images for the *Safety Zone* panel. Most of these images focus on atrocities enacted by the Japanese in Nanjing in the 1930s. As the Japanese marched closer to Nanjing in 1931, most foreigners

---

16   Carolyn Barnes, 'Towards a Layered Imaginary', in *John Young* (Fisherman's Bend, Victoria: Craftsman House, 2005), 61.
17   John Young, cited in Thomas J. Berghuis, 'John Young: Situational Ethics', *Art & Australia* 48, no. 3 (2011): 440.

10. Australia's Other Asia in the Asian Century

left the city, except for 15 Americans and Europeans who stayed behind and formed the International Committee to protect the Chinese. They set up a Safety Zone of some 3.85 square kilometres. At the height of the Nanjing invasion, the International Committee protected some 200,000 civilian Chinese. In this essay I focus on two foreigners whose stories especially resonated with Young.

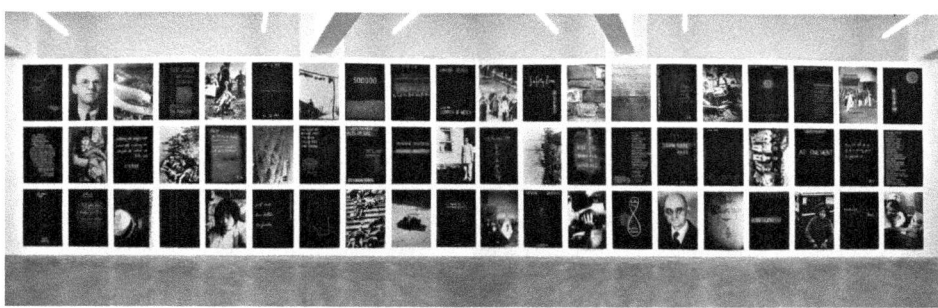

John Young, *Safety Zone* 2010; installation view, 60 works, digital prints and chalk on blackboard paint on paper, 3.2 x 15.9 m overall.

Collection of the artist. Image courtesy of the artist

John Rabe was a businessman working for the German electronic and engineering company Siemens. He was appointed leader of the International Committee largely because he was a member of the Nazi Party, which afforded him negotiating capacity with the Japanese, as the Germans were then allies with the Japanese as part of the Anti-Comintern Pact. When the Safety Zone was disestablished in 1938, Rabe was sent back to Berlin. After Hitler's reign, however, he and his family encountered great hardship because of his Nazi association; he was first held by the Gestapo and then, after the war, by the Soviet NKVD (The People's Commissariat for Internal Affairs), and later by the British army. He was forced to undergo an arduous de-Nazification process and lost his job at Siemens. He and his family lived in poverty to the point of starvation until the citizens of Nanjing heard of his situation. They sent money and later monthly food packages to help the family. Rabe died in 1950 in pitiful circumstances.

In the panel inscribed with 'You have the heart of a Buddha' (*Du hast das Herz einer Buddha*), the interplay of two languages operates dialogically. Written in Chinese is 'This is a drawing for John Rabe'. Text under erasure denotes: 'You have saved thousands of poor people from danger and want', which is juxtaposed against Rabe's own writing, 'Everyone thinks I am a hero and that can be very annoying. I can see nothing heroic about me or within me'. Then, in Chinese, 'for Mr. Rabe'.

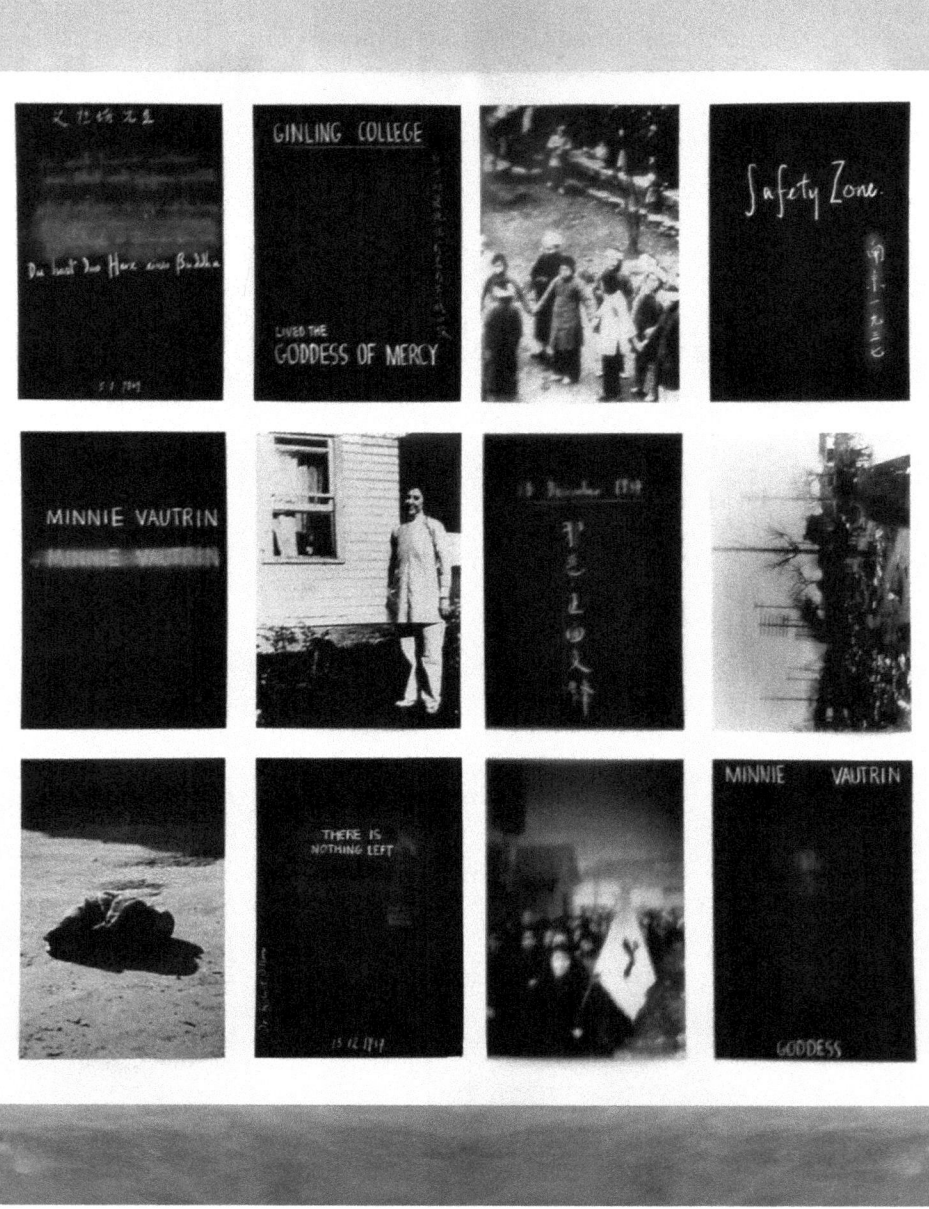

John Young, *Safety Zone* 2010 (detail).

Collection of the artist. Image courtesy of the artist

Another person of note who is explored in Young's work is Minnie Vautrin, an American who established the Ginling Girls College and saved hundreds from rape and worse fates. The inkjet photograph of Vautrin shows her in the college compound in what appears to be a uniform. Ultimately Vautrin could not prevent numerous incursions by Japanese soldiers, who came into the college and raped girls as young as three, as well as their mothers and grandmothers. Vautrin was sent home along with other foreigners in 1938, when the Safety Zone was abolished after the Japanese army claimed formal control of the city. Traumatised by the events she had witnessed and feeling responsible for the lives she could not protect, Vautrin committed suicide by turning on the gas stove in her apartment in Indianapolis in 1940.

An inkjet portrait, of girls playing in the Safety Zone compound are identified with the caption 'Ginling College'. Dietrich Bonhoeffer's quote is reproduced in Chinese: 'The test of the morality of a society is what it does for its children'. For this writer, these words are all the more chilling when accompanied by the image of youth. The image with 'Victim' inscribed depicts the only full-face portrait of a Chinese subject in Young's panel and, thus, is an important assertion of embodied Chinese agency and resistance to the violence of the time. It is likely that this young girl was the victim of rape and a patient of the only foreign doctor who stayed behind at the University of Nanking Hospital, Robert Wilson.

The affective images in *Safety Zone* provoke us to reflect on humanitarian actions that transcend narrow ethnic and nationalist sentiments. The sensitivity and immediacy of the works reveal Young's own position and anxiety as a Chinese Australian. He poses a profound challenge to Asian Australians: perhaps it is not what one identifies 'as' or how one is categorised 'with', but rather what one chooses to 'do,' that truly matters.

New Narratives for an Asian Century?

The works of Asian-Australians, such as Wing and Young, point to more nuanced ways of engaging with the complexities of Asia 'out there', but also the ways in which an understanding of 'Asia within' can enrich our understanding of who we are as a nation, and how we can relate in more meaningful ways with our near-neighbours. As Asian Australians, the artists are not prescriptive in either politics or poetics, but they proffer alternative narratives of being both within and without normative Asia *and* Australia. By focusing on the impact of an older contact history, Wing challenges and supplements the transactional logic of Asian regional integration as exemplified by the *Australia in the Asian Century* white paper and positions Australian–Asian engagement within an unresolved postcolonial context. Young, on the other hand, brings a transnational approach to nationalised histories of war and trauma. The humanitarian acts witnessed by his artwork defy exclusive national and cultural ownership, and testify to how everyday people rise up to assist each other in periods of extreme moral deficit.

The works of the artists and scholars represented in this collection of essays point to the potential (as well as pitfalls) of assuming a simplistic portrait of contemporary Asian visual culture. Instead, the intellectual and cultural complexities, as well as the self-reflexive models of interrogation, that are gathered in this volume, raise the stakes in asking us to rethink what lessons might we, as artists, scholars, activists and citizens, activate and emplace in our engagement with the political imaginary.

Acknowledgements

Excerpts from this essay previously appeared in catalogues for the following exhibitions: *Passages*, Brian Castro, Khai Liew & John Young, Tarrawarra Museum of Art, Healesville, Victoria, 2012; and *John Young: The Bridge and the Fruit Tree*, Drill Hall Gallery, The Australian National University, Canberra, 2013. My thanks to Jason Wing and John Young for permission to use images of their work. Research for this essay was supported by a grant from the Australian Research Council DP08: 'Being Asian in Australia and the United States'.

Epilogue — 'My Future is Not a Dream':[1] Shifting Worlds of Contemporary Asian Art and Exhibitions

Michelle Antoinette

If Asian art of the 1990s offered glimpses into the shifting conditions of Asian societies, especially those of newly industrialised, globalising status, the essays gathered in this collection suggest that art at the turn of the century was poised to take on a different project. They collectively ask *what are we to make of this newly changed Asia, for the present and for the future, for Asia itself and for the world?*

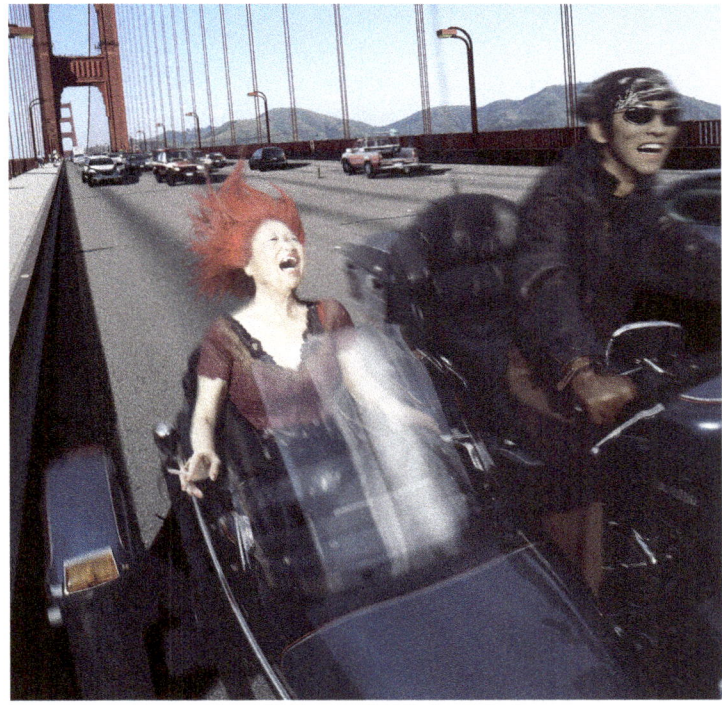

Miwa Yanagi, *Yuka* from *My Grandmothers* series 2000; C-print between plexiglass; 160 x 160 cm.

© The artist; image courtesy of the artist

---

1 'My Future is Not a Dream' is the title of Part III of Chinese artist Cao Fei's video, *Whose Utopia?* (2007).

At the Introduction to this volume, Caroline Turner's essay foregrounds the dramatic shifts in the world of contemporary art at the closing decade of the twentieth century and the new significance of contemporary Asian art within this. As Turner and other authors in this volume have described, the art world began to admit a variety of contemporary art practices from all over the globe, not least Asia, with contemporary Asian art now a thriving presence in international exhibitions. Indeed, alongside Asia's renewed influence in matters of global economics and politics, it has likewise been impossible to ignore Asia's revived cultural influence in the world. This includes the explosion of contemporary art from Asia—the now ubiquitous and striking array of avant-garde, experimental or transforming art practices, which communicate not only the vitality of contemporary Asian art practice, but also reflect the rapidly changing social circumstances of Asia.

Part of the motivation behind Asian art production in the twentieth century was to explore the possibilities of the new Asia and the new art and, in turn, to assert its place in the global art landscape and help convey the new Asia to the world. As the essays in this volume suggest, there is now, however, an increased focus on Asian art for Asia itself, not only so as to continue to nurture and develop a self-defined vocabulary for Asian art, but also increasingly, to address issues of local and regional relevance to Asian societies and to communicate such issues to local and regional audiences—audiences now more accustomed to contemporary art as a feature of urban Asian realities and an increasing part of Asia's newly established cultural industries. Highlighted in Oscar Ho's essay in this volume is the growing attention being given to 'cultural' development within Asia, most strongly demonstrated by newly established cultural projects supporting developing cultural industries and creative economies across various parts of Asia,[2] with contemporary art being a key part of this. Moreover, as Charles Merewether's essay in this volume registers, contemporary art offers a means for developing new transnational networks across Asia, encouraging renewed regional connections across national borders and divides of colonial making. In addition is the variety of new intercultural projects that work *with* and *through* the diversity of cultural difference within the region: in this volume, the 'West Heavens' project, the focus of Chaitanya Sambrani's essay, and the Japan Foundation 'Under Construction' project mentioned by Turner, are key examples of such transnational and intercultural, regional initiatives that at the same time argue for Asia-based exhibition frameworks and perspectives. Meanwhile, projects such as the 'Asia-Pacific Triennial of Contemporary Art' exhibition, discussed by Turner and Pat Hoffie, and Asialink's art-focused

---

2   Lily Kong, 'From Cultural Industries to Creative Industries and Back? Clarifying Theory and Rethinking Policy' (paper presented at the Inter-Asia Cultural Studies International Conference 'Beyond the Cultural Industries', National University of Singapore, 3–5 July 2013) (The *Inter-Asia Cultural Studies* journal, in which Kong's paper will appear, is forthcoming).

intitiatives in Asia discussed by Alison Carroll, point to continuing Australian interest in engaging with Asia's contemporary art and the strengthening significance of Asia's art to international audiences in the twenty-first century.

Indeed, the changing circumstances of Asia and its art, as the authors in this volume have suggested, also bear relevance for the world, necessarily showing Asia as enmeshed in, even increasingly at the centre of or directing, global currents and transnational networks. Politics, the economy, and environmental issues, for instance, may relate directly to local Asian concerns, but also have consequences for the world and international engagements with Asia. Similarly, as Asian art has taken hold in Asia, it has also captured international attention and affects currents of international art. In this sense, as essays by Marsha Meskimmon, Francis Maravillas and Jacqueline Lo highlight, Asian art exemplifies the conditions of 'contemporary art' practice in that it simultaneously speaks to both local and global concerns, is capable of communicating and connecting with audiences near and far across borders of all kinds, and is distinctive in its emergence from or influence by particular Asian cultural contexts of production with concurrent relevance and relation to the world.[3]

These antinomies lie at the heart of the developing field of art historical enquiry surrounding 'contemporary art' practice. As the field continues to be debated and theorised, contemporary Asian art has helped to expand the field's possibilities, revealing Asia-based histories for contemporary art in the world and refuting an exclusively Euro-American paradigm for understanding art developments of the last two to three decades. Contemporary Asian art reveals how the world is made increasingly smaller and connected by the currents of globalisation, but nevertheless, unlike those perspectives encouraging a universalising frame of 'world art', contemporary art is increasingly acknowledged as a diversified field emerging from multiple contexts and differentiated histories, including those of Asia. Indeed, even as contemporary art forges new connective currents of 'global' art, it is propelled by the very diversity and difference of the world's contemporary artistic practices. As the authors of this volume have suggested, Asia is not merely a landscape of renewed regional connection in the twenty-first century, but a place from which we must recognise alternative perspectives on and of the world: for instance, John Clark's essay makes this point specifically with regard to the development of Asian art's history; Patrick Flores, via the Philippines, articulates critical Asian positionings embedded in complex national and cosmopolitan belongings; while Hoffie's essay urges the specific contribution of contemporary Asian art practices to broader notions of the 'contemporary'.

---

3 On theorising contemporary art see, among others, Hans Belting, Patrick Flores, Terry Smith, Hal Foster, and the Asia Art Archive ('The And: An Expanded Questionnaire on the Contemporary', *Field Notes* 1 (June 2012), accessed 7 June 2012, http://www.aaa.org.hk/FieldNotes/Details/1167.

In the following, I reflect on new currents of contemporary Asian art and exhibition in the twenty-first century, highlighting the concerns of a new generation of Asian artists, new issues expressed via art, and new modes of art practice and exhibition with regards to Asia. In so doing, I draw from the various themes and arguments explored throughout the essays in this book as a means of reflecting on Asian art's histories, presents and futures.

Reflections on Contemporary Asian Art: Then and Now

The Malaysian artist Liew Kung Yu participated in the seminal international art exhibition, *Cities on the Move* (1997–1999).[4] This travelling mega-exhibition presented some of Asia's rising contemporary artists alongside architects and filmmakers, seeking to show to largely European audiences the circumstances of Asia's dramatically changed societies and urban landscape under intense industrialisation and globalisation in the late twentieth century. Like other key exhibitions of this time, such as the New York-based Asia Society's *Contemporary Art in Asia: Traditions/Tensions* (1996), it also sought to situate Asia's artistic landscape as part of contemporary currents in the world, moving beyond Western stereotypes of an unchanging, traditional and exotic Asia devoid of contemporary art.

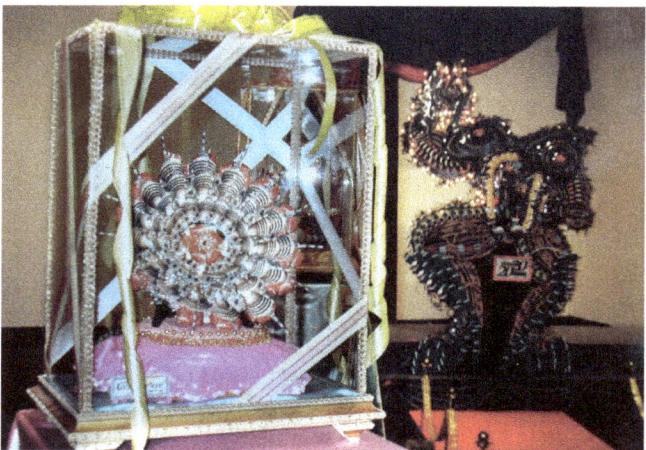

Liew Kung Yu, *Pasti Boleh/Sure Can One* 1997; installation view, for *Cities on the Move* exhibition; installation with red carpet, trophies, photo booth; collage.

© Liew Kung Yu; image courtesy of the artist

---

4   *Cities on the Move* (1997) was curated by Hou Hanru and Hans-Ulrich Obrist and first presented in Vienna with different versions thereafter in London, Helsinki, Bordeaux, Copenhagen, New York, and Bangkok. See Hou Hanru & Hans–Ulrich Obrist, eds, *Cities on the Move*, exhibition catalogue (Ostfildern–Ruit: Gerd Hatje, 1997).

Liew's contributions to the exhibition reflected Malaysia's newly prosperous economic status in the mid-1990s as one of the rising 'Asian tiger' economies—a position that was famously argued by then Malaysian Prime Minister Mahathir Mohamad as resulting from unique 'Asian values'. Liew's installation *Pasti Boleh/ Sure You Can* (1997)[5] comprised five photo-collage 'trophies' presented in neatly gift-wrapped glass vitrines, and reworked the symbols of Malaysia's economic strength and global status in the race to be 'bigger and better'. These trophies straddled a long stretch of red carpet and suggested the treasured monuments and achievements of the modern Malaysian nation. Among the icons of Malaysian modernity appropriated by Liew were the Kuala Lumpur Tower and the famed Petronas Twin Towers—the latter notable for being the world's tallest skyscrapers at the time of completion in 1999. But Liew's artwork was not necessarily an unequivocal celebration or veneration of Malaysian progress, since its garish vision of the newly urbanised Asia might also be read as a parody of all things shiny and novel: indeed, at the end of the red carpet, visitors were met with a monstrous if alluring idol of modernity at this symbolic altar of progress. Bearing the sign 'Vision 2020', it heralded the further progress of the Malaysian nation striving towards the future. Continuing to trace Malaysia's modernist 'progress', in 2009 Liew exhibited *Cadangan Cadangan Untuk Negaraku* (*Proposals For My Country*), at the Twin Towers' Galeri Petronas. The exhibition presented four large-scale photo-collages in Liew's typically garish and kitsch style, based on photographs of Malaysian icons, sculptures and monuments that he had sighted while touring the country. They convey vivid images of Malaysia's future landscapes as a spectacular if chaotic assemblage of modernity and history.

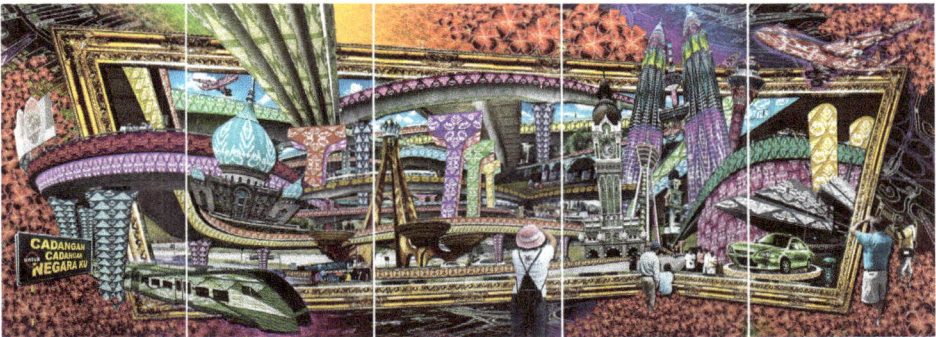

Liew Kung Yu, *Cadangan Cadangan Untuk Negaraku (Proposals for My Country) series: Metropolis Warisan* 2009; photo-collage.

© Liew Kung Yu; image courtesy of the artist

---

5   Liew also presented the performance *Selamat Datang to Malaysia* (1998–1999) with Lena Ang.

In 2012, 15 years after Liew's participation in *Cities on the Move*, artist Phuan Thai Meng offered another vision of Malaysian urbanisation, but one which is decidedly bleak and seemingly less ambivalent about the effect of economic 'progress' in Malaysia. His canvas *The Luring Of //流水不腐, 户枢不蠹* (2012) depicts some of the massive concrete bridge structures that define Malaysia's cityscapes, but this is a deserted landscape, an urban dystopia, unpeopled and lifeless. Far from the busy, colourful kitsch of Liew's imagination, this is a grey, barren and ominous scene with apocalyptic overtones. A faded sign greets visitors with 'Selamat Datang' ('Welcome'), provocatively recalling a former thriving cityscape that is now decayed and abandoned. The enormous six-part panel also addresses formalist concerns of painting, with its ripped canvas spilling onto the gallery floor, reminding its audience of the connectedness of contemporary art to issues of everyday reality. Eventually the façade of the new must give over to the old, as surfaces fade, begin to crack and peel off to reveal the plain and often brutal realities of everyday life, mimicking the economic collapse, which affected many parts of Asia in the late 1990s, and which demanded a re-examination of the dreams and hopes for Asia's futures.

Liew and Phuan's works together reflect the twin contrasting images of Asia at the beginning of the twenty-first century which have recurred throughout this volume: on the one hand, Asia is characterised by glitzy spectacle, glittering skyscrapers, dazzling prosperity and all things new, the excitement and thrill of modernity, economic progress and development; on the other, by degeneration and regretful loss of the old and the past, the disappearance of traditions and former ways of life, the continuing political and economic struggles of everyday people and ongoing socio-economic disparity between the rich and the poor, the urban and rural classes. As with artists of the past, contemporary artists of this century provide us with critical reflection on the positive and negative aspects of living in present-day Asia. Increasingly artists are attentive to the antinomies of progress, and present these contradictions in their art as part of the everyday conditions of Asian experience in the twenty-first century. Often this is so as to highlight multiple and overlapping perspectives on Asia's stories—its presents and futures, its distinct and shared experiences—and to register Asia's modernity as an unfinished project of diverse possibilities and potentialities.

Epilogue — 'My Future is Not a Dream': Shifting Worlds of Contemporary Asian Art and Exhibitions

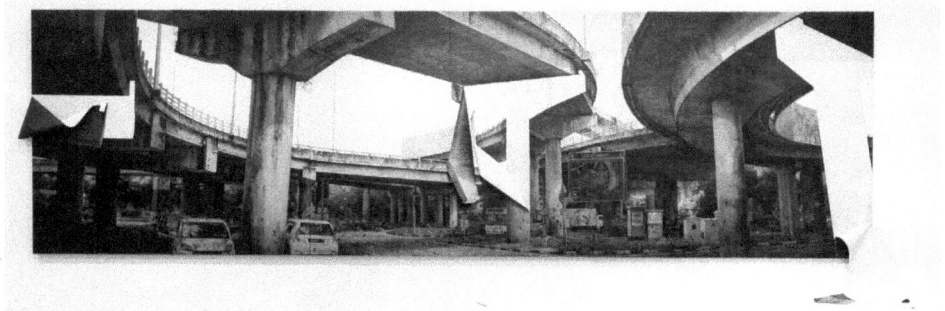

Phuan Thai Meng, Malaysia, b. 1974. *The Luring of [ ]*. 流水不腐, 户枢不蠹 2012; synthetic polymer paint on canvas mounted on plywood; six panels: 300 x 996 cm (overall), 300 x 166 cm (each).

Acc. 2012.442a-f; purchased 2012; Queensland Art Gallery; Collection: Queensland Art Gallery; © Phuan Thai Meng; photograph: Natasha Harth, QAGOMA

The exquisite filmic works of Chinese artist Chen Qiulin, also discussed by Merewether in this volume, are marked by such contradictions: the pessimism and hope which characterises China today. Her art considers the effect of recent industrial progress in China on the everyday lives of individuals, their redefined relationship to changed environments, and their disappearing memories of place. The artist suffered the loss of her hometown of Wanxian when the nearby Yangtze river was flooded for the Three Gorges Dam project, constructed between 1994 and 2008. This incident, alongside other effects of urbanisation, has been powerful subject matter for her films including *River River* (2005) and *The Garden* (2007). In *Peach Blossom* (2009), Chen reflects on another kind of destruction adding to the already changed environment following the Three Gorges Dam project—that of the devastating earthquake which affected Sichuan in 2008. In a kind of fantastical, surrealistic self-ethnography the artist casts herself in the role of a bride and she and her surrogate groom wander amid the ruins of this derelict landscape, as if ghosts in a suspended future, out of time and place. In their dreamlike wandering they evoke the kinds of trauma that people endure following such natural disasters. In fact, the artist went to visit the Sichuan countryside in search of a location for her real-life wedding, but was met with a still severely dishevelled landscape a year on from the earthquakes, despite government reports suggesting the area's restoration and resumption of order. In the photographs, the wedding couple represent the hopes and dreams of the community that once peopled this landscape, longing for the reappearance of a familiar place they once called home, but their romantic attempts seem futile. Human interference, followed by environmental destruction, has rendered the landscape barely recognisable. Yet, as with much of Chen's art, hope and will are registered through the artist's intimate and personal attempts at reconnection with this place and, always, there is some beauty to be revealed or made anew. As with Liew and Phuan, Chen illuminates the consequences of development, thus registering commonalities of experience across contemporary Asian societies and between the motivations of artists as they reflect present-day social concerns in Asia.

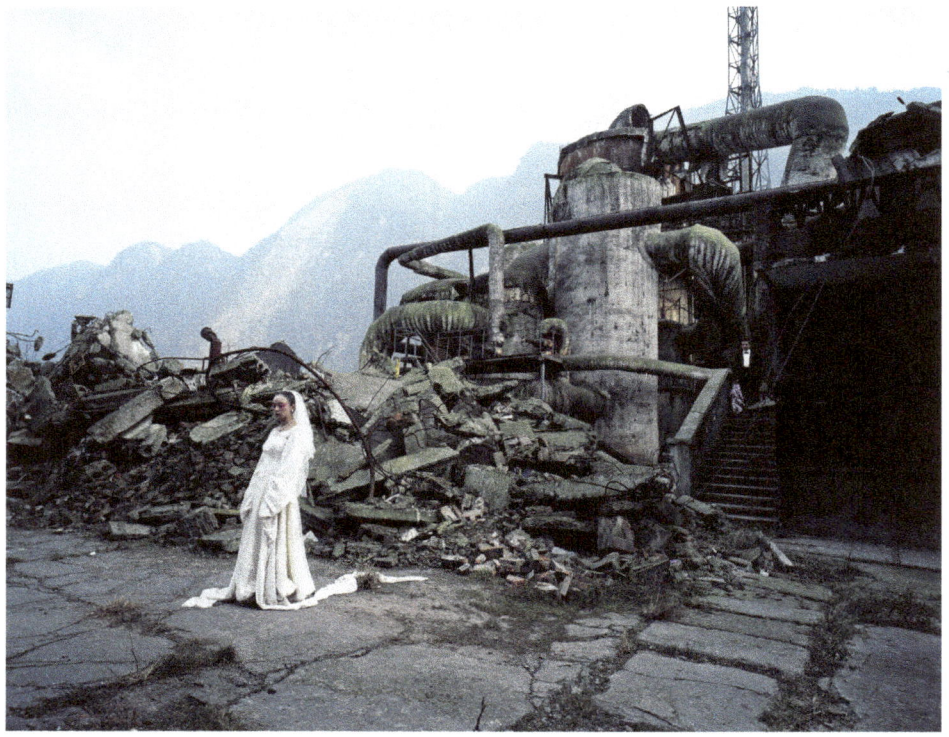

Chen Quilin, *Solidified Scenery* (from 桃花 *Peach Blossom*) 2009; 录像 video; 16 min, 37 sec; photograph, 154 x 124 cm.

Courtesy of the artist and Beam Contemporary Art, New York and London

Contemporary Asian Art: Asian and International Currents

Exhibiting Asian Art

As I intimated earlier in this epilogue, exhibitions of Asian art have been a major focus of this book, discussed especially in essays by Turner, Sambrani, Hoffie, Ho and Carroll. As Turner's essay discusses, besides country-focused or thematic exhibitions, a burgeoning number of Asia-based art biennale and triennale exhibitions—major international recurring exhibitions[6]—sprouted across Asian urban centres in the 1990s, which prior to then were only to be found in Japan, India and Bangladesh (Tokyo Biennale, 1952–1990; Triennale India, 1968–; Asian Art Biennale Bangladesh, 1981). Many of these act as important sites for the exhibition of contemporary Asian art to international audiences, some even arguing their mutual influence in shaping the new Asian art markets. As the Biennial Foundation describes, 'Biennials have become, in the span of a few decades, one of the most vital and visible sites for the production, distribution, and public discourse around contemporary art.'[7] The new Asia-based biennales have not only attracted international curatorial expertise, but also increasingly, the creativity of a new force of Asian curators, and new intra-Asian collaborations and networks.[8]

These globalised art exhibitions have been key driving factors in encouraging new kinds of contemporary art, with art and artists constantly on the move as part of developing global trajectories of art production, exhibition, and cultural exchange projects.[9] Undoubtedly, globalisation has played an enormous part in shaping contemporary art everywhere.

New Asian Art Markets and Cultural Industries

Asian art has also acquired a spectacular new commercial value in global markets, arguably at such an accelerated and commanding pace as to now be a dominating influence on the kinds of art being produced and in shaping artists' careers. Part of this stems from the emergence of art markets that are based in Asia itself and which have developed as a result of new Asian prosperity among the upper middle classes. This increasingly commercially valuable art is registered especially in the unprecedented exhibitions of Asian art in major commercial galleries in the United Kingdom and Europe, such as the London-based Saatchi Gallery's *Indonesian Eye: Fantasies & Realities* (2011) and, in Paris, *Transfigurations: Indonesian Mythologies* (2011) at the Espace Culturel Louis

---

6   'Biennials and large-scale periodic exhibitions constitute a sizeable part of the production and distribution system of artistic products, an instrument of the economic strategy of the worldwide cultural industry, and a vehicle for the development of cities' (1st Athens Biennial, *Gallery Online*, 6 July 2007, accessed 26 October 2013, http://gallery.esquare.it/press/index.asp?idp=79).
7   Biennial Foundation, 'About', accessed 19 September 2013, http://www.biennialfoundation.org/about/. See also Asia Art Archive & Art Map Ltd, 'All You Want To Know About International Art Biennials', http://www.aaa.org.hk/onlineprojects/bitri/en/didyouknow.aspx#fn1
8   For instance, the Biennale Jogja XI – Equator # 1 (2011–2012), saw the meeting of Indian and Indonesian curators and artists, while the Japan Foundation exhibition *Under Construction* (2002–2003) was premised on intraregional collaborations between curators from China, India, Indonesia, Japan, Korea, the Philippines, and Thailand.
9   The antecedent of these exhibitions is the Venice Biennale, established in 1895, which has notably boosted its Asian representation since the 1990s, with national pavilions of China, Singapore, Indonesia, and Thailand being added in the early 2000s.

Vuitton. Famously, Japanese artist Takashi Murakami began his long-standing artistic alliance with luxury fashion house Louis Vuitton in 2002, collaborating on the design of their merchandise; and, as Clark describes in his essay in this volume, Sudarshan Shetty was commissioned by Louis Vuitton to produce *House of Shades* (2009/2010) for the Women's Fashion Week in Milan, installed at Galleria Vittorio Emanuele II. Ironically, the controversial installation by Xiao Lu, which prompted the closure of the famous *China Avant-Garde* exhibition at the National Art Gallery, Beijing, in 1989, forcing Chinese avant-garde art to go back underground, sold in 2005 at the China Guardian auction in Beijing for 2,310,000 yuan,[10] indicating both the ideological and monetary force of the market in giving new value to Asian art.

The strength of Asia's art industries is most obvious in Hong Kong's new status as the site for one of the world's leading commercial art fairs, featuring modern and contemporary art from all over the world. After the success of the Hong Kong International Art Fair, launched in 2007, the fair was taken over by the longer standing 'premier' international art fair, Art Basel. For the inaugural Art Basel in Hong Kong in 2013, '53 per cent of the 245 galleries on show [were] from Asia and the Asia-Pacific.'[11] According to the organisers, this 'confirm[s] Art Basel's desire to build a cultural bridge between the long-established Western artworld and the vibrant new scenes of the entire [Asian and Asia-Pacific] region.'[12] Meanwhile, the former Singapore Art Fair was surpassed by newer commercial initiatives such as Art Stage Singapore (est. 2010, with its first show in 2011)[13] focusing on Asian art, and especially South-East Asian art, and the Affordable Art Fair that takes place in both Hong Kong (since 2013) and Singapore (since 2010) and other major cities around the world. Reflecting the renewed economic importance of India, the India Art Summit was established in 2008—and rebranded in 2012 as the India Art Fair—to meet the world's interest in modern and contemporary Indian art but also includes international art. Coinciding with the India Art Summit 2011, the Lisson Gallery, representing world-renowned sculptor Anish Kapoor, presented the artist's first exhibition in India—the self-titled *Anish Kapoor* (2010–2011)—nearly 40 years after the artist's departure to England from India, his country of birth. Evidently, these new sites of commercial exchange across Asia have created connections within the region, and between the region and global art market networks.

---

10   See Payal Uttam, 'A Shot in the Dark', *Prestige Hong Kong*, 18 January 2013, accessed 26 October 2013, http://prestigehongkong.com/2013/01/shot-dark.
11   'Magnus Renfrew, Art Basel HK Director', *Australian*, 3 May 2013, accessed 24 June 2013, http://www.theaustralian.com.au/executive-living/luxury/magnus-renfrew-art-basel-hk-director/story-e6frg8io-1226631745312.
12   Art Basel, 'About Art Basel: Our History', accessed 24 June 2013, https://www.artbasel.com/en/About-Art-Basel/History.
13   The Founder & Fair Director of Art Stage Singapore, Lorenzo Rudolf, was director of Art Basel (1991–2000) and launched *ShContemporary* in Shanghai in 2007, mainland China's first international art fair.

Epilogue — 'My Future is Not a Dream': Shifting Worlds of Contemporary Asian Art and Exhibitions

Independent and Localised Engagements

Alongside the commercial growth of Asian art, a phenomenal array of new art galleries and museums has been established across Asia. These include commercial spaces, state-supported projects, private initiatives, artist-run initiatives and independent projects. The government-supported M+ museum in Hong Kong, as Ho discussed in his essay in this volume, seeks to be a centre for the collection and exhibition of 'local' art (see Ho, this volume); the Gillman Barracks in Singapore serves as a contemporary art hub connecting diverse art galleries and a Centre for Contemporary Art; and the National Art Gallery Singapore as a centre for modern South-East Asian art. Alongside these larger state-supported projects, the presence of smaller independent or 'alternative' initiatives has been instrumental in nurturing contemporary Asian art, a point also emphasised by Ho. This was especially so in the 1990s when, throughout Asia, there was far less state-supported infrastructure or even interest in contemporary art.[14] Together these initiatives form a dynamic intra-regional network for alternative art practices across Asia that are concurrently embedded within transregional, global art networks.[15] While such independent initiatives are often short-lived or shift in their 'alternative' value, the relative longevity of these in the Asian context is testimony to their vital part in the contemporary art scene.

Despite the force of the art market, or perhaps because of its influence, a new generation of artists is embedding itself in community-based art activities, which are often removed from commercial imperatives. This kind of art, typically connecting with and engaging everyday communities as participants and creative agents in the art-making process, resonates with the 'relational', 'participatory' or 'collaborative' art engagements variously theorised and famously debated in art circles by Nicolas Bourriaud, Claire Bishop, Grant Kester and others (see also Maravillas, this volume). While these art historical debates erupted around the early 2000s, following publication of Bourriaud's 1998 *Esthétique relationnelle* (*Relational Aesthetics*),[16] as early as 1993, artist FX Harsono

---

14 Prominent 'alternatives', past and present, include Cemeti Art House (Yogyakarta) and Ruangrupa (Jakarta); 798 Art District and Long March (Beijing), Vitamin Creative Space (Guangzhou); 1a space and Para Site (Hong Kong); Surrounded by Water, Big Sky Mind and Green Papaya (Manila); Salon Natasha and Blue Space (Ho Chi Minh); The Artists' Village and the Substation (Singapore); commandN (Tokyo); About Studio / About Café (Bangkok), The Land Foundation (Chiang Mai); Alternative Space Loop (Seoul); Khoj (Delhi), Open Circle (Mumbai); and Theertha (Colombo), alongside newer spaces and collectives such as SA SA BASSAC (Phnom Penh) and Sàn Art (Ho Chi Minh).
15 The Aar-Paar project beginning in 2002, involving the 'cross-border' exchange and exhibition of artworks between Indian and Pakistani artists, demonstrates the capacity of such independent projects to make political interventions and implement social change by negotiating national borders and connecting people across physical and ideological constraints.
16 See Nicolas Bourriaud, *Esthétique relationnelle* (*Relational Aesthetics*) (Dijon: Les Presses du réel, 2002 (1998)). The term 'relational aesthetics', however, was first used in Bourriaud's 1996 catalogue for the exhibition *Traffic* at the CAPC musée d'art contemporain de Bordeaux, France.

suggested the particular relevance of a socially engaged art practice within the Indonesian context: 'The resulting art installation is known as participative art. In this type of art, the participation of the public is vital.'[17] These types of performative, community-engaged, participatory practices are witnessed in the work of other contemporary South-East Asian artists as early as the 1960s and 1970s—for instance, the Conceptual art forms signalled by Merewether in this volume—and some have argued their distinctive affinities to traditional South-East Asian cultural practices.[18] The turn to community via contemporary art is particularly pertinent in the twenty-first century as contemporary art becomes a more familiar communicative tool and popularised cultural practice in Asian societies. Whereas prior to the 2000s the communities for contemporary art in Asia arguably targeted more elitist and art-specific audiences, the last decade has witnessed an increased mainstreaming of contemporary art in public spaces.

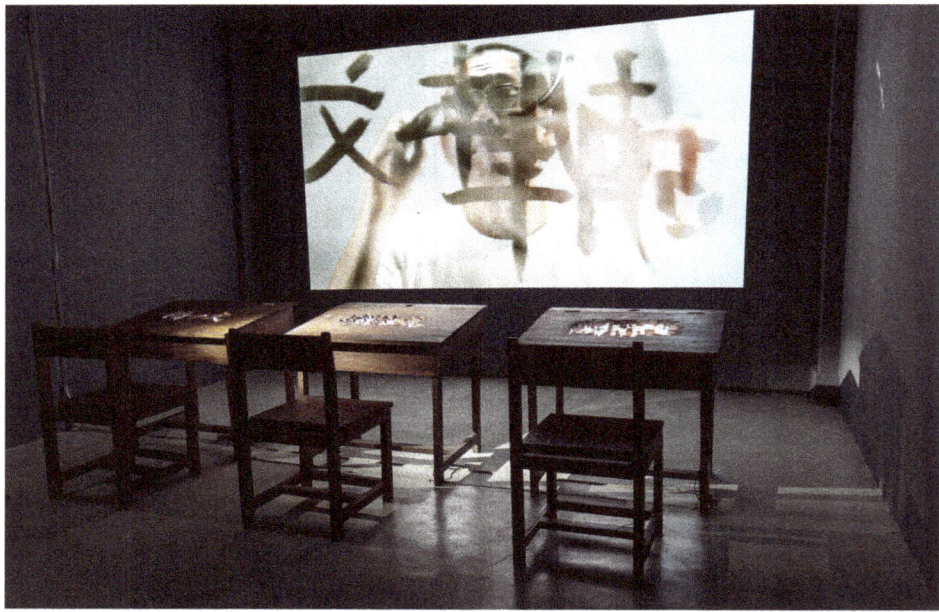

FX Harsono, *Writing In the Rain* 2011; single-channel video performance.

© FX Harsono; image courtesy of the artist

---

17 FX Harsono, 'The Installation as the Language of Social Concern', in *The First Asia–Pacific Triennial of Contemporary Art. Identity, Tradition and Change: Contemporary Art of the Asia Pacific Region (QAG, Queensland Cultural Centre, South Bank, Brisbane, 17–20 September 1993)*; unpublished conference papers & list of attendees; Queensland Art Gallery et al. (Brisbane: Queensland Art Gallery, 1993).

18 See Raymundo R. Albano, 'Installations: A Case for Hangings', in *ASEAN Art Exhibition: Third ASEAN Exhibition of Painting and Photography 1984*, ed. ASEAN Committee on Culture and Information (Manila: Cultural Center of the Philippines, 1984); Julie Ewington, 'Five Elements: An Abbreviated Account of Installation Art in South-East Asia', *ART and AsiaPacific* 2, no. 1 (1995): 108–15.

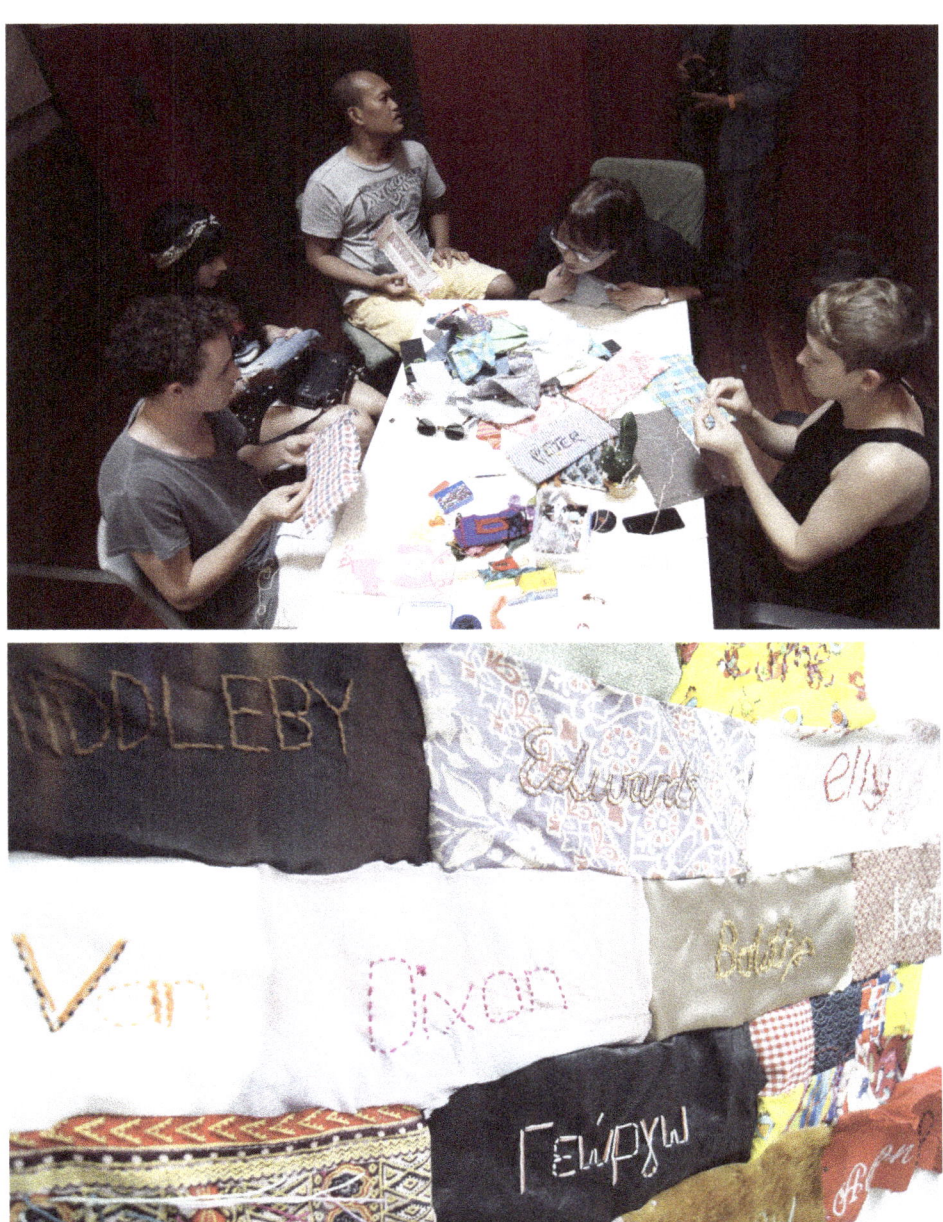

Elly Kent, *Nee (Born As)* ongoing participatory project January 2012 – ; (top) participants stitching and conversing at 4A Centre for Contemporary Asian Art, 18 February 2012; (bottom): the physical artefact of the first conversation/stitching session held in the artist's garage, 26 January 2012.

Photography: Elly Kent; image courtesy of the artist

Between 2010 and 2013, Harsono participated in the *Edge of Elsewhere* exhibition project (a curatorial collaboration between the Campbelltown Arts Centre and 4A Centre for Contemporary Asian Art), which invited Asian and Pacific contemporary artists to engage with Sydney's everyday suburban communities in forms of community-engaged art.[19] Harsono initiated a public curatorium entitled *In Memory of a Name*, inviting participants to reflect on the memorialisation of names.[20] The project took inspiration from his previous artwork *Rewriting the Erased* (2009), a film depicting Harsono repeatedly inscribing his original Chinese name, responding to its erasure under the Suharto regime when Indonesians of Chinese descent were forced by government decree to adopt 'Indonesian' names. This action was also demonstrated in his subsequent film-performance *Writing in the Rain* (2011). Australian artist Elly Kent, a participant in Harsono's curatorium, in turn developed her own participatory conversation project: *Née (Born As)* invited participants to tell and stitch the stories of their names—names 'left behind, names "embraced"'[21]—registering the social, material and affective significance of art to illuminate forgotten histories and to communicate narratives of shared human experience between people across cultures.

Projects such as *Edge of Elsewhere* can be situated within the familiar frame of international exhibition projects which seek dialogue between cultures. Unlike traditional nation state-to-nation state exchanges or collaborations emphasising the display of one culture to another, however, a new stream of collaborative projects seeks to create more experimental and flexible platforms for art's production and exhibition *within* and *by* localised communities and emphasise art's possibilities for everyday, grounded community engagement. This return to community and local concerns is a means of redressing the oversights of global and regional views in cross-cultural projects where a localised basis can afford different perspectives. *Edge of Elsewhere* foregrounded the value of the localised community in representing suburban community perspectives on globalisation's massive cultural transformation affecting people and major cities in all parts of the world. This intersection of the local, national and global demonstrates 'important new models for placing communities at the centre of contemporary art development ...',[22] which in turn illuminate the everyday realities and cultural entanglements of Asia's diasporas, migratory flows and their legacies in all parts of the world. As mentioned at the Introduction (Part 2) and as Lo discusses in her essay in this volume, 4A Centre for Contemporary Asian Art[23] has established

---

19   *Edge of Elsewhere* was supported by the Australia Council for the Arts and the NSW Government.
20   See the 'Edge of Elsewhere' blog, http://edgeofelsewhere.wordpress.com/category/fx-harsono-in-memory-of-a-name/ (accessed 23 September 2013).
21   Elly Kent, *Née (Born As)*, accessed 26 October 2013, http://ellydotkent.blogspot.com.au/p/nee-born-as.html.
22   Kon Gouriotis & Frank Panucci, 'Creative Adaption and Continuing Conversations ...', *Artlink* 3, no. 1 (2011): 53.
23   The '4A' alliance (the Asian Australian Artists' Association) was established in 1996 as a non-profit organisation to support the differently positioned cultural concerns and challenges of multi-disciplinary

an important profile in Australia, but also Asia, as a significant independent art space for the development of contemporary art at the intersection of Asian, Australian and Asian–Australian concerns. It has undertaken art projects in Australia and Asia that build experimental and collaborative contemporary art platforms between Asian and Australian artists and audiences. Echoing Lo's hopes for new 'Australian' narratives for engaging with 'Asia', 4A's mappings of contemporary art, I suggest, bring complexity to otherwise simplistic identitarian notions of art, challenging what is meant by contemporary 'Asian', 'Australian', and 'Asian–Australian' art.

Transnational Vectors, Responding to the World

The art-focused essays by Meskimmon, Maravillas, and Lo in this volume point to contemporary Asian art practices that are deeply informed by specific issues of localised meaning, but which at the same time respond to and resonate with transnational issues and audiences. The focus of Wong Hoy Cheong's art has over the last few decades constantly shifted between local concerns of Malaysia and South-East Asia, and issues of transnational, global relevance, including the significance of Islamic identifications around the world following the September 11 terrorism attacks of 2001, and the subjecthood of contemporary migrants and refugees in a world of intensified globalisation and continuing global conflict. What remains an ongoing thread in Wong's practice is his illumination of power struggles that are inherent to identity formation, whether in Malaysian or wider global contexts. In so doing, he reveals themes of human connectedness across cultures reflecting the multi-layered cultural positioning of people. For the Australia–Malaysia collaboration, *The Independence Project*[24] (Gertrude Contemporary Art Spaces, Melbourne and Galeri Petronas, Kuala Lumpur) Wong offered a work that, at first glance, bore no relationship to Australia–Malaysia cultural crossings. He presented his film *Aman Sulukule Canim Sulukule* (*Oh Sulukule Darling Sulukule*) (2007), first shown at the *10th Istanbul Biennial*, the result of his time working with children of the Roma community of the Sulukule quarter in Istanbul, Turkey. By positioning this work as part of *The Independence Project*, Wong also set up a deliberate cultural 'transfer' of sorts, situating the Australia–Malaysia collaboration in the 'third space' of Turkey, thereby reinforcing issues of universal, transnational human concern and connection. By bringing disjunctive regions into proximate dialogue on seemingly distant global concerns, Wong's projects rather reveal the intersection and adjacencies of local

---

Australian artists of Asian ethnic heritage, then at the margins of a largely Anglo-centric Australian arts scene. The independent art space now known as 4A Centre for Contemporary Asian Art developed from the earlier organisation. See 'About 4a', accessed 8 October 2013, http://www.4a.com.au/about-4a/.

24   *The Independence Project* was the first in a series of Australia–Asia cultural exchange projects beginning in 2007, between Gertrude Contemporary Art Spaces, Melbourne, and independent art spaces in Kuala Lumpur, Singapore, Beijing and Seoul.

and global influences, evincing possibilities for more fluid imaginations of Asia and Asian networks of transnational, cosmopolitan belonging. He also registers a particular trait of contemporary art at the turn of the twentieth century in evoking local issues that are contingent to global currents.

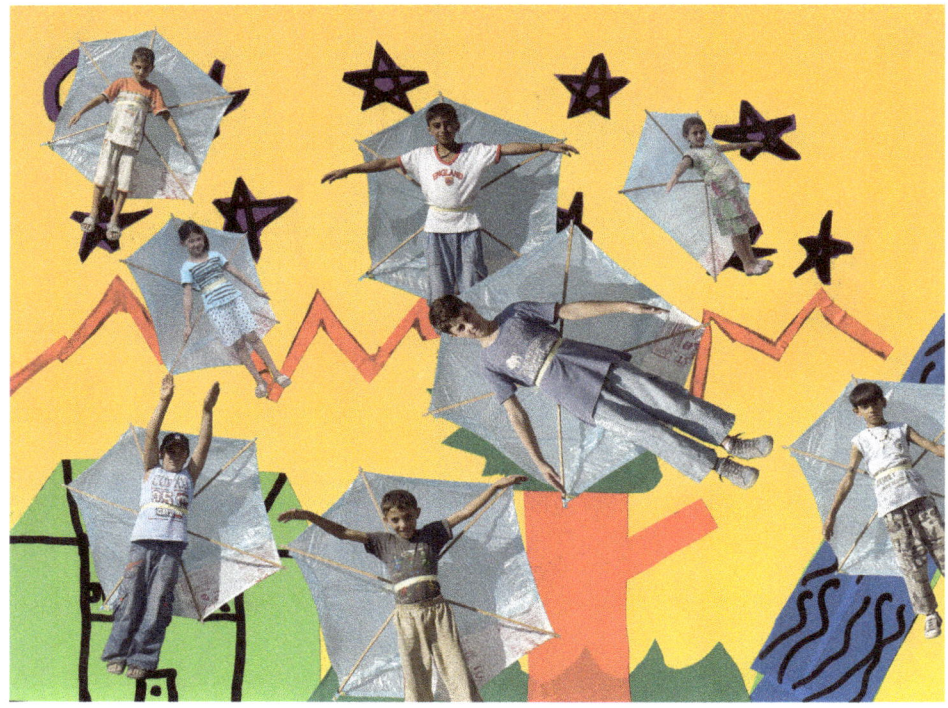

Wong Hoy Cheong, *Aman Sulukule Canim Sulukule* (*Oh Sulukule Darling Sulukule*) 2007 (video still); 13 min, 52 sec, PAL (in Turkish with English subtitles). Video installation produced with the Roma community of Sulukule, Istanbul, Turkey, for the 10th Istanbul Biennale, 2007.

© Wong Hoy Cheong; image courtesy of the artist

Similarly, India-born artist N.S. Harsha draws us into the entangled worlds of people everywhere, their struggles and injustices, their daily lives, as well as their ambitions and hopes. Best known for his intricate figurative works evoking the miniature-painting tradition, Harsha's art conveys the shared stories of the masses, but concurrently focuses on individual lives. For instance, his painting *Mass Marriage* (2003) reflects such tendencies, exploring the ritual of marriage, especially its new complexities and entanglements across contemporary cultural contexts worldwide. Through the artist's use of repetition, a seemingly infinite number of couples are depicted in multiple linear patterns, techniques that are commonly employed across the artist's oeuvre to reinforce themes of human connection across spatial and temporal zones. Harsha's installations and community-based collaborations engage similar themes and modes, including in his workshops with children in India, such as *Our Bridge* (2011), which invited children to draw their 'dream village' onto 277 pillars of the bridge between Bodh Gaya and Sujata Village in southern Bihar, and the outdoor installation *Ambitions and Dreams* (2005) in Tumkur, in which long, connective shadows were cast in the spaces between children dotting the landscape. The installation *Leftovers* (2008), presented in Tokyo, was inspired by the elaborate and hyper-real plastic food replicas displayed in the windows of Japanese restaurants. Harsha's installation, however, replicated traditional Indian meals—of curry, rice and beans served on a banana leaf. The meals were laid out on the floor, the scene suggestive of the aftermath of a mass banquet, where everyone has been served the same meal, but experienced it uniquely, with different 'leftovers' at the meal's end. Alongside each 'meal', lay a white mat imprinted with the imagined diner's feet, a further individual trace left behind. In this linking of Japanese and Indian cultures, the artist suggests the human commonalities and differences in the aesthetic and ritual patterns of food consumption, but also highlights both individual and shared responsibility in global consumption and waste.

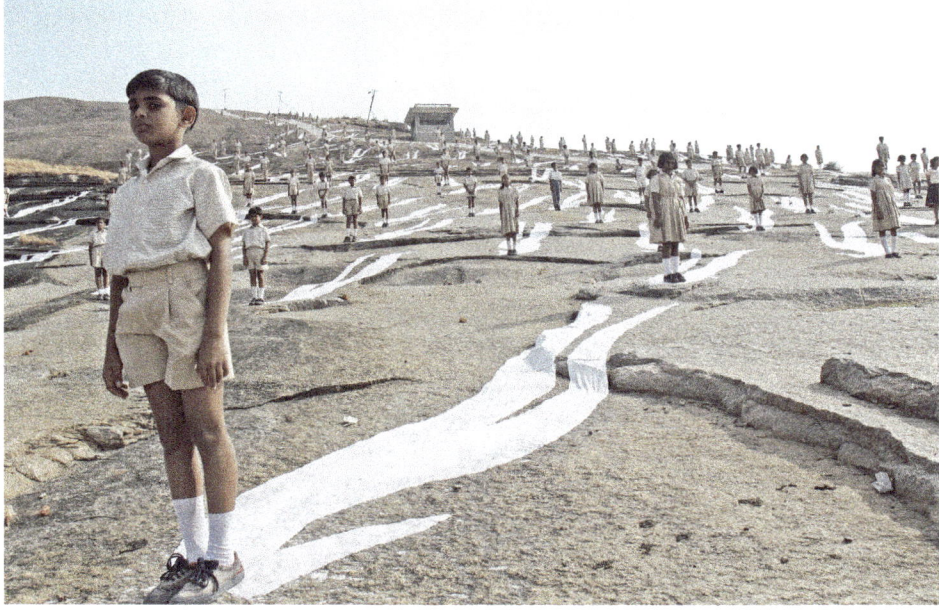

N.S. Harsha, *Ambitions and Dreams* 2005; cloth pasted on rock, size of each shadow 6m. Community project designed for TVS School, Tumkur, India.

© N.S. Harsha; image courtesy of the artist; photograph: Sachidananda K.J.

And the Future?

How do we think through the futures of contemporary Asian art? If Asian art at present shows general tendencies to the past, uncovering hidden histories and remembering forgotten stories, the essays in this volume suggest that it often does so as a means of understanding the present and to carve a trajectory for the future.

Contemporary artists point to shared future concerns, especially via tropes of memory, time and history. They invoke common issues of life and death, youth and ageing populations, the surreal experience of rapid development, and consequences for the future. They also register personal and individual stories of Asian experience, especially via intergenerational change and continuities: Miwa Yanagi's iconic photographic series *My Grandmothers* of the early 2000s (see first figure, this essay) captures the self-perceptions of young Japanese women asked to imagine themselves in 50 years' time; Fiona Tan's film *Cloud Island* (2010) (see figure, Introduction Part 2) portrays the quiet, slow-paced life of a diminishing and ageing community on Inujima, an island in Japan's Seto Inland Sea; in Jun Yang's film *Seoul Fiction* (2010) we accompany an elderly couple taking a bus trip from a rural area to Seoul, experiencing their conflict and confusion in a surreal journey through space and time; in its intimate portrayal of everyday life in suburban Taiwan, Yuan Goang-Ming's three-channel video, *Disappearing Landscape—Passing II* (2011), suggests the passing of time, cycles of life, and intergenerational connections of human experience.

Alongside such artistically driven projects mapping the present and the future are growing initiatives to document and archive contemporary Asian art, given the breadth and richness of material now available, over two decades after its international emergence. Since 2000, the Hong Kong-based Asia Art Archive (AAA) (see figure, Introduction Part 2), a private, non-profit organisation, has been a pioneering force in the collection and generation of physical and online resources on modern and contemporary Asian art, guided by a critical, self-reflexive and open approach to archiving the still evolving field of 'contemporary art'. Significant digitisation projects undertaken by the AAA include 'Another Life: The Digitised Personal Archive of Geeta Kapur and Vivan Sundaram'; the Salon Natasha archive (documenting Vietnamese art since 1990); 'The Chabet Archive: Covering Fifty Years of the Artist's Materials' (tracing the Filipino artist Roberto Chabet's personal archives and larger influence); and a number of China-focused archives including 'Materials of the Future: Documenting Contemporary Chinese Art from 1980–1990'.[25] Other important archives include

---

25 See Asia Art Archive, 'Special Collections', accessed 23 September 2013, http://www.aaa.org.hk/Collection/SpecialCollections.

the Australian Centre of Asia Pacific Art at the Queensland Art Gallery | Gallery of Modern Art (QAGOMA),[26] the Fukuoka Asian Art Museum (FAAM) research library, and a growing number of country-based archives, such as the Indonesia Visual Art Archive (IVAA, Yogyakarta, formerly Cemeti Art Foundation, est. 1995) and the Cambodian Visual Art Archive (at the Phnom Penh based art space SA SA BASSAC, est. 2011). The politics of archiving—which art and artists should be collected and documented, and on what grounds—are important topics for the critical development of such archives, crucial to the question of Asian art's futures and its canonical histories.

Critical scholarship about Asian art has challenges in keeping apace with the changes in Asia and developments in art. Nevertheless, significant critical dialogue, inquiry, documentation, and historicisation of contemporary Asian art occurred during the 1990s and earlier via the important work of key art historians, curators, institutions, organisations and journals for instance, forming pioneering work which must be built upon. As essays in this volume by Turner, Clark, Sambrani and Ho emphasise, there continues to be a widening field of art historical work that takes into account the important modern and contemporary art histories of Asia and which, up until recently, was overshadowed by hegemonic Western art histories.[27]

Academic work and other scholarly enquiry regarding Asian art is certainly being increasingly pursued, especially as a gradual accumulation of Asian art documentation now demands critical reflection. Moreover, the historical lack of public resources and support to develop art history departments and professional arts and culture training programs in many parts of Asia[28] is being challenged at the beginning of the twenty-first century, via a mounting desire across the region to match the rapid growth in the cultural industry sector with locally based knowledge and expertise (see Ho, this volume). Exhibitions have themselves been a significant site for the generation of critical knowledge and documentation about contemporary Asian art. Indeed the educative and critical purpose of exhibitions—including their catalogue essays, related symposia and conferences and reviews—has been instrumental in the development of critical dialogues for the field of Asian art.[29] Art writing often develops in

---

26 For *The Seventh Asia-Pacific Triennial of Contemporary Art* (2012–2013), QAGOMA presented 'The 20-Year Archive' project, inviting artists to engage with the archives of QAGOMA and marking the APT's 20-year anniversary.
27 See also John Clark, ed., *Modernity in Asian Art* (Sydney: Wild Peony, 1993); and Caroline Turner, ed., *Tradition and Change: Contemporary Art of Asia and the Pacific* (St Lucia: University of Queensland Press, 1993).
28 See T.K. Sabapathy, *Road to Nowhere: The Quick Rise and the Long Fall of Art History in Singapore* (Singapore: The Art Gallery at the National Institute of Education, 2010).
29 In this regard the Asia Art Archive organised the symposia 'Sites of Construction: Exhibitions and the Making of Recent Art History in Asia', 21–23 October 2013, see http://www.aaa.org.hk/Programme/Details/409.

tandem with art exhibitions. Notably, the task of writing about Asian art is often one undertaken by those who also curate Asian art or are practitioners of it, connecting art practice, curatorship and art writing.[30]

One of the key questions for Asia now is how to encourage creativity within society at large. As a number of Asian governments establish new cultural initiatives, it has been argued that a critical education is lacking not only for the development of art and other creative expertise within Asia itself,[31] but also for the development of creative minds that are able to contribute to rapidly changing societies via new ways of creative thinking and solutions. Related to this, the influence of commercial imperatives has led to serious concerns in some sectors about the future of contemporary Asian art as having less to do with creative integrity and urgent social issues and instead concerned with the demands of commerce and fashion.[32]

Reflecting on the changing conditions of 'creativity' through the phases of industrial to post-industrialisation, cultural theorist Sarat Maharaj has argued for a necessary reconfiguring of 'creativity' in order to reclaim its generative potential. Maharaj contends that 'as the "conditions of creativity" undergo change today, they have increasing bearing on what we consider as "work"—how we define labour, knowledge, creativity and art practice.'[33] Recognising the newly institutionalised and instrumentalised relationship of art to the assembly line growth of the 'knowledge' and 'cultural' industries in advanced capitalist societies, he poses the question, 'In the "creativity pandemic" where almost all activities are increasingly revamped as "creative" is anything actually so?'.[34] As Maharaj also reminds, not everything in the universe is wrapped up and regulated. Despite the machine rhythms of industrialisation and the regulated strictures of capitalist economies, creativity keeps doors open.[35]

The conceptual art of Pak Sheung Chuen involves subtle interventions in Hong Kong's everyday urban reality. Pak's performative-piece *Waiting for everyone to fall asleep* (2006) involved the artist's contemplation of everyday life within a 13-storey apartment complex at Hong Kong's Sham Shui Po area. There, the artist stood outside from 10.38 pm until just past 5 am, recording the visual play

---

30 See Patrick Flores, *Past Peripheral: Curation in Southeast Asia* (Singapore: NUS Museum, National University of Singapore, 2008).
31 Sabapathy, *Road to Nowhere*.
32 Mella Jaarsma and Nindityo Adipurnomo, 'The Point: What Are We Waiting For?', *ArtAsiaPacific* 81 (Nov/Dec 2012): 47.
33 Sarat Maharaj, 'Know-How and No-How: Stopgap Notes on "Method" in Visual Art as Knowledge Production', *Art & Research: A Journal of Ideas, Contexts and Methods* 2, no. 2 (Spring 2009): 9, accessed 24 June 2013, http://www.artandresearch.org.uk/v2n2/pdfs/maharaj.pdf.
34 Sarat Maharaj, 'Know How & No How: Thinking Through "Art as Knowledge Production" in a Time of "Creativity Cholera"' (keynote address at the 5th Auckland Triennial, 10 May 2013).
35 Sarat Maharaj, 'Sounding Asia Pandemonium' (Inaugural Burger Collection Keynote Lecture, Asia Art Archive Backroom Conversations, Hong Kong International Art Fair, 26 May 2011).

of lit and unlit windows patterned across the face of the building at various times throughout the night, as tenants gradually turned off their room lights and presumably went to sleep. The concrete and glass of an ordinary apartment complex became infused with humanity as Pak took note of the persons living within, humanising the city and recognising beauty in the seemingly impersonalised nightscape of Hong Kong's concrete jungle. These are the hidden social relationships or correspondences of community life, which may otherwise go unnoticed, subtly disappearing from consciousness as people become preoccupied with the meta-realities and rhythms of rapid social change in Asian mega-cities. Even as Hong Kong represents a cultural space of shifting coordinates, transforming subjectivities and uncertain futures in the new century, especially in relation to China, Pak reminds us of the inter-subjective connections and creative possibilities of the present in Hong Kong's reality of here and now. He harnesses the political, aesthetic and affective potential of the everyday so as to reimagine and resensitise us to the extraordinary within seemingly ordinary experiences of human observation, encounter and connectedness.

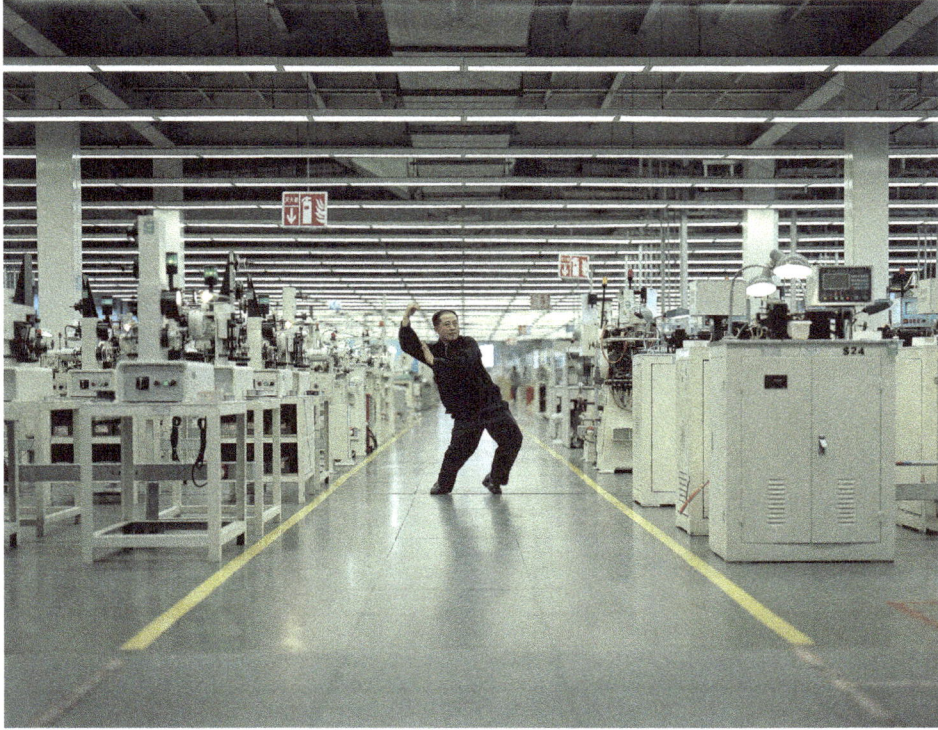

Cao Fei, *Whose Utopia* 2006; video; 20 min.

Courtesy the artist and Vitamin Creative Space 2013

In his essay in this volume, Merewether points to what art does in society in terms of documenting and creating new future possibilities. It is in this vein that artist Cao Fei explores the possibility for the extraordinary within everyday life. Interested in the different worlds of reality and fiction, her art often reflects themes of the future, of utopias, of make believe and fantasy, of the surreal reality of contemporary urban life in China. In her video, *Cosplayers* (2004), (see Figure, Introduction Part 2) the artist draws attention to China's 'cosplay' scene in which participants carry out 'costumed play' representing fictional Japanese anime characters who battle each other and then return home to the routine of everyday life. For her later video *Whose Utopia* (2006–2007), filmed at an Osram lighting company factory in China's Pearl River Delta region, the artist invited the company's factory workers—emigrants from inland China—to share their aspirations and hopes for the future. She filmed them acting out their dream roles within the factory space, the workers interrupting the usual rhythms of factory life to momentarily perform the roles of, for instance, rock musicians, break dancers and ballerinas. Here, imagining the possibilities of the future is not the stuff of mere fantasy and unattainable utopias; it is given actual form in the space of everyday life in contemporary Asia, where the 'future is not a dream', but made real in the present. In foregrounding these connected worlds of the real and the possible, Cao also offers critical visions about the changed realities of Asia, the differently positioned, but shared utopias of Asian people—be they the new urban working class or upper middle class—as they navigate the social and political challenges of the present, recalling their individual and collective dreams and hopes for the future in a rapidly changing Asia.

Selected Reading on Contemporary Asian Art

See also references in individual essays in this volume.

Andrew, Brook, Berghuis, Thomas J., Havilah, Lisa & Seeto, Aaron. *Edge of Elsewhere* (Campbelltown Arts Centre, 2010).

Ang, Ien et al. (eds). *Alter/Asians: Asian-Australian Identities in Art, Media and Popular Culture* (Sydney: Pluto Press, 2000).

Antoinette, Michelle. *Reworlding Art History: Encounters with Contemporary Southeast Asian Art after 1990* (Amsterdam & New York: Rodopi, 2014).

Art Asia Pacific (1993–).

ArtAsiaPacific Almanac (annually from 2005).

Asia Art Archive, www.aaa.org.hk.

Asia Art Archive. 'The And: An Expanded Questionnaire on the Contemporary', 'Field Notes' 1 (June 2012), http://www.aaa.org.hk/FieldNotes/Details/1167.

Asia Art Archive & Art Map Ltd. 'All You Want To Know About International Art Biennials', http://www.aaa.org.hk/onlineprojects/bitri/en/didyouknow.aspx#fn1.

Asia-Pacific Triennial of Contemporary Art. Catalogues of the First, Second, Third, Fourth, Fifth, Sixth and Seventh Asia-Pacific Triennial of Contemporary Art (Brisbane: Queensland Art Gallery, 1993–2012).

Asia-Pacific Triennial, http://www.apt3.net (Third APT).

Asia Research Institute & National University of Singapore. 'Our Modernities: Positioning Asian Art Now', international conference, Singapore, February 2004. Online conference papers: http://www.ari.nus.edu.sg/conf2004/asianart.htm.

Australian Government, Department of Prime Minister and Cabinet. *Australia in the Asian Century*, White Paper (Canberra, 2012), http://pandora.nla.gov.au/pan/133850/20130914-0122/asiancentury.dpmc.gov.au/white-paper.html.

Bauer, Uta Meta & Hanru, Hou (eds). *Shifting Gravity: World Biennial Forum No 1* (Ostfildern: Hatje Cantz, 2013).

Belting, Hans. 'Contemporary Art as Global Art: A Critical Estimate', in *The Global Art World: Audiences, Markets, and Museums*, eds Hans Belting & Andrea Buddensieg (Ostfildern: Hatje Cantz, 2009), 38–73.

Berghuis, Thomas. *Performance Art in China* (Hong Kong: Timezone 8 Limited, 2006).

Binghui Huangfu (ed.). *Text and Subtext: Contemporary Art and Asian Women Artists* (Singapore: Earl Lu Gallery, 2000).

Blazwick, Iona (ed.). *Century City: Art and Culture in the Modern Metropolis* (London: Tate Gallery, 2001).

Bydler, Charlotte. *The Global Art World, Inc.: On the Globalization of Contemporary Art* (Uppsala: Acta Universitatis Upsaliensis, 2004).

Carroll, Alison. *The Revolutionary Century: Art in Asia 1900–2000* (South Yarra: Macmillan Australia, 2010).

C-Arts: Asian Contemporary Art and Culture Magazine, http://www.c-artsmag.com/betac-artsmag.

Chang, Tsong-Zung & Li Xianting. *China's New Art, Post-1989* (Hong Kong: Hanart T Z Gallery, 1993).

Chiu, Melissa & Genocchio, Benjamin (eds). *Contemporary Art in Asia: A Critical Reader* (Cambridge, Mass. & London, England: MIT Press, 2011).

Clark, Christine (ed.). *Beyond the Self: Contemporary Portraiture from Asia* (Canberra: National Portrait Gallery, 2012).

Clark, John. Bibliography of Asian Modern and Contemporary Art to 2011: http://www.arts.usyd.edu.au/departs/arthistory/Courses%202002/pdf/Bibliography.pdf.

——. 'Art and its "others" — recent Australian-Asian visual exchanges', in *Australia and Asia: cultural transactions*, ed. Maryanne Dever (Surrey: Curzon Press, 1996).

——. *Asian Modernities: Chinese and Thai Art Compared, 1980 to 1999* (Sydney: Power Publications, 2010).

—— (ed.). *Chinese Art at the End of the Millennium* (Hong Kong: New Art Media, 2000).

——. *Modern Asian Art* (Sydney: Craftsman House G+B Arts International, 1998).

—— (ed.). *Modernity in Asian Art*, The University of Sydney East Asian Series Number 7 (Sydney: Wild Peony, 1993).

Clark, John, Peleggi, Maurizio & Sabapathy, T.K. (eds). *Eye of the Beholder: Reception, Audience, and Practice of Modern Asian Art*, The University of Sydney East Asian Series Number 15 (Sydney: Wild Peony, 2006).

Count 10 Before You Say Asia. Asian Art after Postmodernism. International Symposium 2008 Report (Tokyo: Japan Foundation, 2009).

Ctrl+P: Journal of Contemporary Art and Culture, http://www.ctrlp-artjournal.org (2006–).

Desai, Vishakha (ed.). *Asian Art History in the Twenty-First Century* (Williamstown, Mass.: Sterling and Francine Clark Institute, 2007).

Dysart, Dynah & Fink, Hannah (eds). *Asian Women Artists* (Sydney: Craftsman House, 1996).

Erickson, Britta. 'The Rise of a Feminist Spirit in Contemporary Chinese Art', *Art AsiaPacific*, Issue 31, 2001, 65–71.

——. *Bibliography of Contemporary Chinese Art*, http://www.stanford.edu/dept/art/china/.

Flores, Patrick. *Past Peripheral: Curation in Southeast Asia* (NUS Museum, National University of Singapore, 2008).

——. 'Position Papers: Turns in Tropics: Artist–Curator', in *The 7th Gwangju Biennale: Annual Report: A Year in Exhibitions*, ed. Okwui Enwezor (Gwangju Biennale Foundation, 2008), 262–85.

——. *Painting History: Revisions in Philippine Colonial Art* (Manila: University of the Philippines, Office of Research and Coordination, and National Commission for Culture and the Arts, 1998).

Flores, Patrick D., Cajipe-Endaya, Imelda, Cruz, Joselina & Koh, Jay, convenors. *Locus: Interventions in Art Practice* (Manila: National Commission for Culture and the Arts, Lopez Museum & Pananaw ng Sining Bayan, 2005).

Flores, Patrick D. & Kee, Joan (guest eds). 'Special Issue: Contemporaneity and Art in Southeast Asia', *Third Text: Critical Perspectives on Contemporary Art & Culture* 25, Issue 4.

focas: Forum On Contemporary Art & Society (Singapore, 2001–2007).

4A Centre for Contemporary Asian Art. 'About 4a', http://www.4a.com.au/about-4a/.

Fukuoka Asian Art Museum. Catalogues of the Asian Art exhibitions, Fukuoka Art Museum to 1999 and catalogues of the First, Second and Third Fukuoka Asian Art Triennale, Fukuoka, from 1999–ongoing (Fukuoka Asian Art Museum).

———. *The Birth of Modern Art in Southeast Asia: Artists and Movements* (1997).

Furuichi, Yasuko (ed.). *Alternatives 2005: Contemporary Art Spaces in Asia* (Kyoto & Tokyo: Tankosha Publishing Co., 2004).

———. *Asian Contemporary Art Reconsidered* (Tokyo: Japan Foundation Asia Center, 1998).

Gao Minglu et al. *The Wall: Reshaping Contemporary Chinese Art* (New York and Beijing: The Albright Knox Art Gallery and China Millennium Museum of Art, 2005).

Gao, Minglu et al. *Inside Out: New Chinese Art*, exhibition catalogue (Berkeley: University of California Press, 1998).

George, Kenneth M. *Picturing Islam: Art and Ethics in a Muslim Lifeworld* (Chichester, West Sussex, U.K.; Malden, Mass.: Wiley Blackwell, 2010).

Glass, Alexie, Joseph, Rahel & Jegadeva, Anurendra (eds). *The Independence Project/The Project* (Fitzroy, Vic.: Gertrude Contemporary Art Spaces; Kuala Lumpur: Galeri Petronas, 2007–2008).

Glass, Alexie, Mashadi, Ahmad, Chong, Heman, Cormack, Emily, Doughty, Jacqueline & Lim, Qinyi. *And the Difference Is: The Independence Project.* Fitzroy, Vic.: Gertrude Contemporary Art Spaces; Singapore: NUS Museum, 2008–2009).

Guillermo, Alice. *Image to Meaning* (Ateneo de Manila University Press, 2001).

———. *Protest/Revolutionary Art in the Philippines 1970–1990* (Quezon City: University of the Philippines Press, 2001).

Harris, Clare. *In The Image of Tibet: Tibetan painting after 1959* (London: Reaktion Books, 1999).

Hashmi, Salima. *Hanging Fire: Contemporary Art from Pakistan* (New York: Asia Society, 2009).

———. *Unveiling the Visible: Lives and Works of Women Artists of Pakistan* (Lahore: Sang-i-Meel Publications, 2002).

Hassan, Salah & Dadi, Iftikhar (eds). *Unpacking Europe* (Rotterdam: NAI Publishers, Museum Boijmans Van Beuningen, 2001).

Hjorth, Larissa, King, Natalie & Kataoka, Mami (eds). *Art in the Asia-Pacific: Intimate Publics* (New York & London: Routledge, 2014).

Ho, Hing-kay Oscar. 'Government, Business and People: Museum Development in Asia', in *The Global Art World: Audiences, Markets and Museums*, eds Hans Belting & Andrea Buddensieg (Ostfildern: Hatje Cantz, 2009), 266–77.

Hoffie, Pat. 'A New Tide Turning: Australia in the Region, 1993–2003', in *Art and Social Change: Contemporary Art in Asia and the Pacific*, ed. Caroline Turner (Canberra: Pandanus Books, 2005), 516–41.

Hou, Hanru. *On the Mid-Ground; Selected Texts Edited by Yu Hsiao-Hwei* (Hong Kong: Timezone 8, 2002).

Hou, Hanru & Obrist, Hans–Ulrich (eds). *Cities on the Move*, exhibition catalogue (Ostfildern–Ruit: Gerd Hatje, 1997).

Huangfu, Binghui (ed.). *Text and Subtext: Contemporary Art and Asian Woman* (Singapore: Earl Lu Gallery, 2000).

Japan Foundation Asia Center (ed.). *The Japan Foundation 30th Anniversary International Symposium 2002: 'Asia in Transition: Representation and Identity' Report* (Tokyo 2003).

———. *Under Construction* (Tokyo: The Japan Foundation Asia Center & Tokyo Opera City Cultural Foundation, 2002).

Jurriëns, Edwin & de Kloet, Jeroen (eds). *Cosmopatriots: On Distant Belongings and Close Encounters* (Amsterdam & New York: Rodopi, 2007).

Kapur, Geeta. *When Was Modernism: Essays on Contemporary Cultural Practice in India* (New Delhi: Tulika, 2000).

Kee, Joan. 'What is Feminist about Contemporary Asian Women's Art?', in *Global Feminisms: New Directions in Contemporary Art*, eds Maura Reilly & Linda Nochlin (London: Merrell Publishers Ltd., 2007), 107–22.

Kim, Young-Na. *Modern and Contemporary Art in Korea: Tradition, Modernity and Identity* (Elizabeth, New Jersey: Hollym Corporation, 2005).

———. *Korean Art of the Twentieth Century* (Seoul: Yekyung Publisher, 1994).

Kwok, Kian Chow. *Channels & Confluences: A History of Singapore Art* (Singapore Art Museum, 1995).

Lee, Yong Woo. 'Globalism and the Vanity of its System', in Japan Foundation Asia Center, *Asia in Transition* (Tokyo: 2002), 292–308.

Lenzi, Iola (ed.). *Negotiating Home, History and Nation: Two Decades of Contemporary Art in Southeast Asia 1991–2011* (Singapore Art Museum, 2011).

Li Xianting & Jose, Nicholas. *Mao goes Pop: China post-1989*, exhibition catalogue (Sydney: Museum of Contemporary Art, 1993).

Lo, Jacqueline. 'Diaspora, Art and Empathy', in *John Young: The Bridge and the Fruit Tree*, exhibition catalogue (Canberra: Drill Hall Gallery, The Australian National University, 2013), 19–43.

Lo, Jacqueline, Chan, Dean & Khoo, Tseen. 'Introduction — Asian Australia and Asian America: Making Transnational Connections', *Amerasia Journal* 36, no. 2 (2010): xii–xxvii.

Lynn, Victoria et al. *India Songs: Multiple Streams in Contemporary Indian Art*, exhibition catalogue (Sydney: Art Gallery of New South Wales, 1993).

Maravillas, Francis. 'Cartographies of the Future: The Asia-Pacific-Triennials and the Curatorial Imaginary', in *Eye of the Beholder: Reception, Audiences and Practice of Modern Asian Art*, eds John Clark, Maurizo Peleggi, T.K. Sabapathy, The University of Sydney East Asian Series Number 15 (Sydney: Wild Peony, 2006), 244–70.

———. 'Constellations of the Contemporary: Art / Asia / Australia', *Journal of Australian Studies* 32, no. 4 (2008): 433–44.

MAAP-Media Art Asia Pacific, http://www.maap.org.au/about-maap/.

Merewether, Charles. 'The Spectre of Being Human', in *Art and Social Change: Contemporary Art in Asia and the Pacific*, ed. Caroline Turner (Canberra: Pandanus Books), 101–43.

Meskimmon, Marsha. *Contemporary Art and the Cosmopolitan Imagination* (London & New York: Routledge, 2011).

Munroe, Alexandra (ed.). *Scream Against the Sky: Japanese Art after 1945* (New York: Harry N. Abrams, Inc., 1994).

Museum of Contemporary Art, Tokyo. *Art in Southeast Asia: Glimpses into the Future* (Tokyo: Museum of Contemporary Art & Hiroshima: Hiroshima City Museum of Contemporary Art, Japan, 1997).

Nadarajan, Gunalan, Storer, Russell & Tan, Eugene. *Contemporary Art in Singapore* (Institute of Contemporary Arts Singapore, 2007).

Nakamura, Fuyubi, Perkins, Morgan & Krischer, Olivier (eds). *Asia through Art and Anthropology: Cultural Translation Across Borders* (London; New York: Bloomsbury Academic, 2013).

Nanjo, Fumio, Friis-Hansen, Dana, Sontag, Susan & Fuse, Hideto. *Of the Human Condition: Hope and Despair at the End of the Century* (Tokyo: Spiral/Wacoal Art Centre, 1994).

Nur Hanim Bt Mohamed Khairuddin & Yong, Beverly, with Sabapathy, T.K. (eds). *Narratives in Malaysian Art* (Kuala Lumpur: RogueArt, 2012–).

Osaka, Eriko & Kline, Katy (eds). *Against Nature: Japanese Art in the Eighties* (New York: Grey Street Gallery and Study Center, New York University, 1989).

PANANAW: Philippine Journal of Visual Arts (Manila: The National Commission for Culture and the Arts, 1997–).

Piyadasa, Redza. 'Modernist and Post-Modernist Developments in the Post-Independence period', in *Modernity in Asian Art*, ed. John Clark (Sydney: Wild Peony, 1993).

Poshyananda, Apinan. *Contemporary Art in Asia: Traditions/Tensions* (New York: Asia Society Galleries, 1996).

———. *Modern Art in Thailand: Nineteenth and Twentieth Centuries* (Oxford University Press, 1992).

Roberts, Claire (ed.). *Go Figure! Contemporary Chinese Portraiture* (Canberra: National Portrait Gallery & Sherman Contemporary Art Foundation, 2012).

———. *New Art from China: Post-Mao Product*, exhibition catalogue (Sydney: Art Gallery of NSW, 1992).

Rodboon, Somporn. 'Notes on the Revival of Traditional Art in Thai Contemporary Art', paper delivered at Symposium on Southeast Asian Art History and Regional Aesthetics, SPAFA/SEAMEO, March 1995, Singapore.

Sabapathy, T.K. *Intersecting Histories: Contemporary Turns in Southeast Asian Art* (Nanyang Technological University, 2012).

———. 'Developing Regionalist Perspectives in South-East Asian Art Historiography', in *The Second Asia-Pacific Triennial of Contemporary Art* (Brisbane: Queensland Art Gallery, 1996), 13–17.

——— (ed.). *Modernity and Beyond: Themes in Southeast Asian Art* (Singapore Art Museum, 1996).

Sabapathy, T.K., Flores, Patrick D. & Rajah, Niranjan (eds). *36 Ideas from Asia: Contemporary South-East Asian Art* (Singapore Art Museum, 2002).

Saidon, Hasnul J. & Yong, Beverly. *Between Generations: 50 Years across Modern Art in Malaysia* (Kuala Lumpur & Penang: University of Malaysia, Valentine Willie Fine Art & Universiti Sains Malaysia, 2007).

Sambrani, Chaitanya (ed.). *Edge of Desire: Recent Art in India* (London: Philip Wilson Publishers, 2005).

SentAp! (Perak: Teratak Nuromar, 2005–).

Sheikh, Gulammohammed (ed.). *Contemporary Art in Baroda* (Delhi: Tulika, 1997).

Singapore Art Museum. *Visions and Enchantment: Southeast Asian Paintings*, exhibition catalogue (Singapore Art Museum in association with Christie's Singapore, 2000).

Stanhope, Zara & Antoinette, Michelle. 'The World and World-Making in Art: Connectivities and Differences', *World Art* 2, no. 2 (2012): 167–71.

Sullivan, Michael. *Art and Artists of Twentieth Century China* (Berkeley: University of California Press, 1996).

———. *The Meeting of Eastern and Western Art* (Berkeley: University of California Press, 1989).

Supangkat, Jim. *Indonesian Modern Art and Beyond* (Jakarta: Yayasan Seni Rupa Indonesia/ The Indonesian Fine Arts Foundation, in cooperation with Museum Universitas Pelita Harapan & Edwins Gallery, 1996).

Supangkat, Jim, et al., *Outlet: Yogyakarta within the Contemporary Indonesian Art Scene* (Yogyakarta: Cemeti Art Foundation, 2001).

Tatehata, Akira, Mizusawa, Tsutomu & Shioda, Junichi (eds). *Asian Modernism — Diverse Development in Indonesia, the Philippines, and Thailand* (Tokyo: The Japan Foundation Asia Centre, 1995).

Taylor, Nora Annesley. *Painters in Hanoi: An Ethnography of Vietnamese Art* (Honolulu: University of Hawaii Press, 2009).

Taylor, Nora A. & Ly, Boreth (eds). *Modern and Contemporary Southeast Asian Art: An Anthology* (New York: Cornell University, 2012).

Turner, Caroline. 'Cultural Transformations in the Asia-Pacific: The Asia-Pacific Triennial and the Fukuoka Triennale Compared', in *Eye of the Beholder: Reception, Audiences and Practice of Modern Asian Art*, eds John Clark, Maurizo Peleggi, T.K. Sabapathy, The University of Sydney East Asian Series Number 15 (Sydney: Wild Peony, 2006), 221–43.

—— (ed.). *Art and Social Change: Contemporary Art in Asia and the Pacific* (Canberra: Pandanus Books, 2005).

—— (ed.). *Tradition and Change: Contemporary Art of Asia and the Pacific* (St Lucia: University of Queensland Press, 1993).

Turner, Caroline & Devenport, Rhana (eds). *Present Encounters: Papers from the Conference of the Second Asia-Pacific Triennial of Contemporary Art, 1996* (Brisbane: Queensland Art Gallery, 1996).

Turner, Caroline & Low, Morris (eds). *Beyond the Future: Papers from the Conference of the Third Asia-Pacific Triennial of Contemporary Art, 1999* (Brisbane: Queensland Art Gallery, 1999).

Turner, Caroline, Antoinette, Michelle & Stanhope, Zara (eds). 'The World and World-Making in Art', special issue, *Humanities Research* 19, no. 2 (2013) http://press.anu.edu.au/titles/humanities-research-journal-series/volume-xix-no-2-2013.

Universes-in-Universe, http://universes-in-universe.org/eng/ (1997–).

Ushiroshoji, Masahiro. *New Generation of Asian Art* (Fukuoka Art Museum, 1997).

Webb, Jen. 'The Asia-Pacific Triennial: Synthesis in the Making' (with Tony Schirato), *Continuum* 14/3 (Special issue: 'Synthesis') (November 2000): 349–58.

Weerasinghe, Jagath. 'Made in IAS: An Exhibition of Paintings, Sculpture and Installation Works by 16 Artists from the Institute of Aesthetic Studies of the University of Kelaniya' (introduction to catalogue), Gallery 706, Colombo, 11–20 July 2000.

'West Heavens' project website, http://westheavens.net/en.

Wright, Astri. *Soul, Spirit, and Mountain: Preoccupations of Contemporary Indonesian Painters* (Kuala Lumpur & New York: Oxford University Press, 1994).

Wu Hung (ed.). *Chinese Art at the Crossroads: Between Past and Future, Between East and West* (Hong Kong: INIVA and New Art Media, Hong Kong, 2001).

——. *Transience: Chinese Experimental Art at the End of the Twentieth Century* (University of Chicago Press, 1999).

Contributor Biographies

Michelle Antoinette is a researcher of modern and contemporary Asian art, currently affiliated with the Centre for Art History and Art Theory at The Australian National University (ANU). She was recently an Australian Research Council (ARC) Postdoctoral Fellow (2010–2013) and she has been convenor and lecturer at ANU for courses on Asian and Pacific art and museums. Her ARC project, 'The Rise of New Cultural Networks in Asia in the Twenty-First Century' (DP1096041), together with Caroline Turner, explored the emergence of new regional and international networks of contemporary Asian art and museums. Her ongoing research focuses on the contemporary art histories of South-East Asia on which she has published widely including her book, *Reworlding Art History: Encounters with Contemporary Southeast Asian Art after 1990* (2014).

Caroline Turner is an Adjunct Senior Research Fellow in the Humanities Research Centre, Research School of Humanities and the Arts at ANU. Prior to joining ANU in 2000 she was deputy director of the Queensland Art Gallery (QAG) and organised and curated many international exhibitions, including from the Louvre, the Shanghai Museum, and the Idemitsu Museum, as well as co-curating *Matisse* in 1995 with works from 50 collections worldwide. She was co-founder and project director in the 1990s for the Asia-Pacific Triennial exhibitions (1993, 1996, 1999) at QAG and scholarly editor of the three major catalogues for the first three triennials. Her books include *Tradition and Change: Contemporary Art of Asia and the Pacific* (1993); and *Art and Social Change: Contemporary Art in Asia and the Pacific* (2005). She has written extensively on contemporary Asian art and museums as well as lecturing on this subject internationally and is currently completing a jointly authored book with Jen Webb on art and human rights for Manchester University Press.

Alison Carroll has been an academic, critic, writer, curator and administrator of art exhibitions and artist exchanges with Asia for over 30 years. In 1990 she established and was director (until June 2010) of the Arts Program at Asialink, University of Melbourne, which became the main program for arts exchange between Asia and Australia for visual arts, performing arts, literature and arts management practice. She received the Visual Arts Board of the Australia Council's Emeritus Medal 2006 and was made a Member of the Order of Australia (AM) in 2010 for her work at Asialink. She is the author of *The Revolutionary Century: Art in Asia 1900–2000* (2010). Her most recent project is Guest Editor of 'This Asian Century', *Artlink* 33, no. 1, 2013.

John Clark was Professor of Asian Art History at the University of Sydney and, after his retirement in 2013, Professor Emeritus. He is currently completing a draft of volume one of *The Asian Modern*; to do the research for this project he received an ARC Professorial Fellowship in 2008–2012. His books included *Modern Asian Art* (1998), the co-edited *Eye of the Beholder* (2006), *Modernities of Chinese Art* (2010), *Asian Modernities: Chinese and Thai Art in the 1980s and 1990s* (2010), and *Modernities of Japanese Art* (2013).

Patrick D. Flores is Professor of Art Studies in the Department of Art Studies at the University of the Philippines, which he chaired from 1997 to 2003, and Curator of the Vargas Museum in Manila. He is Adjunct Curator at the National Art Gallery, Singapore. He was one of the curators of *Under Construction: New Dimensions in Asian Art* in 2000 and the Gwangju Biennale (Position Papers) in 2008. He was a visiting fellow at the National Gallery of Art in Washington, D.C. in 1999 and an Asian Public Intellectuals fellow in 2004. Among his publications are *Painting History: Revisions in Philippine Colonial Art* (1999); *Remarkable Collection: Art, History, and the National Museum* (2006); and *Past Peripheral: Curation in Southeast Asia* (2008). He received a grant from the Asian Cultural Council (2010) and was a member of the Advisory Board of the exhibition *The Global Contemporary: Art Worlds After 1989* (2011) organised by the Center for Art and Media in Karlsruhe and member of the Guggenheim Museum's Asian Art Council (2011). He co-edited the South-East Asian issue with Joan Kee of *Third Text* (2011). In 2013 in Manila he convened the conference 'Histories of Art History in Southeast Asia' on behalf of the Clark Institute and the Department of Art Studies of the University of the Philippines.

Oscar Ho Hing Kay is currently Associate Professor in cultural management at the Chinese University of Hong Kong, formerly exhibition director of the Hong Kong Arts Centre and founding director of MoCA Shanghai. He curated numerous exhibitions of Hong Kong and Asian art, including co-curating *China New Art, Post 1989*; *Designing Identity: Hong Kong Sixties*; and served as guest curator for the 2nd and 3rd Asia-Pacific Triennial of Contemporary Art. He is the founder of the Hong Kong chapter of the International Association of Art Critics, board member of the Asia Art Archive, and he was organiser of the Asian Curatorial Network in 2011. He was a member of the Advisory Committee, responsible for conceiving the plan of M+.

Pat Hoffie is a visual artist based in Brisbane where she is a Professor at the Queensland College of Art, Griffith University. She is Director of SECAP (Sustainable Environment through Culture, Asia-Pacific). She exhibits regularly and has worked with Caroline Turner on the series of exhibitions and publications on *Art and Human Rights*.

Jacqueline Lo is Director of the ANU Centre for European Studies and Adjunct Fellow of the International Centre for Interweaving Performance Cultures at the Free University of Berlin. Her research focuses on issues of race, colonialism, diaspora and the interaction of cultures and communities across ethnic, national and regional borders. Publications include *Staging Nation* (2002), *Performance and Cosmopolitics* (2007, with Helen Gilbert). Her latest publications include editing a special issue of *Crossings: Journal of Migration and Culture* focusing on transnational memories in Germany and Australia (2013). She is Chair of the Asian Australian Studies Research Network and serves on the executive of the International Network for Diasporic Asian Art Research.

Francis Maravillas is Associate Researcher at the Transforming Cultures Research Centre at the University of Technology, Sydney, where he also lectures in cultural studies. His research interests focus on contemporary art and visual culture in Asia and Australia, curatorial practice and international art exhibitions, socially engaged art and new media. His current research examines the role of food in contemporary Asian art, collaboration and community engagement in contemporary Asian and Pacific art, and art and the cultural industries in Hong Kong. His work appears in various journals and exhibition catalogues as well as edited collections including *In the Eye of the Beholder: Reception and Audience for Modern Asian Art* (2006); *Cosmopatriots: On Distant Belongings and Close Encounters* (2007); *Crossing Cultures: Conflict, Migration and Convergence* (2009); and *New Vision, New Voices: Challenging Australian Identities and Legacies* (2012). He has been a board member of the 4A Centre for Contemporary Asian Art, Sydney (2004–2007).

Charles Merewether is an art historian, writer and curator. He was director of the Institute of Contemporary Arts, LASALLE College of the Arts, Singapore, from 2010 to 2013. Born in Scotland, he was educated in Australia where he received his BA in literature and doctorate in art history at the University of Sydney. From 2007–2008 he was deputy director of the Cultural District, Saadiyat Island, Abu Dhabi, and artistic director & curator of the Biennale of Sydney (2004–2006). Merewether has taught at the University of Sydney, Universidad Autonoma in Barcelona, and University of Southern California. His recent book publications include *The Archive* (2006); *Art, Anti-Art, Non-Art: Experimentations in the Public Sphere in Postwar Japan 1950–1970* (2007); *Under Construction: Ai Weiwei* (2008); a co-edited volume of essays *After the Event* (2010); and *After Memory: The Art of Milenko Prvacki, 40 Years, ISSUE: Land* (2012).

Marsha Meskimmon is Professor of Modern and Contemporary Art History at Loughborough University (United Kingdom). Meskimmon's research focuses on contemporary art, with a particular emphasis on feminist theory, and her publications include: *The Art of Reflection: Women Artists' Self-Portraiture in the Twentieth Century* (1996); *We Weren't Modern Enough: Women Artists and the*

Limits of German Modernism (1999); *Women Making Art: History, Subjectivity, Aesthetics* (2003); *Contemporary Art and the Cosmopolitan Imagination* (2010); and *Women, the Arts and Globalisation: Eccentric Experience* (co-edited with Dorothy Rowe) (2013). With Amelia Jones, she edits the series *Rethinking Art's Histories* and, with Phil Sawdon, she is currently writing a book exploring gender, sexual difference and drawing.

Chaitanya Sambrani is an art historian and curator with special interests in modern and contemporary art in Asia. He completed his MA in art criticism in the Faculty of Fine Arts, M.S. University, Baroda, and his PhD in art history and curatorship at ANU. His work has been featured in major publications, exhibitions and conferences in Australia, India, China, Korea, Singapore and the United States. His curatorial projects include *Edge of Desire: Recent Art In India* (Perth, New York, Mexico City, Monterrey, Berkeley, New Delhi, Mumbai, 2004–2007); *Place.Time.Play: Contemporary Art from the 'West Heavens' to the 'Middle Kingdom'* (Shanghai, October–December 2010); and *To Let the World In: Narrative and Beyond in Contemporary Indian Art* (Chennai, 15 March–10 April 2012). He is currently Senior Lecturer in Art Theory at ANU School of Art, Canberra.

www.ingramcontent.com/pod-product-compliance
Lightning Source LLC
Chambersburg PA
CBHW040545220526
45473CB00017B/3031